TO

...ica's working men and women, union and ...nion alike, whose bedrock support of our ...etitive enterprise system and belief in individ- ...berty constitute the greatest obstacle to those ...ng to transform us into a collectivist society.

...NDRED MILLION DOLLAR PAYOFF

...t © 1974 and 1976 by Douglas Caddy

... by the Public Policy Press, a division of the ...licy Research Corporation, 1721 DeSales Street, ...shington, D.C. 20036.

...d to the book trade by:
... Publishers, Inc.
... Box 738
...inois 61350

...red in the United States of America.

...Congress Catalog Card Number: 74-5348

...6054-30-6

The questions Americans should be asking—and most likely will be doing if they read Caddy's book—is whether or not they have been· given the full story. In particular, have campaign violations even more serious than Watergate been covered up by the union-dominated media.

Knoxville Journal

It is political dynamite if enough people hear about it . . . The book is an eye-opener . . . This is a damning report on illegal union political spending.

Charleston *News Courier*

The abuses cited by Caddy read like a weekly grocery shopping list . . . Its allegations by the author, however, are not made lightly for he offers substantial documentation for each.

Ripon Society Quarterly

Add it all up, and count what labor spends on state and local elections, and it may well be that Mr. Caddy is not too far wrong in titling his book *The Hundred Million Dollar Payoff*.

National Review

In this volume we have full documentation of specific funds and services transmitted, the methods employed for "laundering" contributions, and devices used for getting around the law. We also have the record of pledges by senators such as Lee Metcalf (D.-Mont.) and Harrison Williams (D.-N.J.) voting fealty to the labor chieftains in thanks for these political favors.

Columnist M. Stanton Evans

DOUGLAS CADDY is a graduate of the Georgetown University School of Foreign Service and New York University School of Law. He is an attorney-at-law in Washington, D.C. and is a member of the American Bar Association, the District of Columbia Bar Association, the District of Columbia Bar, the American Judicature Society, and the Federal Bar Association. His articles have appeared in *National Review, Barron's,* and *Human Events.* He is the author of *How They Rig Our Elections* (Arlington House, 1975).

THE HUNDRED MILLION DOLLAR PAYOFF

DOUGLAS CA

Ame
nonu
comp
ual li
strivi

PUBLIC POLICY
WASHINGTON

THE HU

Copyrigh

Published
Public Po
N.W., Wa

Distribute
Green Hill
Post Office
Ottawa, Ill

Manufactu

Library of

ISBN: 0-91

Contents

Appendices

Tables

THEN . . .

"A United States Senator . . . represented something more than a state, more even than a region. He represented principalities and powers in business. One Senator, for instance, represented the Union Pacific Railway System, another the New York Central, still another the insurance interests of New York and New Jersey. . . . Coal and Iron owned a coterie from the Middle and Eastern seaport states. Cotton had half a dozen senators. And so it went.

> —A description of the U. S. Senate of 1899, in William Allen White, *Masks in a Pageant* (New York: Macmillan Co., 1928)

. . . AND NOW

"I owe everything to you. . . . What you want you've got. I owe that much to you."

> —Senator Harrison A. Williams, Jr. (D.-N.J.), chairman of the Senate Labor and Public Welfare Committee, addressing leaders of organized labor in 1970 after his re-election victory

"A liberal Democratic senator on Capitol Hill: 'They have the power because they have the money and the manpower. There are damn few free men on this Hill.' "

> —Haynes Johnson and Nick Kotz, *The Unions* (New York: Pocket Books, 1972)

Preface to Revised Edition

From there I drove to the White House annex —the old Executive Office Building, in bygone years the War Department and later the Department of State.

Carrying three heavy attaché cases, I entered the Pennsylvania Avenue door, showed my blue-and-white White House pass to the uniformed guards, and took the elevator to the third floor. I unlocked the door of 338 and went in. I opened my two-drawer safe, took out my operational handbook, found a telephone number and dialed it.

The time was 2:13 in the morning of June 17, 1972, and the five of my companions had been arrested and taken to the maximum-security block of the District of Columbia jail. I had recruited four of them and it was my responsibility to get them out. That was the sole focus of my thoughts as I began talking on the telephone.

But with those five arrests the Watergate Affair had begun. . . .

After several rings the call was answered and I heard the sleepy voice of Douglas Caddy. "Yes?"

"Doug? This is Howard. I hate to wake you up, but I've got a tough situation and I need to talk to you. Can I come over?"

"Sure. I'll tell the desk clerk you're expected."

"I'll be there in about twenty minutes," I told him and hung up.

From the safe I took a small money box and removed the $10,000 Liddy had given me for emergency use. I put $1,500 in my wallet and the remaining $8,500 in my coat pocket. The black attaché case containing McCord's electronic equipment I placed in a safe drawer that held my operational notebooks. Then I closed and locked the safe, turning the dial several times. The other two cases I left beside the safe, turned out the light and left my office, locking the door.

E. Howard Hunt, Undercover—Memoirs of an American Secret Agent (Berkley, 1974)

1

When my telephone rang on that fateful Saturday morning, little did I dream that the act of merely picking up the receiver and answering it was the beginning of a chain of events that not only would completely alter the course of my life, and many other lives, but would also eventually change the course of the history of the world.

A commonly heard phrase is that life turns on being in the right place at the right time. The possibility must also exist of being in the wrong place at the wrong time, or variations of that. In any event, my entrance into the drama of Watergate took place when I was awakened from a sound sleep by my ringing telephone. A more inauspicious method of being thrust into such a dynamic affair can hardly be imagined. Whether my being in bed on that morning was being in the right place at the right time or the opposite, only the years that lie ahead of my present thirty-seven will reveal.

Howard Hunt was both a client whom I had advised on legal matters over the years and a person whom I counted among my close friends, as were his wife Dorothy and their four children. I had known Howard since just before his retirement from the CIA, and when later I entered private practice with a Washington law firm, Howard became one of my first clients.

About half an hour after he called on that June 17, Howard arrived at my apartment, which was located just five minutes from both the White House and Watergate. It took me only a short time to grasp the significance (and horror) of what he had to relate. Apparently, as subsequent events were to reveal, I was the first person after the arrests—next to the seven conspirators themselves—to learn what had really occurred at Watergate and to understand its terrible meaning.

A short time after he arrived, Howard placed a telephone call to G. Gordon Liddy, with whom I had become acquainted in my professional capacity on three or four previous occasions. Howard handed the telephone to me and I too had a conversation with Gordon. Both Howard and Gordon retained me as their legal counsel on that Saturday morning. Later, at about 10:30 A.M. the same day, I—along with my co-counsel—visited the cellblock of the Second Police Precinct; after conversing with the five individuals incarcerated there, we were asked to represent them in the case. The five—James McCord, Bernard Barker, Eugenio Martinez, Frank Sturgis, and Virgilio Gonzales—had been arrested some eight hours earlier within the headquarters of the Democratic National Committee in Watergate.

I served as attorney for the Watergate Seven—the only attorney in the original case to represent all of the defendants

2

—until permission was granted to me to withdraw as counsel in order to avoid a potential conflict of interest in my representing all seven. The issue arose after I had been subpoenaed to appear before the grand jury in an attempt by the prosecution, among other things, to link Hunt and Liddy (who had not yet been arrested or charged with a crime) to the arrested five individuals. This effort by the prosecutors took the form of attempting to extract from my lips as Hunt and Liddy's attorney incriminating information that could be used against them, which information I maintained, and still do, is protected by the attorney-client privilege (which protects communications a client has with his attorney) and by the Sixth Amendment, the right to counsel. So strongly did I feel the prosecution was mistaken in this improper course of action that I adopted the legal strategy, after consultation with five senior members of the District of Columbia Bar (including a past president of the District of Columbia Bar Association), of being held in civil contempt by Judge John Sirica in order to obtain an immediate review of the issues by the U. S. Court of Appeals.*

At the first Watergate Seven trial, in January 1973, I was called as a witness by both the prosecution and the defense. After the trial my name did not emerge again publicly until the Senate Watergate Committee held its televised hearings, which disclosed that I had been the first person approached soon after the break-in to transmit coverup money to the seven defendants.

The overture was made by Anthony Ulasewicz, a former New York City police detective, acting upon the instructions of Herbert Kalmbach, President Nixon's personal attorney. Here is the testimony of Mr. Kalmbach before the Ervin Committee:

> *Mr. Dash.* Now, what was the first instruction you received to give the money?
> *Mr. Kalmbach.* Again, as I have tried to reconstruct this, Mr. Dash, the first instruction that I received, which I passed to Mr. Ulasewicz was to have Mr. Ulasewicz give $25,000 to Mr. Caddy. I don't know much of Mr. Caddy, I understand he is an attorney here in Washing-

---

* I lost on appeal, and on July 19, 1972, went before the grand jury and reluctantly answered questions put to me on matters I felt fell within the attorney-client privilege. The incredible pressures that were brought to bear on me by the prosecutors and by Judge Sirica to violate what I believed to be the sanctiity of the attorney-client privilege involve a story about Watergate that has never fully been disclosed publicly.

ton. And, as I recall it, this was probably from approximately July 1 through July 6 or 7. There were a number of calls. I would either talk to either Mr. Dean or Mr. LaRue. I would then call Mr. Ulasewicz who, in turn, would call Mr. Caddy. He would have some response from Mr. Caddy, and I would call back up to either Mr. Dean or Mr. LaRue.

Mr. Dash. What was the response from Mr. Caddy?

Mr. Kalmbach. Well, the sum and gist of it was that Mr. Caddy refused to accept the funds.

Mr. Dash. In that manner?

Mr. Kalmbach. That is correct. That was the end-all. There were several telephone calls, but the final wrap-up on it was that he refused to receive the funds. [*Hearings before the Select Committee on Presidential Campaign Activities of the U. S. Senate,* July 16, 1973, pp. 2103–4]

Later, Kalmbach was again to testify about the circumstances of my being approached to transmit "hush" money. The testimony this time was at the Watergate "coverup" trial of Mitchell, Haldeman, Ehrlichman, Mardian, and Parkinson. As the *Washington Post* of November 13, 1974, reported:

Judge Sirica waited until he had sent the jurors home for the day to voice his incredulity. Taking over the questioning after the lawyers for all sides were done, Sirica made it plain he could not accept Kalmbach's claims to a slow awakening. The Judge pointed out all of the trouble Kalmbach had with the first $25,000 payment, beginning with Caddy's refusal to take it.

"Didn't that arouse your suspicions somewhat?" the Judge demanded. "Didn't it indicate to you that there must be something wrong?"

"Well, your honor," Kalmbach replied, "I simply felt that there was a misunderstanding in some way."

I had no misunderstanding as to why I believed Kalmbach and his associates wanted me to transmit the coverup money to the defendants. That is precisely why a partner of my law firm was sitting in my office at the time the final telephone call came in, so that I would have a witness to my end of the conversation that I had turned down the solicitation to become part of the conspiracy. Still I found irony in the fact that the same Judge Sirica who held me in contempt of court two years earlier when I sought to exercise my ethical duty to protect the attorney-client privilege—and was ever so vicious in disparaging my professional reputation to the packed courtroom—subsequently held up as a standard to Kalmbach my

4

refusal to accept the "hush" money and become a part of the conspiracy. Legal scholars and history will ultimately judge Judge Sirica on whether he gave the original Watergate defendants a fair trial.

One thing is certain: Watergate for me was a rude awakening to the corruption that permeates American politics today. Much of what the average citizen had long suspected was confirmed as the sordid details of Watergate unfolded. The letdown brought on by the scandal was all the more severe to those of us who had supported the Nixon administration in its early years because of our hope that it would succeed in reversing the trend toward a regimented, collectivist society and begin the march back to individual liberty.

Shocking as Watergate was to me in revealing the corruptness of the Republican Party, even more shocking was the deceit of some who vigorously condemned the excesses of power as revealed by Watergate while wrapping themselves in innocence and virtue. It was this patent hypocrisy and deceit, especially by the pliant tools in Congress of the labor bosses, that has prompted me to write *The Hundred Million Dollar Payoff.*

Two dramatic examples of the hypocrisy that surrounds campaign reform in the wake of Watergate came to my attention as I was finishing this preface to the revised edition. The first is an article from *The Washington Star* of February 19, 1976 titled "Wayne Hays 'Conversion' Should Save FEC" which disclosed how Rep. Wayne Hays (D.-Ohio), powerful chairman of the House Administration Committee, was changing his tune regarding revising the Federal Election Commission along the lines mandated by the U.S. Supreme Court in its landmark decision issued a month earlier in the case challenging the constitutionality of the Federal Election Campaign Act Amendments of 1974. States the news article:

> Organized labor, which originally showed little interest in the fate of the FEC after the Supreme Court ruling, last week lined up with reform advocates and began pushing for a bill to reconstitute the commission.
>
> Hays spent last weekend in Miami, talking with key labor officials at the AFL-CIO convention there, and when he returned he had given up his battle to destroy the independent election agency . . .
>
> The big bonus for organized labor—and the one provision which Ford told Hays he may oppose—would overturn a controversial FEC ruling viewed as favorable to big corporations . . .
>
> At this morning's committee meeting, Rep. Bill

Frenzel (R.-Minn.), warned Hays this particular portion of the bill "is going to be sticky."

The chairman swiftly retorted, "It isn't gonna be sticky because every Democrat is gonna vote for it, and we have two-thirds of the House.

"If you think this Congress is going to give corporations the right to solicit their stockholders, management and employes—and check it all off—you need to see a shrink!"

The second example is another news article which also appeared on February 19, 1976, this one in *The New York Times*. Headlined "Labor's Highest Chiefs Planning 'Tremendous Effort' for Election," the article stated:

Bal Harbour, Fla.—Organized labor's top leaders have been making plans here this week to mount what they say will be the most effective political action in the history of the AFL-CIO.

In a special report on the outlook, Alexander E. Barkan, director of the federation's Committee on Political Education, said that 1976 was going to be a "tough year" in which to elect additional liberals to the United States House and Senate.

"It will require a tremendous effort—an all-out registration drive among union members, a full-scale educational effort in which voting records can be a key instrument, and on Election Day a get-out-the-vote program that exceeds anything we've ever done before," he said.

Albert Zack, director of public relations for the AFL-CIO, reported that George Meany, federation president, Mr. Barkan, and other leaders reviewed plans and prospects for the 1976 election campaign at a closed meeting here today of the 130-member administrative committee of COPE, the federation's political arm.

One key device the federation is using, Mr. Zack explained, is a computer that contains the names, addresses, local union and other pertinent information for 14 million members and retired members in 45 different states. These will be matched against voter registration lists, he said, to provide printouts of those registered and unregistered, to use for mailings, to provide telephone call lists, and to use for getting out the labor vote on Election Day.

The costs of these efforts and the computer, Mr. Zack said, can be paid for by members' dues money under the law that permits such expenditures by organized labor for reaching its own members. Voluntary contributions

6

from members can be later used to assist particular candidates within the limits of the Federal Election Campaign Act Amendments of 1974.

It is becoming increasingly clear to thoughtful Americans that the Watergate scandal has not led to true election reform, to the thorough cleaning up of illegal, unconstitutional and unethical campaign practices. Instead it has brought about a conspiracy by liberal politicians, union bosses, and radical self-styled "public interest" groups to rig our elections and to deny the freedoms of the American people to choose in the election process.

The only way this conspiracy can be defeated and real reform achieved is through public exposure and public education. Such real reform should include, among other things, getting both Big Business and Big Labor out of political bankrolling by enacting new, stringent laws that would effectively bar corporate and union contributions in any form. It is toward this end that this book has been written.

March 1, 1976,
Washington, D.C.

Introduction

> At any given moment there is an orthodoxy, a body of ideas which it is assumed that all right-thinking people will accept without question. It is not exactly forbidden to say this, that or the other, but it is 'not done' to say it. . . . Anyone who challenges the prevailing orthodoxy finds himself silenced with surprising effectiveness. A genuinely unfashionable opinion is almost never given a fair hearing, either in the popular press or in the highbrow periodicals.
> —GEORGE ORWELL, *Animal Farm* (1945)

This book challenges the prevailing orthodoxy that maintains that labor unions today engage essentially in collective bargaining and are not primarily political organizations, and that the political spending of organized labor is minuscule when compared with the campaign contributions pouring forth from the business community. The truth is that the *raison d'être* of organized labor has become partisan politics, resulting in its wielding political influence far disproportionate to the number of members it represents.

The evidence marshaled in this volume proves beyond a reasonable doubt, not merely by its weight, that:

(1) Organized labor ranks among the most powerful and active political forces in the United States. Indeed, its leaders refer to it, quite credibly, as the most effective political machine in the country and as the most influential single voice in national policymaking, since almost two thirds of the members of the United States Senate and House of Representatives, as well as a large number of state and local political officials, owe their offices in material part to election support, financial and other, furnished by organized labor.

(2) To a great degree, the funds that support organized labor's political activities come from the dues paid by union members, most of whom are under compulsory-unionism contracts, and those funds are committed to partisan political purposes by the union bosses without regard to the normally conflicting political sentiments, loyalties, and wishes prevailing among union members.

Despite an existing federal statute prohibiting labor unions from spending their dues money for partisan political activities, organized labor today directly and indirectly is contribut-

9

ing tens of millions of dollars to candidates it supports, most of whom are of a single political party. The federal statute that to date law-enforcement authorities have enforced only rarely against unions is the Federal Corrupt Practices Act as amended by the Federal Election Campaign Act of 1971, and the Act's Amendments of 1974, found in title 18, section 610 of the United States Code. The act—applicable to corporations, national banks, and labor unions—is reproduced in full at the conclusion of this Introduction, but the following excerpt is key to the discussion here:

> Sec. 610. It is unlawful for . . . any labor organization to make a contribution or expenditure in connection with any election at which Presidential and Vice-Presidential electors or a Senator or Representative in, or a Delegate or Resident Commissioner to Congress are to be voted for, or in connection with any primary election or political convention or caucus held to select candidates for any of the foregoing offices, or for any candidate, political committee, or other person to accept or receive any contribution prohibited by this section.
>
> Every . . . labor organization which makes any contribution or expenditure in violation of this section shall be fined not more than $25,000; and every . . . officer of any labor organization, who consents to any contribution or expenditure by the . . . labor organization . . . and any person who accepts or receives any contribution, in violation of this section, shall be fined not more than $1,000 or imprisoned not more than one year, or both; and if the violation was willful, shall be fined not more than $50,000 or imprisoned not more than two years, or both.

Barkan Speaks

Labor leaders, of course, vigorously protest what they characterize as the "myth" of their powerful political apparatus and of their generous spending from tax-exempt treasury funds on political activities. One of the top chieftains leading the protest is Alexander Barkan, director of the AFL-CIO Committee on Political Education (COPE), the overt political arm of the giant labor federation. Fair play dictates that Barkan's viewpoint on labor's political spending be given equal time here, before evidence is presented—mostly from union documents and material—that, I believe, overwhelmingly refutes his position. The following views are from Barkan's letter to syndicated labor columnist Victor Riesel; they appeared in the latter's newspaper column of February 15, 1973:

Dear Vic:

The 1972 political campaign proved anew how widespread is the media—and consequently, the public—misconception of the role of AFL-CIO COPE in politics. Now that most of the heat of the campaign is cooled off, I'd like to correct these misunderstandings—myths, if you will. Anything you can do to make the record clear will certainly help the public's understanding in future elections.

First, there is no "massive labor slush fund" for politics. There never was. We operate quite openly and did so long before the new reporting laws. We file our reports of financial contributions to candidates to the penny, and on time, with appropriate authorities. As of Nov. 2, 1972, the most recent filing date, we find contributions of $1,128,300.31. The final report reflected another $100,000-plus in contributions.

These funds—contrary to some reports—do not come from union treasuries, but from small voluntary donations by union members.

Despite these publicly available figures, a political functionary in California in 1972 fantasized a COPE budget of $72 million and tried to pass it off as genuine. Incredibly, his monumentally exaggerated figure was picked up and given currency by major elements of the media. Thus myth can become entrenched as fact and molehills are turned into mountains.

Lest any persons are genuinely alarmed over National COPE contributions of over $1 million, let me point out that political contributions of one Chicago millionaire alone equaled it.

So there is the misconception of massive labor funds in politics when, in fact, labor's funds are really quite modest, given over-all campaign spending running into the hundreds of millions of dollars.

COPE functions quite openly, as well, in the manner of its endorsements of candidates. The only endorsement power of the National AFL-CIO is in the matter of presidential and vice presidential candidates. The 35-member Executive Council has the initial responsibility and, as is already widely known, in 1972 it decided by a vote of 27 to 3, to make no presidential endorsement.

All other endorsements are made at the state, congressional district and community levels, by the state or local

11

COPEs. They are made openly and democratically. We here in COPE headquarters don't make that decision: it is made by the people who will be represented by the candidate.

In 1972, 408 candidates for U.S. House and Senate and governor were endorsed in this fashion. I should point out, endorsements are not made whimsically, nor are they made on the basis of a candidate's party affiliation. The platform and public records of candidates, especially their voting records, are studied closely and form the basis of endorsement.

It is true that most of the candidates endorsed are Democrats, and the media often suggests that this shows COPE is merely an appendage of the Democratic Party. We are not. The fact is—I repeat—candidates win endorsement from the state or local COPE on the basis of their record as individuals, not their party affiliation. In 1972, in fact, some 25 Republicans were endorsed for high federal office, among them Sens. Clifford Case (N.J.), Edward Brooke (Mass.) and James Pearson (Kansas).

Somehow, too, there has been planted in the public mind the vision of "labor bosses" directing a vast paid army into political battle. Nothing could be further off the mark. On election day, COPE fielded about 110,000 get-out-the-vote workers nationwide. All but a handful of these were volunteers. What political effect we have is achieved by the thousands and thousands of union men and women, and their family members, who volunteer their time to the COPE program. Volunteers conduct our registration and education efforts and get-out-the-vote drives. Some members of our COPE Women's Activities Department have contributed upwards of 10,000 hours of volunteer time to COPE. Obviously, the image of a paid host of mercenaries often portrayed in the media doesn't square with this reality.

Incidentally, COPE has been scrutinized, examined, turned upside down and inside out more than once since 1956 by federal agencies, and the basis for a formal charge, though zealously searched for, has never been found. This sustains, I believe, our claim that we operate openly and scrupulously within the law.

I hope this helps lay to rest at least the major and most persistent myths about labor in poliitcs. Our primary purpose is to engage union members in the political process—to get them registered, to help inform them on issues and the records of candidates, to get them out to vote.

We think working to increase the political participa-

12

tion of our members is important. We think it's good work in our democracy and FOR our democracy. That's what we do. . . and we're proud of it.

Sincerely,
/s/ Al
ALEXANDER E. BARKAN
National Director

The authoritative labor columnist, however, does not find Barkan's views to be in accord with his own. On the contrary, Riesel realistically recognizes that the token figures of labor's cash contributions tossed around by Barkan are only the tip of the iceberg—that organized labor in each national election year actually spends tens of millions of tax-exempt dollars on candidates it endorses. Riesel estimates that union officials actually spent some $60 million in the 1968 elections and $50 million in 1972. Predictably, union officials have challenged the accuracy of Riesel's estimates. On November 3, 1973, Riesel publicly responded to one such challenge when requested to do so by the *Orlando* (Fla.) *Sentinel-Star:*

"In measuring the value of campaign contributions, the unions do not admit that there is far more than cash gifts to be considered," Riesel said.

"If you apply cost accounting to what the unions do in a political way," he said, "you will find that the non-cash contributions consist of staff time—meaning union officials who are assigned to compaigns for months on end—printing costs, postage, telephone and various other support services financed entirely with compulsory union dues and fees.

"For example, during the recent Democratic telethon, the Communications Workers of America furnished 10,000 telephone operators to take calls. They were supposed to be volunteers, but were they? Who paid their carfare?

"How do you 'cost out' the value of 72,000 house-to-house canvassers by labor in the 1968 election, or the 95,000 election day car pool drivers and baby sitters?

"The carpenters' union sent letters to 900,000 people urging them to vote Democratic. Think of the expense of that. There were 600 political organizers from the steel-workers, a similar number from the auto workers. In 638 localities throughout the country there were 8,000 telephone banks manned by a total of 25,000 persons. There were 94,000 distributors of material.

"It is time and services, not just cash contributions alone, which I consider in making my estimates. I know my estimates are right. I know they spent the time and money. Let them open their books if they say they didn't."

This, then, is the hundred-million-dollar payoff, how big labor buys its candidates! In the 1972 elections Riesel estimated organized labor spent $50 million. In reviewing the vast outpouring of union funds pumped into the 1974 elections, Riesel commented that he "stopped counting when it passed $25 million." (See Appendix I for a Common Cause study concerning $74 million spent by Congressional candidates in 1974.) In 1976 organized labor is expected to spend a record amount to elect a labor government composed of a liberal in the White House and a two-thirds liberal block in both the Senate and the House.

1974

A good deal of evidence has been amassed with regard to the effectiveness of union political activity in the 1974 special and national elections. (See Appendix 2 for a speech by Congressman Robert Michel [R-Ill.] exposing union "in-kind" contributions in four special congressional elections in 1974.)

In its report to the 11th AFL-CIO biennial convention in October 1975 held in San Francisco, the AFL-CIO Executive Committee boasted of the victories of labor-backed candidates in the 1974 national elections:

Labor's political programs in 1974 were more effective than any previous election effort.

This high level of effectiveness contributed tremendously to a major shift in Congress toward the progressive, pro-worker position on issues and correspondingly away from the reactionary economic and social policies of the Nixon years.

Obviously, circumstances played a major role in the 1974 results—widespread citizen disgust over Watergate, deep anxiety over jobs, inflation and the health of the economy.

But the fact is, never before did the COPE operation work so effectively among our own members and voting-age-members of their families in every phase of the program—funding, special manpower, volunteers, registration and get-out-the-vote, communications, materials and the involvement of Executive Council members and allied organizations.

These many components of victory helped produce a

COPE record of 70 percent success in election of its endorsed candidates for U.S. House, U.S. Senate and governor. In the House, 270 of 389 endorsed candidates won; in the Senate, 25 of 33; in gubernatorial races, 26 of 33.

The success rate in marginal districts was lower, as expected. But even here, a large majority of endorsees were elected, particularly in the House. In the process, dozens of conservatives and ultraconservatives who had held their seats for many years were defeated. In Indiana alone, five new representatives—all COPE-endorsed—were elected, replacing congressmen who had a cumulative COPE voting record of 40 "right" and 292 "wrong" votes.

The impact of COPE's over-all effort goes far beyond the vote tallies, since many other factors were involved last November. One important example is that COPE was able—through its register-and-vote programs—to reach union members and voting-age members of their families and produce a comparatively good voting performance among union members.

Though only 38 percent of eligible voters turned out nationally, among our own membership and their families the voter turnout exceeded 50 percent, and in many areas went far above that. In New Jersey's 2nd District, for example, where conservative Rep. Charles Sandman was defeated, 60 percent of eligible union members and voting-age members of their families voted on election day.

This pattern was present in many of the key districts and states where major House gains were made, or friendly seats held, including the Indiana 2nd and 8th Districts, Colorado 2nd, Connecticut 2nd, Oregon's 1st and 4th, Utah's 1st and 2nd. Even in a couple of losing causes—the Maine 1st and Arkansas 3rd—a high percentage of union members voted. In Arizona, where a friendly governor was narrowly elected, the turnout of union members in five key Phoenix precincts ranged from 70 to 84 percent.

This aspect of 1974, perhaps more than any other, demonstrates the increasing growth and effectiveness of COPE organization. It shows that in a year in which many voters were turned off, the labor movement was able to reach and motivate a respectable percentage of its members. While 50 percent is not satisfactory, in the context of 1974 it is an achievement of no little note, and indicates that in a healthier political climate substantially higher percentages than that—or than in any previous year—can be achieved.

Labor's Role in the 1974 Elections

For the labor movement, the 1974 campaign began soon after the 1972 campaign ended. Marginal or potentially-marginal U.S. House and Senate seats were quickly identified and recognized as the areas in which major gains or losses would occur in 1974. Hence, concentration on these districts began early, and it was these, indeed, that provided the large gains in progressive candidates elected November 5.

While substantial attention was of course paid to other congressional and senatorial contests, the focus on marginal races dictated more emphasis on recruitment of volunteers, assignment of full-time staff, special attention to registration and get-out-the-vote programs, improved precinct organization and extra effort to generate informational materials for distribution to members.

In these districts, too, the efforts of the A. Philip Randolph Institute and the COPE minorities department, Frontlash, the Labor Council for Latin-American Advancement and senior citizens were concentrated where appropriate.

In addition, the special program under which members of the Executive Council assumed responsibility for guidance and assistance to COPE's programs in various states was centered on marginal House and Senate contests.

Sixteen members of the council participated in assigned key states, working with state and local councils and helping to coordinate their COPE efforts. The 16 were Vice Presidents Abel, Bommarito, Dennis, Finley, Grospiron, Guinan, Hall, Hardy, Housewright, Keenan, Lyons, Raftery, Sidell, Shanker, Stetin and Ward.

COPE funding in 1974 reached an all-time high, totalling more than $3.3 million for all programs, including direct contributions, and far exceeding the $2.7 million total in 1972.

Contributing significantly to the growth in effectiveness of overall COPE activities was further development of the computer program and the related critical path method, which charts an accurate schedule of all the activities and responsibilities associated with political action and education. As of the 1974 election period, there were 36 states in the COPE computer program, representing nearly 11 million membership records, compared with the 1972 figures of 23 states and 7.7 million records.

In 1974, the computer produced for COPE more than 30 million print-outs in the form of mailing labels, listings and 3-x-5 cards and performed sortings of local union listings of non-registered members, telephone bank listings, precinct street lists for election day and labels for specific marginal district elections.

The readiness of material through the computer, plus the added sophistication of the critical path method, made possible the relatively strong union-member registration and voting performance as contrasted with the apathy of the general voting citizenry.

More than 110,000 volunteers contributed millions of hours to COPE programs at the community level during register-and-vote campaigns, staffing telephone banks, polling, canvassing, checking registration, distributing materials and getting out the vote—mostly under the aegis of the COPE Women's Activities Department.

Approximately 20,000 phones were installed specifically for phone bank use in COPE-WAD workshops, and some 10,000 more were made available in union offices and homes.

COPE programs in association with several coalition allies achieved considerable impact among specific population groupings. The COPE minorities department and A. Philip Randolph Institute helped produce relatively high voter turnout in black communities within many marginal districts, as did the newly-formed Labor Council for Latin-American Advancement in Latin communities. Frontlash carried out its most far-reaching election year program, concentrating on registration and get-out-the-vote in union and central city areas in 65 marginal districts. In addition, Concerned Seniors for Better Government functioned effectively in marginal House and Senate contests in 23 states, including 16 Senate and 50 House races.

(Note: See Appendix 3 for a list of members of Congress endorsed and supported by COPE and their 1975 voting records as compiled by the Americans for Democratic Action and the American Conservative Union.)

Watergate

One of the most significant revelations of the multifaceted Watergate scandal has been the number of corporations (perhaps as many as thirty) that contributed illegal corporate funds to politicians in both major political parties.

These contributions from corporate treasuries are indefensible. Violations of the Federal Election Campaign Act should be prosecuted no matter who is involved—corpora-

17

tions, national banks, or labor organizations, all of which are covered by the act.

Nevertheless, there are some important differences between these political contributions made from corporate treasuries and those from union treasuries. First, the corporations involved were for-profit business organizations, which pay an annual corporate income tax. Labor unions are tax-exempt organizations under section 501(c) of the Internal Revenue Code and pay no taxes. Second, the corporate funds were derived principally from voluntary purchases by customers of the corporations' products and services, whereas the union treasury funds were derived from compulsory dues money of union members, who must pay the dues or lose their jobs. Finally, virtually no evidence indicates that additional funds from these corporations were utilized to pay for campaign aid such as manpower, transportation, partisan voter-registration and voter-turnout programs, telephones, signs, brochures and pamphlets, and other resources, However, labor organizations routinely mobilize all of these means to aid partisan political campaigns. Senator Robert Packwood (R-Oreg.), responding not long ago to Senator Walter Mondale (D-Minn.) in a Senate debate on campaign spending, observed:

The Senator from Minnesota has indicated that, in his estimate unions do not contribute to political campaigns. In my experience, again in poliics, that is not true. Unions do contribute extraordinarily in the form of property, they do give the use of their buildings, trucks or telephones. Almost any night in a political campaign one can go to a labor temple and see the supporters of a candidate working at telephone banks, paid out of the fees, assessments and dues. That is a contribution from the union out of the dues that have been paid.

The influential role of in-kind contributions in campaigns was noted in the message of the President to Congress on campaign reform on March 8, 1974, the eve of the Senate debate on the legislation. The message declared:

In recent years there has been a proliferation of "in-kind" contributions in the form of campaign workers, printing supplies, the use of private aircraft, and other such nonmonetary campaign assistance. Because there is as much room for abuse with "in-kind" contributions as with financial ones, I believe we should prohibit all "in-kind" donations by any organization other than a major political party.

18

Any "in-kind" contribution by an individual would, of course, continue to be permissible, but would have to be disclosed as to both donor and recipient, with an open report of its reasonable value. These personal "in-kind" donations would come within the same ceiling limitations as monetary contributions and would apply towards the ceiling amounts for Senate, House, and Presidential elections.

Sources of Union Power

One object of this book is to trace the sources of organized labor's financial support of political activity. Summarizing, one may divide organized labor's political fund sources into two main categories: voluntary political contributions, and involuntary or compelled payments by union members. No matter how broadly one may construe the category "voluntary," or how narrowly the category "involuntary," two facts are clear: (1) Voluntary contributions by members are sizable but inadequate to the total needs of organized labor's political activities. (2) In order to fill those needs, organized labor relies heavily on "taxes" or assessments imposed upon the dues paid by union members, and on dipping into tax-exempt union treasury funds, which are derived from the same compulsory dues. (See Appendix 4 for affidavit of Jerry Wurf, president, AFSCME, on using union dues for political activity.)

Supreme Court Decision

On January 30, 1976, the U.S. Supreme Court issued its long awaited opinion in the case that had been brought to test the constitutionality of the Federal Election Campaign Act of 1971 as amended in 1974 (Public Law 93–443). The decision in the case, *Buckley, et al.* v. *Valeo, Secretary of the United States Senate, et al.* (—U.S.—, 44 U.S.L.W. 4127) both upheld and struck down a number of key provisions of the campaign reform act, which had been passed in the wake of the Watergate scandal.

The Court in its decision attempted to fashion a new balance between union and corporate political action. In a statement of significant importance in the decision, the Court wrote:

While providing significant limitations on the ability of all individuals and groups to contribute large amounts of money to candidates, the Act's contribution ceilings do not foreclose the making of substantial contributions to candidates by some major special interest groups through the combined effect of individual contributions from adherents or the proliferation of political funds each authorized under the Act to contribute to candidates. As a prime example, Section 610 [of Title 18 of the U.S. Code] permits corporations and labor unions to establish segregated funds to solicit voluntary contributions to be utilized for political purposes. Corporate and union resources without limitation may be employed to administer these funds and to solicit contributions from employers, stockholders and union members. Each separate fund may contribute up to $5,000 per candidate so long as the fund qualifies as a political committee under Section 608(b)(2). See Senate Report No. 93–1237, pp. 50–52 (1974); Federal Election Commission Advisory Opinion 1975–33 (Nov. 24, 1975).

The Act places no limit on the number of funds that may be formed through the use of subsidiaries or divisions of corporations, or of local or regional units of a national labor union. The potential for proliferation of these sources of contributions is not insignificant. In 1972, approximately 1,824,000 active corporations filed federal income tax returns. Internal Revenue Service, Preliminary Report Statistics of Income—1972, Corporation Income Tax Returns, p. 1. (It is not clear whether this total includes subsidiary corporations where the parent filed a consolidated return.) In the same year, 71,409 local unions were chartered by National Unions. Department of Labor, Directory of National Unions and Employee Associations, p. 87 (1973).

The Act allows the maximum contribution to be made by each unit's fund provided the decision or judgment to contribute to particular candidates is made by the fund independently of control or direction by the parent corporation or the national or regional union. See Senate Report No. 93–1237, pp. 51–52 (1974).

In the wake of the Court's decision, leaders of organized labor and liberals in Congress announced their determination to enact new legislation that would again tilt the balance of power towards the unions by bestowing new political advantages upon them while denying these same advantages to corporate political action committees.

In writing this book, I have, in my own mind at least, arbitrarily broken its contents into three segments. This, I hope, facilitates you, the reader, to make your own determination whether union leaders are guilty or not guilty of using the compulsory dues money of their members for partisan politics. In the first segment, which is this Introduction, I have sketched the general allegations levied against organized labor for its political spending and pointed to the Federal Election Campaign Act as being circumvented by the unions. Also in this segment I have permitted organized labor, through the carefully chosen words of COPE director Al Barkan, to make its own "opening statement" of its position.

In the book's second segment, Chapters 1 through 8, I will present evidence showing how labor unions, pretty much as everyday practice, use their tax-exempt treasury funds derived from compulsory dues for politics. The evidence covers scores of illustrations and ranges from assigning paid union manpower to candidates' campaigns to even paying for the printing of congressional newsletters, which many congressmen regularly send to their constituents. The evidence in the second segment is presented with minimal commentary; you, the reader, as a juror in the court of public opinion, can reach your own verdict.

The final segment, Chapter 9, is devoted to a review of the large number of remedies that are available to correct labor's campaign spending abuses. Foremost among these remedies, and the one I most strongly advocate, is the appointment of a special prosecutor, as in Watergate. I have reluctantly concluded, after an intensive and thoughtful review of the situation, that the present Department of Justice is too easily influenced and pressured to mount an effective investigation into union political corruption. The 48,000 outstanding employees of that department all possess sufficient personal integrity and rectitude to be unresponsive to anyone offering a bribe to influence a criminal or civil case being handled by the department. However, at the top echelon of the Justice Department, as recent events have shown, are some officials who are too easily influenced by political considerations when it comes to prosecuting or not prosecuting a criminal case of a political nature involving labor unions. For example, consider how the department handled the strange case of the Seafarers International Union. The facts are as *Time* reported in its issue of December 3, 1973:

> In 1970 the Justice Department under Attorney General John Mitchell indicted [Union President Paul] Hall and seven other Seafarers' Union officials for violations of the Corrupt Practices Act, which makes it illegal for corporations or unions to donate money to political campaigns. The case against Hall was strong. The Government reportedly had witnesses ready to testify that the union forced them to contribute to political causes, a practice so widespread within the union that the Seafarers' Political Activity Donation Fund (SPAD) was the

21

richest such fund within the AFL-CIO and enabled Hall to disburse nearly $1,000,000 in campaign donations in 1968. At the time of the indictment, union officials did not even bother to refute the charges. Rather, they claimed that the Government's aciton was political, as most of the campaign money had gone to Democrats, including President Nixon's 1968 opponent, Hubert Humphrey.

While Hall and his lieutenants waited for the ax to fall, however, the Government unaccountably sat on its hands. Curiously, the Justice Department of the same time was preparing its case against United Mine Workers Boss Tony Boyle under the same Corrupt Practices Act. But while the Boyle case ended in prosecution and conviction, the one against Hall was dismissed by the court in May last year on the ground that the Government had not pushed it in prompt fashion. The Justice Department did not appeal the decision, in effect simply dropping the case.

Just days before the 1972 presidential election, Hall provided a token of his gratitude to the Nixon Administration in the form of a $100,000 SPAD donation to the Commitee for the Re-election of the President. The gift bore a striking similarity to one Hall made in 1968 when the Democratic Administration of Lyndon Johnson rejected a Canadian attempt to extradite High Seafarers Official Hal Banks to Canada on charges of perjury. Hall at that time immediately donated $100,000 to the presidential war chest of Hubert Humphrey. In neither case was there any suggestion of prior bargaining between the Government and the union.

As the Seafarers' case shows, enforcement of the law by the Department of Justice may be temporized as political consequences are evaluated.

Some final words need to be said on my research material used in this work and why I have chosen the format I have. The prevailing orthodoxy that minimizes the real political muscle flexed by unions has left an apparent void in the knowledge of how organized labor exercises it political power, which is founded in its use of tax-exempt compulsory dues money. A dramatic example of this occurred on the floor of the U.S. Senate in December 1973 when the Senate Watergate Committee requested a supplemental appropriation to carry out its probe into the campaign activities of the 1972 Presidential campaign. Senator Paul Fannin (R-Ariz.) pointedly asked committee chairman Sam Ervin (D-N.C.) "if this investigation will probe contributions of unions, which amount to hundreds of millions of dollars." The venerable senator from North Carolina responded: "If the Senator or anyone else will give us any information that union funds were contributed out of union treasuries, we would be glad to have that information."

My aim in this book is to supply that information, not only to the U.S. Congress but to the American people as well. (See Appendix 5 for the ACA study, released January 23, 1976, on unions' contributions to members of Congress who voted for the prounion Common Site Picketing Bill.)

I am an attorney by profession. If this manuscript has an obvious weakness on its face, it is that it reads like a lawyer's brief with supporting evidence being cited wherever possible. This aspect may also be regarded by some as the manuscript's strength, since much published criticism of union political activity in the past has been long on rhetoric and short on facts.

Rather than risk being accused of making allegations without the proof to back them up, I have deliberately gone to the other extreme—that of letting pertinent union correspóndence, documents, publications, and materials (all in the public domain) speak for themselves. Where spelling, punctuation, and grammatical errors appear in the unions' correspondence and documents, I have left these undisturbed and uncorrected in the interest of authenticity. Few liberties have been taken with the documents' texts, save those which scholarly opinion in general approves.

Some of the internal union documents cited in the book have come to public light only recently as the result of a suit by a group of courageous workers forced to pay compulsory union agency fees, protesting the use by their union of their union fees for political purposes. The case is *George L. Seay, et al.* v. *Grand Lodge International Association of Machinists, et al.*, filed in the United States District Court for the Central District of California. The suit is being appealed to the U.S. Court of Appeals after having been dismissed on December 19, 1973, by the trial judge. Plaintiff employees are being represented in their litigation by the National Right to Work Legal Defense Foundation, a public foundation supported by citizen contributions, with offices at 8316 Arlington Boulevard (U.S. 50), Fairfax, Virginia 22030.

The cause of original research into the subject of union political spending is tremendously indebted also to an affidavit of unprecedented documentation. I refer to that which Professor Sylvester Petro of Wake Forest School of Law, the internationally distinguished labor law authority, submitted in

23

the case of *Gerald M. Marker, et al.* v. *John B. Connally, et al.*, filed in 1972 in the United States District Court for the District of Columbia. This book draws extensively upon Professor Petro's affidavit.

Title 18, Section 610 of the U.S. Code
Contributions or expenditures by national banks, corporations or labor organizations

It is unlawful for any national bank, or any corporation organized by authority of any law of Congress, to make a contribution or expenditure in connection with any election to any political office, or in connection with any primary election or political convention or caucus held to select candidates for any political office, or for any corporation whatever, or any labor organization to make a contribution or expenditure in connection with any election at which presidential and vice presidential electors or a Senator or Representative in, or a Delegate or Resident Commissioner to Congress are to be voted for, or in connection with any primary election or political convention or caucus held to select candidates for any of the foregoing offices, or for any candidate, political committee, or other person to accept or receive any contribution prohibited by this section.

Every corporation or labor organization which makes any contribution or expenditure in violation of this section shall be fined not more than $25,000; and every officer or director of any corporation, or officer of any labor organization, who consents to any contribution or expenditure by the corporation or labor organization as the case may be, and any person who accepts or receives any contribution, in violation of this section, shall be fined not more than $1,000 or imprisoned not more than 1 year, or both; and if the violation was willful, shall be fined not more than $50,000 or imprisoned not more than 2 years or both.

For the purposes of this section "labor organization" means any organization of any kind, or any agency or employee representation committee or plan, in which employees participate and which exist for the purpose, in whole or in part, of dealing with employers concerning grievances, labor disputes, wages, rates of pay, hours of employment, or conditions of work.

As used in this section, the phrase "contribution or expenditure" shall include any direct or indirect payment, distribution, loan, advance, deposit, or gift of money, or any services, or anything of value (except a loan of money by a national or State bank and made in accordance with the applicable banking laws and regulations and in the ordinary course of business) to any candidate, campaign committee, or political party or organization, in connection with any election to any of the offices referred to in this section; but shall not include communications by a corporation to its stockholders and their families or by a labor organization to its members and their families on any subject; non-partisan registration and get-out-the-vote campaigns by a corporation aimed at its stockholders and their families, or by a labor organization aimed at its members, and their families; the establishment, administration, and solicitation of contributions to a separate segregated fund to be utilized for political purposes by a corporation or labor organization: *Provided*, That it shall be unlawful for such a fund to make a contribution or expenditure by utilizing money or anything of value secured by physical force, job discrimination, financial reprisals, or the threat of force, job discrimination, or financial reprisal; or by the dues, fees or other monies required as a condition of membership in a labor organization or as a condition of employment, or by monies obtained in any commercial transaction.

PART I

The American Federation of Labor and Congress of Industrial Organizations (AFL-CIO) and the Committee on Political Education (COPE)

An Inside Look at the Nation's Most Powerful Political Machine

1

COPE: The Nation's Most Powerful Political Machine

Organized labor in America has always engaged in political activity, although it has been only in recent years that the union movement has molded itself into the nation's most effective pressure group. At its first convention, in 1886, the American Federation of Labor (AFL) urged support for "the independent political movement of the workingman" and in 1895 it established a legislative committee in Washington, D.C., to follow legislation before Congress and influence votes in both houses.

Samuel Gompers, at first a strong believer that collective bargaining was the best means for the workingman to achieve economic gains, eventually became an advocate of overt political action. He personally campaigned in 1906 against a Republican congressman in Maine who the AFL felt was opposing its vital interests on the House Judiciary Committee. Two years later Gompers publicly urged that the labor movement give strong support to the Democratic Party in the national elections.

In 1936 a major step was taken when key labor leaders formed Labor's Nonpartisan League, two of whose spokesmen were Sidney Hillman and John L. Lewis. The League supported President Franklin Roosevelt for reelection that year. Lewis's United Mine Workers pumped $460,000 into the Democratic Presidential campaign and Lewis himself toured the country speaking in behalf of Roosevelt. The AFL denounced Labor's Nonpartisan League two years later, regarding it as a tool of its new rival, the Congress of Industrial Organizations (CIO), and antagonistic to the federation. However, it was not actually until 1943 that the CIO formally established its own Political Action Committee (PAC) with headquarters in New York City and with 14 regional offices. Sidney Hillman became PAC's principal leader and soon was embroiled in a controversy about James F. Byrnes getting the Democratic Vice Presidential nomination. The controversy was sparked when FDR was overheard telling Byrnes to "clear it with Sidney." This little drama cogently revealed the full extent of labor's influence on FDR and the Democratic Party by the mid-1940s.

In 1948 PAC was split when Henry Wallace ran for President on a third-party ticket. The CIO Executive Board voted 35 to 12 to endorse Truman. While the AFL did not endorse any Presidential candidate in 1948, the election did serve to stimulate the federation to establish on a permanent basis its Labor's League for Political Education (LLPE).

Four years later, when Dwight Eisenhower was opposed by Adlai Stevenson in the first of their two Presidential races, the two giant labor organizations worked closely through their political organizations to elect Stevenson. When in 1955 the AFL and the CIO merged, becoming the AFL-CIO, the Committee on Political Education (COPE) was created to carry on the functions of PAC and LLPE.

In a legal document co-signed and filed in federal court in 1973 by Thomas E. Harris, associate general counsel of the AFL-CIO (who was appointed a member of the Federal Election Commission in 1975), the following statements concerning the national federation were stipulated as being true:

> The AFL-CIO is a labor federation. It has many functions which are set out in Article II of its Constitution, a number of which include political and legislative activities, including the advocacy of legislation which it deems to be in the interest of organized labor and the election of candidates favorable to its legislative policies. One of its largest departments, the Committee on Political Education, is devoted exclusively to such maters. In addition to the activities carried on by COPE, the President and the Secretary-Treasurer and some other representatives and employees of he AFL-CIO devote a portion of their time to furthering the political and legislative objectives of the organization and in pursuing activities designed to secure maximum support for these objectives by affiliated unions, and state and local AFL-CIO councils and committees, including their involvement in and planning and preparing for political activities. . . .

> National COPE seeks to coordinate the political activities of the national and international unions affiliated with the AFL-CIO and of state and local AFL-CIO central bodies. COPE's national staff is headquartered on the 6th floor of the AFL-CIO building in Washington, D.C. The Administrative Committee of COPE is headed by the President of the AFL-CIO, and consists of members of the AFL-CIO Executive Council. The operations of COPE are under the immediate direction of Alexander E. Barkan, its national director, Joseph M. Rourke, Deputy Director, and John Perkins, Assistant Director. The headquarters staff includes a research director and

an assistant research director, a national field coordinator, a data processing director, a publications director and various other staff assistants. COPE currently has 18 area directors and field representatives stationed in various areas of the country, and having responsibility for COPE activities in specific states. Included among the 18 field staff are field coordinators for minority groups and women. . . .

With minor exceptions, the expenses of COPE, including salaries of the COPE staff personnel, travel expenses, office supplies, telephone and telegraph, printing, and general overhead expenses, are paid by the AFL-CIO out of the general fund of the AFL-CIO, a fund which is drived principally from per capita taxes received from affiliated national and international unions. . . .

In addition to the expenditures of COPE referred to in the foregoing paragraph, some of the other departments of the AFL-CIO, including the public relations department, the publications department, the research department, the education department, the civil rights department and the legislative department, carry out some functions and activities which are integrated with the political and legislative activities of the AFL-CIO and COPE. No records or accounts are maintained by AFL-CIO in a manner which would permit a proportionate allocation of the expenses of these various departments to the political and legislative activities and functions of AFL-CIO and COPE.

The official newspaper of the AFL-CIO, the *AFL-CIO News,* and some of the printed materials prepared and distributed by the Education Department and other departments of the AFL-CIO seek to influence the reader toward political and ideological positions favored and supported by AFL-CIO and COPE. . . .

AFL-CIO and COPE officials seek to maintain close liaison with political party officials in various states and in various congressional districts, and COPE officials sometimes participate in the process of selecting candidates, campaign planning and policy decisions respecting the mechanics and strategy of the election campaigns of candidates for national, state and local offices. Through coordination with affiliated international unions and their state and local representatives, COPE assists in providing financial, organizational and manpower resources for the campaigns of such candidates. In congressional and senatorial election years COPE divides the marginal congressional districts and key Senate races and approximately 10 of the major national and international unions affiliated with AFL-CIO generally accept special responsibility for specific congressional districts or Senate races. These affiliated unions, in turn, assign staff representatives to these strategic areas. In order to provide these staff representatives with necessary training in political strategy and techniques COPE conducts political seminars and conference at various locations throughout the country at various times during the year. Such conferences and seminars are held in off-years as well as in election years in order to insure the existence of a large corps of politically trained union staff personnel available for assignment to actual campaign operations. . . .

A portion of COPE Educational Fund monies, derived ultimately from membership dues, are frequently used for the preparation, printing and dissemination of political brochures and other materials which support particular candidates for federal office. Such funds are also used for the purpose of making direct cash contributions to candidates for non-federal offices, such as state gubernatorial races. . . .

One of COPE's major operational tools is voter registration. By using its computerized voter identification program, COPE seeks to determine whether union members are registered and to which political party the union member belongs. The use of this program greatly facilitates the registration of union members and their families. COPE registration drives are now carried on in various states according to the laws of such states, throughout the year, utilizing staff personnel made available by affiliated unions. . . .[1]

No Party Can Match

Alexander Barkan, 65, director of COPE, has said:

We're kind of proud of our organization. We've got organizations in 50 damn states and it goes right down from the states to the cities. There's no party can match us. Every election it gets better and better. Give us ten years or fifteen years and we'll have the best political organization in the history of this country. We're at it the year 'round. We've got full time people in every state in the union.[2]

George Meany, a year before the 1972 Presidential election, boasted to a group of five hundred union leaders: "We've got the finest political organization in the nation right now in the AFL-CIO." [3] Two years later, in October 1973, addressing the AFL-CIO Tenth Biennial Constitutional Convention, Meany stated in his keynote speech:

Today, one year after one of the most divisive election years in our history, I think it is accurate to say that the labor movement is more widely respected for its political clout than ever before. And, I mean, by both parties. And, I think, our COPE operation is stronger and more effective today than ever before.

We have a lot going for us—and we have got to put it all to work next year to elect a Congress that can get the country back on the track again.

We need a Congress that has the numbers and the will to override every veto the President can throw at us [applause]—to liberate every dollar he impounds.[4]

COPE engages in practical politics. Director Al Barkan put it bluntly: "COPE does not engage in the cosmetic side of politics. We do not appear on network television, do not finance expensive media advertising, do not even make many speeches, except to our own union members. We perform the nuts-and-bolts basics of politics. We engage more in registration than rhetoric, more in organization than oratory, more in getting out the vote than getting into headlines." [5]

National COPE is duplicated in every state. The national and state COPEs serve as the eyes and ears of organized labor in gathering political intelligence. Their roles go far beyond this too, as COPE area director Daniel M. Powell stated in an interview. Powell acknowledged that there are campaigns in which COPE, not the political party's leadership, is actually in charge. "In some cases," he told the interviewer, "behind the scenes, I'm the campaign manager." [6]

The role of COPE as a candidate's campaign organization is admitted also by Meany:

Q. What do you do in these Congressional elections? Do you set up your own machinery in most places?

A. Oh yes, we set up our own machinery.

Q. Do you bypass . . . ?

A. Neil, they are not there to bypass. There just isn't anybody to bypass. Now, in the past few years, we have in some cases, sort of went in and picked up the stragglers who had some experience and really put them to work for us in getting out the vote and registration. We may do that in a number of cities. But, actually, we are not concerned with reviving the party, we are concerned with a specific campaign for a specific individual. This is where we use whatever money we have got and whatever talents we have got. . . .[7]

COPE's Research Department

COPE's research staff is composed of five full-time employees. Their work includes studying not only the issues raised in campaigns but also the background and positions of candidates:

The research workers maintain individual files on all five hundred and thirty five Members of Congress, the fifty Governors, Congressional candidates and the political campaigns in each state.

"Normally, the people we oppose are the ones we keep extensive files on," said Margaret T. Cronin, assistant research director. "It's not worth our time and energy to keep extensive files on liberals." She pointed to a file bulging with information about Rep. Joel T. Broyhill, Rep.-Va., whom COPE considers hostile to labor. A nearby folder on Rep. George A. Brown, Jr., Dem.-Calif., a friend of labor, was almost empty.

If COPE-endorsed candidates seek information about their foes, the researchers are happy to oblige. Often, members of COPE's field staff advise candidates of the files and make arrangements for getting materials to them.[8]

Financing COPE

Once voluntary political contributions by union members to COPE dollar drives are excluded, the main source of the revenues supporting the political expenditures of COPE is union dues, the bulk of which are paid under the pressure of compulsory-unionism agreements.

Table I
1975 Expenses, AFL-CIO COPE

Salaries	$ 870,065.03
Travel expenses	147,288.88
Printing	94,986.99
Supplies	11,052.28
Telephone and telegraph	13,982.93
Subscriptions	3,215.00
Postage	32,106.42
Field offices	29,146.50
Consultants' fees and expenses	(15,654.57)
Educational Fund	600,000.00
Matching funds for state political education activity	99,165.08
Other	(1,158.25)
TOTAL	**$1,884,196.29**

While COPE in a number of ways gets political money that traces ultimately to dues funds, present purposes are best served by observing the clearest, most formal, and most systematic method by which it receives political funds—the provisions in state AFL-CIO constitutions that allow for per capita taxes and assessments. Such provisions require local AFL-CIO unions in a given state to set apart a certain percentage of the dues they collect for transmittal to COPE either directly or indirectly, under the heading of "political" or "educational" budget accounts.

For example, *The New York Times* on November 2, 1975, in the article "State AFL-CIO Votes Raise in Dues to Push Political Action," reported:

> The State AFL-CIO voted today to double its dues to pay for stepped-up political activity. . . .
> Officially, the convention, representing two million workers throughout the state, voted to increase the per capita tax from 5 cents a month to 8 cents a worker this Jan. 1, and to 10 cents a worker the following Jan. 1. The extra money—$100,000 a month—will go to pay for a statewide committee on political education comparable to the national committee of the AFL-CIO.
> The statewide committee will have a full-time staff of 8 to 10 people and will be able to draw on computerized lists of union members by ward and precinct.

A sampling of other such provisions from state AFL-CIO councils across the nation follows (in each case the provision quoted is from that state AFL-CIO's constitution, with article and section cited, in that order):

CONNECTICUT, VI, 2: "Each local union affiliate shall pay a monthly per capita membership tax at the rate of eight cents ($.08) for each dues-paying member. . . . Two cents ($.02) of this amount shall be expended only for the COPE program."

LOUISIANA, III, 2(c): "The per capita tax payable to the Louisiana AFL-CIO shall be thirty cents ($.30) per member per month. . . . Provided that . . . eighteen cents ($.18) shall be used for education, public relations, legislative and political education and activity."

MARYLAND AND DISTRICT OF COLUMBIA, XI, 1(a): "Affiliated organizations shall pay dues to the Md. State and D.C., AFL-CIO as follows: (a) Local unions sixteen cents (16¢) per member per month on all dues-paying members, of which seven and one-half cents (7½¢) shall be allocated to COPE. . . ."

NEW JERSEY, XI, 2: "Local unions shall pay a per capita tax of forty (40¢) cents per member per annum. . . . The Executive Board shall have the authority to increase the per capita tax by an amount not to exceed an additional ten (10¢) per annum. . . . The President and Executive Board are empowered to establish the procedure for disbursing such additional revenue for a program of the Committee on Political Education (COPE), through the state, county central labor unions and their Committees on Political Education."

VIRGINIA, XI, 2(b): "Beginning January 1, 1970, and continuing through December 31, 1974, each affiliate, except subordinate bodies, shall pay a dedicated assessment of one dollar and thirty-eight cents ($1.38) per member per year. The dedicated assessment shall be used exclusively to finance the COPE–Public Relations–Legislative Program of the Virginia State AFL-CIO except as provided in Section 2(c) and 2(e) of this Article." [2(c) confines 25 percent of COPE funds to "educational purposes"; 2(e) that one-and-one-half cents of the $1.38 shall be allocated to a building fund.]

WISCONSIN, VII, 1: "Commencing with January 1, 1969, each union shall pay into the treasury of the Wisconsin State AFL-CIO a per capita tax of twelve (12) cents per month for each member in good standing, of which eleven (11) cents shall be for general fund purposes and one (1) cent shall be set aside for Political Education Purposes. . . ."

It is beyond dispute, then, that the expense of sponsoring COPE is borne extensively by tax-exempt union dues. The constitution of the AFL-CIO state councils clearly reflect this. So does the following 1970 communication from the director of the Machinists Non-Partisan Political League to the general secretary–treasurer of the International Association of Machinists:

The figures you saw in Miami were in error. I have just checked with COPE and they failed to include a $5,000 contribution which we sent in January to be credited to 1969. Our total for 1969 on their record is now $52,624 or 58.6 percent of our $89,000 quota.

Other unions make treasury donations in their educational fund quota to bring their totals up. Steel is almost all educational.[9]

As the above letter makes clear, unions affiated with the AFL-CIO use their tax-exempt treasury money to meet their Cope quotas, although they recognize that the money is destined for political activity. The AFL-CIO's most recent financial report shows that the AFL-CIO's expenditure of dues

36

money for COPE was $1.9 million for 1975.[10] This figure does not include the dues money spent on politics by the many AFL-CIO state and local central bodies, nor does it include the expenditures of any of the individual unions affiliated with the AFL-CIO.

One of the principal tasks of national COPE is to stimulate political activity at the local, regional, and international levels of affiliated unions. Here is a checklist of suggested activities at these levels, as contained in a COPE publication titled "Operation Win": [11]

. . . At the Local Union Level
Your local union COPE Committee should:
- Make sure all members, and members of their families are registered
- Get out your local's vote on Election Day
- Collect COPE dollars
- Develop year-around local union COPE educational program
- Develop corps of effective, informed political workers
- Distribute national COPE and international COPE materials to all members
- Report regularly to local union members on activities and progress
- Participate in district-wide and AFL-CIO COPE area-wide political programs and election campaigns
- Include, and involve, union women and the wives of members

. . . . At the Regional Level
- Develop coordinated programs for all locals in the district
- Guide and to the extent necessary supervise local union COPE register and get-out-the-vote programs and dollar drives
- Develop printed materials specifically for district use
- Implement political education program developed by international union COPE and localize it where possible for special application to your district
- Help locals build effective between-election programs
- Build support within locals for state and national legislative goals of international union
- Keep locals alerted to constructive accomplishments and votes of incumbent friends in state and national legislatures to build voting support for them
- Help arrange visits to locals for friendly incumbents and potentially friendly candidates
- Advise locals of use of funds retained by or returned to, regions in COPE dollar drive

37

- Develop materials for district and local union COPE use—printed matter, visual aids, research data, other educational and campaign materials
- Develop education and action programs; help implement them at local and district levels
- Assign specific functions for local union COPE Committee members as guides to their action
- Test sentiment of members on issues and friendly incumbents and potential friendly candidates. Advise liberal legislators of members' viewpoints
- Encourage local and district COPEs to do all they can between elections, as well as during elections, for liberal friends

Since 1966, COPE has placed primary emphasis on its marginal congressional district program, in which friendly incumbents or candidates in key districts are provided with campaign funds, manpower, and other union resources. On this marginal district program in 1968 COPE lavished attention equal to what it accorded the Presidential candidacy of Hubert Humphrey. And the program rated even higher priority in 1972, when COPE sat out the McGovern race. The development of the marginal congressional district program, the support provided in Presidential elections, and other key elections are traced below, beginning with 1966.

1966

In its report to the AFL-CIO Seventh Constitutional Convention in 1967, the AFL-CIO Executive Council stated:

> In the first reaction to the loss of more than 40 liberal House members, three liberal Senate seats, including that of the symbolic figure of Paul Douglas, and six liberal governors, the negative aspects of the 1966 elections were overemphasized. To maintain a proper perspective, it must be remembered that the pendulum pattern in American politics is standard. The extent of the 1964 presidential swing of the pendulum was abnormal, sweeping into office an extraordinary number of new congressmen and other elected officials from areas which are normally and traditionally conservative.

> The return swing of the pendulum in 1966 was actually less than might reasonably have been expected. For example:

> 1. The number of COPE-endorsed House members elected in 1966 (182) was only eight fewer than the number (190) elected in 1962, regarded as a very suc-

cessful year for liberals. (In strictly party terms, Democrats elected one more House member outside the South in 1966—165—than in 1962.)

2. Two COPE-endorsed, incumbent senators lost in 1966 (Bass, Tennessee; Douglas, Illinois). Only two COPE-endorsed, incumbent senators lost in 1962 (Carroll, Colorado; Hickey, Wyoming). COPE-backed senators made a better total showing in 1962, because 17 (compared to 10 in 1966) were incumbents, and most of these were strongly entrenched.

3. Thirty-four congressmen in marginal districts increased the liberal share of the vote over the 1962 figure, and 13 performed the extraordinary feat of increasing the liberal share over the 1964 vote.

4. Almost half the liberal "Class of '64" won reelection. Seven of them increased their margins over the 1964 figure.

Surely, without COPE's best efforts, the 1966 swing of the pendulum would have been more extreme, considering the nature of the unfavorable forces at work. . . .

Labor can never account for more than a minority of votes. In a close situation it can provide the margin of victory. In a situation such as in 1966 we can take satisfaction in having prevented worse disaster. Two major ingredients contributed to that achievement. They were:

1. a higher degree of involvement in the COPE operation at every level of the AFL-CIO from the national level down through the ranks of the state and local central bodies and, from international unions, more cooperation, more manpower, membersip lists for data processing pilot projects, all adding up to the best organizational effort ever mounted by COPE;

2. an unusually early start in planning and organizing for the 1966 elections and close and continuing cooperation with candidates.

1967

Although this was not a national election year, labor was active in local contests. One of these was the mayoralty race in Philadelphia, in which labor boasts that its support was pivotal. In the article "Labor Claims Credit for Victory, Tate Agrees It Played Key Role" in the *Philadelphia Evening Bulletin* of November 8, 1967, Edward H. Tooley, president of the Philadelphia AFL-CIO Council and its COPE, is quoted as saying:

"I don't want to sound like I'm bragging, but I would say

labor was fifty percent of the strength of the Democratic Party yesterday. . . .

"We had well over 1,500 paid workers on the street and at least 2,000 more union members who worked during key evening hours," Tooley said. "Some one million pieces of literature was given out during the past few months and over 100,000 letters. . . . Some 200,000 telephone calls were made in a voter canvass." [12]

According to the same *Evening Bulletin* article, unions spent $200,000 on the mayoralty campaign; national COPE contributed $25,000 of the total. The same article quoted William Ross, a member of the Philadelphia Board of Education and manager of the Dress Joint Board of the Amalgamated Clothing Workers of America, as stating: " 'We were canvassing and preparing for Election Day weeks ahead of time. We rang the door bells and asked the people to come out to vote. . . . We did the leg work the trained politicians are supposed to do.' " [13]

If COPE and organized labor unleash such vast union resources in a mere municipal campaign, it is not hard to imagine the power they wield in state and federal campaigns.

1968

In no other Presidential campaign in modern times has there been such an outpouring of union funds, manpower, and resources for a labor-backed candidate as there was in the Humphrey-Nixon race. According to COPE director Al Barkan:

No discussion of the 1968 presidential campaign is relevant if it ignores the role of the labor movement in helping Hubert Humphrey come within a whisker of a political miracle of the magnitude of the New York Jets' subsequent football miracle. Excluding only his own courage, drive, and effectiveness as a first-rate campaigner, the trade union movement's support was the biggest thing Vice President Humphrey had going for him.[14]

Barkan is frank to say that COPE activities were in fact AFL-CIO activities, which involved pressing both union funds and union personnel into service:

Negro trade unionists were mobilized at a series of conferences in the spring of 1968 which led to the formation of units in 31 big cities to increase the vote in the black

40

community. Three and a half million pieces of literature, especially prepared for the Negro community, were distributed. We were the major national organization working at registering black voters and getting out their vote. The Negro vote for Humphrey exceeded 80 percent.

The labor movement mobilized Mexican-American farmworkers; and the AFL-CIO funded an operation which included a million leaflets, radio spots, and hundreds of election day workers in California alone. Farmworkers' ballot boxes in the state also exceeded 80 percent for Humphrey.[15]

In the 1968 national campaign, "Labor's nationwide registration drive put 4.6 million voters on the registration rolls," according to Barkan. Of these 4.6 million voters, Barkan reveals—to almost nobody's surprise—"most were Humphrey supporters." He continues: "The figure not only represents trade union members and members of their families, but reflects the results of labor's registration drives in the Negro, Puerto Rican, and Mexican-American communities. In many states, labor did the registration job for Humphrey singlehandedly; the Democratic Party had abandoned the field." [16]

Throughout our states and cities countless union personnel worked for Humphrey, some full time, some part time; some were paid out of union treasuries, many, according to Barkan, worked as unpaid volunteers:

By actual count, prior to and on election day COPE groups operated telephone banks in 638 locations with a total of 8,055 telephones manned by 24,611 volunteers, union men and women, and members of their families. . . .

In many states, a house-to-house canvass was conducted as part of our get-out-the-vote effort, particularly in selected labor areas and in minority group areas where there are relatively few telephones. The number of persons involved in this operation was 72,225.

On election day, 94,457 COPE workers did the bread-and-butter jobs as poll-watchers, baby-sitters, telephoners, materials distributors, and car-poolers. All but a small percentage were volunteers.

The results speak well of the effort. In Michigan, labor's campaign enrolled 690,000 new registrants. On election day, 30 phone banks with 275 telephones operated by 550 volunteers were in action. Five hundred union people conducted a house-to-house canvass to get out the vote, and 6,000 functioned in other election day activities. Vice President Humphrey carried Michigan 49 to 41 percent over Mr. Nixon.

41

In Pennsylvania, labor's role was more clearly decisive in Humphrey's narrow 47–45 statewide victory. Our registration drive added 492,000 voters to the rolls, 600 phones were manned by 1,800 volunteers in sixty locations, 4,000 unionists worked the precincts in house-to-house canvassing. On election day itself, 13,127 persons participated in COPE's activity.[17]

Excerpts of a report by COPE on its 1968 "AFL-CIO Register and Vote Program" can be found in Appendix 6. The report contains significant information, including this statement:

And thus the story went in state after state, pointing up the fact that in 1968 the AFL-CIO mounted its best COPE effort in history. It also proves the point that labor, a minority group in co-operation with another minority group, which includes sub-minorities, such as the Negro, Spanish-American, Puerto Rican communities, is not enough to be predominantly persuasive to carry the majority vote in the nation. What this campaign lacked was the effort and vote of dissident Democrats which came back to the fold either too late or not at all.[18]

Union publications and printed matter are integral to organized labor's political strategy. Commenting on the Humphrey campaign, Barkan discloses:

Not that we slight the educational and propaganda aspects of campaigning, essential ingredients of any political effort. Evidence of the intensity of labor's political activity in 1968 was the 55 million pieces of printed matter distributed by national COPE to union members and an additional 60 million-plus distributed by state AFL-CIO bodies and international unions. It is unlikely that any organization—including the two major parties—ever produced so much political literature in any one campaign.[19]

An unusual factor in the 1968 election was George Wallace, who threatened to siphon off a significant portion of votes that might have gone to Humphrey. Leaders of the AFL-CIO decided they had to meet the Wallace issue head-on. Barkan describes this strategy:

Between the time of the early polls and election day, the labor movement's anti-Wallace campaign took effect in these ways: International unions instructed their staffs to speak on the Wallace question before local unions and to help distribute anti-Wallace literature; united labor committees formed in important industrial states and made specific campaign assignments to deal with the Wallace threat; national COPE material flowed to union members often supplemented by anti-Wallace literature produced and tailored for specific states or individual unions (more than 200 million pieces of literature on Wallace were distributed by the labor movement); hundreds of thousands of letters were sent to members by presidents of international unions; union journals and regular publications of the AFL-CIO carried hard-hitting well-documented stories and features on the Wallace record.[20]

George Wallace's candidacy in 1968 evokes, as it was to do again four years later, a sense of panic among the AFL-CIO hierarchy. The cause of this was the realization by the hierarchy that Wallace was able to appeal to the rank and file over their heads and strike a responsive chord. For example, when legal representatives of the AFL-CIO in 1973 stipulated certain political activities of the federation in a legal document filed in federal court, they agreed that the following paragraph and the quotation attributed therein to federation secretary-treasurer Lane Kirkland from Theodore H. White's book, *The Making of the President 1968,* were substantially correct:

In a sense, the challenge of Wallace had been a challenge to the leadership of labor itself. Their own membership had, as early as midsummer, shown Wallace picking up 25 percent of the labor vote in Pennsylvania, 32 percent in Connecticut, in Maryland even higher. By September, in Flint, Michigan, at the large Buick plant there, a poll of the 8,000 autoworkers in Local 599 showed Wallace outstripping both other candidates with 49 percent of the total; in Norfolk, Virginia, the Wallace challenge within the union was the springboard in an attempt to overthrow the local's internal leadership; in Pennsylvania, in Baltimore, in Gary, steelworkers were breaking to Wallace. Totally dismayed by the early confusion in Humphrey's headquarters in Washington, the AFL-CIO leadership considered its support of the Democrat and its drive against Wallace almost a mission of its own. "We had to do what we did," said Lane Kirkland, executive assistant of the AFL-CIO's president, "because the Party was bankrupt intellectually and financially. I reached the point where I said I'd never go into Democratic headquarters. I'd go in feeling good and come out feeling terrible. The only useful thing they did was television, in the last couple of weeks; and beyond that they didn't do a god-damned thing except cry.[21]

An example of the mobilization of labor's resources to knock out Wallace's candidacy is contained in a memorandum of September 23, 1968, from COPE director Al Barkan to international union presidents and secretaries, the text of which is found in Appendix 7.[22]

Although Humphrey lost to Nixon, AFL-CIO leaders were almost jubilant in assessing their effect on the election's final results. The AFL-CIO Executive Council in its report to the federation's 1969 Constitutional Convention declared:

At every level the AFL-CIO was involved in the campaign to an unprecedented degree.

The trade union movement, on the heels of President Johnson's announcement he would not seek re-election, was quick to organize a Labor Committee for Humphrey, co-directed by I. W. Abel and Joseph Keenan, and listing as sponsors principal officers of most internationals. This committee helped build popular support and increase support within the labor movement for Humphrey's candidacy for the Democratic nomination. Subsequently, at Chicago, labor delegates to the convention worked hard within their delegations to secure the nomination for Humphrey.

Members of the Executive Council served with distinction in their assignments to oversee the labor operation in individual states.

Special COPE co-ordinators assigned to 16 states bolstered the efforts of state COPEs in California, New York, Ohio, Pennsylvania, Georgia, Indiana, Maryland, Michigan, New Jersey, Oklahoma, Missouri, Utah, Minnesota, Massachusetts, Texas and Iowa.

Two factors came through clearly during the campaign and on election day:

1. The labor movement established itself more than in any previous presidential election as a major factor in American politics.

2. Union members listen when presented with factual, effective materials in a political campaign. This was underscored by the turn-around in the Wallace sentiment within union ranks and by the strong support given Humphrey on election day by union members.

The *Wall Street Journal* of Nov. 11, 1968, reported that "organized labor is alive and well, after all," and could "sway its members, mount a mammoth campaign

44

against strong opposition and poor odds to come within a millimeter of total victory."

At the Women's National Democratic Club on Monday, Nov. 11, 1968, former Census Bureau Director Richard Scammon addressed the group on the subject of "Voting Patterns for the 1968 Election." In the course of his remarks he made the following comment: "The real untold story of this election is the role of the labor unions in it. This is a remarkable story and should be told soon. There is no question but that the trade union movement effort materially affected the outcome and contributed substantially to Mr. Humphrey's total vote."

Scammon did not exaggerate. The labor movement was the single biggest factor Vice President Humphrey had going for him. In Connecticut, Maryland, Michigan, New York, Pennsylvania, Texas and Washington—all big states which he carried by close margins—the trade union movement was the decisive factor. In California, Illinois, Missouri, New Jersey, Ohio and Wisconsin— big states which he lost narrowly—the efforts of the labor movement brought him close. Only 300,000 more votes in Illinois, Ohio, Missouri and New Jersey would have turned the election around and won for Humphrey.

The two areas most often noted as revealing striking labor success were 1) limiting the net loss of liberals in Congress to four Senators and two House members, and 2) turning back the threat of massive defections to George Wallace.

COPE's selection of vulnerable districts shortly after the 1966 elections and two years' attention to those districts played a major role in saving all but seven incumbents and electing five new liberals to replace conservative incumbents.

Labor's 1968 Spending

How much did labor spend in 1968 in attempting to elect Humphrey President? The exact amount is in dispute: while labor political committees reported the disbursement of voluntary contributions received from their members, they failed to report the dollar value of paid union manpower and other union resources thrown into the campaign. Perhaps the most realistic amount attributed to union political spending is that advanced by syndicated labor columnist Victor Riesel, who seems to be aware that the directly visible and reported dollar contributions and expenditures of the unions constitute no more than the tip of the iceberg. In his column of November 6, 1968, immediately after the election, Riesel declared that "America's labor movement poured out well over $60 million for Hubert Humphrey." Riesel stated that the amount "on the record" spent by individual unions

is petty cash when compared with the local spending from the kickoff, massive Labor Day Parade up Fifth Avenue here to the last-minute caravans and get-out-the-vote telephone squads.

There were hundreds of radio and television broadcasts. Mr. Labor himself, George Meany, hit a network of some 330 stations five times. The Ladies' Garment Workers put on four national broadcasts. Thousands of locals hit the airwaves with their own appeals. There were special drives for the "nationalistic" vote—sometimes known as the foreign language appeals. From labor's point of view, it was their most splendid hour.

All these are on-the-record expenditures. There are thousands of indirect costs. No Humphrey caravan, on land, sea, or in the air, by ship, jet or truck, was without its share of international union presidents. They were seafarers, longshoremen, plasterers and electricians, building service leaders and retail clerks. They were the advance men—though some of them lead unions of a million members in less political moments. They were fellow travelers. And they stayed behind to make certain the candidate's visit would not be forgotten.

"It was the most all-out effort that the Labor movement ever had made," said Al Zack, one of a handful of men close to George Meany. "It was more intense than the effort to beat Barry Goldwater. I never saw anything like it. I saw more evidence of union signs, sound tracks, billboards, union registration drives, than ever before. We even had union registration headquarters deep in Watts. It was American Labor's greatest political push." [23]

COPE, it should be remembered, is only one of labor's national committees. Herbert Alexander of the Citizens' Research Foundation of Princeton, New Jersey, tabulated 37 political committees of labor that were active in the 1968 campaign. Their receipts and expenditures are listed in Alexander's incisive book *Financing the 1968 Election* (Lexington, Mass.: D.C. Heath & Co., 1971). In this work Alexander concludes:

In gross disbursements, labor committees expended 92 percent more [in 1968] than they had in 1964, and they spent more of it themselves. . . .
    . . . The contribution of labor committees . . . accounted for 61 percent of Democratic [senatorial and

46

congressional] candidates' funds and only 5 percent of Republican candidates' funds. . . .

. . . labor committees gave Democrats almost as much money as party committees gave to Republicans. . . .[24]

The United Automobile Workers (UAW) had withdrawn from the AFL-CIO by election day 1968. Under Walter Reuther's liberal leadership the union was still, of course, deeply committed to electing Humphrey. Victor Riesel, one of the few labor columnists who really takes the time to dig into union records, commented in 1969 on the UAW's 1968 financial report:

> The small print reveals that Mr. Reuther and his board of directors spent mightily last year to defeat Richard Nixon. Virtually all of the union's $2.1 million "Citizenship Fund" went for political stakes in the '68 race. This does not include the pay and expenses for 916 national headquarters field men known as "International Representatives." In the final months of the campaign, virtually all of these men spent virtually all their time campaigning against the Republican front runner. On the cost line, as the accountants say, this would come to many millions of dollars.
>
> Nor does the "Citizenship Fund's" $2.1 million spent last year include the monies poured out by the national union's regions and its 1,383 locals.[25]

1969

The American Federation of State, County and Municipal Employees is the nation's fastest-growing union, recruiting government employees. Jerry Wurf, AFSCME's president, is a dynamic liberal who maneuvers his union's resources where they'll do the most good in a labor candidate's campaign. The printed proceedings of AFSCME's 18th convention, held in 1970, contain a section, "AFSCME Political Action—1969," describing the union's accomplishments in this off-election year:

AFSCME POLITICAL ACTION—1969
WISCONSIN—April 7—the new Secretary of Defense had to resign his 7th District Congressional seat which had not been in Democratic hands in the 20th Century. A member of the International staff recruited bus loads of college students from outside the district to participate in the massive door-to-door campaign that propelled Democrat Dave Obey into an upset victory with 51.5 percent of the vote.

MONTANA—June 24—A Republican Congressman resigned his seat in the 2nd District. At the request of the Democratic candidate, John Melcher, through COPE, AFSCME arranged for the full-time release of two local union leaders to the campaign. Melcher won election in the normally Republican District with 50.9 percent of the vote.

MASSACHUSETTS—September 30—The Republican incumbent died in office in the 6th Congressional District, a seat that had never been held by a Democrat. A dozen AFSCME Council and International staff plus an International Vice President worked full-time in the closing weeks of Democrat Michael Harrington's campaign. He won with 52.4 percent of the vote.

NEW YORK CITY—November 4—The central labor body had overwhelmingly endorsed the ultra-conservative survivor of the Democratic mayoralty primary; but AFSCME and a few smaller unions stuck with Liberal Party Candidate John Lindsay. Council 37 supplied much of the leadership and muscle in an all-out campaign that returned Mayor Lindsay to office.

Of the two major gubernatorial races in 1969 one was in Virginia. State Senator Henry Howell, a self-styled liberal populist, was the labor-backed candidate for governor. In his public utterances in 1969, as well as in his 1973 gubernatorial campaign, Howell persistently pictured himself as the champion of the downtrodden and the "little people." However, there is another side to Henry Howell, one not generally known: that of the ambitious office seeker who openly courts labor support and earnestly solicits compulsory dues money from the unions' tax-exempt treasuries.

On May 7, 1969, Howell wrote the following letter on his Virginia State Senate letterhead to the director of an international union's political arm:

Since our meeting of January 15, in Washington, I have heard from only a few of America's great international unions, whose representatives met with me there, notwithstanding the fact there are only two statewide elections this year, that is for the Governorship of Virginia and of New Jersey. Those of you who were with me at the meeting know that the International Organization of Masters, Mates and Pilots and the Marine Engineers Beneficial Association each contributed $10,000.00 to my campaign.

I have a record of twenty years of commitment to the welfare of the people of Virginia. My involvement on behalf of the people of Virginia has most recently resulted in the first reversal of the State Corporation Commission of Virginia. I requested and received the complete cooperation of the Virginia State AFL-CIO, who joined with me in the appeal of the case. My services were rendered as a State Senator. The AFL-CIO paid the necessary Court costs. This is the type of economic and social involvement that will bring a breakthrough for labor in Virginia. . . .

Right now I need to raise $150,000 to project my record on television. We have received substantial assistance from state labor, but practically none from national labor.

If you do not like my record, write and let me know. If you like my record, write me your check that is consistent with a viable labor movement in this country dedicated to the betterment of the conditions of mankind and the structuring of a more civilized society. P.S. Don't wait! Do it today! [26]

In his unsuccessful 1969 gubernatorial race, Howell received more than $50,000 solely from local unions within Virginia. Four years later, when he lost the governorship by less than 1.5 percent of the vote, Howell received close to $300,000 in union money from within and outside the state. In both of these gubernatorial races union contributions were primarily from dues money. In effect, Howell's campaigns were run at the taxpayer's expense, using tax-exempt funds. And the above amounts do not include the cost of union manpower and other resources assigned to Howell's campaigns

The story of Henry Howell's races for governor of Virginia is not unique. There are thousands of other public office-seekers in all parts of the country who have requested and received tax-exempt compulsory dues money from union treasuries for their campaigns. In return they vote for and implement the public policies demanded by leaders of organized labor, ignoring the fact that many of these policies do not reflect the true sentiment of the rank and file.

1970

Organized labor approached the 1970 national elections with trepidation. As the AFL-CIO Executive Commitee commented later in its report to its members, "The arithmetic of 1970 was heavily weighted against liberal candidates, most notably in the United States Senate races. Of 35 Senate contests, 25 involved incumbent Democrats, only 10 incumbent Republicans. Twenty-one seats were held by good friends of the labor movement with solidly progressive voting records.

Of these, more than a dozen fell in the marginal category, with re-election considered a toss-up."

Despite the uphill battle it faced, COPE came through with an astounding record. It endorsed a total of 31 candidates for the U.S. Senate; 19 were elected. Of 336 candidates endorsed for the U.S. House of Representatives, 203 won. Of 28 gubernatorial candidates endorsed, 19 were victorious.

By far the two most important races to COPE were those of Senator Ralph Yarborough (D-Tex.) and Senator Harrison Williams (D-N.J.). Yarborough, chairman of the Senate Labor and Public Welfare Committee, was regarded by labor as its closest confidant and ally in the Senate.* Senator Williams, who was in line to succeed Yarborough as committee chairman, was equally esteemed by union leaders.

This is why COPE received a rude shock in 1970 with the defeat of Yarborough by Lloyd Bentsen in the Texas Democratic primary. With Yarborough as chairman of the Senate committee that has principal jurisdiction over labor affairs, COPE's strategic base from which it could implement its economic and political policies and block hostile legislation had been secure.

In the wake of Yarborough's primary defeat, COPE director Al Barkan ordered his research department to analyze the reasons for the loss.[27] In his covering memorandum to President Meany, which accompanied the report, Barkan stated:

After studying all the data carefully, I have reached the following conclusions about the Yarborough debacle and the lessons to be learned from it:

1. Labor's campaign was excellent. The candidate's was not. He began late and campaigned tepidly. In his own campaign post mortem, Yarborough admitted this, and warned fellow liberal senators and congressmen to spend less time in Washington and more time campaigning at home or they, too, will go down the drain.

2. Yarborough was ill-prepared for the nature of Bentsen's attack and responded to haymakers only with light jabs.

a. Bentsen employed all the passion-rousing issues—school prayer, busing, student unrest, ghetto riots—and linked Yarborough to them crudely, but effectively. The tactic kept Yarborough off balance all the way.

b. Yarborough apparently felt a sufficient response

---

* For a fascinating peek into power politics à la LBJ, see Appendix 8, a report from a Machinist political operative to the union's international president on Yarborough's reelection problems in 1964.

was reference to his seniority, and to other issues of little immediate public concern.

3. Bentsen outspent Yarborough 3–1, and this was evident early. That fact alone should have moved the Senator into high gear, but didn't.

4. Despite our excellent effort, our own members were affected by the Bentsen campaign and unmoved by the Yarborough one.[28]

Barkan, continuing his analysis of the Yarborough defeat, relayed to Meany what he felt were its lessons for the labor movement:

A. It is not enough for us to have excellent organization alone. We had it in Texas, and we lost.

B. Our educational campaigns must hit harder at the opposition. We must, of course, continue to stress the positive accomplishments of our friends. But we must show—in the struggle for the minds of our members—that behind all the phony issues raised by the opposition is a genuine threat to the well-being and security of working people.

C. In Texas, vast quantities of material were distributed by the State AFL-CIO. International unions ran inserts on Yarborough in their journals. International Union presidents sent personal letters to their members appealing for support of Yarborough. . . .

D. We have to hit the opposition in the same fashion we hit George Wallace in 1968—to hammer away at unemployment, high prices, the threat to members' unions and contracts implicit in the election of a conservative Congress.

E. The single concern common to all union members is their economic security. It is this theme that we can strike most effectively—your job, your wages, your contract are on the line.[29]

With Yarborough's defeat in the Texas primary, labor's political strategists hit the panic button. No matter what the cost, they decided, they must work to ensure the reelection of Senator Williams, who at the time appeared to be facing a tough battle in New Jersey. Within two weeks of the Texas setback, Barkan sent the following letter to international union presidents:

Dear International Union President:

As you know, our good friend Sen. Harrison Williams of New Jersey faces an extremely dangerous challenge in the June 2 Democratic primary election.

The recent defeat of Sen. Ralph Yarborough in the Texas primary brings home forcefully that we must "run scared" wherever a friendly incumbent faces primary opposition.

President George Meany already has appointed a special five-member committee of the AFL-CIO Executive Council to accept the responsibility of helping in the crucial New Jersey campaign. Members are Vice Presidents Joseph A. Beirne, Hunter P. Wharton, Peter Fosco, Max Greenberg, and Paul Jennings.

As a result of a meeting this week of this special committee with New Jersey AFL-CIO President Charles Marciante, it was agreed each International Union will be asked to accept responsibility for mobilizing its own members in New Jersey in a full-scale effort to get out the vote for Senator Williams by:

1. Assigning a full-time man to work among your New Jersey members to assure a maximum vote;

2. Mailing the special letter (enclosed) to all members in the state (the phrasing of the letter is offered only as a suggestion—you might wish to make changes in it);

3. Distributing a four-page supplement we have produced on Senator Williams to all your members in New Jersey. Your locals or the full-time man you assign should be advised these are available through COPE Area Director Charles McMahon, New Jersey AFL-CIO, 744 Broad St., Newark, N.J. Phone (201) 621-8150.

4. Coordinating all efforts with Area Director McMahon.

Please help us in this extremely important effort.[30]

The special letter that Barkan enclosed and recommended be sent to union members read:

Dear Member:

On June 2, the most important primary election in the recent history of New Jersey politics will be held.

Senator Harrison A. Williams, a good friend of our members and our union, is seeking election to his third term in the U.S. Senate.

I'm sure that you are fully aware that his return to office is vital for your own security and welfare and for our union's.

As a ranking member of the Senate Labor Committee, who may well become its chairman, Senator Williams is in the unique position of helping to advance legislation that is good for all working people, and to guard against legislation damaging to working people and their unions.

52

His voting record is one of the best in the Senate in terms of promoting the interests of workers.

He has stood the test on issue after issue over the years and has been a leader in the Senate in enacting such laws as minimum wage improvements, medicare for the elderly, aid to education for your children, anti-pollution measures, war on poverty, and many other proposals that benefit all of us.

I hope you will be sure to vote June 2 and that you will keep uppermost in your mind that a good friend, a very good friend, needs your help and that of all your fellow workers.[31]

Senator Williams was victorious in the Democratic primary and went on to win in November. After his reelection he addressed a group of key labor leaders, declaring sincerely, "I owe everything to you. . . . What you want you've got. I owe that much to you." [32] Williams spoke the truth, for he indeed owed everything to union support—to labor cash contributions and tax-exempt union funds, tax-exempt union personnel, and tax-exempt union resources, all of which were mobilized to win his reelection so labor could continue to control the Senate Labor and Public Welfare Committee. Here is the list solely of labor's *cash* assistance to Williams' campaign, which list does not include in-kind contributions:

Labor's Cash Assistance to the Williams Campaign

• The following contributions were filed with the secretary of state in Trenton, New Jersey:

National Committee to Reelect Harrison A. Williams

6/30/70	United Auto Workers COPE (Michigan)	$ 2,500.00
8/14/70	United Steelworkers of America	1,000.00
8/14/70	IBEW-COPE (D.C.)	220.00
9/17/70	ILGWU (NYC)	2,000.00
5/21/69	COPE	2,500.00
8/8/69	United Auto Workers COPE	2,500.00
10/20/60	COPE	2,500.00
2/12/70	Machinists Non-Partisan Political League	1,000.00
3/26/70	Machinists Non-Partisan Political League	2,500.00
4/2/70	Carpenters Legislative Improvement Committee	2,000.00
5/9/70	DRIVE	5,000.00
5/15/70	COPE	5,000.00
10/19/70	Amalgamated Meat Cutters	500.00
10/19/70	United Steelworkers of America	2,000.00

10/26/70	COPE	5,000.00
10/26/70	United Steelworkers of America Legislative Committee of New Jersey PAC	500.00
10/30/70	New Jersey State Carpenters Non-Partisan Political Committee	1,500.00
9/29/70	Active Ballot Club	5,000.00
9/29/70	UAW-Region O PAC Acc't. (Camden, N.J.)	5,000.00
10/1/70	DRIVE Political Fund (D.C.)	5,000.00

• The following contributions were filed with the secretary of the U.S. Senate and with the clerk of the U.S. House of Representatives:

Harrison A. Williams, D.C. Committee

1969	Machinist Non-Partisan Political League	$ 500.00
1970	Machinist Non-Partisan Political League	2,500.00
10/10/69	IBEW-COPE	500.00
4/24/70	IBEW-COPE	500.00
10/20/69	Laborers' Political League	500.00
5/11/70	Laborers' Political League	2,000.00
10/12/70	Laborers' Political League	500.00
10/20/69	Transportation Political Education League	500.00
4/29/70	Transportation Political Education League	500.00
10/1/70	Transportation Political Education League	3,000.00
5/6/70	Communication Workers of America	1,000.00
8/24/70	Fireman and Oilers Political Fund	500.00
10/24/69	MEBA #1	1,000.00
1970	Maritime Action Committee	2,000.00
1969	Carpenters Legislative Improvement Committee	1,000.00
10/2/69	National Martime Union	200.00
10/17/69	Building and Construction Trades	1,000.00
10/14/69	I.L.G.W.U.	2,000.00
5/4/70	I.L.G.W.U.	100.00
1970	United Rubber, Cork et al.	200.00
5/27/70	Industrial Union Department	1,000.00
8/31/70	Brotherhood of Maintenance of Way Employees	500.00
1970	International Typographical Union	200.00
12/3/69	Textile Workers Union	200.00
10/20/69	Railway Clerks Political League	1,000.00
5/18/70	Railway Clerks Political League	2,000.00
6/8/70	Railway Clerks Political League	2,000.00

7/24/70	Railway Clerks Political League	1,000.00
1969	Active Ballot Club	400.00
1970	Active Ballot Club	1,000.00
1/20/70	American Federation of Musicians	100.00
5/24/70	American Federation of Musicians	1,000.00
6/30/70	United Steelworkers of America	2,000.00
7/2/70	United Steelworkers of America	2,000.00
8/3/70	United Steelworkers of America	1,000.00

D.C. Friends of Williams
| 1970 | Machinist Non-Partisan Political League | 1,000.00 |
| 1969 | Maritime Action Committee | 3,000.00 |

Labor for Williams
| 1970 | Machinist Non-Partisan Political League | 2,500.00 |

Committee to Re-elect Harrison A. Williams
| 10/14/70 | IBEW-COPE | 780.00 |

LaSalle Letter Co. (Williams printing)
| 5/20/70 | Textile Workers Union | 1,200.00 |
| 6/15/70 | Textile Workers Union | 544.00 |

Williams for Senate
10/21/69	Communication Workers of America	500.00
9/29/70	Communication Workers of America	1,000.00
9/29/70	I.L.G.W.U.	3,000.00
1970	United Rubber, Cork et al.	500.00
1970	International Chemical Workers	3,000.00
5/25/70	Textile Workers Union	1,000.00
10/21/70	Textile Workers Union	500.00
4/29/70	Amalgamated Political Education Committee	1,000.00
5/28/70	Amalgamated Political Education Committee	3,000.00
9/23/70	Amalgamated Political Education Committee	2,500.00

Citizens for Williams
1970	MEBA #2	500.00
1970	Maritime Action Committee	2,000.00
9/16/70	I.L.G.W.U.	500.00
1970	United Rubber, Cork et al.	500.00
5/11/70	AFL-CIO COPE	5,000.00
5/21/70	United Steelworkers of America	2,500.00
9/11/70	IBEW-COPE	1,000.00
7/13/70	Teamsters DRIVE #688 (St. Louis)	500.00

H. A. Williams Campaign Fund
| 5/20/70 | Oil, Chemical and Atomic Workers | 100.00 |

| 10/7/70 | United Steelworkers of America | 2,000.00 |

Williams Campaign Committee
10/9/70	National Martime Union	5,000.00
4/9/70	Amalgamated Meat Cutters	500.00
11/11/69	United Auto Workers	200.00

Independents for Williams
| 10/19/70 | AFL-CIO COPE | 10,000.00 |

Williams Testimonial Dinner
| 1970 | United Rubber, Cork et al. | 500.00 |

Merkle Press (Leaflets for Williams)
6/10/70	AFL-CIO COPE	2,700.00
6/29/70	AFL-CIO COPE	1,674.00
9/28/70	AFL-CIO COPE	2,148.00
	TOTAL	$150,966.00

Senator Williams was not the only member of Congress from the Garden State who benefited in 1970 from labor's largesse. The *New York Times* of March 19, 1972, in an article titled "2 Jersey Democrats Received Biggest Labor Fund Gifts in '70," reported: "Senator Harrison A. Williams, Jr. and Representative Frank Thompson, Jr., both liberal New Jersey Democrats, received larger campaign contributions from organized labor than any other Congressional candidates in the 1970 elections, a survey of political spending by special interests groups disclosed. . . . Mr. Thompson was reported to have received the largest of any 1970 candidate for the House—$22,500, or three-fourths of the amount he received from organizations."

Thompson, the second-ranking Democrat on the House Committee on Education and Labor, is chairman of its Special Subcommittee on Labor. William V. Shannon, a member of the board of editors of the *New York Times,* has observed:

> Like its counterpart in the Senate, the House Education and Labor Committee is also a stacked committee. In deference to the AFL-CIO, every single Democrat on the committee is safely pro-labor. Except for one lone Republican from North Carolina, it does not have any members in either party from the South. Because it is not representative of the actual range of opinion in the House, the committee has trouble putting together legislation which can pass. The Labor Committee is not a place where one learns the rudimentary legislative lesson that it is wiser to give an inch in committee to save a yard on the floor.[33]

In the earlier cited stipulation signed by AFL-CIO associate general counsel Thomas E. Harris and filed in federal court in 1973, it was conceded, "In congressional and senatorial election years COPE divides the marginal congressional districts and key Senate races and approximately 10 of the major national and international unions affiliated with AFL-CIO generally accept special responsibility for specific congressional districts or Senate races." (Excerpts of a significant COPE document on 1969–70 COPE aid to congressional and state legislature campaigns appear in Appendix 9.) One of these unions is the Steelworkers, whose political action director, James Cuff O'Brien, began working on the 1970 elections a year early. The Steelworkers had been assigned political responsibility for Montana by COPE.

In carrying out his responsibilities, O'Brien submitted the following report on Montana to the Marginal District Committee of national COPE:

The second of the State Marginal Congressional District meetings for which steel was responsible was held in Helena, Montana, on August 21, 1969. In attendance were:

James C. O'Brien, United Steelworkers of America
Joe Crosswhite, President, Montana State AFL-CIO
James W. Murry, Exec. Secretary, Montana State AFL-CIO
James J. Leary, Director, Region #21, AFL-CIO
Mitchell Mihailovich, COPE Chairman, Butte COPE Committee
J. P. Mooney, Int. Rep., United Steelworkers of America
Ernest Post, COPE Director, Montana State AFL-CIO
Jack McCoy, Area Director, COPE, AFL-CIO
Vincent Bosh, President, Cascade County Trades & Labor Assembly
Joseph Meyer, President, State Council of Retail Clerks
Billy Brothers, Exec. Secretary, Montana Carpenters District Council
Vesta Shaw, President, State Council of H&RE & Bartenders
Russell Williams, Int. Brotherhood of Electrical Workers
Allie Cole, United Brotherhood of Carpenters & Joiners
Edgar Cozad, International Association of Machinists
Bernhard Merkel, Montana State Council of Carpenters
Gordon Twedt, President, Montana Farmers Union
Dave Fuller, Exec. Secty., Montana Democratic State Central Committee

The discussion that followed the introduction of the

national COPE views on both congressional contests, early registration, state legislative races and coordinated activities was positive and helpful. There was not a single representative present who dissented or challenged in any way the soundness of the recommendations on the approach to be made as viewed by national COPE in cooperation with the state and central bodies.

First Congressional District

The same team that has been so effective in promoting through organized labor's participation close cooperation with the Democratic Party in Montana is conscious of the difficulties to be encountered and is preparing early for the fight. Dave Fuller, Executive Secretary of the Montana Democratic Committee, was present and he is integrating his efforts completely with ours. There seems to be an absence of jealousy or friction and a common confidence and excellent working relationship.

Second Congressional District

Obviously, John Melcher, having won by such a very close percentage of the vote, will face a stiff Republican challenge. It is most fortunate that Ernie Post, who had been one of several of the people most effective in John Melcher's original victory, is the newly appointed state COPE director, for both the congressional districts involved. He is already working hard on a compilation of lists for checking, and he has found nearly all Internationals cooperative. It has been only two weeks that he has been on the job; and, as soon as he ascertains where there is a failure to obtain adequate lists he will notify the National COPE Marginal District Committee and seek their assistance. I outlined to the fellows present the approach being newly inaugurated in New Mexico where Sherman Miles, with the cooperation of the state body, has arranged to have all checking done through a central state facility; and, after the initial work has been done, supply the names of the non-registered to the local unions, making them responsible for the follow-through. Many of the fellows present, and again I must single out the building trades, felt that not only was it a good idea to follow this pattern but thought they could furnish in many of the smaller communities the names of two, three, or more individuals who would clearly take responsibility with Montana's liberal registration laws for handling fifty or one hundred registration assignments as a contribution to their belief in COPE. The Melcher fight will require our constant attention and will undoubtedly need some financial assistance from outside the state if we are to have real hope of retaining the seat.[34]

The Steelworkers were not the only union working hard for specific candidates. Evelyn Dubrow, secretary of the ILGWU Campaign Committee, wrote the political director of the Machinists:

> As you know, the International Ladies' Garment Workers' Union has been assigned the 19th Congressional District in Pennsylvania in the marginal district project of the AFL-CIO COPE.
>
> We have assigned staff to work for Arthur L. Berger who is the Democratic candidate running against Representative George A. Goodling, the incumbent Republican. . . .
>
> . . . I am writing you to ask if your International Union could send a contribution to the Berger for Congress Labor Committee 19th Congressional District. . . .[35]

Another key race was that for control of the executive mansion in Albany, which pitted former AFL-CIO counsel Arthur Goldberg against Governor Nelson Rockefeller. Victor Gotbaum, officer for the New York district of AFSCME, boasted: "This union was the biggest contributor to Goldberg's campaign. When we go in, we go all out. I think in terms of printing and money, we spent about $250,000 before it was over." Was it members' voluntary contributions or dues money that Gotbaum gave to Goldberg? "No, this was legal union money," Gotbaum asserted. "It came right out of the treasury, you know. It's the difference between soft money and hard money. On state campaigns, you can use union treasury money. On federal campaigns, you can't." [36]

How did labor-backed candidates fare in 1970? Shortly after the election, COPE director Al Barkan offered his private assessment:

> . . . In spite of the few scattered disappointments and in spite of the "Alice in Wonderland" claims of the White House the recent election was generally a satisfying one. On all levels, with some exceptions, of course, we did well.
>
> In my judgment, it was made possible by the best organized effort in COPE's relatively young history. In spite of weaknesses here and there . . . we were able in 1970 to continue the record of COPE fielding a better organization effort than in any previous campaign.
>
> I told President Meany and the Executive Council in my report that programmatically 1970 was our best year. They agreed.[37]

The official COPE report on the 1970 "AFL-CIO Register and Vote Program" supports Barkan's views.[38]

At the 1971 Constitutional Convention of the AFL-CIO, held in Bal Harbour, Florida, the Executive Council presented the following report on the federation's 1970 political activity:

Labor's successful political effort in 1970 overcame both adverse arithmetic and the calculated use of emotional issues raised to obscure more basic ones.

The anticipated 7–10 seat conservative gain in the Senate dwindled to a net gain of three, and in the House liberals actually picked up 10 seats, solidifying their control. Democrats turned an 18–32 deficit in governorships into a 31–19 advantage. . . .

The results of the 1970 elections were largely due to the political activity and education programs of the labor movement. In no previous election year had the AFL-CIO's political arm, COPE, at every level, functioned as effectively. In terms of funding, manpower, communications, registration and get-out-the-vote apparatus, and precinct-level organization—by any yardstick, 1970 was labor's finest campaign effort.

The special program developed in 1968 assigning members of the council to coordinate COPE's program in key states was once again eminently successful. Council members served effectively in many states where crucial Senate races occurred.

National COPE was able to give more financial assistance to endorsed candidates than ever, despite the fact that 1970 was not a presidential year.

Significant progress was achieved also in the bread-and-butter operations of labor's political programs, registration and getting out the vote. Much of the progress was a result of Voter Identification Programs inaugurated in key states and integrated into COPE's data processing system. The success of this program was made possible by the cooperation given national COPE by state COPEs, state and local central bodies and by participating international unions and their locals.

The entire labor movement heeded the Executive Council statement of August 1970 that "We must make registration and get-out-the-vote a priority activity . . ." and which called on "all segments of organized labor to make this year's election drive the best in labor's history."

The successful registration and get-out-the-vote campaigns reflected the urgency with which the labor movement at-large took the call to action. More than 35,000 union members and members of their families participated in the nationwide registration campaign. On election day itself, more than 81,500 participated in COPE's get-out-the-vote drive.

In the 26 states reporting results of the special Voter Identification Program, more than 5.7 million members' names were checked. (An additional 1.4 million names were checked in nine other states that reported on their registration programs.) The program increased member registration in these states from 53 percent before the registration campaign to 69 percent eligible to vote on election day.

The massive effort among trade union members generally was carried over into the minorities community, where the A. Philip Randolph Institute again effectively mobilized black trade unionists to conduct register-and-vote campaigns in their communities. The success of this program was clear in the election day results that showed minority groups voting overwhelmingly for COPE-endorsed candidates.

The register-and-vote campaign was complemented by a full-scale communications effort by international unions, state and local central bodies and national COPE, an effort which concentrated union members' attention on the real issues of 1970—their jobs, the prices they paid, their family's security. Scores of international unions used their journals, and other special materials, to relate these key issues to labor's endorsed candidates. State and local central bodies produced millions of pieces of printed materials on the issues and on candidates. The entire labor movement—including its journals—generated more than 100 million pieces of political matter.

The results of 1970 elections testified to the effectiveness and impact of the political programs of the trade union movement. COPE endorsed a total of 31 candidates for the U.S. Senate, and 19 were elected. Of 336 candidates endorsed for the U.S. House of Representatives, 203 were elected. Of 28 gubernatorial candidates endorsed, 19 were elected.

Several conclusions may be drawn from the 1970 campaign:

• The labor movement's political programs mature and increase in effectiveness with each campaign.

• Union members, by their votes, showed again—as they had in 1968 by voting overwhelmingly for our endorsed presidential candidate—that they vote their genuine interests, not their interests as defined by demagogues. An open effort was made by the Administration and its candidates to appeal to passions it felt were widespread in workers' ranks. In one Senate race after another, new lows were reached in the conservatives' use of the politics of hate and fear. But, union members —provided by their unions with the facts on issues and candidates—rejected the demagogues.

• These facts together provide helpful signs that 1972 will produce even more successful results at the polls.

Council Recommendation

All levels of the leadership and staff of the labor movement should make political action a priority activity from now to Election Day 1972, to cooperate with COPE in every way possible and thereby to assure that everything that can be done to achieve political victory will be done.

How much did labor spend to support its candidates? The *Washington Post* of October 21, 1970, said its latest investigation revealed that "Democratic candidates for the Senate are receiving five dollars from unions and liberal fund-raising groups for every dollar from their party's national campaign committees."

Americans for Constitutional Action (ACA), in a separate analysis, found that labor's "contributions actually totaled $4,297,297.04, including $1,767,044.73 for candidates to the Senate, $1,521,939.92 for House candidates and $1,008,312.39 for Gubernatorial candidates.' Democratic candidates in the three categories received the lion's share of contributions, the Democratic total being $4,153,746.52 as against the total for Republicans of $143,550.52."

1971

Most union publications devote considerable space to political news propaganda and activities. The *Public Employee,* a publication financed by the dues of AFSCME members, is the house organ of a union that proudly boasts of its political prowess. In its January–February 1971 issue, under the headline "Candidate for Congress says AFSCME Won Primary for Him," the *Public Employee* said in part: "For the first time in nearly 100 years the District of Columbia will have its own Congressman next March, and in all probability he will be a Negro Democrat who frankly declares that he could not have won the nomination without the votes of and support of AFSCME Local I."

COPE began working toward the defeat of President Nixon early in 1971. An example of its early organizing efforts appeared in the *Chicago Tribune* of June 17, 1971, which reported:

Union members are bearing the brunt of the fight against inflation and must work to elect a Democratic president in 1972 to reverse the trend, two speakers told the 37th annual convention of the Hotel and Restaurant Employees and Bartenders Union yesterday.

The speakers were Al Barkan, National Director of the AFL-CIO's Committee on Political Education, and Rep. Daniel D. Rostenkowski (D.-Ill.). . . .

Barkan shouted to the delegates, "Don't tell me about your contract negotiations next year. The most important thing you have to do next year is to organize your members and win the election."

1972

This was a tumultuous year for COPE. The roll of the political dice came up with so many surprises for labor that it is difficult to know just where to begin to catalog them. Perhaps the best course is to trace what COPE did in a few key Senate and House races, then discuss why Meany refused to support McGovern after the Democratic National Convention, and wind up by summarizing—in COPE's own words—the year's results.

A campaign of singular interest to labor was Senator John McClellan's battle for reelection in Arkansas. McClellan, then 75, had served 30 years in the Senate and had earned the enmity of labor's chieftains because of his courageous investigations of union corruption in the late 1950s that led ultimately to enactment of the Landrum-Griffin Act. COPE was determined to find a liberal Democratic candidate to oppose McClellan in the Arkansas Democratic primary and, with union backing, defeat him. The first step was taken in August 1971—10 months before the primary—when the political strategist for a major international union wrote the following memorandum to members of his executive committee:

A private poll that will not be published has just been taken by John Kraft Associates in Arkansas for Congressman David Pryor. It deals with issues people are interested in, rating of Nixon and others, and trial heats against McClellan in the Senate race.

The total cost of the poll was $8,000. Congressman Pryor is short $750 in paying for the poll. He contacted us and asked if we could help. This money would be charged against any contribution we would give to Congressman Pryor.

Educational money can be used for this and the poll would save us money in the future by our knowing who the strong candidates would be against McClellan, if there are any.[39]

63

The next step in COPE's strategy took place on December 1, 1971, when the director of the Machinists Non-Partisan Political League wrote COPE director Al Barkan the following memorandum:

The committee on Arkansas met at the IAM office at 9:30 a.m. on December 1. The following people were present: Chuck Caldwell, UMWA; Jim Kennedy, BRAC; John Pecoraro, Painters; Jim Harris, AFSCME; Peter McGavin, Maritime; Jack Waller, Firefighters; Joe Cribben, Plumbers; Dick Murphy, SEIU; Dean Clowes, USA; Frank Wallick, UAW; Mel Boyle, IBEW; Dave Sweeney, Teamsters; Al Loewenthal, AFT; Joe Miller, MEBA; Don Ellinger and Bill Holayter of IAM.

We reviewed the current political scene in Arkansas with particular relation to the Senate race. McClellan, who escaped a runoff in 1954 by 2,300 votes, was unopposed in 1960, and had an unknown opponent in 1966 who spent $2,000 on his campaign but got ¼ of the vote. He will be 76 years old next February. In 1954 the incumbent Governor was a conservative ally of McClellan's and in 1972 there is a moderate liberal who at least will be neutral. In 1954 there was still a poll tax in the state and a very small black vote. Of course, no 18 to 20 year olds were registered.

The Kraft Poll in July shows that in a heads up race between McClellan and Congressman David Pryor, McClellan got 42 percent, Pryor 20 percent, and 38 percent were undecided. Pryor ran ahead of McClellan in the 4th Congressional District in which he is known.

A meeting called by the Arkansas State AFL-CIO was held in Little Rock on October 31 with all major unions in the state represented. They were unanimous in support of Pryor. Pryor reported to the group that a substantial effort was being made among the 237,000 senior citizens and that the Concerned Seniors had been consulted about the program. A meeting has been held with Frontlash to work out a program to supplement Pryor's own voluntary youth campaign. He assessed his chances as even assuming a candidate to the right of McClellan gets in the race. He emphasized his confidence in that he is giving up a safe House seat to make the race. The formal announcement will come in February. Filing date is April 27 and the primary is June 27, but Pryor expects the legislature to set the primary up into early June.

Organizations were asked to estimate what resources they would make available to a campaign in Arkansas and some were unable to commit at the present time. Others made the following estimates: BRAC—$2,000,

Painters—$1,000, Maritime—$5,000, Steelworkers—$5,000, UAW (who has made an initial contribution)—$10,000, Teamsters—$5,000, MEBA—$2,500, Service Employees—$1,000, IBEW—$2,500, IAM—$6,000, and COPE is prepared for a $10,000 contribution. The IAM has assigned one full time staff member to the state. Teamsters indicated they would be able to put 2 in, the Steelworkers will consult with their Director, and UAW will make personnel available.

A D.C. Committee for Pryor has been established and can receive funds through his Congressional office. The Concerned Seniors, 1346 Connecticut Avenue, N.W., is prepared to accept money for the Arkansas campaign.

Other organizations indicating interest but who were not represented are: ILGWU, Retail Clerks, Pulp and Sulphite, CWA, and OCAW.[40]

The full list of labor political operatives present at the December 1, 1971, meeting is reproduced in Appendix 10.[41] One of those present was Joseph Miller, of the Marine Engineers Beneficial Association, to whom Congressman Pryor wrote the following letter two days after the meeting:

Just a short note to tell you how much I enjoyed meeting with you on Wednesday. I look forward to meeting again in the near future, both on a group and an individual basis, and toward working with you in the weeks and months ahead. As you know, it is my firm conviction that together we can work to bring about a new direction in both our State and National policy.[42]

On December 13, 1971, an IAM political operative wrote Kenneth Germanson of the Allied Industrial Workers of America, to bring him up to date on the conspiracy to defeat McClellan:

Again, my apologies for overlooking you and your organization on the Arkansas situation. I am enclosing some material for you to look over.

To bring you up-to-date more fully, let me give you the information we got from the meetings. In early October a very small group of union political operatives from Washington met with Bill Becker and Congressman Pryor about his plans. At that time Congressman Pryor was 99 percent sure that he would run against Senator McClellan. Bill Becker and two other international union people from Arkansas felt that if anyone could beat McClellan it was Pryor, and we agreed at this meeting to have a meeting of Arkansas labor leaders to evaluate the situation and to get some kind of idea of how much financial and labor help would be available to Pryor in a Senatorial race. A meeting was held in Little Rock on October 31, 1971, attended by state leaders of the Teamsters, CWA, UTU, Pulp & Sulphite, ACWA, IBEW, Retail Clerks, UMW, Steelworkers, UAW, and Machinists. Also attending were Bill Becker and Congressman Pryor. We discussed Pryor's candidacy against McClellan, the problem of endorsement, and evaluated Pryor's chances of winning.

We then had another meeting of COPE Operating Committee members here in Washington on December 1, to further analyze the situation. The meeting was attended by representatives from UMW, BRAC, Painters, AFSCME, Maritime Trades Dept., Firefighters, Plumbers, SEIU, Steelworkers, UAW, IBEW, Teamsters, AFT, MEBA, and Machinists. At this time we talked more about the state and the possibility of beating McClellan, and what we could do both with financing and staff people. As an example, Al Barkan has previously pledged the full COPE donation, we have pledged to match it, and some of the other larger organizations have done likewise. Our Vice President for the territory has also pledged two full time people for the campaign with a good possibility of two additional full time people. Other organizations present also pledged some staff.

I hope this information will bring you up-to-date on the situation. We feel that this is a real opportunity to knock off a proven, long-time enemy. I have informed Ken Schanzer, who is in Pryor's office, of my conversation with you and he will be in touch with you at a later date.[43]

The rest is political history. In May 1972 the Democratic primary was held in Arkansas. Pryor got 200,133 votes, McClellan 216,221, and Ted Boswell got 61,538. This necessitated a run-off, which was held in June. McClellan was the victor by a slim margin and today attributes his reelection victory in part to the public exposure given the above labor documents by the press in the closing days of the campaign. When Congressman Pryor, while campaigning, was confronted by reporters with copies of the correspondence, he admitted that "to the best of my knowledge they are true." With the exposure of the whole sordid story of how unions outside the state tried to buy the election, Arkansas voters rebelled, and Pryor lost.

What makes Senator McClellan's campaign story different from most is that while labor political strategists are constantly working to defeat conservative legislators in both major parties, it is only on the rare occasion—such as this one—that their plotting ever comes to light. For example, here is a letter—never publicized by the press—written to Al Barkan by the president of the Mississippi AFL-CIO shortly after McClellan's win:

Enclosed you will find a financial report on all monies spent by the State AFL-CIO during the three months prior to and during the Democratic Primaries (April–June). The Second Primary was conducted on June 27, 1972. As you will note, most of this money was spent on voter registration and voter education with our members and friends.

As you know three incumbent Congressmen did not seek reelection in Mississippi this year. They were: William Colmer in the 5th District, Charles Griffin in the 4th District and Thomas Abernathy in the 2nd District. With three incumbents stepping down, we felt we had a golden opportunity to elect three friendly Congressmen and, therefore, concentrated our efforts in this direction.

I am happy to report to you that we were successful in all three situations. We were instrumental in electing Ben Stone in the 5th, Ellis Bodron in the 4th and David Bowen in the 2nd. Unfortunately, our work is not through by any stretch of the imagination. Each of these gentlemen has a Republican opponent in November. Now that McGovern has won the Democratic nomination for President, our problems are magnified. With Wallace out of the picture as an independent, this state's electoral votes will probably go to Richard Nixon. Obviously these three Republican candidates for the House of Representatives plan on riding Nixon's coat tails into the Congress.

Be that as it may, we do not intend to roll over and play dead in the situation. Fortunately we now have a Governor who is more than willing to work with us and with his help I believe we can make the grade. As usual our major problem is money or the lack of it. Even though we received a nice contribution from your office and several International Unions, we virtually went broke in the Primaries. We intend to put on a fundraising campaign in the state but we know we can not raise the money necessary to win all three positions. As a matter of necessity we must once again call upon you [National COPE] and our other friends in the Labor Movement for assistance.

We intend to continue our voter registration and education efforts up to 30 days prior to the November 7 election date. This means we can use the treasury money for this phase of our program. Free money for the candidates is also badly needed. All three candidates have rather large deficits from the Primaries and will need all possible help to finance the current campaigns, as well as pay off the deficits.

Any and all contributions will be greatly appreciated. I would suggest that free money for the candidates be channeled through our office. By following this procedure we will not run the risk of a situation similar to that which occurred in Arkansas recently. We will inform the candidates where the money came from and ask them to write a letter of appreciation to you or any one else who makes a similar contribution.[44]

Table II
1972 AFL-CIO Voter Registration

The following table, based on preliminary data released by the AFL-CIO, indicates by state the number and percentage of its members registered to vote in the 1972 election. In states where the number of registered union members was unavailable, the percentage figure is marked by an asterisk (o) indicating the public registration percentage.

	Membership	% Registered	Total Registered
Alabama	100,000	80	80,000
Alaska	15,000	75	11,250
Arizona	59,250	75	44,437
Arkansas	74,787	70	52,350
California	1,300,000	75	975,000
Colorado	74,441	75	55,830
Connecticut	172,000	75	129,000
Delaware	19,117	80	15,293
Florida	180,243	75	135,182
Georgia	115,000	57	65,550
Hawaii	50,682	84	42,572
Idaho	24,770	90	22,293
Illinois	800,000	72	576,000
Indiana	322,283	75	241,712
Iowa	69,000	80	55,200
Kansas	74,500	75	55,875
Kentucky	167,000	67*	
Louisiana	157,000	75*	
Maine	42,540	75	31,905
Maryland	204,000	65	132,600
Massachusetts	440,000	70*	

Michigan	307,000	75	230,250
Minnesota	200,000	80	160,000
Mississippi	40,000	75	30,000
Missouri	309,823	70	216,876
Montana	34,000	83	28,220
Nebraska	60,000	80	48,000
Nevada	35,718	75	26,788
New Hampshire	34,002	75	25,501
New Jersey	583,000	73*	
New Mexico	20,802	93	19,346
New York	1,246,995	72*	
North Carolina	78,245	70	54,771
North Dakota	15,000	100	15,000
Ohio	752,000	70	526,400
Oklahoma	74,002	75	55,501
Oregon	160,000	70	112,000
Pennsylvania	1,031,000	70	721,700
Rhode Island	63,367	80	50,694
South Carolina	50,019	70	35,013
South Dakota	12,000	82	9,840
Tennessee	194,000	73*	
Texas	316,000	75	237,000
Utah	36,880	91	33,561
Vermont	12,972	75	9,729
Virginia	93,000	65	60,450
Washington	309,000	70	216,300
West Virginia	70,000	92	64,400
Wisconsin	304,000	75	228,000
Wyoming	12,000	92	11,400

Why COPE Sat out the McGovern Race

After the Democratic National Convention in Miami Beach nominated Senator George McGovern to be the party's Presidential candidate, Meany held a press conference and announced: "I will not endorse, I will not support and I will not vote for Richard Nixon for President of the United States. I will not endorse, I will not support and I will not vote for George McGovern for President of the United States."

Because of Meany's adamant position, the AFL-CIO did not assist either of the two Presidential candidates. Meany's dislike of McGovern was intense and personal:

You know, I'll give McGovern credit for accomplishing one thing. . . . Ten years ago, he was broke. Now, he's got a big house, expensive works of art, a swimming pool, a big bank account. He's done all right for himself. . . . I wonder where he got it all. Oh, I know he gets fees for speeches, but let's say he makes 35 of them a year, at $1,000 a speech. That's about $35,000 above his pay as a Senator. After he pays his taxes, how much would he have left? [45]

One McGovern Senate vote is remembered by Meany as particularly galling: in 1965 he voted against labor's position on section 14(B) of the Taft-Hartley Act—the right-to-work section. "Christ," a Meany aide has complained, "labor got George McGovern elected in the first place. . . . When he first ran for the Senate, back in 1962, he lost. He wanted a recount. But recounts cost $30,000 in South Dakota. And he didn't have it. So he came to Al Barkan and asked him for it. Al went to Meany and Meany said, 'Give it to him.' We did and McGovern ended up the winner by about 65 votes." [46]

At the heart of Meany's break with McGovern was his passionate belief that the candidate intentionally tried to freeze labor out of the ruling circle within the Democratic Party:

. . . But it was mainly the people he brought to control of the decision-making process of the Democratic Party and our people who he shut out from any role in that decision-making. It's not unreasonable to say that we contributed—when I say we, I mean not myself personally, but our members who were Democrats—to the victories of the Democratic Party in the past. All of a sudden under McGovern's leadership, under McGovern's maneuvering he maneuvered the rules of the party so that we were shut out of that convention and those who had never done anything for the party except split and weaken it gained control.[47]

Meany's opposition notwithstanding, McGovern did receive a great deal of support from many union leaders, although not from the rank and file. *Newsday* of September 20, 1973, reported:

McGovern's labor effort is being coordinated in Washington, not in his campaign headquarters, but across the street in the offices of something called the National Labor Committee for McGovern. . . .
The Committee had budgeted only $250,000 for the campaign, but that figure is deceptively low. The entire staff including Director Howard Samuel is on loan from member unions, which still are paying their salaries.

Along with Samuel, who is an official of the Amalgamated

70

Clothing Workers, another key labor strategist high within the McGovern campaign was William Dodds, the political action director of the Autoworkers. Dodds was named the new executive director of the Democratic National Committee. Carl Wagner, formerly of the UAW-backed Alliance for Labor Action, became manager of McGovern's grassroots operation.

By election day, 40 major unions had brushed aside Meany's personal wishes and endorsed McGovern. The internal leadership of these unions constitutes the bedrock of the Democratic Party. Joseph Keenan, general secretary of the International Brotherhood of Electrical Workers, was named chairman of the National Labor Committee for McGovern, and Joseph Beirne of the Communication Workers became secretary-treasurer. The unions that endorsed McGovern are listed in Table III.

Table III
National Labor Committee for the Election of McGovern-Shriver

Joseph D. Kennan	Joseph Beirne	Howard Samuel
IBEW	CWA	Amalgamated Clothing
Chairman	Secretary-Treasurer	Executive Director

American Postal Workers
International Union of United Automobile, Aerospace and Agricultural Implement Workers of America (UAW)
Bakery and Confectionery Workers International
International Union of United Brewery Workers
International Chemical Workers Union
Cigarmakers' International
Amalgamated Clothing Workers of America
Communication Workers of America
Coopers International Union of North America
Distributive Workers
Graphic Arts International
International Union of Electrical, Radio and Machine Workers
United Electrical Workers
United Furniture Workers
United Glass and Ceramic Workers
United Hatters, Cap and Millinery Workers International Union
Allied Industrial Workers
International Jewelry Workers
International Association of Machinists and Aerospace Workers

71

Amalgamated Meat Cutters and Butcher Workmen of North America
International Molders and Allied Workers Union
National Alliance of Postal and Federal Employees
The Newspaper Guild
Oil, Chemical and Atomic Workers International Union
International Brotherhood of Pottery and Allied Workers
International Printing Pressmen's and Assistants' Union of North America
Retail Clerks International Association
Retail, Wholesale and Department Store Union
United Rubber, Cork, Linoleum and Plastic Workers of America
Service Employees International Union
United Shoe Workers of America
American Federation of State, County and Muncipal Employees
American Federation of Teachers
Teamsters Local 688
American Federation of Technical Engineers
Textile Workers Union of America
Transport Workers Union of America
Upholsterers' International Union of North America
West Coast Longshoremen
International Woodworkers of America

It is highly debatable, putting the question of ethics aside, whether the unions listed as members of the National Labor Committee for the Election of McGovern-Shriver actually represented the sentiment of a majority of their members. In most cases the decision to commit the union's name and resources to McGovern was made by a few top leaders without any consultation with the rank and file. For example, in the thought-provoking column "How 'Labor' Endorses," in the *San Francisco Examiner & Chronicle* of July 20, 1972, newspaperman Dick Nolan wrote:

The question has long since become rhetorical: Who decides whom "labor" will back for political office?

In my own union, the Newspaper Guild, which endorsed Senator McGovern, the top lads kind of asked each other first. They did not consult me. I might have voted for it, but they didn't ask.

What they did was, they passed a resolution at the last national convention, authorizing the executive board to pick us a candidate, if the executive board wished.

The board dusted off this resolution the other day and

said, "McGovern!" It did not precipitate a landslide of labor endorsements for our man.

Even less than in our Newspaper Guild, which is reasonably democratic much of the time, do people like the organized plumbers . . . and all the organized rest ever get to choose a man, officially.

Plump George Meany took a firmer chomp on the mandatory $2 cigar without which all really big labor leaders are considered out of uniform. "I do not like Nixon," he said. Chomp, chomp. "On the other hand, I do not like McGovern either."

Thus spoke organized labor?

The alienation between union leaders and their membership was never greater than on the question of supporting McGovern. George Hardy, international president of the Service Employees International Union, observed that 90 percent of the "activists" in the labor movement were for McGovern despite the neutrality of Meany.[48] Yet Nixon got 54 percent of the vote of union members on election day.

Table IV
How Union Families Have Voted Since 1952**

1952		1956		1960	
Stevenson	Ike	Stevenson	Ike	JFK	Nixon
61	39	57	43	65	35

1964		1968			1972	
LBJ	Goldwater	Humphrey	Nixon	Wallace	McGovern	Nixon
73	27	56	29	15	46	54

** Based on Gallup poll survey data.

There was a considerable range of moods among those union leaders supporting McGovern in 1972. One union official was quoted as saying, "I'm not for McGovern and that crowd of his either. Like everybody else, I wanted Humphrey or even Muskie. But now we got to play the game right. You can't elect Democrats to Congress by being neutral about the Democrats' presidential candidate in a presidential year." [49]

Another mood was reflected by Edward Swayduck, head of the Amalgamated Lithographers, who praised McGovern's campaign declaration that he was "fed up with old men dreaming up wars for young men to die in." Swayduck coupled McGovern's statement with an attack on Meany:

Old men like Meany who support new and wider wars, just naturally hate McGovern for saying it. But it's hard

73

to keep from wondering, if Meany approves warfare so much, where was this great warrior when they were passing out uniforms in World War I? He was 23 years old when the U.S. entered that War—a fine age for a good patriot to tote a rifle—and he chose to work in a shipyard.[50]

After the election, which saw McGovern defeated in a landslide, Meany issued a statement in which he declared:

We are proud of our Committee on Political Education. We think COPE did a magnificent job under very difficult conditions. The results in the Senate and the House more than adequately reflect the effectiveness of COPE's efforts.

We have said many times that while we are non-partisan, we are not non-political. We are very political, and we intend to continue to be political.[51]

In October 1973, in his president's report to the Tenth Biennial Constitutional Convention, Meany told the assembled AFL-CIO delegates:

The AFL-CIO Executive Council, correctly interpreting the mood of the menbership, took no position on the 1972 presidential election. Indeed, subsequent polls and other data showed union members split nearly 50–50 on the two presidential candidates. Therefore the Council concentrated labor's united efforts on the election of congressmen and senators who were proven friends of working people.

The affiliated national and international unions were free, of course, to make their own decisions in the presidential election. Many unions endorsed McGovern, others supported Nixon. The vast majority of unions adopted the position of the Executive Council.

Today, the labor movement is stronger politically than it has ever been in its history. Many unions that had no political action programs before have good programs now.

COPE did its best job ever in 1972 and already is gearing up for 1974. Its mission then will be to elect a Congress dedicated to social progress in America.

Meany's maneuvering of the AFL-CIO toward neutrality in 1972 even drew faint praise from his internal critics, once the election results were in. Jerry Wurf, liberal activist and head of AFSCME, commented, "If they say Meany doesn't look bad, they're right."

Another key labor strategist, Gus Tyler of the ILGWU, thought that Meany's strategy and the election results prove that "while labor backing does not guarantee the election of a Democrat, no Democrat can win without the unions." [52]

COPE and the 1972 Congressional Elections

After McGovern's nomination, COPE switched its attention and resources from the Presidential picture to Congress. The *Wall Street Journal* of July 14, 1972, reported:

As part of its "save Congress" operation this year, the AFL-CIO will expand its program of giving extra aid to House candidates in especially tight races. This program aims to help candidates in districts where the previous election was decided by a margin of less than five percentage points. "Now," predicts an AFL-CIO official, "the criteria for what makes a 'marginal district' will change appreciably" to compensate for the McGovern impact on Democratic chances. As a result, the number of House candidates eligible for special help will increase from the current 70.

During the campaign, organized labor as a whole threw 75 percent of its direct cash contributions into the battle for Democratic control of the 93rd Congress. The remaining fourth went into the Presidential campaign of McGovern.

COPE alone reported spending nearly $2 million on the election, despite the fact that some unions withheld their per capita COPE payments because of the McGovern flap. "It's more than we've ever given in the past," Barkan was quoted as saying.[53] "We did better than we ever did before. We concentrated on saving the Congress." [54]

The *AFL-CIO News* of November 18, 1972, in a special supplement titled "COPE in '72," disclosed:

COPE's representatives were everywhere during the campaign. The number of full-time workers in the field was 15 percent higher than in previous years. Representatives of 31 international unions worked for a period of up to four months with local unions and central bodies in 45 states covering the marginal races.

The Rubber Workers, for example, assigned 76 members to various campaigns. The Steelworkers had 67; the Meat Cutters, 54; Carpenters, 24; International Brotherhood of Electrical Workers, 23; Machinists, 19; Communications Workers, 15; and Oil, Chemical & Atomic Workers, 10.

All this manpower and effort helped realize some stunning upsets across the country.

In Delaware, an August poll showed veteran Sen. J. Caleb Boggs (R) with a 47–19 lead over COPE-endorsed Joseph R. Biden, Jr., a young Wilmington lawyer. COPE workers blanketed the state with leaflets and mailings to union members giving Biden's liberal views on tax reform, health care and ecology.

By the second week in October, the 29-year-old Democrat cut Boggs' lead in the polls to 43–40, and the race went down to the wire. On Election Day, Biden passed his opponent with about 2,500 votes to spare.

Again, in '72, as in earlier campaigns, COPE heavily promoted its voter-registration and turnout programs. Actually, these programs began taking shape 18 months before the election, as columnist Paul Hope reported in the *Washington Star-News* of July 5, 1971:

> National Democratic Chairman Lawrence F. O'Brien has set up a special unit to coordinate the party registration effort. But the big push from the Democratic side is coming from labor unions. Union leaders like to claim their activity is nonpartisan, but it would be hard to convince the Republican National Committee that labor has the welfare of the GOP at heart.
>
> . . . In the youth bracket, COPE is working with and helping to finance Frontlash, Inc., a coalition of 18 liberal, nonpartisan youth organizations.
>
> The Alliance for Labor Action, sponsored primarily by the United Auto Workers and the Teamsters, is working on high school students in several states. Spokesmen for this group say that registration is going overwhelmingly Democratic. The ALA said recently that figures in some high schools in California are running 3 to 1 Democratic, and in one black area the ratio was 100 to 1.

The results of labor's political activities in 1972 were impressive. Of the 361 candidates for House seats endorsed by COPE, 217 won and 144 lost. In addition, 13 other House winners not formally endorsed by COPE were deemed friendly to labor. Of 29 candidates for the Senate endorsed by COPE, 16 won and 13 lost. In addition, three other winners and 38 senators who were not up for election in 1972 were regarded as friendly to labor.

What was the total spent by labor on the 1972 Presidential and congressional campaigns? Columnist Victor Riesel estimates it was $50 million—ranging from cash contributions to paid union manpower.[55]

Common Cause, in its summary of cash contributions to congressional candidates reported:

National Republican Committees that gave to Congressional candidates distributed twice as much money as did the Democratic committees—$3,280,986 to $1,504,659.

The Business/Professional and Labor interest groups contributed roughly equal amounts to candidates and the parties' Congressional fund-raising committees, $4.4 million and $3.8 million respectively. The miscellaneous groups, among which are the liberal National Committee for an Effective Congress, Democratic Study Group Campaign Fund, and Stewart Mott's Vote for Peace, as well as the American Conservative Union's Conservative Victory Fund, distributed $1.5 million to candidates and party committees.

Business money went to Republicans over Democrats by a 2 to 1 ratio; labor money and that from liberal-oriented groups in the miscellaneous category went overwhelmingly—8 to 1—to Democrats.

This was the distribution by party:

	To Congressional Democrats
Interest groups	$5,787,726
Party committees	1,504,659
	$7,292,385
	To Congressional Republicans
Interest groups	$2,662,014
Party committees	3,280,986
	$5,943,000 [56]

Executive Committee Report on 1972

In its report to the AFL-CIO 1973 Constitutional Convention, the federation's Executive Committee boasted: "The political programs of the trade union movement in 1972 achieved their primary goal: to retain a progressive Congress." The report continued:

Success was gained in the face of a massive presidential landslide which normally would have created a sweeping congressional majority for the winning presidential candidate. In fact, despite President Nixon's near 2–1 triumph, which carried all but one state and the District of Columbia, his party actually lost two seats in the U.S. Senate and gained only 13 in the U.S. House.

The results bore out the effectiveness of labor's political role in 1972. Uncommitted in the presidential campaign, the AFL-CIO was thus enabled to devote all of its time, energy and political resources to the critical battle for Congress. As a consequence, though according to polls a majority of union members voted for the re-election of President Nixon, in overwhelming numbers they cast their ballots for House and Senate candidates endorsed by COPE.

In non-federal elections, too, the presidential outcome failed to reflect itself. Democrats actually gained one governorship and won control in several previously Republican-controlled state legislatures.

Overall, COPE endorsed a total of 408 candidates for the U.S. House, U.S. Senate and governor. Of these, 244 won their contests, a percentage just shy of 60. In House races, 362 endorsements were made; 217 were winners. In the Senate, endorsements were made in 29 contsts; 16 won. There were 11 winners among the 17 gubernatorial endorsements.

By any standard of measurement, the COPE program in 1972 exceeded any previous year—more volunteer manpower and womanpower and more full-time staff assigned by international unions; increased funding; more effective and better-organized registration and get-out-the-vote campaigns; improved precinct-level organization.

COPE-supported non-partisan programs aimed at union members in the minorities community under the aegis of the A. Philip Randolph Institute, in the youth community under Frontlash, and among seniors through the National Council for Senior Citizens, all functioned with great effect and impact in their respective areas.

In addition, the special program under which members of the Executive Council assumed responsibility for guidance and assistance to COPE's program in states with marginal Senate and House races contributed significantly to successful election results. The U.S. was divided into 10 geographic regions, with one or more members of the Executive Council assigned to work with state and local councils in each region.

With the help of the council members and a special COPE project that provided early organization of COPE programs in marginal districts, 51 of 83 candidates endorsed in marginal House races, and 10 of 19 in Senate races, won. Most of these were extremely close elections, and the margin of victory was clearly provided by labor's efforts.

Council members participating in the special program were Vice President Hall, chairman of the special council subcommittee, and Vice President Abel, Bommarito,

Hardy, Lyons, Jennings, Chesser, Dennis, Ward, Sidell and Guinan.

Major progress was achieved in the nuts-and-bolts programs that are essential to any successful political effort, registration and getting out the vote, and in these areas COPE's computerized Voter Identification Project was of immense value. Twenty-three states participated in the data processing program which permitted sorting and printing of nearly 10 million names in a format compatible with local registration records. The over-all percentage of union members registered nationally set a new high of between 75 and 80 percent, reaching the 90 percent range in five states and in the 80s in nine states, compared to a 65 percent registration in 1970.

In COPE's registration campaign, and the election period get-out-the-vote effort, more than 110,000 volunteers—union members and members of their families—participated, devoting more than a million hours to checking lists, canvassing, telephoning, preparation and distribution of materials, conducting election day carpools and baby-sitting operations. This was the highest number of volunteers ever involved in COPE activities.

Total funding of COPE programs, including contributions to endorsed candidates, reached a record high of more than $2 million, 25 percent over the best previous year of 1970. Many international unions reached or exceeded 100 percent of the voluntary COPE quota.

Besides manpower and money to conduct an effective political education campaign, COPE assisted state and local central labor bodies by providing other tools needed to reach and motivate members.

Hundreds of thousands of leaflets and flyers, special radio announcements in support of labor-backed candidates, a million copies of voting records in various marginal races—these were some of the services COPE made available to AFL-CIO members.

Layouts and photographs of the candidates were prepared for use by unions as special inserts in their official journals.

The AFL-CIO Department of Public Relations helped in developing and producing informational materials on COPE-endorsed candidates. The hundreds of thousands of letters and other literature generated under this program were paid for, signed and distributed to their members by local unions.

In its coverage of the youth vote the media dwelt largely on college students. But a labor-supported program, Frontlash, focused its attention on those newly enfranchised young union voters between the ages of 18 and 21 who hold down jobs.

Actually larger than the college vote, the young worker bloc proved of critical importance in several closely contested congressional races.

Frontlash helped organize non-partisan register-and-vote campaigns in 25 states and hundreds of communities. More than 930,000 young and working-class voters were added to the voting rolls through the efforts of Frontlash.

To carry out an effective non-partisan voter-registration and get-out-the-vote campaign among black trade unionists, COPE availed itself of the personnel, facilities and services offered by the A. Philip Randolph Institute.

COPE's senior-citizens operation—geared to work through the National Council of Senior Citizens and its hundreds of local chapters—worked for the election of labor-endorsed candidates in 31 states, a fourfold increase over past years.

Former Machinist Sec.-Treas. Matt DeMore volunteered to head the operation, and set up a liaison between COPE and local NCSC chapters.

COPE coordinated the compilation of lists of thousands of names of union retirees across the country. Senior citizens then organized non-partisan drives to get them to vote. Operating at a far higher level than ever before, senior citizens held kaffee-klatsches for endorsed candidates, set up phone banks to call retired members, and mailed out thousands of brochures.

More women were involved in COPE's 1972 operation than in any previous year. The Pell campaign in Rhode Island illustrates women's increasing role in political efforts.

Sixty women members of the Ladies' Garment Workers, Steelworkers and Communication Workers, coordinated by a WAD director, worked full-time with the Rhode Island COPE, and did an outstanding job.

During the 1972 campaign, there were 14 full-time state WAD directors, plus 11 full-time acting WAD directors. In addition, there were 87 local central council WAD directors.

Thousands of women volunteers from AFL-CIO affiliates checked registration lists, helped contact unregistered voters, canvassed neighborhoods, distributed materials through mass mailings, and handled countless other assignments.

COPE in 1974

"What Do You Do for an Encore?" read the headline

of the post-1974 election issue of *Memo from COPE,* official publication of the political machine. The opening sentence beneath the headline appropriately stated, "It's a good question: What *do* you do for an encore after a day like November 5?" The publication continued:

COPE rang up its best results ever November 5 in terms of victories for endorsed candidaters.

Over-all, 455 candidates for U.S. House and Senate and for governor were endorsed, with 321 of them winning, a 70.5 percent record.

In the House, 389 endorsements were made, with 270 winning for 70 percent; in the Senate, 25 for 33, 76 percent, and in the gubernatorial races, 26 for 33, 79 percent.

Mary Zon, COPE director of research, provided this analysis of the 1974 election in the December 1974 issue of AFL-CIO *American Federationist:*

In 1974 state COPEs endorsed more candidates than in any earlier election and a higher percentage of COPE-endorsed candidates for Congress and for Governor were successful in 1974 than in any previous election. The 70.5 percent score in 1974 compared to 60.9 percent in 1970 and a dismal 51.8 percent in 1966, the two preceding non-presidential years.

Overall, the figures were good enough for liberals to look forward to the 1976 campaign—which began on the morning of Wednesday, November 6, 1974.

United Automobile Workers

When the UAW, under Walter Reuther's leadership, withdrew from the AFL-CIO in 1968, "we lost $100,000 a month in dues and 50 percent of our political clout," several key AFL officials commented.[57] No discussion of organized labor's political activities, therefore, would be complete without a brief look at how the UAW conducts its political program.

At present the main vehicles of UAW political action are its district councils and its Community Action Program—both financed at least in part by per capita taxes on compulsory membership dues funds. Article 34, sections 1–9, of the UAW constitution establishes the district councils, sets forth their functions, provides for their financing, and defines their administrative procedures. Section 3 provides that the district councils shall have political functions, among others. Section

5, dealing with the financing of the councils, reads as follows: "Activities of the District Councils shall be financed by the payment of a per capita tax by each Local Union affiliated with the District Council, which shall require the approval of the International Executive Board." Section 6, which specifies the political uses to which the district councils may put the funds so acquired, states: "The per capita tax may be used to assist in organizational work, prepare educational literature, lobby for legislative programs and programs of benefit to its affiliated Local Unions."

The current UAW constitution, adopted April 1970, does not fix a precise per capita tax in favor of the Community Action Program. Instead, article 23, section 3, provides for a "National UAW Community Action Advisory Council" and declares that it is "the duty of such council to advise and counsel the International Executive Board on programs and policies, including the per capita tax requirements of each local Union to the CAP Councils." In May 1969, when he created CAP, Reuther set a three percent figure as the beginning per capita tax.[58] He announced then:

> The International Executive Board determined that each Local Union will be required to set aside a minimum of three percent (3%) of each member's monthly membership dues as prescribed in the International Constitution, as per capita to the UAW Community Action Program established, and will remit the per capita payment to the Community Action Councils in accordance with the instructions and procedure established by the International Secretary-Treasurer in consultation with the Regional Director (or Regional Directors) in each area.

In a transparent effort to stem criticism of its use of tax-exempt compulsory dues money for political activity, the UAW in 1972 established procedures for rebating a portion of the dues to members who objected. UAW officials arbitarily determined the amount at $3.68 per member per year. This, of course, was an unrealistically low figure. Still it was a tacit admission by the union that $5.3 million a year of tax-exempt compulsory dues money was being used for politics.

In 1975, the union revised its amount subject to rebate. UAW Administrative Letter No. 2 of June 5, 1975, declared:

> The dues income of the International Union for 1972, 1973 and 1974 respectively was $94,460,720, $108,395,519, and $114,521,890 for an average per year of $105,792,709.

The dues income of the Local Unions for 1972, 1973 and 1974 respectively was $55,476,930, $63,660,860, and $68,714,449 for an average per year of $62,617,413.

The combined annual average dues income of both the International Union and the Local Unions was $168,410,122.

The total average annual disbursements for partisan political activity . . . is $6,150,869. This represents 3.652 percent of the total average annual dues income.

Average annual membership dues, based on 1974 figures, was approximately $132.84 ($11.07 per month on the formula of two hours pay per month).

Since the proportion of annual expenditures for partisan political activity is 3.652% of total dues income, we apply this 3.652% to the individual member's average annual dues of $132.84, which comes to $4.85.

Therefore, the amount subject to objection under Article 16, Section 7 of the Constitution is $4.85 per year. We will hold this figure through 1977.

Conclusion

The conclusion for this chapter is adopted verbatim from the "summary and conclusions" of the exhaustively documented affidavit, filed by Professor Sylvester Petro of the Wake Forest School of Law in his capacity as an expert witness in the case of *Marker, et al.* v. *Connally, et al.:*

1. Organized labor is prodigiously committed to partisan political activities.

2. Its political efforts rival in scope, character, persistence, and expertise those of the traditional political parties.

3. By the frank admission of union officials and agents themselves, as well as by the agreement of all observers, the political activities of organized labor are strictly partisan in character; "nonpartisanship" is merely on assumed guise, not a practical reality; in fact, organized labor is in partnership with the Democratic Party, where, indeed, it is now the senior partner.

4. Though supported in part by voluntary contributions, the massive political activities of organized labor are financed in major part out of the dues paid by the twenty million persons who belong to unions in the United States.

5. Of twenty million union members, at least thirty percent and perhaps as many as forty percent are either Republicans or Independent by personal convictions; and the diversion of their dues to the support of Demo-

cratic Party political candidates and policies therefore infringes upon their political autonomy, their political rights.

6. A reasonable estimate placed at one in eight the union members who contribute voluntarily to organized labor's political activities; nevertheless, by various devices the leaders of organized labor avail themselves of involuntary political contributions from *all* dues-paying members.

7. Owing to the prevalence of compulsory-unionism agreements throughout unionized industry, i.e., agreements which require maintenance of union membership as a condition of employment, union members are compelled to tolerate the diversion of their dues to political purposes, unless they are willing to sacrifice their jobs, their skills, and sometimes even their homes by resigning from their unions.

8. Organized labor diverts dues-funds to political ends in two general ways: (a) by per-capita taxes in favor of affiliated political-action committees such as AFL-CIO COPE; and (b) by the direct use of dues-financed physical facilities and union personnel in political activities.

9. Dues-funds diverted to political committees are often earmarked for "educational purposes" but in fact, as revealed in union documents, pay all salaries and overhead costs, thus releasing the "voluntary" funds of the political-action committees for direct campaign contributions.

10. Unions make dues-supported direct-money contributions to candidates for state and local political office, thus releasing still more of the "voluntary fund" of their political-action affiliates for federal campaign contributions.

2

The AFL-CIO Today

Organized labor today presents a paradox: total union membership is only slowly growing, having increased by 1.1 million since 1972. Yet labor's political influence is pervasive, far disproportionate to its membership.

At the end of 1974 in the U.S., membership in unions and employee associations was 22,807,000. The total membership for international unions, national unions, and employee associations was 24,163,000 (reflecting membership outside the U.S., primarily in Canada).

Most of the increase in U.S. membership occurred in public employee unions. In 1974 there were 447,000 more union members in government jobs than there were two years earlier —an 18 percent gain. Most of the increase was largely because of successful organizing drives at state and local levels.

AFL-CIO affiliates reported 16.9 million members in 1974, compared with 16.5 in 1972. The federation represented 78 percent of all union members in 1974 compared with 79 percent in 1972 and 77 percent in 1970.*

Structure of the AFL-CIO

The federation's constitution, adopted at its founding convention in 1955, establishes an organizational structure closely resembling that of the former AFL, although it vests in the federation more authority over affiliates than the AFL had. The chief members of the federation continue to be the national and international unions, the trades departments, the state and local bodies, and the directly affiliated local unions.

The supreme governing body of the AFL-CIO is the biennial convention, the most recent being held in 1975. Each union is entitled to convention representation in proportion to its membership of which the per capita tax has been paid.

Between conventions, the executive officers, assisted by the Executive Council and the General Board, direct the affairs of the AFL-CIO. In brief, the functions of the two top officers and of the structural bodies are as follows:

* The preceding statistics appear in the U.S. Department of Labor release of August 12, 1975, titled "Labor Union and Employee Association Membership, 1974."

EXECUTIVE OFFICERS The president, as chief executive officer, has authority to interpret the constitution between meetings of the Executive Council. He also directs the staff of the federation. The secretary-treasurer is responsible for all financial matters.

EXECUTIVE COUNCIL Delegates to the 1969 biennial convention added six new members to the Executive Council, which now consists of 33 vice presidents and two executive officers. It is the governing body between conventions and meets at least three times each year. Among the duties of the Council are proposing and evaluating legislation affecting the labor movement.

GENERAL BOARD This body consists of all 35 members of the Executive Council and a principal officer of each affiliated international and national union and department. The General Board acts on matters referred to it by the executive officers or the Executive Council.

TRADE AND INDUSTRIAL DEPARTMENTS The AFL CIO constitution provides for six trade and industrial departments. An Industrial Union Department was added to the five departments that were carried over from the AFL. Affiliation with departments is open to all national and international unions belonging to the AFL-CIO, and affiliates must pay a per capita tax based on the number of their members.

DEPARTMENT OF ORGANIZATION AND FIELD SERVICES The scope of activities encompassed by this department was broadened by the Executive Council in 1973. The department will play a pivotal role in implementing federation political strategy in the coming years. This role is discussed in greater detail below.

STANDING COMMITTEES AND STAFF The constitution authorizes the president to appoint standing committees to carry on legislative, political, educational, and other activities. These committees operate under the direction of the president and are subject to the authority of the Executive Council and the convention. Fifteen standing committees are operating at present. Staff departments are established as needed.

DIRECTLY AFFILIATED LOCAL UNIONS At the time of the formation of the AFL-CIO, local trade and federal labor unions (AFL) and local industrial unions (CIO) had a combined membership of 181,000. These local unions, having received charters from the federation, became directly affiliated with the AFL-CIO. In 1973 there were 161 of these locals unions directly affiliated with the AFL-CIO, with a total membership of 55,200.

STATE AND CENTRAL BODIES The AFL-CIO constitution authorizes the Executive Council to establish central bodies upon a city, state, or other regional basis. Central bodies comprise locals of national unions, organizing committees, and directly affiliated local unions. In 1973 there were 50 state central bodies and 735 local central bodies in existence.

The federation held its Eleventh Biennial Constitutional Convention in San Francisco in October 1975. George Meany, 81, was reelected president and Lane Kirkland, 54, secretary-treasurer. Thirty-three federation vice presidents were also elected.

Significant Development

One of the most significant developments in the AFL-CIO's history occurred on the eve of the 1973 convention. The Executive Council voted to change the Department of Organization to the Department of Organization and Field Services and selected W. J. Usery, Jr., director of the Federal Mediation and Counciliation Service, to be the director of the new department. (After submitting his resignation in October 1973 as director of the Federal Mediation and Conciliation Service, Usery changed his mind in January 1974 and announced his intention to remain in the Nixon administration as special assistant to the President. In 1976 President Ford appointed Usery Secretary of Labor.)

The importance of the new department is seen in the report of the AFL-CIO Standing Committee on Organization, headed by Paul Hall of the Seafarers Union, to the Executive Council in August 1973. Excerpts of the report follow:

For some time, the Executive Officers and the Committee on Organization have been reviewing the status of the AFL-CIO Department of Organization and considering steps which might be taken to integrate it more closely with the general work of the Federation and to equip it to serve more fully the current needs and requirements of all sectors of the labor movement. . . .

With the exception of a substantial attrition in personnel and some consolidation of regions, the basic structure and functions of the Department of Organization have remained essentially unchanged since the merger. Within the limits of the circumstances, the Department has ably and efficiently performed its assigned duties, developed coordinated organizing campaigns, trained staff, provided strike and boycott support, and rendered substantial assistance to the organizing campaigns of individual affiliates.

At present, the staff consists of a Director and Assistant Director at headquarters, 16 Regional Directors, 4 Assistant Regional Directors and a field staff of 90, together with 29 secretaries in the field and five at headquarters. . . .

The cost of maintaining this structure is in excess of $4 million per year and comprises some 30 percent of total AFL-CIO operating expense. . . .

The years since merger have seen the development and expansion of other AFL-CIO programs and activities in the field, unrelated to the Department of Organization and its staff.

An Office of Coordinator of State and Local Central Bodies has been established in headquarters as a point of contact with Central Bodies and a channel of service to their needs.

The AFL-CIO Committee on Political Education now has a field staff of 12 area directors, 2 WAD directors, and 4 field coordinators and directors working with civil rights and Spanish-American groups.

The AFL-CIO Community Services Department maintains a close relationship with 185 full-time labor representatives employed by community service agencies in 145 communities.

The AFL-CIO Department of Urban Affairs oversees programs which reach out into the field: A Mortgage Investment Trust, which finances low and middle-income housing projects, and a Human Resources Development Institute which is engaged in local manpower training and job placement activities. The Human Resources Development Institute (financed by a Labor Department grant but AFL-CIO directed) has 54 field offices manned by 7 field directors and 58 area representatives. In terms of other AFL-CIO-related activities, there are now 115 local chapters of the A. Philip Randolph Institute, which is supported by the AFL-CIO. A close relationship is also maintained with Frontlash, as an avenue of work with young people, and there are 56 local groups of that organization. . . .

While all of this manpower and skill is not available for every AFL-CIO activity, some advantage could and should be gained by a better coordination of these resources in the field, without impairing their necessary channels to the responsible national office staff. This would clearly also require the more systematic coordination of the Department of Organization with other headquarters departments.

While there are advantages in specialization, it should be possible, without sacrificing those advantages, to develop a structure that is fully responsible to objectives uppermost at any given time, in the labor movement's order of priorities. *For example, in a crucial election year, labor's interests may be best served by placing greater emphasis on political action assignments, and the field staff should be fully prepared to perform such assignments as an integral part of their mission. . . .*

The role and prestige of the AFL-CIO Regional Director in relation to State and Local Central Bodies as well as all AFL-CIO programs and activities in his region should be strengthened and enhanced, as well as his capacity to perform a broader role. *He should be equipped and prepared, for example, to help organize maximum local support for the legislative position of the AFL-CIO when crucial votes are pending in the Congress, which means that he should be fully tuned in on the legislative process.*

In short, the Regional Offices should be made an integral part of the full range of the AFL-CIO operations and programs.

The committee feels that the department and its field offices should be reorganized in such a way as to serve that objective.

Organizing does not take place in a political, legislative and climatic vacuum. *There are clearly times when the most effective organizing that can be done is the organizing of support for amendments of the National Labor Relations Act, or for a shift in the balance of power in Congress.* The strengthening of the capacity of a local central body to perform its responsibilities in a community has organizing consequences. Conversely, of course, all of the purposes and aims of the labor movement are served by a continuing healthy growth in the organized labor force.

With these considerations in mind, we offer the following recommendations:

1. The Department of Organization should be renamed "Department of Organization and Field Services," to reflect a broader mission. The present functions and staff of the Coordinator of State and Local Central Bodies should be transferred to that Department. The Director and staff of the Department should maintain a close and continuing liaison with all other Departments of the Federation, particularly those—such as COPE, Legisla-

tion, Community Services and Urban Affairs—which have activities in the field or which rely upon strong field support. His responsibilities should include the development of regular and effective working relationships between each Regional Director and all AFL-CIO operations in the field, and of methods to assure that all Regional Directors are thoroughly familiar with AFL-CIO policies and programs.

2. The present 16 Regions should be consolidated to a maximum of 7 Regions. The directors of those Regions should be selected on the basis of their ability to perform as general representatives of the full range of AFL-CIO interests and policies in their regions, and should be brought into a closer relationship with and participation in the work of the national AFL-CIO.[1] [Italics added.]

At the heart of the federation's decision to create its new department was the realization that the growth of organized labor has reached a plateau and that now is the time to switch emphasis from organizing the work force to maximizing political effectiveness. In an interview, George Meany was asked whether it was a problem that "fewer than something like one out of four workers today are AFL-CIO members. . . ." He replied:

No. No, that's never been a problem. You see, the millions of unorganized workers have no political power whatsoever, merely because they're unorganized. The only way they could ever have political power is to get themselves organized. So they're not organized. So the people who have the political punch are those who are organized, whether they're businessmen, whether they're farmers . . .[2]

Meany believes that the AFL-CIO is the most powerful political organization in the country today, and hopes to make it even more effective. Al Zack, the federation's director of public relations, has declared that in Meany's opinion, "COPE is as fine a piece of political machinery as ever existed in the United States, and is far more effective than either the Republican National Committee or the Democratic National Committee."[3]

Meany and other federation leaders believe that with their new department, they can further strengthen the political muscle of organized labor. According to a *Business Week* article on the Hall committee report,

The new reorganization plane is not meant to replace existing state and local AFL-CIO organizations. However, the new regional directors will be sent into the field to make the state federations more responsive to national AFL-CIO policies. The aim is to avoid in the future what happened during the 1972 Presidential election. The Federation was formally neutral, but several state and local bodies—notably in Colorado—objected and actively supported Democratic nominee George S. McGovern. Meany, backed by the Council, took a tough stand against the recalcitrants. His insistance that they follow AFL-CIO policies and his ouster of the Colorado State Federation President are expected to be a convention issue this October.[4]

The struggle between the Colorado Labor Council and the national federation, which began in August 1972 and lasted more than a year, provides an unusual inside look at the internal political operations of the AFL-CIO. The dispute arose after the AFL-CIO Executive Council on July 19, 1972, adopted the following statement:

> Under the circumstances, the AFL-CIO will refrain from endorsing either candidate for the office of President of the United States.
> Those circumstances call, rather, for the maximum concentration of effort upon the election of Senators and Representatives whose records commend them to the working people of America. Affiliates are, of course, free to endorse and support any candidate of their choice.[5]

About three weeks later the Executive Board of the Colorado Labor Council, and that council's COPE, adopted a resolution endorsing McGovern for President. When Meany heard of this action, he threatened the Colorado council with disciplinary proceedings unless the endorsement of McGovern was rescinded. Subsequently, the AFL-CIO's Executive Council did take disciplinary action against the Colorado group and in its decision declared:

> The political effectiveness of the AFL-CIO depends upon its speaking with one voice, and when its governing body determines that, because of lack of any consensus within the organization, or for whatever other reason, the AFL-CIO shall remain neutral, that determination is binding on the AFL-CIO's subordinate state and local central bodies. Any other rule would be destructive of the AFL-CIO's political effectiveness.[6]

The Colorado council appealed the decision of the Executive Council to the delegates at the federation's 1973 convention in Bal Harbour. The appeal fell upon deaf ears despite praise of the Colorado group from the floor from such as the Typographical Union delegate, who pointed out that, after all, in 1972, "The Colorado Labor Council under the leadership of Herrick Roth, was able to successfully defeat the Republican candidate for Senator and elect a Democratic Senator. It was successful in helping to elect a number of Democratic Representatives in the House of Representatives." The Colorado Council defended its action in endorsing McGovern as being justified since, as its appeal to the Tenth Biennial Constitutional Convention declared, "The three and one-half years preceding July 19, 1972, was an increasing crescendo of AFL-CIO and AFL-CIO COPE policy to 'Dump Nixon' (the Colorado Labor Council, alone received over 50,000 fliers from AFL-CIO COPE between July 25 and August 8, 1972, detailing the AFL-CIO policy stand and calling for DUMP NIXON.)" [7]

As expected, the pro-McGovern Colorado Labor Council leadership lost in a vote on the floor of the federation's convention.

Labor's Lobbying Apparatus

One of the goals of the new Department of Organization and Field Services is that of mobilizing all of the federation's resources to assist the AFL-CIO Department of Legislation in lobbying more effectively on Capitol Hill.

Andrew J. Biemiller is director of the Department of Legislation, which also has an assistant director. Kenneth Young, and five legislative representatives. Biemiller, 69, "is a former history teacher, AFL organizer and Wisconsin legislator. He has been a member of the Socialist, Progressive and Democratic parties. During World War II he worked for the War Production Board. He was elected to the U.S. House of Representatives from Wisconsin in 1944 and 1948 and was twice defeated for re-election." [8]

Table V
1975 Expenses, AFL-CIO Department of Legislation

Salaries	$376,849.07
Travel expenses	12,278.84
Printing	1,561.18
Subscriptions	5,082.02

Pamphlets	25,782.67
Other	6,569.35

TOTAL $428.123.13

Biemiller says, "I have tried to act as a lobbyist by the standards I appreciated in lobbyists when I was their target." [9]

Although the AFL-CIO Executive Council serves as the Committee on Legislation, the real lobbying strategy is developed by the Administrative Committee, which is appointed by Meany and which meets every Monday morning. The Administrative Committee includes over 30 legislative representatives of affiliated unions and AFL-CIO departments in addition to the representatives of the Department of Legislation. The Executive Council report to the 10th Convention declares:

> From 1971 through September 1973, the Department of Legislation was concerned with more than 100 separate legislative issues. These issues included such subjects as economic controls, trade, tax reform, education, occupational health and safety, civil rights, consumer protection and other measures affecting living and working conditions. During this same time the director and legislative representatives of the Department of Legislation made more than 100 formal appearances before Congressional committees as well as countless informal personal contacts with individual members of Congress to explain AFL-CIO policies. . . .
> The department maintains a complete and up-to-date file on all Congressional bills, resolutions, committee reports and public laws enacted as well as the voting records and other relevant information on individual members of Congress. This recourse material and other pertinent publications obtained by the department on a subscription basis enables the department's legislative representatives as well as those of affiliated departments and unions to perform more effectively in their day to day consultations with individual members and the committees of Congress.[10]

Over 60 international unions and employee associations now have their headquarters in Washington, D.C., for the purpose of having maximum impact on Congress and other branches of government. In the fall of 1973 the AFL-CIO opened the $5 million addition to its national headquarters (already valued at $6 million) located at 815 16th Street, N.W only a short distance from the White House across Lafayette

Park. The eight-story addition, which expands space by 85 percent, also provides for seven new tenants, including the Washington office of the United Steelworkers of America and the international office of the Wood, Wire and Metal Lathers International Union. Another new union building is the eight-story United Unions Building, 1750 New York Avenue, near the Corcoran Gallery of Art. Its joint owners are: International Association of Bridge, Structural and Ornamental Iron Workers; International Brotherhood of Painters and Allied Trades; International Association of Firefighters; and Sheet Metal Workers' International Association. The building cost $10 million.

In 1970 the Retail Clerks International Association dedicated an 11-story office building at 1775 K Street, N.W. Its innovative features include all-electric facilities, ice-melting devices in the sidewalks, and a chapel.

In 1971, the International Brotherhood of Electric Workers moved into a 12-story granite building at 1125 15th Street, N.W.

The Communications Workers of America is erecting an eight-story addition to its headquarters at 1925 K Street, NW., costing $4.5 million.

The Teamsters and Carpenters internationals are among the early owners of buildings, the Teamsters with a $4 million marble-faced headquarters not far from the Capitol, and the Carpenters with a $6 million home of Georgia marble and fine interior woodwork on Constitution Avenue.

Diverging Labor Views

Although the AFL-CIO, its affiliates, and the nonaffiliated unions are almost always united in their strategy on domestic legislation before Congress, their views cover the spectrum on foreign policy. It was this divergence of opinion on foreign affairs that, in part, led the United Automobile Workers to leave the AFL-CIO in 1968. It was this same divergence that led Meany to withhold the federation's support from Senator McGovern in 1972; he felt the Democratic Presidential candidate was not anti-Communist enough.

Victor Reuther, brother of Walter—the late UAW leader—and a UAW official today, declared: "George Meany has been to the right of every Secretary of State and every President from Foster Dulles and Eisenhower on. And that is very sad." [11]

Another UAW official, Irving Bluestone, put it this way: "By and large, the Cold War efforts of the post–World War II era live untarnished in the AFL-CIO and from the start we have been in disagreement with this." [12]

Despite the differences on foreign policy, forces are at work to unite the union movement under one head. Jerry Wurf, of the American Federation of State, County and Municipal Employees, believes the solution lies in a series of mergers to consolidate collective-bargaining strategy. Collective-bargaining strategy leads quickly, of course, to political strategy. Wurf notes that the potential for consolidation is there:

> The Teamsters are not members of the AFL-CIO, having been expelled for corrupt practices in 1957. But with 2 million members they have a substantial potential for achievement and could be a valuable ally, if that were structurally possible. The United Automobile Workers left the Federation in 1968 under the leadership of the late Walter Reuther; UAW has some 1.4 million members. The National Education Association, with 1.3 million members and 700,000 more loosely affiliated members, has never been an AFL-CIO body, but in recent years, it has become as militant and more effective than the AFL-CIO's smaller American Federation of Teachers. At last they are talking merger.[13]

Wurf observes that labor "has considerable clout in Congress and in political campaigns," but its "influence is far from what it could or should be." [14] Merger, Wurf feels, would maximize this influence.

Conclusion

The AFL-CIO, which already possesses the finest political machine in the nation, has reorganized itself, consolidating its internal operations as the prelude to renewed political activity more ambitious than it has previously undertaken. Federation strategists recognize that organized labor's membership of one out of every four working Americans has stabilized and will show little real growth in the immediate future. However, the fact that about 25 percent of the work force, even though stabilized, is *organized* offers top labor leaders a built-in base for political action and influence that is not duplicated elsewhere in our society.

Practical politicians in both political parties know that the AFL-CIO has 50,000 locals that swing into action at election time, and that should each of these locals spend merely $1,000 apiece on an election, the total comes to $50 million. They know that the federation has some 140 experienced organizers who work with regional directors and that the United Steelworkers—to single out one union from among many—has over 600 field organizers who become campaign workers at election time.

For these reasons, no political observer today underestimates the potential impact that organized labor will have at the ballot box in future elections.

Labor and the Democratic Party

Under the title "Labor and the Liberals," the late *Newsweek* columnist Stewart Alsop perceptively described the internal dilemma faced by the Democratic Party:

> . . . The liberal millionaires are much influenced in their views by the left intellectuals, who are fashionable people, and hardly at all by the views of machinists or autoworkers, who are not fashionable people. There are a great many more autoworkers and machinists than there are Norton Simons or Stewart Motts. Yet an aspiring Democrat must, if he wishes to emerge from obscurity and onto the national television screens, pay assiduous court to the liberal millionaires.
>
> The money power of labor is feeble by comparison. But the organization and manpower of labor are not feeble at all. Labor very nearly achieved the miracle of making Hubert Humphrey President in 1968, after the left had wrecked his chances in Chicago. In Richard Scammon's analogy, the Democratic Party without labor is like a car without an engine—the upholstery and the body work may be handsome, but the car won't run.
>
> "That's right," says Lane Kirkland. "And the intellectuals think they should be at the wheel, and that we should stay under the hood." [1]

An example of the enginelike work performed by labor for the Democratic Party is registering sympathetic voters and getting them to the polls on election day. The primary function of any political party's precinct organization traditionally has been to see that party supporters are registered to vote and, through telephone exhortations, car-pool arrangements, and other available means, to follow up on election day. This function, once performed by Democratic Party volunteers, is now carried on by union staff personnel, whose salaries are paid out of union membership dues, as are also the expenses of poll workers, telephones, cars, and various precinct activities.

One of labor's most brilliant strategists, Gus Tyler of the ILGWU, believes that there will soon begin an "organic evolution" toward the creation of labor precinct organizations, as labor and the Democratic Party become more coterminous.[2]

Because the AFL-CIO and COPE operate year round, labor's forces can quickly and efficiently gear up whenever a sudden political opportunity or challenge arises. No other group in the country is as well organized. The *Wall Street Journal* of September 25, 1972, in an article on Al Barkan, reported how labor's resources can be mobilized:

"And Mr. Barkan can crank up his COPE machinery in a hurry," Senator Lee Metcalf, a pro-labor Democrat from Montana, testifies. "It was right in this room," the Montanan recalls, sitting in his comfortably cluttered Senate office. "I told Al we had a fellow (now Rep. John Melcher) in mind to run in a special election for this Republican seat. Al asked, 'Can he win?' I said he was the best man to take the seat away from the Republicans. And Al said yes without going to the phone or consulting anybody."

Mr. Barkan delivered. A little while later, when Sen. Metcalf drove by Melcher headquarters in Montana, he saw "a whole line of cars out front with Arkansas and Oklahoma license plates." The out-of-state labor support was so obvious the Senator feared Mr. Melcher's opponent would make it an issue. The Senator had to call Mr. Barkan and ask him to get some of the cars off the street.

In most states, the Democratic Party organization is financed and run by organized labor. Michigan is a prime example. The *Detroit Free Press,* in a series analyzing labor's influence in the Wolverine State, concluded:

Organized labor's large membership funds and plentiful campaign manpower make it the most powerful single force in Michigan politics.

Unions pour huge sums of money into the campaign committees of candidates they favor. The candidates are usually Democrats.

Labor, in fact, contributes a major share of the funds used to finance the day-to-day operations of the Michigan Democratic Party.

Unions in Michigan also have a small legion of adept political workers operating year-round under cover of citizenship and community action groups. The workers are on union payrolls.

Voter registration drives that favor Democrats are conducted and financed by unions.

Millions of pieces of political literature are printed and distributed, particularly during election years, by labor's manpower.

Labor dominates the Michigan Democratic State Central Committee and the party's conventions.

In the past two decades, labor has been the main influence in changing Michigan from a Republican stronghold to a heavily Democratic state.[3]

Still another illustration is this letter sent by Victor Bussie, president (who currently serves on the Democratic National Committee), and F. J. Bourg, Sr., secretary-treasurer, Louisiana AFL-CIO, on December 22, 1971, to "All Affiliated Locals, Councils, and International Representatives":

Let us not forget, however, that we can lose it all in the General Elections on February 1, 1972. Not only do the Democratic nominees for Governor and the other statewide offices have Republican and American Party opposition, but approximately 50 members of the Legislature also have opposition.

We must do everything in our power to win this final round or else all of our efforts up to this time will be wasted. We must inform our members of the critical situation and urge them to go to the polls and vote for our friends on February 1, 1972.

And we must have some financial assistance from your organization. We spent all of our available funds on literature and other political expenses in the first and second primaries—and have absolutely nothing left in the treasury to face this last critical campaign.

Please make every effort to assist us financially now. We must have contributions at the earliest possible moment if we hope to win.

Funds may be contributed directly from your union funds in this campaign. Please make checks payable to the Louisiana AFL-CIO and mail them as soon as possible to Post Office Box 3477, Baton Rouge, Louisiana 70821.

We must have this special help now!!

As labor's political strength grows stronger, COPE's public stance becomes bolder. No longer do labor's strategists try to hide their deep-seated political bias behind a facade of non-partisanship. The *AFL-CIO News* routinely carried this article, "Democrats Retain Senate in California," in its March 10, 1973, issue:

Democrats still control the California state Senate— thanks to a massive labor-effort for a COPE-endorsed candidate in a Los Angeles area special election.

A Democratic primary split and a well-financed GOP

candidate had raised Republican hopes for capturing the Los Angeles seat as well as scoring an expected victory in a normally Republican district in San Diego. A double victory would have given the GOP organizational control of the Senate.

The San Diego seat went to the GOP as anticipated. But Democrat Allan Robbins held the Los Angeles district with a 41,395 to 37,347 victory.

National COPE Director Al Barkan reported that more than 1,000 union members were involved in precinct organization in the Robbins campaign. Hundreds of other union members, joined by Frontlash volunteers, took part in the get-out-the-vote effort. Cars and drivers were provided through the Los Angeles Building & Construction Trades Council.

A special effort was mounted in 53 predominantly Chicano precincts with the help of Chano Marino of the COPE staff. In another area, black union members put on a successful get-out-the-vote drive.

While the Senate has a 20–20 party tie, a Democrat is president pro tempore of the Senate and state law provides that the party holding that office organizes the Senate.

Labor's Role in Seven Senate Campaigns

Although it is generally acknowledged that organized labor provides funds, manpower, and other union resources to endorsed candidates, what is not as widely known is that labor's strategists also frequently play key and indispensable roles in the early planning and execution of many campaigns. In the U.S. Senate today, the AFL-CIO claims to be able to control the votes of 62 of the 100 senators. Most of these 62 senators owe their election to organized labor. To show how labor provided campaign support and why these senators are now in bondage to labor's chieftains, let us examine the campaign plans of seven senators. Three of these Senate races took place in 1970: those of Senators Philip Hart (D-Mich.), Frank Moss (D-Utah), and Howard Metzenbaum (D-Ohio). Metzenbaum ran for the U.S. Senate in 1970 but was defeated by Senator Robert Taft, Jr. However, in 1974 Metzenbaum was appointed by Ohio Democratic governor John Gilligan (also a recipient of lavish union support) to fill the seat of Ohio's other Republican senator, William Saxbe, who resigned after being appointed Attorney General of the United States by President Nixon. Three other Senate races that we will discuss were run in 1972 and are those of Senators Claiborne Pell (D-R.I.), Lee Metcalf (D-Mont.), and Dick Clark (D-Iowa).

100

The seventh race we'll review is that of John Durkin (D-N.H.) in 1975.

Philip Hart

The planning of the campaign of Senator Philip Hart, who was up for reelection in 1970, began in early 1969. On May 8, 1969, Senator Hart wrote the following letter to Don Ellinger, director of the IAM's Machinists Non-Partisan Political League:

> Some weeks ago you were kind enough to meet with me, Senators Fred Harris and Gaylord Nelson and others to talk about the 1970 Senate race in Michigan. No need to tell you that I'm grateful—but I say it.
>
> Since that time we've been reviewing carefully the things we'd like to do for the rest of 1969, keeping in mind the suggestions made at our meeting.
>
> Now we're ready to move. On Thursday, May 15, at 3:00 P.M., in Room 155, Old Senate Office Buidling, Washington, we will be meeting again to review plans. It would be most helpful if you could attend. Can you let Sid Woolner know if you can come? [4]

At the earlier meeting, referred to in Senator Hart's letter, held on March 19, 1969, the following persons are listed as being "Invited to March 19 Michigan Campaign Planning Meeting":

Sen. Philip A. Hart
Sid Woolner
AA to Senator Hart
Cong. Charles Diggs
Cong. James O'Hara
Mrs. Mildred Jeffrey
Democratic National
   Committeewoman
The Hon. Coleman Young
Democratic National
   Committeeman
Stuart Hertzberg
Democratic State Treasurer
The Hon. Neil Staebler
Sam Fishman
United Auto Workers—
   Michigan
Gus Scholle & Bill Marshall
Michigan AFL-CIO

James McNeeley
Democratic State Chairman
Mrs. Patti Knox
Democratic State Vice
   Chairman
Ken Harding
Ted Henshaw
House Campaign Committee
Don Ellinger
IAM
Jim O'Brien
USW
Dave Anderson
CWA
Walt Davis
SIA
Democratic National
   Committee
Sen. Fred R. Harris

Stan Arnold
Michigan Building Trades
Al Barkan & Mary Zon
COPE
Sen. Daniel Inouye
Nordy Hoffman
Senate Campaign
   Committee

Bill Welsh
George Bristol
Mark Shields
Al Spivak
Harriet Cipriani [5]

The "Agenda: Michigan Campaign Planning Meeting" of March 19 was as follows:

I. Opening remarks by Chairman Harris
II. Assessment by Senator Hart on the situation in Michigan and outlook for his own campaign—strengths, weaknesses and needs
III. Reports from Michigan people
IV. Discussion of what efforts can be made in 1969 to aid the campaign [6]

It is interesting to note that of the 30 persons invited to the campaign planning session on March 19, fully one third (or 10) were representatives from organized labor. This may not be too surprising; the article in the *Detroit Free Press,* cited earlier in this chapter, had charged its investigation showed that "organized labor's large membership funds and plentiful campaign manpower make it the most powerful single force in Michigan politics."

On election day, Senator Hart went on to score an impressive victory, the credit for which can go in large part to the support of labor. It should also be observed that all 10 labor representatives at the March 19 planning meeting drew salaries from the tax-exempt treasuries of their unions, a fact which means that Senator Hart's campaign from its inception drew support from the tax-exempt compulsory dues money of union members.

Frank Moss

Another prominent liberal Democrat up for reelection in 1970 was Senator Frank Moss of Utah. Like his colleague from Michigan, Senator Moss began his campaign planning early. The first strategy meeting was held on March 5, 1969, and its "Agenda: 1970 Utah Campaign Planning" was as follows:

I. Introduction—opening remarks of DNC Chairman Fred R. Harris (5 mins.)

II. Report by Senator Ted Moss assessing the overall Utah political situation (10 mins.)
III. Report from Utah (5 mins.)
John Klas, Democratic State Chairman
Wayne L. Black, National Committeeman
Jean Westwood, National Committeewoman
Norma Thomas, State Democratic Vice Chairman
Phil Cowley
Don Holbrook
IV. Identification of needs during remainder of 1969
United States Senate race
Congressional races
Building Democratic Party
V. Open discussion by all present concerning plans for meeting needs in 1969 and laying plans for 1970 [7]

The list of "Participants: 1970 Utah Campaign Planning Meeting," March 5, 1969, follows:

Democratic National Committee:
Chairman Fred R. Harris
Vice Chairman Geri Joseph
Bill Welsh
George Bristol
Al Spivak
Senate Campaign Committee:
Sen. Daniel Inouye
Nordy Hoffman
House Campaign Committee:
Rep. Ed Edmondson
Ken Harding
Ted Henshaw
Utah Democratic Party:
Wayne L. Black, National Committeeman
Jean Westwood, National Committeewoman
John Klas, Democratic State Chairman
Norma Thomas, Democratic State Vice Chairman
Phil Cowley
Don Holbrook

National Labor:
COPE—Al Barkan, Mary Zon, LaMar Gulbransen
USW—James O'Brien
IAM—Don Ellinger
Utah State Labor:
E. C. Berger, President, State AFL-CIO
Michael Durkson, United Oil, Chemical & Atomic Workers
NRECA:
Kermit Overby
National Farmers Union:
Blue Carstenson [8]

Of the 25 participants in Senator Moss's meeting, one quarter (or 7) represented organized labor. Not many days later, on March 14, 1969, Senator Moss wrote one of the labor participants:

> I can't tell you how much I appreciate your making the effort and taking the time to come to the meeting to discuss the Utah political situation on Wednesday, March 5 at the Democratic National Committee. Personally, I felt it was a most fruitful meeting at which many problems of coordination between national and state committees and organizations were resolved.
>
> I know that we must follow on vigorously on all of the fronts that we talked about. I have already thanked those from Utah who attended, stressing the importance of setting up a state meeting soon, and of continuing with other meetings when I am in Utah.
>
> Your assistance will be of great importance in the months ahead, and I am hopeful that we will get together frequently.[9]

Senator Moss's "Utah Senate Campaign 1969 Activities," a campaign document that was developed at meetings in which labor representatives actively participated, is found in Appendix 11.[10] Of far greater significance, however, is the memorandum on the subject "Utah Senate Race and Related Matters," prepared by James Cuff O'Brien and Dean Clowes, director and deputy director respectively of political action for the United Steelworkers of America. The entire memo is in Appendix 12.[11]

Howard Metzenbaum

In January 1974 Howard Metzenbaum became the junior senator from Ohio, thereby fulfilling a lifetime ambition. With labor's support he had run for governor in 1968 and was defeated. Two years later he ran for the Senate and lost. In 1970, however, Democrat John Gilligan was elected governor and when Senator William Saxbe resigned his seat to become U.S. Attorney General, organized labor moved quickly to pressure Gilligan to appoint Metzenbaum. Gilligan acquiesced, of course. Metzenbaum was defeated in the Democratic senatorial primary in 1974 by John Glenn, who was to go on to win in the general election in November.

When Metzenbaum made up his mind to run for the Senate in 1970, he quietly informed a key Machinist strategist in advance:

> I have made the dicision to take the plunge. I will be announcing next Wednesday. My decision is based prin-

104

cipally upon two factors. One being the amount of support I have been developing from labor and political leaders and other groups, and some other factors which convinced me that I can win both the primary and the general election. Obviously I am extremely grateful to the Machinists for their support and of course this is an important consideration in my decision. I hope that we can work closely together during the campaign.[12]

For his 1970 campaign, Metzenbaum developed a $750,000 budget; of this amount he designated $100,000 to be raised by the Machinists. Although he did not get the full $100,000 in cash, he did receive ample Machinist funds and manpower. The Executive Committee of the Machinists Non-Partisan Political League

reviewed the Metzenbaum race and approved an additional $5,000 check and agreed that we would project an additional $5,000 depending on available money. The total amount of contributions in the Gilligan campaign from our general fund was about $15,000. The check is made payable to the Labor Committee for Metzenbaum because there is a $5,000 limitation to any one committee in support of a candidate. Howard undoubtedly has established such a committee and if not, he can very easily do so.[13]

Claiborne Pell

Democratic Senator Claiborne Pell of Rhode Island is the third-ranking member of the Senate Labor and Public Welfare Committee. He consistently votes on issues before the committee as he is directed by Andrew Biemiller, director of the AFL-CIO Department of Legislation. For this reason, when Pell came up for reelection in 1972, COPE mobilized its resources quickly to aid him. These resources are described in an internal union political document titled "R.I. Meeting":

1. Organized labor should supply 6 full-time organizers for political-educational purposes in Rhode Island.
2. All union newspapers, newsletters, etc., should have one complete story on CP's voting record, biography, etc. Also another story pre-election, of CP's pro-labor activities.
3. All members of organized labor should receive the labor brochure.
4. A political action office should be set up with a

secretary, telephone, desks, etc., preferably in AFL-CIO Headquarters.

5. There should be appointed a coordinator for all CP union activities in Rhode Island from the ranks of organized labor.

6. One member of organized labor should be responsible for a series of press commentaries by organized labor.

7. Local unions should be putting out a barrage of endorsements: i.e., Local 29 today endorses Senator Pell because of "his excellent voting record in support of the working man in Rhode Island, etc."

8. Union political activists should be attacking the anti-labor record of opponent, specifically, and not trying to attach him to the Nixon Administration.

9. COPE should have a "Dollars for Pell" Committee to try to get one dollar contributions from the union membership. (STRICTLY VOLUNTARY)

10. Money: Where, when, how much?? [14]

The above steps were not the only ones taken to aid Senator Pell's campaign. On August 5, 1971, Hamilton E. Davis, chief of the Washington Bureau of the *Providence Journal*, authored an article titled "Pell, Labor Chiefs Plan Campaign":

Washington—Sen. Claiborne Pell has sharply accelerated the pace of his early campaign for reelection, moving on several fronts to overcome the gap between himself and his likely opponent, Navy Secretary John Chafee.

The most important of the moves was the decision to take an in-depth poll immediately to find out why Pell ran so far behind Chafee in a Channel Six poll last spring. That survey showed Pell running behind Chafee by a margin of 53 to 25.

The poll will be taken by the Oliver Quayle Organization, starting any day, with the results due sometime around mid-September. The study, whose cost will be split by Pell and by organized labor, will show not only how far Pell is running behind Chafee now, but more importantly why he trails. These results will shape the remainder of the campaign.

The decision to take the poll was made at a secret strategy meeting here last week, involving both political leaders and representative of organized labor. Those attending included Pell, Ray Nelson and Paul Goulding, both of Pell's staff; Al Barkan of COPE, the political arm of the AFL-CIO; a handful of COPE staffers; Thomas Policastro; an AFL-CIO official from Rhode

Island; Major Joseph Doorley of Providence; and James McKenna of Sen. John Pastore's staff.

Pell flatly refused to comment on the meeting other than to admit it took place, but a general outline can be deduced from other sources. . . .

There was a consensus that while Pell is in desperate trouble politically, he can be reelected. The AFL-CIO committed itself to that proposition in terms of both financial support and technical campaign assistance.

Lee Metcalf

Senator Lee Metcalf of Montana, up for reelection in 1972, was the recipient of lavish labor support in his campaign. The initial steps in planning his campaign are described in this confidential memorandum of February 23, 1972, from the director of IAM's Machinists Non-Partisan Political League to an IAM vice president:

I recently attended a meeting with Senator Lee Metcalf, Al Barkan, Bob Maurer of Maurer, Fleisher and Zon, and several other union political operatives.

Bob Maurer offered to be of help to the Senator through the COPE program, with services and material including still pictures and film for television; work on materials that would be appropriate for inserting in union publications, telephone polls, designs for billboards and other signs.

The Senator will have primary opposition from Merrill Riddick, a Phillsbury prospector, and Jerome Peters, a Martin City hotel owner, but does not feel they are much of a threat at this time. He does, however, anticipate problems in the general election. Earlier he thought former Governor Babcock (R) would be his opponent in the general election, but Babcock plans to run for Governor again. Metcalf's probable opponent now, in the general election, will be State Senator Henry Hibbard, a Helena rancher, director of the largest bank in Montana, and owner of the largest sheep operation in the State.

Metcalf says he is being hurt in the lumber and sawmill regions because of his supposed stand on conservation. He feels, however, that conservation is not hurting the sawmill industry but rather, Nixon's economic policy.

With regard to the Governor's race, Senator Metcalf said that Lt. Governor Tom Judge is by far the leader on the Democratic side and that Babcock will face a tough race. He further stated that Judge, in his opinion, is not to be trusted.

In the first Congressional District he said almost anyone could beat the Republican Congressman Shoup. The only other contender he mentioned besides Arnold Olsen was Harriet Miller of Helena, former Public Instructions Superintendent. He feels certain Olsen could win both the primary and the general election, if he would only straighten out.[15]

Washington Post reporters Haynes Johnson and Nick Kotz, in their superb book *The Unions,* quote Senator Metcalf as telling a COPE meeting called to discuss his campaign strategy:

> I've never made any secret about it. They can say Lee Metcalf's campaigns are financed by organized labor, that I'm too close to organized labor. Well, I'm as close as I can get and if I can get any closer, or if I start straying away, you guys better come around and tell me. Nobody has to come to my office to tell me what to do on a bill. In fact, I've been ahead of you guys on a number of pieces of legislation.

Dick Clark

One of the big upsets of the 1972 election was the defeat of the Republican Senator Jack Miller of Iowa. He was upset by Democrat Dick Clark, who in the early days of the campaign was given scant chance of pulling off a victory. Clark strongly believed Miller could be beaten. He knew that if he was going to do it he would need the funds, manpower, and other resources that could only be supplied by organized labor. He indicated this in his letter of March 13, 1972, to Machinist George Kourpias in the nation's capital:

> I do want you to know how very much I appreciated your kind hospitality when we met in Washington several days ago.
> Your generosity in offering to set up a luncheon with representatives of international labor unions in Washington is particularly thoughtful and useful. It can very well mean the beginning of substantial and meaningful assistance and support. It will provide us with an opportunity to "make our case" and to reveal how careful planning, organization, and execution can give us a good opportunity to defeat Jack Miller.
> We had a good visit with Jim Wengert and Bill Fenton

in Des Moines upon our return and both were very helpful. Jim and Hugh feel that the first week of April would be the best time for them to come in to the luncheon because the legislative session may continue as late as the end of March. Jim called and said that he had talked with you and that this later date was agreeable to you.

I am in the process of finalizing my schedule for April and May and wonder how April 3, 4, 5, 6, or 7 would work for you and the Washington people. I would like to start an extensive campaign tour in western Iowa on April 10 (Sioux City—Council Bluffs, etc.) which would last several weeks. If Al Barkan and the others can be present as well as the Iowa leadership, that would seem feasible. Al's presence is certainly essential to a successful meeting and I know he will want to be there. He has been outstanding in his support from the outset and arranged the meeting with the COPE committee in Bal Harbour.

You mentioned the possibility of bringing Bill Dodds into the arrangements and I agree that it would be excellent to get him involved if that proves possible.

Bill Fenton has been most helpful with the Watts line and has been friendly and enthusiastic in his support and assistance.

Your list of important officers around the state was at my office when I arrived home and we will be visiting with each as we travel the state. Thank you for being so prompt.

When we met, you mentioned that you might want to talk with Jim O'Brien about my campaign manager, Dr. J. C. Smith. He is available for consultation in the area of data processing and systems analysis. Jim is going to engage him for some work and this may be something you will want to consider.

Let me tell you, in closing, how much your interest and enthusiasm has meant to me personally; it is just what a candidate needs and it is most encouraging. The campaign is going very well and with your continued interest, advice, and assistance I believe we can upset Jack Miller. We know that our campaign must be the most carefully planned, organized and executed effort in the country if we are going to be successful and that is just what it is going to be.

John Durkin

Citizens interested in learning how the labor bosses use their unions' resources to elect senators should study carefully yet another race, that between Democrat John Durkin and

109

Republican Louis Wyman in the 1975 special election in New Hampshire. Durkin was the winner and owes his Senate seat today to the key support provided him by organized labor.

The Washington newspaper, *Human Events* was among the first publications to expose the outpouring of union help in Durkin's behalf. The article "Unions Exploiting Holes in Campaign Reform Law," in its September 13, 1975, issue, stated:

> Aside from pouring large sums of money into the Durkin campaign, sums which are, in fact, regulated by the new law, the unions have amassed an extensive army of full-time paid workers for Durkin, are pumping out huge quantities of propaganda on his behalf and are engaged in extensive direct-mail operations (using cheap, bulk rates allowed for "nonprofit" organizations), activities so far out of reach of the campaign reform law.
>
> Congress intended to bar limitations on such "in kind" aid on the premise that the unions should not be checked in their right to "communicate" with their members. And they are "communicating" with a vengeance.
>
> The New Hampshire State Labor Council president, Thomas J. Pitarys, for instance, has mailed pro-Durkin letters to 47,000 union members in the state affiliated with the AFL-CIO. The presidents of the nation's most powerful AFL-CIO unions have also swung into action. The heads of the International Union of Electrical, Radio and Machine Workers (IUE), the United Association of Journeyman and Apprentices of the Plumbers and Pipefitting Industry, the Service Employes International Union, and the Textile Workers of America are bombarding their individual members with pro-Durkin literature. . . .
>
> But this represents only a fraction of what Big Labor is doing for Durkin in New Hampshire. Both the United Steelworkers of America and the Sheetmetal Workers had a joint meeting in Concord on August 28 in the New Hampshire Highway Hotel in which members were openly discussing how to organize workers, distribute literature, man telephone banks, advance Durkin's trips and get out the vote.
>
> Meanwhile, the national AFL-CIO has dispatched to Manchester from COPE headquarters in Washington, D.C., a Miss Ruth Colombo, Eastern Director of COPE's Women's Activities Department. She has set up shop in Manchester at Local 2320 of the International Brotherhood of Electrical Workers.
>
> "Durkin was endorsed by the labor movement, he is our endorsed candidate, and we're hoping our union mem-

bers will come and vote for Durkin," Miss Colombo told reporters. She is setting up nine telephone banks in New Hampshire, calling out union members, and urging them to vote for Durkin on September 16. Miss Colombo is using a computer printout as a guide in her phone operation.

When *Human Events* tried to contact Miss Colombo, she was out, but we did get hold of Miss Madeline Matchko, the area COPE director, who is working with her. Miss Matchko said that none of these operations had to be reported or included in Durkin's overall spending limitations because the campaign "reform" law specifically exempted this type of union contribution. David Prosser, a lawyer who works for Wyman, laments that Miss Matchko is probably right, for that's the way Congress appeared to draft the law.

In brief, then, Durkin is benefiting from an enormous loophole in the law. While his opponent is subject to strict expenditure limitations, Durkin is receiving thousands of dollars' worth of critical, unreported "in kind" contributions that could spell the difference in this hotly fought contest.

Following Durkin's defeat of Wyman, John Chamberlain wrote in his syndicated column, "Well, John A. Durkin won his senatorial seat legally. But whether he won it fairly and squarely is another question. The campaign expenditure laws demonstrably favor labor unions over corporations, who would be accused of the worst kind of propagandizing if they tried to rally their stockholders behind a political candidate."

Labor's Internal Dispute about Its Role in the Democratic Party

Organized labor today has almost fully recovered from the wounds it received in the 1972 fight that centered around the McGovern nomination. Forty of the 177 national and international unions supported McGovern, while the majority followed Meany's lead and refused to support either Nixon or McGovern.

The storm warnings about potential fratricidal political warfare were up months before McGovern locked up the sufficient delegate votes for the nomination. As early as December 23, 1971, a prominent member of the COPE Operating Committee, James J. Kennedy, Jr., national legislative counsel for the Brotherhood of Railway, Airline, and Steamship Clerks, advised COPE Director Al Barkan:

111

It seems to me that we are at a critical point. I believe that we either take steps necessary to make a defeat of President Nixon a strong possibility or cause a tremendous rift in the Democratic Party. It is my judgement that any of a number of democratic candidates are acceptable to the labor movement, that at the present time on his own, Senator Muskie has gotten far enough ahead of the field that the added support we would give him would virtually assure his nomination and make the same obvious to all of the other important candidates.[16]

Despite the early warning signals picked up by Kennedy and others, Meany and Barkan were caught flatfooted when Democratic National Convention time rolled around. Subsequently, the AFL-CIO secretary-treasurer Lane Kirkland, in response to the question "Did you let the delegate-selection process get away from you last year?" provided the following illuminating answer:

As a rule we haven't made an effort to put "labor" delegates on state delegations. We haven't had to, because the party structure in the past was run by professional politicians. And they would consult us. We could be pretty sure that whatever came out of the process wouldn't be too offensive to us. . . . We were aware of the McGovern reforms, but the "quota" business took us by surprise. And we didn't get serious enough about the state conventions until it was too late. McGovern really won the nomination in those conventions. The whole world is run by a handful of people who are willing to sit until the end of the meeting.[17]

After the 1972 election, which saw families of union members cast their ballots 54 percent for Nixon and only 46 percent for McGovern, the real shakeout began within the Democratic Party's leadership. McGovern himself was quick to let his feelings be known:

. . . I see nothing to be gained about airing these differences publicly. I want some chance to talk with other key Democrats around the country, to see what their thinking is. I'd like to be kind of a reconciling influence. I would do whatever I could to make sure that the wreckers, like Barkan and Meany, don't come back into a dominant role in the Democratic Party.[18]

Meany and Barkan, for their part, wasted no time either in formulating plans to recapture the Democratic Party structure.

On December 7, 1972, full-page advertisements were placed in major newspapers around the country by a Barkan-inspired group called the Coalition for a Democratic Majority, crying "Come Home, Democrats" to those who supposedly had been aliented by the McGovern candidacy and the "New Politics." The signers included Peter Bommarito, president, Rubber Workers; Walter Burke, secretary-treasurer, Steelworkers; C.L. Dennis, president, Railway, Airline, and Steamship Clerks; William DuChessi, secretary-treasurer, Textile Workers-Velma Hill, vice president, American Federation of Teachers; S. Frank Raftery, president, Brotherhood of Painters & Allied Trades; A. Philip Randolph, vice president, AFL-CIO; and Albert Shanker, president, United Federation of Teachers (New York City).

A founder of the coalition, author Ben Wattenberg declares, "It was our view that labor and regular Democrats were not getting a fair shake. We want to make sure that the next Convention is more representative of the Party as a whole." [19]

Whether the Meany-Barkan-Wattenberg strategy will succeed remains to be seen. One party technician has been quoted as follows:

> Barkan and his people think that if they can win the delegate selection commission they can control the convention. Well, they are wrong. It won't be a controlled convention in 1976; it will never be controlled again.
>
> What labor still has to learn is what they really must do is go out and broaden their political base on a precinct-by-precinct basis around the country. It's not enough any more to make deals with the party leadership.[20]

Tom Wicker, in a column titled "Will 1976 Be Like '68 or '72?" in the *New York Times* of October 9, 1973, observed:

> Ultimately the real test will be whether the convention is reasonably representative, rather than dominated by a handful of labor chieftains, state chairmen and other "leaders." Another rule will work to that end: mandated by a 1972 convention vote barring "winner-take-all" primaries, it will assure that Presidential candidates win delegates proportional to their strength at precinct, Congressional district and state levels.

Black political leaders, many of whom have been elected to public office with union support, support continuance of the McGovern "quota" system. Congressman Louis Stokes (D-Ohio) says it is "imperative that black people not relinquish gains" made under party reforms put into effect in 1972. "We could not afford as minority citizens to revert back to the guidelines of 1968." [21] Black congressman Parren Mitchell (D-MD.) warns: "Don't mess with the guidelines. This is an attempt to turn back the clock. Until the time when we achieve economic and political parity, I'm going to insist on quotas for blacks." [22]

The simmering debate over the representative makeup of delegates to the next Democratic National Convention is not without its humorous side. Liz Carpenter, former press aide to Lady Bird Johnson, suggests that the ideal delegates would be "polka-dot Jewish hermaphrodites who carry an AFL-CIO card, spend their summers chopping lettuce heads off with a tomahawk, and keep in constant touch with Mayor Daley." [23]

Despite some minor disagreements, Barkan and Robert Strauss, the Democratic national chairman, have developed a close working relationship since the latter assumed the post in December 1972. Victor Riesel, in a column titled "Capture of Democratic Committee by Labor's Man Starts Meany-Nixon Rift," tells how Strauss got elected:

> There's no doubt the charming, urbane ex-FBI agent Robert Strauss, new Democratic National Committee (DNC) Chairman, has a union label on him. . . .
>
> A swing of some 3½ votes from the New York delegation, where Meany had special influence, swung the majority of the 209-man committee to Strauss.
>
> And it wasn't done with the ballroom mirrors. It took weeks of skilled direction. A pro-Strauss high command had met almost daily in Suite 137 of the Old Senate Office Building, Sen. Scoop Jackson's office. The brain trust consisted of Jackson's young men, some from the Humphrey camp, COPE's Robert Keefe, the anonymous Bill Welsh, a brilliant strategist now working for Jerry Wurf's American Federation of State, County and Municipal Employees—and from time to time Al (Low Profile) Barkan.[24]

One of the quarrels between Barkan and Strauss concerned the markeup of labor's representatives on the Democratic National Committee. There are at the present time 13 labor representatives on the DNC, three of whom are believed not to be Barkan's men since they supported McGovern in 1972 and are of the "New Politics" school (see Appendix 13). When one of the three, Floyd Smith,, president of the Machinists Union, was elected over Frank Raftery, president of the Brotherhood of Painters and a founder of Barker's Coalition for a Democratic Majority, Barkan became so incensed that he threatened Strauss: "All I have to do is give the word and off we go, all of us. We'll leave you to your New Politics friends." [25]

The Democratic Party and the Future

Leaders of organized labor will continue to play key roles in the future of the Democratic Party—the leaders, not necessarily the rank and file. This is a distinction that must continually be drawn, for there exists ample evidence that union members and their families are more conservative than union leaders.

In fact, it was this conservatism that worried labor's strategists as they laid plans for the 1972 election. Until George Wallace was shot in Laurel, Maryland, in May 1972, labor leaders feared the effect he might have on the outcome of the Presidential race. On June 8, 1971, Al Barkan wrote James Kennedy, national legislative counsel of the Brotherhood of Railway, Airline and Steamship Clerks:

> As you know there is increasing evidence that Governor Wallace retains considerable support among our members. The IAM poll of their members in Texas, Tennessee and even outside of the South shows a disturbing degree of support among our members for Wallace. I have a feeling that we ought not wait until 1972 before we start facing up to the Wallace infection among our members.
>
> We have scheduled a COPE Operating Committee meeting for July 8th and 9th at Piney Point, Maryland. I would like for you to serve on a Special Committee with Don Ellinger and Mel Boyle to come up with some ideas for the Piney Point meeting as to how we can best meet the Wallace danger in advance of the '72 presidential campaign.
>
> I have asked Don Ellinger to be the chairman of the special Committee and I hope you will serve on it. Please let me know and if there is anything our office can do to help in the work of the committee just call on us.

On June 17, 1971, Don Ellinger, director of the Machinists Non-Partisan Political League, reported back to Barkan:

> Your committee regarding the Wallace problem met Thursday, June 17, and agreed on the following points:
> 1. The Wallace strength among trade unionists is

probably accurately reflected by the Machinists polls, running about 20 percent outside of the south.

2. The high percentage and perhaps a majority of these pro-Wallace unionists are strongly anti-Nixon.

3. We assumed there is a hard core of Wallace racist sentiment that cannot be substantially changed.

4. The trade union movement should emphasize that a vote for Wallace helps Nixon and begin the propaganda as soon as possible.

5. Among the non-trade unionists, the Wallace candidacy probably helps us and can be an asset if we knock out the trade union component.

6. We favor an attitude questionnaire to be distributed nationwide to a random sample of 2 percent of at least 10 international unions which would attempt to measure the strength and source of the Wallace support. The committee is not unanimous as to the timing. I an inclined to favor a poll mailed in August to be analyzed and reported to you in September.

7. We need a current analysis of the Wallace performance in Alabama by a competent writer with a trade union background. This could be done under the aegis of SCOPE, if we want to resurrect it, or someone hired for the purpose, like perhaps Ronnie Dugger.

If you agree, we would be prepared to submit a proposed questionnaire and this general outline to the Operating Committee at Piney Point.[26]

One candidate, Senator Henry Jackson of Washington, currently cultivates the support that Meany and Barkan can provide. When Jackson addressed the AFL-CIO convention in 1973, he declared:

This is a great country and we can do whatever we need to do. . . . The Democratic Party is either the party of the workingman or it has no future. . . . Let the others whine about Big Labor and the labor bosses. I want to see more of you, not less of you, in the center of the Democratic Party where the decisions are made. . . . I think we can do better.[27]

Perhaps the most perceptive contemporary analysis of the relationship of organized labor to the Democratic Party is found in Alice Widener's article, "The 70s Left: Socialists Come out of the Closet," which appeared in the October 1973 issue of *U.S.A.* Excerpts follow (for the full text, see Appendix 14):

116

A major new move of deepest political significance to the entire nation is under way within the Democratic Party. In a split with aging George Meany's concealed socialism called "industrial democracy," the two most influential leaders of the Democratic Left—economist John Kenneth Galbraith, author of *The Affluent Society,* and Michael Harrington, author of *The Other America*—deicded to come out of the closet as avowed socialists. As such they intend to lead a "70s Left" movement within the Democratic Party as the best vehicle for turning our country into a socialist nation.

What authors Galbraith and Harrington want is a non-violent revolution in America, Asia, Africa, and Latin America. The kind of revolution they want is described in Michael Harrington's pamphlet "American Power in the Twentieth Century" (published by the League for Industrial Democracy, New York, 1967). Mr. Harrington wrote:

> "It requires, to use John Kenneth Galbraith's symbolic language, a revolution that would be less than a 'Russian' and yet more profound than a 'French' revolution. . . .
>
> "To make a democratic revolution here and now, it is necessary to go beyond the French model—to institute extensive economic planning, and to ignore the allocation of resources made by the market."

No matter how it is put, what Messrs. Galbraith and Harrington want is what all socialists want: abolition of the free market and the collectivization of our entire society. . . .

On September 10, the *New York Times* reported "Socialists Plan Founding Parley—Harrington and 45 Others in New Group Issue Call." The call is for "a new American socialist organization" and its aim is to "set up a socialist caucus within the Democratic Party."

On September 18, Leonard Silk, economics editor of the *New York Times,* reviewed John Kenneth Galbraith's new book *Economics and the Public Purpose* (Boston: Houghton Mifflin Company, 1973). Mr. Galbraith reveals in it he is a socialist and he describes socialism as "indispensable" for our country. Leonard Silk commented, "So Mr. Galbraith has at last come out of the closet as a socialist." Mr. Silk opined that Mr. Galbraith's coming out, "is publicly useful; it will add clarity and realism to the debate."

It will and it already has. . . .

In the 1972 McGovern campaign, radicals took effective control of the Democratic Party. The new Democratic Socialists intend to form a powerful caucus able to take control of the radicals and use the Democratic Party as an instrument for turning our country into a socialist state. "We are looking to the United States of the 1970's and beyond," says Michael Harrington.

"The new socialism," writes John Kenneth Galbraith, "allows of no acceptable alternatives; . . . The new socialism is not ideological; it is compelled by circumstances."

Both Communists and Democratic Socialists proclaim the inevitability of socialism due to circumstances. Neither Communists nor Democratic Socialists will tolerate the free market, the sole guarantor of individual freedom. What John Kenneth Galbraith and Michael Harrington are trying to do is to force every American to choose between Left and Right. In 1972, Americans— Republicans and Democrats—overwhelmingly rejected the Left. If they do not do so in 1976, our country will begin its third century of existence under a Socialist President.[29]

The Labor Bosses and 1976

A. H. Raskin, labor editor for the *New York Times,* in a January 11, 1976 article, "Labor Has Picked Its Man—Any Democrat," observed:

The leadership of organized labor, which was scattered in every direction in the 1972 Presidential campaign, is all moving in one direction this time. The union chiefs— those who backed Richard M. Nixon, those who lined up behind George McGovern and those who joined George Meany in sulky aversion to both—are now almost unanimously in the Democratic camp for 1976.

Their goal is to get a record number of unionists—at least 500 out of the 3,000 total—chosen as delegates to the Democratic nominating convention in New York City next July. A contingent of that size would give labor plenty of leverage in the brokering which the union leaders are sure will precede the party's final selection. . . .

More important than an endorsement is the union political apparatus, which is able to marshal large numbers of staff members and rank-and-filers to get out the vote, employing a highly sophisticated update of the dragnet method used by the now largely defunct big-city political machines. In a year when campaign spending is under tight new statutory restraints, this "free" help from the unions can be significant.

118

George Meany's position in 1976 is much clearer than it was in 1972. Says Meany in an interview in *U.S. News and World Report* of Sept. 8, 1975,

I'd like to see a liberal Democrat in the White House. . . . I don't have any particular candidate. . . . If the Democratic Party comes up with a candidate who can receive . . . united support, I think the Democratic Party's chance of winning the election in November, 1976, is quite good.

While it appears that Meany is enthusiastic about supporting the 1976 Democratic nominee, whoever he may be, it cannot be ruled out that some unforeseen event may cause him to sit the election out as he did in 1972 when he did not support either McGovern or Nixon. A number of more liberal-radical union leaders are not taking a watching and waiting attitude. Instead they are organizing into a powerful political bloc.

The unions in this bloc, working together as the Labor Coalition Clearinghouse, are the Communications Workers of America (CWA), the United Auto Workers (UAW), the International Association of Machinists (IAM), the Graphic Arts International Union, the American Federation of State, County and Municipal Employees (AFSCME), the International Union of Electrical, Radio and Machine Workers, the Oil, Chemical and Atomic Workers, the United Mine Workers (UMW), and the National Education Association (NEA). All but the UAW, UMW, and NEA are AFL-CIO affiliates.

Nearly all of the nine unions were active for McGovern in 1972, despite the official neutral policy of the AFL-CIO laid down by Meany.

The rise of this powerful coalition of liberal-radical unions will have a significant impact on 1976 and future elections. Liberal activist Alan Baron, who advises McGovern on his labor strategy, declares: "The whole situation puts the unions more and more to the left in the Democratic Party. The politically active unions are the most liberal ones."

The influence of the Labor Coalition Clearinghouse, which is part of the Galbraith-Harrington radical axis working within the Democratic Party, could be considerable when it is realized that there are six million members in the nine coalition unions, representing a total of 200 congressional districts in each of which the unions have a combined average of 20,000 members.

Conclusion

In most states, even in the Deep South, organized labor

119

controls the machinery of the Democratic Party by providing funds and manpower and a political operation that works 24 hours a day, 365 days a year. This control allows labor to influence the selection of the party's candidates at the national, state, and local levels.

It is generally recognized that unions provide funds, manpower, and other goods and services to labor-backed candidates. What is less known is that labor political strategists play indispensable roles in the early planning and execution of these campaigns—even to the point of being key participants in the campaign planning sessions of members of the U.S. Senate.

The liberal-radical unions are those that are the most politically active. With the retirement or death of George Meany it is quite likely that the bulk of the labor movement's leadership will align itself with the liberal-radical element, thus paving the way for the imposition of a labor government in the United States, as has occurred in England.

PART II

The International Association of Machinists and Aerospace Workers (IAM) and the Machinists Non-Partisan Political League (MNPL)

A Case History of How One Major Union Conducts Its Political Program

4

How the IAM and MNPL Are Organized

International Association of Machinists and Aerospace Workers

The International Association of Machinists and Aerospace Workers (IAM) was spawned during the turbulent final quarter of the 19th century when the Industrial Revolution sparked the creation of a number of labor unions, many of which still form the backbone of organized labor today. Unions in America's metal and machinery industry appeared even before the Civil War; one international union, the International Union of Blacksmiths and Machinists, was created in 1859 but failed during the 1877 Depression. Two of its successors, the National Boilermakers and Helpers Protective and Benevolent Union, created in 1881, and the Machinists National League, established in 1886, also were short-lived.

In 1888 the United Machinists and Mechanical Engineers of North America was organized by 19 machinists meeting in a locomotive pit in Atlanta, Georgia, and in 1890 evolved into the International Association of Machinists of America. Its founder was Thomas W. Talbot of Atlanta. Talbot was a railroad machinist with the Eastern Tennessee, Virginia and Georgia Railroad and was elected grand master machinist at the first Machinists convention held in 1889 in the Georgia State Senate chamber. Not long after its birth the union enrolled many of the workers belonging to National Trade Assembly 198 of the Knights of Labor, the forerunner of today's American Federation of Labor and Congress of Industrial Organizations (AFL-CIO).

Although its beginnings were the unindustrialized South, IAM spread quickly northward and its membership steadily grew, especially under the militant leadership of James O'Connell who was elected the Union's president in 1893. In 1895, IAM joined the American Federation of Labor (AFL) after the Machinists had agreed to omit the "white only" membership qualification from the union's constitution. It was not until the 1940s, however, that IAM ceased to exclude blacks from its membership.

Today IAM is the fifth largest labor union in the United States. It currently has over 940,000 members, with representation in all 50 states. Since the IAM's negotiating agreements encourage the inclusion of compulsory union-shop or agency-shop clauses requiring all persons in the bargaining unit to be members of and pay membership dues and fees to IAM as a condition of their employment, it is impossible to determine how many of its members belong to the union on an involuntary as contrasted to a voluntary basis.

Table VI
Ten Largest Labor Unions in the U.S.

Teamsters	1,973,272
Auto Workers	1,544,859
Steelworkers	1,300,000
Electrical Workers (IBEW)	991,228
Machinists	943,280
Retail Clerks	650,876
Laborers	650,000
State, County Employees	648,160
Service Employees	550,000
Meat Cutters	528,631

SOURCE: U.S. Department of Labor release of August 12, 1975, "Labor Union and Employee Association Membership, 1974."

The Grand Lodge is the central body of IAM and has its headquarters in a modern, 10-story office building on fashionable Connecticut Avenue in Washington, D.C. The union owns the building, which is situated in an area abounding with offices of prestigious Washington law firms, powerful trade associations, and influential corporate lobbyists. The building's entrance ostentatiously bears the slogan "One Million Strong."

Basic Organizational Structure

IAM's basic organizational structure is made up of:
* The Grand Lodge
* 167 district lodges
* 1,929 local lodges
* 48 state and provincial councils

The Grand Lodge is the union's central body. Indeed, the labor organization's formal name is the Grand Lodge of the International Association of Machinists and Aerospace Workers. Ultimate power is vested in the 11-man Executive Council, which comprises the international president, the general secretary-treasurer, and nine general vice presidents (GVPs). The Executive Council meets an average of four times a year. The international president's salary per annum is $35,000,

124

that of the general secretary-treasurer $31,000, and that of the GVPs $27,000.

The 11 Grand Lodge officers are elected by the general membership every four years.

The union also holds its convention every four years. The convention coincides with national election years in which the President and Vice President of the United States are elected, and is held after the nominating conventions of the major political parties but well before election day. A major purpose for holding its convention then is to provide the labor organization with the opportunity of formally endorsing one of the Presidential candidates. Each local lodge is entitled to be represented by a convention delegate, and each lodge that has more than 200 members is entitled to another delegate or delegates based on increments of an additional 200 or more members.

A staff of 247 Grand Lodge representatives (GLRs), special representatives, auditors, and organizers is employed by the Grand Lodge. Sixteen GLRs are assigned to IAM headquarters, of whom two lobby for legislation on Capitol Hill. The headquarters staff is composed of 292 persons.*

Under the Grand Lodge, in the next organizational layer, are the 167 district lodges. A district lodge is a delegate body made up of elected representatives from local lodges within the railroad or air transport system, industry, or locality in which the district lodge is situated. Generally, local lodges merge into a district lodge for areawide or industrywide bargaining.

There are 1,929 local lodges scattered throughout the country. A local lodge consists of not less than 35 persons in any locality, qualified for membership, and is organized under a charter issued by the Grand Lodge. A local lodge usually represents members employed at a single plant or facility.

Approximately 48 state and provincial councils have been established. The *raison d'etre* of the state organizations is to implement IAM's political and legislative programs. A state council (sometimes called a conference) is made up of district

* A bird's-eye view of the IAM would also include 662 elected business representatives and general chairmen, 20,960 district and local lodge officers, 292 professional supervisory, clerical, and custodial employees, and 13,038 contracts with employers. IAM is active in almost every industry and maintains agreements with almost every major employer in the U.S. and Canada.

IAM is affiliated with these organizations: AFL-CIO and most of its departments (14,000,000 members), Canadian Labour Congress (1,800,000 members), Railway Labor Executives Association, International Metalworkers' Federation (11,000,000 workers in 60 nations), and the International Transport Workers' Federation (7,000,000 workers in 80 nations).

and local lodges within that state which have chosen voluntarily to affiliate.

Table VII
Receipts and Disbursements of IAM Grand Lodge

Year	Receipts	Disbursements
1963	$16,740,647	$14,239,218
1964	17,968,717	14,623,440
1965	17,505,849	14,188,145
1966	22,419,693	16,801,533
1967	27,119,243	20,070,320
1968	25,517,999	21,835,832
1969	29,584,665	24,039,918
1970	31,188,939	24,861,829
1971	35,267,663	37,109,861
1972	36,983,825	34,046,942

SOURCE: Figures for 1963 through 1970 were obtained from the union's records by A. Dudley Benson, Certified Public Accountant, Los Angeles, California. Receipts include contributions to the union's Strike Fund. Figures for 1971 and 1972 were obtained from IAM reports filed with the U.S. Department of Labor.

The Grand Lodge exercises a substantial degree of supervision and control over the 662 business representatives and general chairmen attached to district and local lodges. It shares on a 50–50 basis with the district and local lodges the cost of the salary of each of these business representatives and general chairmen so long as the individual's salary does not exceed $19,000 a year. The Grand Lodge also contributes $300 a month to pay the salaries of 500 organizers employed by district and local lodges. District and local lodge treasury funds pay the salaries and other compensation that may be received by approximately 21,000 district and local lodge officers, as well as any other staff personnel employed at the local level.

Dues Revenue

A Machinist's dues usually average $7.00 per month. In a typical case, such a member's dues are remitted directly to the district lodge, which forwards $3.30 to the Grand Lodge, remits 25¢ to the local lodge, and retains the rest. The amount retained by the district lodge is drawn upon to pay various per capita assessments and contributions, primarily to political organizations such as the Machinists Non-Partisan Political League (MNPL), state and local MNPLs, and state AFL-CIO Committees on Political Education (COPE).

In 1972, for example, the Grand Lodge received $36,983,825 in dues income from its members. One dollar of each member's $3.30 monthly dues received by the Grand Lodge is allocated to the Strike or Defense Fund. Although agency employees must pay the same amount of dues as full-fledged union members and although $1.00 of their monthly dues goes into the Strike Fund, the union denies them a claim to benefits from the fund when a strike takes place.

The Grand Lodge also allocates a portion of the $3.30 monthly dues received from each member to other organizations, either on a per capita tax basis or on a contributory basis. The groups that primarily enjoy support drawn from dues monies are the national MNPL, AFL-CIO, national COPE, National Council of Senior Citizens, League of Women Voters, Group Research, Frontlash, NAACP, Institute for American Democracy, and similar liberal and Left organizations promoting political action.

Two Chief Officers

International President Floyd E. Smith and General Secretary-Treasurer Eugene Glover are the union's two chief executive officers.

Smith's roots in the IAM go back to 1945, when he joined as a member. That same year saw him appointed as one of the union's business representatives. He has devoted his professional life to IAM and the union movement. Having joined the Grand Lodge staff in 1952, he ascended to the general vice presidency in 1961 and served in this post until his election as international president eight years later.

Smith acknowledges that he first became aware of the political activity engaged in by the union during the first year he was a member, two years before the MNPL, the union's political arm, was established in 1947. Smith asserts, however, that the union has been engaged in political action to one extent or another since its birth on May 5, 1888.[1]

International President Smith does not mince words in explaining the union's political posture to its members. In a letter on IAM stationery to members in 1971, Smith attacked the Nixon administration's economic stabilization program, declaring, "We have no confidence in the man President Nixon has placed in charge of this program, former Governor John Connally of Texas, and we are determined to clean out this administration, if possible, in 1972. We are seeking the largest political fund because we think it is the biggest challenge we have ever faced. . . ." [2]

General Secretary-Treasurer Glover, like Smith, has devoted much of his professional life to unionism. He served as a Grand Lodge representative and a business representative before becoming the GVP for the Midwest territory. As general secretary-treasurer, he sits on the IAM Executive Council and is co-chairman of MNPL along with the international president and resident GVP.

Glover is as outspoken on politics as Smith. In a 1972 letter he wrote:

> 1972 will be the most political year in the history of the labor movement. The present administration is carrying on an all-out attack on labor and our collective bargaining structure. Unemployment, inflation and tax loopholes are still major problems that face every working man and woman in America. The worn-out cliche "We can't stand four more years of Nixon" becomes clearer and clearer as election day nears. We must make 1972 our greatest and most effective political effort.[3]

Machinists Non-Partisan Political League

Much of the IAM's overt and covert political activity is conducted through the Machinists Non-Partisan Political League (MNPL). The league has its suite of offices on the fourth floor of the IAM headquarters building in Washington, D.C., and the officers of the Grand Lodge and MNPL work in tandem to implement the union's political programs.

The *Machinist,* official IAM newspaper published 48 times a year for the membership, has described the relationship between IAM and MNPL, a description which Floyd Smith has termed accurate:

> The MNPL is the political arm of the International Association of Machinists and Aerospace Workers and is created by and subordinate to the Executive Council of the IAM. The Constitution of the MNPL rests authority for the operation of the national headquarters of the League in a 9-man Executive Committee with the International President, General Secretary-Treasurer and Resident General Vice President as Co-Chairmen.

> The National Planning Committee is the basic advisory group to the Executive Committee and consists of IAM leaders throughout the country nominated by the General Vice Presidents of the IAM, approved by the

Executive Committee and appointed by the International President.[4]

The director of MNPL is William Holayter, who assumed the position upon the unexpected death of his predecessor, Don Ellinger. Ellinger was a skilled professional who had spent many years in politics. He had served as COPE director for the Southwest prior to the merger of the AFL and CIO in 1955 and later manned the labor liaison desk at the Democratic National Committee, where he attempted to make tighter the knot that binds labor to the Democratic Party.

Ellinger brought Holayter into the MNPL as assistant director in 1969. Holayter, who had been a Machinist since 1954, was employed as a business representative by District Lodge 93 in California at the time Ellinger asked him to join the MNPL staff.

Holayter admits he "has been doing political activity for as long as I can remember." [5] Politics was part of his everyday work responsibility as an IAM employee "but it was only a part, because I was first of all a Business Representative for District Lodge 93." [6] One of the campaigns in which he worked was the special election in California's 27th Congressional District in 1969, where his political chores were performed while on the payroll of District 93. Barry Goldwater, Jr., who won that special election, was opposed by IAM.

In 1973 Holayter appointed Machinist Jerry Thompson, formerly state COPE director in Kentucky, as MNPL assistant director. The two full-time MNPL officials carry out their duties with the help of three clerical employees in MNPL's national office. All five MNPL employees are paid directly by the IAM payroll, instead of MNPL maintaining its own payroll. At the end of each month IAM bills MNPL and collects the gross amount of payroll costs of the employees, including pension payments. This procedure, which was adopted in 1966 by the IAM Executive Council, allows MNPL's employees to participate in the union's pension plan and to be eligible for its benefits upon retirement. The funds with which the MNPL reimburses the IAM are dues monies originally given to the MNPL by the Grand Lodge.

Interlocking Relationship

The interlocking relationship between IAM and MNPL is stated candidly and lucidly in two 1968 letters to the postmaster of the District of Columbia, letters that were part of an application for a second-class mailing permit for MNPL.

In the first letter, then MNPL director Don Ellinger enclosed "two copies of the Constitution of the Machinists Non-Partisan Political League, a subordinate division of the International Association of Machinists and Aerospace Workers. The Machinists Non-Partisan Political League is the political arm of the IAM and its officers are the officers of the IAM."[7]

Shortly thereafter the IAM general secretary-treasurer also wrote the postmaster:

> This League was created in 1947 by action of the Executive Council of the IAM. The 3 Co-Chairmen are, by the Constitution, the International President, the General Secretary-Treasurer, and the resident General Vice President of the IAM. All of the League's officers and members of its Executive Committee are Grand Lodge Representatives of IAM.
>
> I assume that this certification is sufficient to establish the relationship between the Machinists Non-Partisan Political League and the IAM as a subordinate body created by and responsible to the Executive Council of the operation of the IAM.[8]

IAM Subsidizes MNPI

At a meeting of the IAM Executive Council early in 1972, the motion was adopted that "the annual contributions to the MNPL be increased by $10,000.00 to be allocated on a monthly basis of $8,333.33 total." [9] Adoption of this motion has increased the contribution from the tax-exempt IAM treasury to MNPL to $100,000 annually.

The increase was not as much as Don Ellinger had hoped for. In a 1972 memorandum to the MNPL co-chairmen, Ellinger noted that of the amounts MNPL had spent in three prior years,

> Direct salary-related items in 1969 were $80,427.98. In 1970 they were $82,312.86. In 1971 these were $103,668.66.
>
> The payment by the IAM to the Political League has been based, before last year, on the amount of the salary-related items, rent and telephone. . . .
>
> We were able to reduce our total administrative outlays in 1971 from 1970, but 1972 is an election year. The items of travel, printing, aid to state councils, political assignments, and contributions to candidates will definitely go up if we are to maintain the program as we have done. . . . I believe the $9,100 monthly figure is

a legitimate one for us to seek from the IAM Grand Lodge.[10]

Five years previously, in 1967, Ellinger had made a similar appeal to the international president in a memorandum he titled "Begging for More Money." He requested that IAM's contribution to MNPL be boosted to $65,000 in 1967 because of increased political activity. He observed in his appeal that in the previous year's national elections, "In 1966, we agreed to put 10 men in the field to help elect our friends in Congress. About $2,000 of this cost was paid in 1967 from our Educational Funds." [11]

As we shall see later, Ellinger's declaration that MNPL Educational Funds were tapped to elect friendly congressmen is significant because such funds are derived solely from the union's dues revenue, which is tax-exempt. Ellinger's statement is an admission that tax-exempt funds were used by IAM MNPL to elect candidates to federal offices.

Local MNPI Groups

The IAM encourages the establishment of affiliated MNPL organizations on the local level, and "most of these Local and District Lodges do have Machinists Non-Partisan Political Leagues or Committees of one type or another." [12] To promote this goal, the national MNPL distributes a brochure titled "Recommended Bylaws" and reviews the bylaws as adpoted by the local group before it grants affiliation. The relationship between IAM, MNPL, and local MNPL groups has been described by an IAM international president as follows:

There exists, as the political action arm of the International Association of Machinists "The Machinists Non-Partisan Political League" of which I am an Executive Officer. Pursuant to this policy and platform the only constitutional and lawful political action committee that can exist within this Union either on an International or Local Lodge level is a Committee or League which is affiliated with The Machinists Non-Partisan Political League. No other group is recognized or authorized to act in behalf of this Union or in its name.

Under our establishment policies each Local Lodge of this Association is encouraged to have its own "local" non-partisan political league or committee and encourage its union officers to participate fully through such a League in such political action as may be lawful under established law.[13]

To develop local MNPL groups, IAM relentlessly propagandizes its members on the need to organize local leagues to increase the impact of the union in national affairs. The *Machinist* regularly publishes articles on politics and MNPL itself issues a political newsletters, *Action,* for its members. IAM distributes brochures and pamphlets showing how local leagues can be established, and the union's leadership stresses MNPL in speeches before the membership. The IAM convention, held every four years, allows MNPL to have an exhibit booth and invites prominent political leaders to address convention delegates. Usually the convention's program includes the presentation of MNPL awards and certificates to publicize the league's activities.

Who Speaks for the Union?

Although the Machinist leadership encourages the development of local MNPL groups and the involvement of its members in politics, the same leadership is careful to make certain that it, and not the membership at large, has the final say on which candidate for President of the U.S. the IAM will endorse and throw its considerable resources behind in the general election.

Opinion surveys taken in 1968 and 1971 of the Machinist membership revealed sharp differences on who should be supported for President. In many states George Wallace received exceedingly strong support from the rank-and-file Machinists. It was an apparent concern, over the possibility of rank-and-file rebellion against IAM's supporting a liberal candidate that led MNPL co-chairmen Floyd Smith and Eugene Glover in June 1971 to spell out the procedure for the union's Presidential endorsements:

1. The authority to speak for the IAM in making a recommendation or endorsement for the office of the President of the United States rests with the IAM Executive Council or the IAM Convention.
2. Subordinate IAM bodies such as state councils, district or local lodges, regional or industry conferences, or their political leagues do not have the authority to speak for the IAM in a nationwide contest.
3. Subordinate bodies may adopt resolutions urging the IAM Executive Council or Grand Lodge Convention to support a particular candidate, but the resolution should make clear that the subordinate body is not acting for the IAM and will support the decision of the Executive Council or Grand Lodge Convention when or if it is made.[14]

According to a recent MNPL brochure titled "MNPL: The Union's Other Arm," the national league operates two separate political funds:

1. *Educational Fund.* Every local and district lodge in the nation is asked to make a 30¢ per member per year contribution from the lodge treasury to the National MNPL educational fund.

The IAM Executive Council also appropriates funds to the educational fund to pay the cost of the routine salaries and operation of the League so that all money contributed by the local or district lodges is used for voting records, issues pamphlets, publications, travel, and support of registration and get out the vote campaigns. Part of the educational fund is contributed to National COPE to assist in meeting the IAM quota.

2. *General Fund.* The general fund of the National League is composed of the individual contributions of IAM members. All members are urged to give at least one hour's pay. Almost all IAM staff members contribute from $25 to $200 per year and become sponsoring members. Many state and district Leagues conduct a wide variety of money raising efforts to increase their individual contributions to the National League.

If a state, district, or local League has been established, the organization sending in the money may request that 25 percent of the individual contributions received by the National League be refunded to the state district or local League for use in accordance with their own bylaws. Only funds contributed individually can be used for federal candidates but the allocation is up to the local, district or state League receiving the refund.

One-fourth of all individual contributions received by the National League are contributed to COPE to meet the IAM quota.[15]

In 1972 the MNPL General Fund receipts totaled $319,684. The Educational Fund receipts totaled $269,866. Even though 1973 was not a national election year, contributions to MNPL were running at nearly a record level. An article in the *Machinist* of August 16, 1973, titled "Watergate Aids MNPL Drive," reported:

For the first seven months this year the MNPL has raised $313,055 for Congressional campaigns. . . .
Holayter reported that during the 1973 first half the

MNPL has received contributions from all but two of the 167 IAM districts. . . .

The league maintains a list of sponsoring members, those who contribute $25 or more. One half of MNPL's sponsoring members are IAM officers, Grand Lodge representatives, and officers of district and local lodges. A higher proportion of full-time officers, full-time subordinate officers, and full-time employees contributes more than does the membership as a whole.

There exists a scale of the amount expected to be contributed to MNPL by full-time officers and employees. Floyd Smith acknowledges only that the union asks each of its officers and employees to contribute more than a nominal sum to the MNPL General Fund. When questioned about an article in the *Machinist* of February 18, 1971, on an MNPL fund-raising drive scheduled for fall 1971 asking for "$5 contributions from 100,000 leaders who should be given honor award certificates," Smith asserted that all persons making a $5 contribution should be regarded as leaders, whether they hold official union positions or not. The article's assertion that "all full-time staff members should be asked to contribute on a proportional basis" is interpreted by Smith as indicating all full-time staff members should be asked to contribute proportionately more than $5, but the actual amount should be left up to the individual. The same article states that "all staff contributions for 1972 should be made no later than January 31, 1972. Those who delay will be asked to contribute $5 for each month after the January 31, 1972 deadline." Smith emphatically denies the article's implication that those staff persons who do not contribute on time will be penalized up to $60 on an annual basis. Even though the same article goes on to state that "all full-time staff members shall freely document their MNPL activity and be answerable for it," Smith explains this away by saying it refers to written, not oral, reports filed by the staff members.[16]

Examination of IAM and MNPL correspondence appears to support the existence of a fairly precise contribution scale. In February 1972 Smith, along with his MNPL co-chairmen, sent virtually identical letters to three different Machinist groups seeking MNPL support. These letters were sent to salaried employees at the Grand Lodge, to members directly affiliated with the Grand Lodge, and to retirees receiving IAM pensions. The letters declared:

Because the outcome of the Presidential election this year is more crucial than ever, we must make a greater

134

effort than ever. In addition to the "Big One" drive—which is specifically aimed at putting an occupant more friendly to labor in the White House—we are going to be carrying on campaigns of voter registration and seeking to mobilize the full political potential of younger members, retirees and women.

Earlier this year the MNPL Planning Committee set up the following formula—based on ability to pay—for MNPL contributions. We hope each of you will adopt it as a guide to your MNPL donation.

Less than $10,000 a year salary (or in pension)	$25.
$10,000 to $15,000.	$50.
$15,000 to $20,000.	$100.
$20,000 to $25,000.	$150.
Over $25,000.	$200.[17]

Pressure to Contribute

Should one of the union's officers or employees fail to contribute to MNPL, he is subtly—and sometimes not so subtly—pressured to come across with his contribution. For example, one business representative received from his GVP a letter that said:

All Business Representative are called to contribute $25.00 to the MNPL each year.

I note that your contribution for 1967 has not been paid and I trust you will send your contribution to Brother G. W. Flinn, Machinists Building, 1300 Connecticut Avenue, Washington, D.C. 20036 by return mail so our Northeastern States staff will be 100 percent.

Kindly furnish me with a copy of your covering letter.[18]

Another GVP wrote a business representative:

A recent report from MNPL Headquarters reveals that you are the only Business Representative in the State of New York who has not as yet made a MNPL contribution for 1969.

You are requested to give this matter your immediate attention and to submit a report to me of your intentions in this regard with a copy to Don Ellinger.[19]

Especially illuminating is the correspondence in 1968 between GVP William Winpisinger and Frank Toccalini, assistant general chairman of District Lodge 89 in California. On June 19, 1968, Toccalini wrote Winpisinger:

135

This will acknowledge your letter dated June 6, 1968 advising that I have not as yet responded to the call for early expedited action by the General Chairman for MNPL Sponsoring Membership contributions in this "double trouble" year. . . .

This failure (to obtain additional MNPL contributions) within District 89 itself cannot and should not be charged to an alleged or implied lack of leadership on my part, but rather to rebellion and outright refusal on the part of the membership to financially support political programs, and their predisposition to reject recommendations and responsibility on issues and candidates in general. Local and National objectives in many instances seem to conflict and veer in different directions. . . .[20]

GVP Winpisinger, who frequently speaks for the union at significant public events, replied to Toccalini on July 26, 1968:

I have studied your letter with considerable intent and concern and am of the opinion that perhaps for reasons of your own, you fail to comprehend the true necessity of teamwork among our leaders in our Union—or irrespective of the facts known to you, you still insist upon a personal course of action rather than majority planning and action developed by the National Planning Committee of our MNPL and subsequently endorsed by the Executive Council members of our Union. . . .

It is not my intention to carry on a lengthy correspondence relative to this subject matter, because in my opinion you know what is right. I am going to rely on your knowledge to do what is right. . . .

It is not my intention to bargain for your support, as I expect this in the same manner as we expect cooperation from all our elected officers.

I am calling upon you again to contribute your share, which as you know is a $25.00 General Chairmen's Sponsoring Membership and an additional $25.00 in the Double Trouble year. Your compliance to this request is a decision that you must make. . . .[21]

Several more letters ensued between a reluctant Toccalini and an adamant Winpisinger, leading to Toccalini's letter of August 23, 1968, which reflects the tone of the most recent communication he had received from his GVP:

I am deeply disturbed over both the implications and expressions contained in the correspondence received to 'date from your office questioning my loyalty generally as a General Chairman and an I.A. of M. member in the political field.

It has always been my firm conviction that a man's political views are as sacred and as subject to respect as are those involving religion. Apparently you do not agree. Compulsory political contributions, moreover, are patently iniquitous and contrary to public policy. . . .[22]

IAM staff personnel have learned not only that they are expected personally to contribute to MNPL, but also that their job description requires them to raise funds for the MNPL from the general membership. Floyd Smith, in a memorandum of February 1970, used his position to emphasize this to the staff;

As the International President I am charged with the direction of the staff to carry out the policies adopted by our convention or the Executive Council. As members of the staff—our fighting force in the field—you are entitled to clear and specific instructions on our duties and obligations, and a definite channel of communication so we can keep each other informed on the progress we must make.

If we are to meet this challenge, each IAM staff member will:

1. Become a sponsoring member of MNPL and, if at all possible, at the "double trouble" rate. . . .

2. Check with every local lodge he services. . . to urge that they make the 30¢ per member contribution to the educational fund of the MNPL.

3. Make certain that every local lodge is participating in raising the voluntary funds from the membership on an organized basis, either using the MNPL receipt books, envelopes, or cooperating in a state or district financial project.

4. Activate political leagues in district or local lodges to begin the registration job in cooperation with COPE, where possible or alone if necessary.

5. Report current developments.

I am attaching . . . a monthly report form which you can supplement by letter. . . .

Some of you will get a more detailed assignment in particular areas from your General Vice President but the assignment covered by this letter applies to everyone. Because the security of our union rests on the success of our campaign—Showdown '70—I must emphasize that this assignment is firm. We will expect a report from each of you about the first of April.[24]

A few months later, as a follow-up to Smith's letter, one GVP wrote to employees in his territory:

The MNPL National Planning Committee has asked the membership, the full-time officers and representatives to *redouble* efforts this year. The International Field staff have all contributed $50.00 each and some have their other $50.00 in. This staff simply must be 100 percent and now.[24]

"The Big One"

With control of the White House at stake in 1972, MNPL began laying the groundwork early in the preceding year to fill the coffers of its General and Educational funds. The combined 1971–72 goal for the General Fund was $1.5 million, all of it earmarked for use in the national elections.

A high-pressure promotional campaign built around the theme "The Big One" was developed, and a carefully orchestrated schedule of publicity was begun in July 1971 through the *Machinist* and *Action.* The goal was to raise $5 each from 100,000 Machinists during the month of October of the same year. Local executive board and stewards meetings were held in September to prepare for the October campaign.

The financial secretary of every local lodge received in August a set of plastic cards, each bearing the inscribed name of a member, the lodge number, and the member's book number. A member was awarded his plastic card when he contributed $5 to MNPL.

MNPL director William Holayter described the disbursement procedure of the big fund-raising drive to an inquiring member:

You also ask how the money raised from the sale of "Big One" cards is being spent. So far, we have spent nothing from this fund. The National Planning Committee of the MNPL has directed that all money raised from the sale of the cards be used exclusively for the Presidential campaign. It is to be allocated according to the following formula: 1/3 of the amount raised is to be a direct contribution to the IAM's endorsed candidate, 1/3 of the money is to be made available to state headquarters for use in strategic states, 1/6 is to be used for the purchase and distribution of campaign literature, and 1/6 is to be used for travel and hotel expenses of Machinists delegates to the National Conventions.[25]

The Big One was not greeted with universal acclaim from all the membership. One local lodge official wrote MNPL:

This letter is in regard to your letter of June 15, 1972 on The Big One, The Battle for the Presidency. The members of our Lodge have voted not to contribute a $5.00 Contribution. We would appreciate your not sending us any cards or instruction.[26]

General Fund Expenditures

The national MNPL, when requested, returns 25 percent of the General Fund contributions it receives to the state council, district, local lodge, or local MNPL that raised it. The national MNPL uses the remaining 75 percent directly to support candidates for federal office. It is up to the local group that receives back the 25 percent to determine how this is to be spent. It usually has gone to candidates for federal offices. Until the Federal Election Campaign Act became effective in April 1972, the ultimate disbursement of the 25 percent was not reported by either the national or the local group. Even under the Federal Election Campaign Act of 1972, few local lodges or MNPLs report how their 25 percent is spent.

State laws in many states allow union dues money or soft money to be used to support candidates for state offices. For example, Don Ellinger, writing to a California union official, declared: "This is the belated acknowledgement of your request for support for the State Legislature in California. . . . Contributions to state legislators in California may be made from dues money and I am sure that the California organization will act promptly on your request."[27]

Only a few states allow corporate funds to be used to support candidates for state offices.

A not uncommon practice by MNPL is to swap General Fund money (or "hard" money) for Educational Fund money (or "soft" money), or vice versa. An example of the swapping of funds is found in this letter to the national league from the Illinois MNPL chairman:

I have enclosed a check in the amount of $4,200.00 which is to be placed in what we refer to as your "hard money" account. This is the money that we had raised on the raffle of the Buick in 1971.

We have forwarded a check in the amount of $800.00 to a Kick-Off Dinner for Congressman Roman Pucinski, who is a Candidate for U.S. Senator, running against Senator Percy. Taking the $4,200.00 and the $800.00, this makes a total of $5,000.00 we will be contributing, which is "hard money."

Last Thursday or Friday, I discussed this with Brother Ellinger and it was agreed that by us sending in this $5,000.00, he would in turn send us a like amount of Educational Fund money which we could use in supporting our State Candidates.[28]

Because of the MNPL procedure of trading off hard and soft money, some of the arrangements made between the national league and local groups become quite complicated. Take a letter Ellinger wrote to a business representative in Wisconsin in 1968:

The Executive Committee of the League has reviewed your letter of May 20 and made the following recommendations:

1. That we contribute $7,000 of educational money to the District 10 MNPL for use in the state races.

2. That the District 10 MNPL deliver to Senator Gaylord Nelson, the additional amounts needed to make up our $5,000 commitment.

3. That the District 10 MNPL contribute $1,000 to the Stalbaum for Congress Committee in the 1st District and $500 each to Kastenmeier and Race in the 2nd and 6th. . . .

The attached check for $7,000 is education money. It should be placed in your education fund.[29]

Educational Fund Uses

The MNPL Educational Fund, which derives its revenues from the 30¢-per-member assessment by district and local lodges and from the IAM general treasury, is—in theory—to be used only for nonpartisan political activity. This is because, in contrast to the General Fund, which derives its revenues from "hard" voluntary contributions, the Educational Fund's income is composed of "soft" tax-exempt dues money. Use of this tax-exempt revenue for partisan political purposes arguably could lead to the union's losing its tax exemption or, at the least, being taxed on that portion used for partisan politics.

Among the overt political uses, some of which are more "nonpartisan" than others, to which tax-exempt educational funds are put are:

• Paying for mailings to union members on voter registration, voting records, and union recommendations on candidates.

140

- Paying for lost time from work and the expenses of persons working for candidates.
- Paying for printing of voting records, materials dealing with the election issues, and election research.
- Paying for the cost of public opinion polls, some specifically for candidates.
- Paying for radio and television time if all candidates for the same office are invited to appear.
- Paying the honoraria of public officials—such as members of Congress—who speak before union meetings.

The MNPL Executive Committee normally makes the decisions on how both General Fund and Educational Fund monies are to be spent. These decisions are reached either at biweekly meetings of the Executive Committe or by casting votes on the subject posed in a memorandum sent to each committee member.

For example, Don Ellinger sent Executive Committee members this memorandum in 1968:

Frank Thompson of New Jersey is willing to address District 15's MNPL kickoff on April 1. They suggest that this would be an opportunity for him to get an honorarium which will help in his campaign. Thompson's district has been redistricted and he will have a tougher time this year than in previous years.

Recommended: That we offer $250 of educational money toward his honorarium if District 15 will put up the other $250.[30]

Upon receiving the approval of his Executive Committee for the Thompson invitation, Ellinger wrote the New Jersey congressman:

This is to confirm our understanding that you will address our District 15 Machinists members at 7:00 P.M. at the District 15 hall, 7 East 15th Street, New York, New York.

There will be an honorarium presented to you at that time in the amount of $500 which we hope will be useful in your campaign.[31]

The honorarium-contribution from tax-exempt educational funds to Congressman Thompson for use in his campaign was to ensure that Machinist influence would continue to be felt on a key committee in Congress. Thompson is chairman of the General Labor Subcommittee of the House Educational and Labor Committee, and is generally regarded by members

141

of Congress on both sides of the aisle as being in the hip pocket of the unions' overalls. He helps them and they help him.

Both the union and the MNPL never cease their efforts to raise tax-exempt money for the Educational Fund. An election is barely over before the machinery is cranked up once again to pressure the lodges to contribute. Many times the pitch for tax-exempt educational funds is tied to a distinctly partisan theme, as it is in this memorandum of December 1968 from the MNPL co-chairmen:

> We are proud of the participation of the International Association of Machinists and Aerospace Workers in the elections of 1968. We had greater unity, harder work, and more money and, although we lost the top spot, we did the best job in the history of the League.
>
> Because union members took the lead in the dark day after the Chicago Convention and stood firm in support of tested union principles, we held the loss in the House and Senate to a historic minimum and came within a hair's breadth of putting labor's friend, Hubert Humphrey, in the White House, . . .
>
> We have raised a record breaking sum in 1968. We have urged every lodge in the country in 1968 to make a contribution based on 30¢ per member to our educational fund. If you have not done so, it would greatly help if we could receive it before the Planning Committee meets on January 27. If you have any voluntary money, we can use it, too. . . .[32]

Use of Tax Exempt Treasury Funds

On occasions, the IAM taps its tax-exempt treasury funds to make a political contribution that even a Philadelphia lawyer would be hard pressed to defend. A typical case is the support provided for Senator Ralph Yarborough of Texas in the period preceding the 1970 primary fight, which saw him defeated by a less liberal Democrat, Lloyd Bentsen. Yarborough was chairman of the Senate Labor and Public Welfare Committee, which is dominated—as is its counterpart in the House—by a majority of members who owe their political survival to the support they receive from organized labor. It was especially important to IAM and the entire labor movement in 1970 that Senator Yarborough be reelected.

MNPL Director Ellinger started marshaling financial help for Yarborough two years before the election. In 1968 he reported to the international president:

Senator Ralph Yarborough called today regarding a money raising event which he wants to have to retire a $6,000 indebtedness which has been contracted for radio and TV reports to the people of Texas. Jerome Keating and E. C. Hallbeck have agreed to serve on the committee and the Senator would very much like permission to use your name. They will plan a reception during the week of May 20 depending on available sites. Since he is not now a candidate and this indebtedness is not part of his campaign, we can use treasury money for the purchase of tickets. Please let me know if you can serve.[33]

A year later Ellinger again attempted to help Yarborough with tax-exempt union treasury funds and was even less subtle as to how their use would benefit the Texas Democrat. Ellinger wrote a Texas AFL-CIO official about a proposed book on Yarborough that he termed "a high prestige item." Ellinger noted that brochures and order blanks had been sent

to each of the national unions urging their purchase of 2,000 copies at $1.98 each. 30,000 purchases will make available to the Senator 50,000 copies of the book, 500 of which will be hardback for big contributors, etc. The purpose of this effort is to make Ralph look so strong in the fall that he would have an aura of invincibility.

The book may be purchased with dues money and we believe major unions should particularly participate in the project out of treasury funds.[34]

It is not only the international union that helps federal candidates by using tax-exempt treasury funds. Subordinate IAM bodies do so too. For example, in 1970 Ellinger received this letter from two officials of District Lodge 12 in Maryland concerning Parren Mitchell's campaign for Congress, a campaign that was eventually successful on election day:

As I told you over the phone last Friday, October 30th, Parren Mitchell's campaign assistant, Dr. Favor, came to us with a last minute desperate plea for financial aid. A number of local Democratic leaders in Baltimore County and Baltimore City were cutting Mitchell from their official tickets because of his race, and Mitchell wanted to get in some last minute radio and TV plugs. Also he did not receive his full share of State Democratic money.

On the strength of your assurance that our plea would be taken up with the MNPL Executive Committee this

143

week, we borrowed $500 from District 12 operating funds and advanced it to Dr. Favor for delivery to Vernon Dobson, Treasurer of the Mitchell campaign.

We believe Mitchell has a fighting chance to win against the white Republican, Peter Parker, and win or lose the Machinists have gained a lot of prestige for our forthright position in this matter—espeically with the black community in Baltimore. Parren Mitchell told me (O'Brien) "I won't forget the Machinists—because you have delivered, while most of the others have given us only lip service."[35]

On-the-Job Political Training

Treasury funds pay the salaries and expenses of union staff personnel whose job descriptions include political activity. The three MNPL co-chairmen (who, remember, are also the chief executive officers of the union) made this duty crystal clear when in 1970 they chastised union staff members for failing to keep headquarters informed of their political activity: ". . . . Far too many have not filed a report and we would like to repeat that the political assignment is part of every staff member's job and we expect a report from each of you." [36]

GVP L. Ross Mathews followed through on the co-chairmen's edict a few months later when he wrote each staff member in his territory:

> You are requested, in instances where you personally service the Lodges. . . to contact the Lodge for the purpose of securing affirmative action to contribute 30¢ per member to the Educational Fund. . . .
>
> Because of the concern this office holds for the success of this fund-raising program, the assignment must be considered as possessing extremely high priority in your work assignments.[37]

Mathews must have been pleased with the response to his 1970 instructions because a year later he decided to put the double squeeze on his territorial staff personnel by soliciting their personal contributions to MNPL and directing them to promote the league among the membership. Mathews' letter began with military crispness:

> Greetings:
> . . . . This office solicits your personal contributions as a sponsoring member of MNPL as the first order of business in this endeavor. The League seeks contributions

144

from Business Representatives and Organizers in a *minimum* amount of $25.00 for 1971. Those in the higher salary scales are, of course, encouraged to contribute an additional $25.00.

A goal of $1,500,000 has been set for the two year period leading up to the national election in 1972. . . .

The educational fund is derived from a 30¢ per member contribution by action of each Local Lodge. Last year 69 percent of the Lodges in the Northeast voted to make contributions of this type. Our goal in 1971 is 100 percent participation by all Local Lodges. Each of you to whom this communication is directed is requested to attend a Lodge meeting in each locality you service for the purpose of securing this donation from the Lodge.[38]

Ellinger was to boast later that yet another GVP, William Winpisinger, "sent his staff throughout the country and reached every railroad lodge; many of them for the first time became contributors to the League." [39]

Conclusion

The IAM, a labor organization enjoying tax-exempt status under section 501(c) of the Internal Revenue Code, regularly engages in political activity. The tax-free dues money received by the union's treasury has underwritten this political activity, which has ranged from paying the salaries of staff personnel assigned to campaigns to using a variety of other union resources.

MNPL, a subordinate organization that is the union's overt political arm, also utilizes tax-free money to finance its operations. The MNPL Educational Fund, to which the treasuries of the Grand Lodge, local, and district lodges contribute tax-free monies, has paid expenses of MNPL staff personnel and of the union members working in campaigns, plus the tabs for a host of other partisan political activities.

Financial support to candidates for federal office is provided through the MNPL General Fund, which is made up of "voluntary" contributions from members and staff personnel. A sliding scale exists of what staff personnel are expected to contribute and subtle coercion is used to stimulate giving. Staff personnel are also assigned to collect the fund's contributions from the membership and, although the General Fund is used directly to support candidates, the salaries of those responsible for collecting the contributions are paid by the union's tax-exempt treasury.

145

The rank-and-file membership exercises little control over the MNPL, which is directly responsible to the IAM Executive Council. Furthermore, the power to grant the union's endorsement of a U.S. Presidential candidate rests not with the rank and file but with the Executive Council and the union's convention that meets every four years.

The MNPL Executive Committee and the National Planning Committee in Action

One indication of the integral relationship existing between the IAM, the parent organization, and the MNPL, its subordinate, is that the three chief executive officers of the union also serve as co-chairmen of MNPL: International President Floyd Smith, General Secretary-Treasurer Eugene Glover, and resident GVP William Winpisinger. The other present members of the MNPL Executive Committee are the committee's vice chairman, GLR George Kourpias, and four trustees: *Machinist* assistant editor Dean Ruth, GVP Paul Peterpaul, GLR Desford D. Smith, and GLR George Nelson, who is also the union's influential lobbyist on Capitol Hill.

Executive Committee members are elected every four years by MNPL sponsoring members residing in the Washington, D.C., area and any other members present at the time the meeting is held. The last election was in May 1972.

Direction of the league's activities rests with the Executive Committee. Virtually no decision affecting MNPL is made unless it is approved by the Executive Committee, which meets approximately every two weeks to discuss items on a proposed agenda that is circulated beforehand.

MNPL director William Holayter and assistant director Jerry Thompson carry out the day-by-day administration of the league's activities, which range from public relations and education to fund raising and organizing local leagues. Holayter and Thompson prepare the proposed agenda of the Executive Committee's meetings and usually formulate in advance a recommendation as to how each item should be disposed of. In most cases their recommendation is adopted by the committee, making the two MNPL staff men—although not officially members of the committee—perhaps the two persons exerting the most influence on the league's actions.

The *MNPL Executive Committee Report 1968*, submitted to the IAM's 27th convention that year in Chicago, expansively discusses the league's operations and achievements. Here are some significant excerpts:

FOUR YEARS OF POLITICAL COMBAT
This report covers the 1964 general election battle which was a great triumph, the 1966 Congressional election

which was a disaster, and the preparation for 1968, a "double trouble" year. . . .

During the 4 years we made contributions in hundreds of political races. Almost of all of them in the marginal category. Many of our state, district, and local MNPLs made additional contributions from the monies refunded to them under the 50 percent return formula. Each year we have raised more money and yet the demands upon us have grown. We are still far from achieving our goal of one hour's pay from each of our members. Our target should be 4 million dollars a year.

In this 4 year period, our relationship to the AFL-CIO Committee on Political Education has become much closer and a substantial portion of the IAM funds have gone to COPE. In return for this enlarged support, our influence in determining COPE policy has been enhanced.

The National Planning Committee, a unique IAM institution, has been expanded since 1964 and has played a greater role in determining and executing the policies of the League.

Each of the General Vice Presidents has designated a member of the Grand Lodge staff in his territory to serve as liaison with the Planning Committee and participate in the January meeting. In the 1968 "double trouble" year, additional staff members have been assigned full or part time to the basic job of money raising, registration, education, and getting out the vote.

The members of the Executive Council have exerted great leadership in securing sponsoring members at an increased figure both in percentage and in 1968 on a doubled basis. This leadership has also been reflected in the educational funds received from more lodges, and in 1968 at the doubled figure. . . .

In the campaign year of 1968, we have added *Action,* a biweekly report to all activists within the union. This report is intended to reach all officers and committeemen who are cooperating on the MNPL effort. . . .

Through the pages of *The Machinist* during the 4 years, most of our members have been reached and stimulated, both to contribute and to participate. Increased cooperation from the state, district and local levels has enabled Gordon Cole and his associates to present a picture of the political development more completely than any other labor publication. The series of objective factual statements regarding the Presidential candidates in 1968 has raised still further the reputation of *The Machinist* which reflects credit on our Political League.

In the last 4 years, members of the Executive Committee and the staff have attended close to 1,000 local, district and regional meetings, presenting the cause of MNPL and, more importantly, listening to the local leaders and members on the political developments in their area.

In 1966, the Machinists cooperated with the AFL-CIO COPE to develop a data processing system using our Univac III at headquarters. This program involved using mailing lists of all union members, locating them by ward and precinct, and determining whether they are registered and in what party. . . .

A special Machinists project using 3 x 5 cards grouped by zip code has been developed for all marginal districts where action meetings have been held. Special mailings targeted to specific districts or portions of the districts have been produced. Howard Dow and his associates are now working on a method to increase the political usefulness of our membership roster. . . .

PRIMARY VICTORIES HOLD OUT HOPE

In accordance with the National Planning Committee recommendation and with the support of state and district leagues, the National League worked hard this year in a number of primary elections where friends were in trouble. . . .

Our box score on primaries shows that we entered 35 primaries. We won 26 and lost 8, with 1 still to be determined.*

GRAND LODGE STAFF ASSISTS

Thirty-four Grand Lodge Representatives have been designated by their General Vice President to assume responsibility in the political field either full or part time. In every area where these men have worked funds have been improved, participation has grown, and registration has increased. Further efforts by all staff members will be needed for the few remaining primaries and the general election in November.[1]

Executive Committee Minutes

The Executive Committee at its meetings usually discusses 15 to 30 topics. Most of these are concerned with what amount of money is to be contributed to which candidate, but the minutes also disclose that a wide variety of political projects surface on one occasion or another.

---

* All 35 primaries, except one, were contests within the Democratic Party, the 1968 report reveals.—D.C.

Below are significant actions taken by the Executive Committee over a five-year span—1968 through 1972. These are summarized directly from the Executive Committee minutes and proposed agendas. When a particularly significant decision is reached, the discussion is reprinted verbatim. The date of the committee meeting is listed following each item. The projects considered were:

1968

- $1,000 for Democrat Charles Vanik for use in his campaign in Ohio's 22nd Congressional District against Congresswoman Frances Bolton. "He is asking for an immediate labor contribution of $12,000 to get him started. He hopes ultimate labor support in the range of $60,000.00." (2/16/68)
- $10,000 from the General Fund for the Committee for the Advancement of Urban Interests, a front organization used by Democrat John Gilligan in his U.S. Senate bid in Ohio. An additional $5,000 to COPE from the Educational Fund; $6,000 to Bardsley & Haslacher, Inc. from the Educational Fund to conduct a public opinion poll in Oregon in behalf of Robert Duncan, Democratic candidate for the U.S. Senate. And exchange of $600 in MNPL General Fund money for $600 in Texas MNPL Educational Fund money, so that the "hard" money can be contributed to the Democratic candidate for lieutenant governor because Texas law does not permit union dues money to be used. (3/13/68)
- "Request of support for a liberal Republican caucus under the leadership of the Amalgamated Clothing Workers have established a means of supporting some research staff work for the small Republican group headed by Brad Morse. The Amalgamated Clothing Workers have agreed to contribute $750 and UAW will match it." Action: Approved $250 each for Congressmen Brad Morse of Massachusetts, Frank Horton of New York, and Charles Whalen of Ohio. (4/5/68)
- 10 tickets at $50 each from the General Fund sponsored by the D.C. Hoosier Committee to help five incumbent Indiana Democratic members of Congress (5/13/68)
- $500 General Fund contribution to Tennessee congressmen Richard Fulton (D) and William Anderson (D) and payment in tax-exempt educational funds of roundtrip airline ticket for Anderson to speak to a Clarksville, Tenn., meeting. (5/13/68)
- Authorization of a $5,000 General Fund contribution to Senator Gaylord Nelson of Wisconsin, of which $2,250

150

had already been donated to the Democratic senator. (5/13/68)

• General Fund contributions of $1,000 to Democratic congressional candidate Stalbaum in Wisconsin's 1st Congressional District, $500 to Congressman Kastenmeier in the state's 2nd Congressional District. (5/23/68)

• $3,500 to the reelection campaign of Senator Henry Jackson (D) of Washington State. (6/20/68)

• $2,000 from the General Fund for the Democratic Study Group, contingent on other pledges at the next COPE Operating Committee meeting. (6/20/68)

• $500 additional contribution to D.C. Hoosier Committee for use by Indiana Democratic Congressmen Brademas, Roush, and Hamilton. (7/1/68)

• $500 in General Fund money to Congressman Fernand St. Germain (D) of Rhode Island. (7/16/68)

• $500 for Congressman William Anderson (D) of Tennessee and $250 each for Ray Blanton's (D) campaign in the 7th Congressional District and Joe Evins' (D) campaign in the 4th Congressional District. (7/16/68)

• Purchase with Educational Fund money of 500 copies at $2 each of a book titled *Liberal Leader in the House,* whose subject is Congressman Frank Thompson (D) of New Jersey. "His district has been changed and he will need financial help. By purchasing and distributing these books, we can be very helpful to him." (7/23/68)

• "Request from [COPE area director] Sherman Miles for a $500 contribution toward a registration and get-out-the-vote campaign in support of Johnny Walker." Action: $250 in Educational Fund money. (8/16/68)

• "Request from Kevin Phillips for a testimonial dinner for Republican U.S. Representative Paul Fino of New York. The request has been referred to District 15 for comment." Action: If District 15 concurs, purchase two tickets at $25. (8/16/68)

• $1,000 to California Democratic senatorial candidate Alan Cranston and $250 each to California Democratic Congressmen Don Edwards, Glenn Anderson, Jim Corman, George Brown, Jr., Richard Hanna and Jack Tunney. $250 each to Democratic congressional candidates Grayson Taketa and Al Ballard. (8/16/68)

• $450 for Democrat Roy Elson for his Senate race against Barry Goldwater in Arizona. (8/16/68)

• Additional $500 for Roy Elson (D) in Arizona. (9/15/68)

• $2,000 from tax-exempt Educational Fund to purchase 8,000 copies of a broadside attacking George Wallace, published by the Southern Committee on Political Ethics (SCOPE). (9/5/68)

• $1,000 for senatorial candidate Thomas Eagleton (D) in Missouri and $500 for congressional candidate Jim Symington in Missouri. (9/5/68)

• $750 contribution to Senator Abraham Ribicoff (D) of Connecticut. (9/18/68)

• $250 contribution to Senator Daniel Inouye of Hawaii. (9/18/68)

• "Letter from Senators Magnuson and Jackson inviting us to a reception for Lloyd Meeds, September 24. We have given Meeds $500 in the general election, but since he is our special charge and on the House Educational and Labor Committee, we should have a good turnout for him." Action: 10 tickets at $25 for Congressman Lloyd Meeds (D) of Washington State. (9/18/68)

• 100,000 copies of "Labor Record of George Wallace" at 7¢ each. (9/18/68)

• $2,200, bringing the total contribution to $7,500, to Democrat John Gilligan, candidate for U.S. Senate in Ohio, $300 to Ohio congressman Michael Feighan (D), and $250 to congressional candidate Pete McCloskey in California. (10/8/68)

• "Request from Phil Hoff, Governor of Vermont, for support of Lt. Governor John Daley. This request is concurred in by Carroll Comstock. This can be educational money." Action: $250 tax-exempt contribution. (10/21/68)

• "Request for dues money for get out the vote operation in support of Humphrey, McNichols and McVicker" in Colorado. Action: $500 tax-exempt contribution to Metropolitan Committee on Voter Education and Registration in Colorado. (10/29/68)

• "As part of the campaign in Florida, a registration and get out the vote operation using computer techniques was established. Several organizations have worked together on this project which can be paid for with dues money. The total cost was $9,000. We have been asked for $1,000." Action: $500 tax-exempt. (10/29/68)

1969

• Place full-time worker at $200 per week for six weeks in Wisconsin's 7th Congressional District, where a special election will be held to fill the seat vacated by Melvin Laird. National COPE will contribute 50 percent of the cost. (2/5/69)

- $3,600 to be spent on airline tickets for a number of U.S. Senators to fly home to their states in the West. (2/5/69)
- "Invitation to attend the Democratic Congressional Dinner on May 12 at $500 a ticket. The new leadership in both House and Senate Committee deserves support. We have a letter from Congressman Bizz Johnson asking that we help him meet his quota. Other Congressmen like Brock Adams have called us. Vice Chairman of the House Committee Ed Edmondson tells me we can earmark any funds we give, but do not have anything in writing on this.

"Recommend: That we establish a list of priority Senators and priority Congressmen. . . . and that we approach them in priority order. Tell them we have $500 to contribute to their campaign, and we can give it to them now to buy a dinner ticket for a member of our Executive Committee or we can contribute it later through our state organizations where it will have more political effect. As soon as Senators and Congressmen say they want it now, we can buy a table with credit to them. . . ." Action: $2,500 approved. (3/18/69)
- "Birch Bayh is seeking funds with which to pay some bills and is urging labor organizations to buy copies of his book at $10 with educational funds." Action: $300 tax-exempt contribution if Indiana State Council of Machinists contributes an equal amount, so that 60 books can be purchased. (3/18/69 and 3/26/69)
- "The Texas MNPL is preparing to get Senator Yarborough before all IAM in the state to help him get home and campaign. I told them I would recommend to you that we split the cost of transportation with them. They are also going to arrange for some honorariums for which they will pick up the tab." Action: $650 to $800 contribution for approximately 10 trips. (3/18/69)
- $1,000 in tax-exempt educational funds for use by Senator Quentin Burdick (D) of North Dakota to program his mailing list on a computer. (5/9/69)
- "Invitation from Averell Harriman and Esther Peterson to honor Senator Frank Moss at the Golden Spike Centennial on May 25. Since Moss is not yet an announced candidate, we can use educational money for this event and later consider this as part of our overall contribution." Action: $1,000 in tax-exempt educational funds authorized. (5/19/69)
- $500 in tax-exempt educational funds to help Congressman Richard Fulton (D) of Tennessee publish his newsletter. (5/29/69)
- $500 contribution in tax-exempt educational funds to Southern Committee on Political Ethics. (6/13/69)
- "Request from Frank Emery and Tom Cheney for $1,000

153

for Mike Harrington in September 30 special election in the 6th District of Massachusetts (Lynn). COPE has endorsed him, Barkan's sending $5,000 and asks each International Union for manpower and contributions." Action: $500 contribution. Request GVP to assign GLR Walsh full-time to the campaign. Request all GLRs and BRs in New England to work in district on weekends of September 20–21 and September 27–28. $250 approved in tax-exempt educational funds to get out the vote. A mailing to all IAM members in the district from MNPL is authorized. (9/8/69)

• Payment of $618.67 in tax-exempt educational funds authorized towards printing bill of newsletter of Congressman Lloyd Meeds (D). (10/6/69)

• "Poetic request from Frank Whiston for support for Senator Montoya and a request of four $250 checks totalling $1,000 to be presented by each New Mexico lodge to the Senator." Action: $1,000 approved. (11/10/69)

• $1,000 in tax-exempt educational money authorized, to be added to $1,700 already contributed toward printing and mailing of publication promoting New Jersey gubernatorial candidate Robert Meyner (D). (11/10/69)

• "Request from James G. Morton for a contribution for Congressman Dick Hanna of California for a cocktail party in Georgetown. Hanna is one of the Congressmen that the IAM has been asked to give special support to." Action: $500 contribution. (11/10/69)

• "Discussion of invitation to Hugh Scott reception, Nov. 18, 1969. $100 tickets. Decided not to participate." (11/17/69)

• "Request from Al Barkan for the IAM to participate in a special pre-election activity made available to certain Senators. The Steelworkers have put $50,000 into this effort and a number of other unions, Railway Clerks, CWA, and IBEW have also participated. Education money may be used for these polls and film development through Maurer, Fleisher and Zon." Action: $16,000 approved for this project: $2,000 each for Democratic Senators Hartke, McGee, Moss, Yarborough, Burdick, Williams, Cannon, and Hart. $5,000 made available immediately in tax-exempt education funds. (11/17/69)

• "Request from the Democratic Study Group for a dinner, Thursday, December 4. President Smith is a sponsor of this event and the money is to be used for support of the legislative research activities." Action: $1,000 in tax-exempt educational funds. (11/24/69)

• $1,000 in general funds and $500 in tax-exempt educational funds for travel approved to aid Senator Albert Gore (D) of Tennessee in his reelection campaign. (12/9/69)

1970

• "Republican Senate-House Majority Dinner. March 11, 1970. Tickets $1,000.00 each." Action: Motion tabled. (1/5/70)

• "Request from Al Barkan and Senator Kennedy for support of last Sunday's TV show answering Nixon's State of the Union Message. Total cost is $59,000. Labor is requested to contribute $20,000. Recommend: $1,000 educational funds." Action: Decision on this recommendation unknown. (2/12/70)

• Fred Purcell has assigned H. A. McClendon to the Albert Gore campaign. McClendon asks for $2,000 educational money to help set up a registration organization among Machinists including stewards meetings with refreshments." Action: $2,000 tax-exempt contribution approved for the project. (2/12/70 and 3/3/70)

• $2,500 in general funds to aid Senator Ralph Yarborough (D). *"The Machinist* featuring Sen. Yarborough this issue. Don [Ellinger] authorized to buy 50,000 reprints." (3/10/70)

• "Report of COPE meeting with Senator Yarborough and request for additional funds. Total contributions to Senator Yarborough in 1969–1970 are $3,750. Support for registration program and other activities in Texas—$4,179. Purchase of Yarborough books—$3,900. Airline tickets—$705.60, for a total expenditure of $12,534.60. Yarborough urges maximum contribution in the primary." Action: Additional $2,500 in general funds approved. (3/25/70

• Purchase of five tickets at $20 each to 23rd Annual Convention of Americans for Democratic Action. (4/21/70)

• $5,000 in tax-exempt educational funds for Group Research, Inc. (4/21/70)

• "Consideration of additional contribution to Senator Montoya so President Smith can bring a contribution with him when he meets him next week." Action $1,000 approved. (4/29/70)

• "Report on Senator Symington's race in Missouri. Recommend: That we consult the Missouri leadership and make an immediate $1,000 contribution to the Symington campaign effort and that we organize a meeting with Al Barkan and the Senator to discuss the race." Action: Proposal approved. (4/29/70)

• "Request by National COPE for the full time services of John Jefferies in the Baltimore political campaign. Jefferies

155

is the Negro leader in our union and has been very helpful there." Action: If District 12 and the Maryland State Council of Machinists will go half, MNPL will authorize up to $1,000. (5/18/70)

• "Howard Metzenbaum met with Fred Purcell, Matt De-More and Bill Holayter to discuss his coming campaign. He suggested an appropriate figure for the Machinists of $100,000 toward his 1¾ million dollar budget. We have allocated $10,000 for this campaign." Action: $5,000 contribution now and the goal of another $5,000 before the end of the summer. (5/28/70)

• $1,000 to the Young Democrats for a voter-registration project. (6/10/70)

• "Request from GLR H. A. McClendon for $4,000 for Senator Albert Gore to be written in 4 $1,000 checks to be presented to the Senator at various meetings in the state." Action: $4,000 in general funds approved. (6/10/70)

• "Request from Congressman John Tunney, candidate for the Senate in California, for early support. We have budgeted $10,000 for him." Action: $5,000 contribution now and $5,000 later. (6/10/70)

• "Request from Phil Zannella for a very substantial contribution to Howard Metzenbaum for the U.S. Senate. The Ohio members believe that we contributed $40,000 to the Gilligan campaign in 1968. The total amount spent from the general fund in that campaign for Gilligan was $15,181.78. An additional amount of education funds was used in connection with the campaign amounting to $15,500. We have projected $10,000 for the campaign and have contributed $5,000." Action: $5,000 contributed now and another $10,000 later if funds are available. (6/17/70)

• "Senator Edward Kennedy requested assistance in his campaign for reelection in Massachusetts at a meeting with members of the COPE Operating Committee. We have projected $1,000." Action: $1,000 contribution approved. (6/17/70)

• "Bill from Merkle Press for $365 for Hubert Humphrey. We had approved $250." Action: $365 approved. (7/6/7)

• "Gordon Cole played some tapes on Registration to Vote used in N.J. for Senator Williams. Proposed to be used in California by mailing to each of 384 Radio Stations and try to obtain as wide use as possible at cost of $500.00." Action: Project approved if International President Smith concurs. (7/6/70)

• "We have received a request to assist in untilizing the services of Rudy Gonzales in the campaign of Congressman Hanna, 34th District, California. Gonzales would work with the MAPA, an Association of Mexican-Americans for a nine-week period of voters registration with the California State Council paying one-third, District 720 one-third and MNPL one-third." Action: Approved if the California State Conference of Machinists and District 720 will also participate. 7/6/70

• "Request from Senator Inouye of Hawaii for attendance at a special fund raiser for Senator Albert Gore on Wednesday, August 12 at the home of Ted Kennedy at $500 a couple. We have received a phone call from H. A. McClendon urging that we make a ticket available to Tom O'Neil, Gore's campaign manager in the 3rd District. We have contributed $5,000 thus far to Gore's campaign." Action: Two tickets to be purchased and made available to O'Neil. (8/4/70)

• "Authorize preparation of voting record folders for Tunney of California, Montoya of New Mexico and Moss of Utah, and a contest of records between Lujan and Chavez in the 1st District of New Mexico." Action: Initial cost of $2,000 approved. (8/4/70)

• "The Montana leaders believe Mike Mansfield is in more trouble than he thinks and recommend we put out a special folder for him for distribution in the state." Action: Up to $1,000 authorized for printing of publications on Senator Mansfield (D) and Congressmen Olsen (D) and Melcher (D). (8 18/70)

• "Request from Senator Daniel Inouye for support for Senator Frank Moss of Utah. We have projected $5,000 for this race and have sent in $1,500 hard money." Action: $1,000 to be sent through the Utah State Council of Machinists, (8/18/70)

• "Request from GLR McClendon to send additional $4,000 for Sen. Gore." Action: Request approved. (8/18/70)

• ". . . The New Democratic Coalition has put 50 people in the summer campaigns including Gore, Duffy, Tunney and Hartke. Birch Bayh and Harold Hughes both recommend some support. The Steelworkers have made some contribution. COPE has not. The UAW has been a substantial contributor." Action: $500 in general funds approved. (8/31/70)

• "Indiana—Senate. We have projected a total of $10,000 for Senator Hartke. We have spent $8,300." Action: $1,700 be sent immediately. (9/14/70)

• "Minnesota—Senate. We have projected a total of $7,500 for the Humphrey campaign. We have sent $4,100. Dale Pommerville has written us asking for $2,000." Action: $1,000 authorized. (9/14/70)

• "Missouri—Senate. We have projected $5,000 for Symington. I recommend we increase that projection to $7,500.

We have sent $1,250 so far." Action: $3,750 to be sent immediately. (9/14/70)

- "Utah—Senate. We have projected $5,000 for Moss. We have sent $2,500." Action: $2,500 to be sent. (9/14/70)
- Washington State: Approval of $800 ($1,200 previously sent) for Congressman Lloyd Meeds (D), $500 ($500 previously sent) for Congressman Brock Adams (D), and $150 ($350 previously sent) for Congressman Thomas Foley. (9/14/70)
- "Request from Averell Harriman and Ramsey Clark for a contribution to the Democratic Study Group. Two years ago we put $2,000 into this fund to strengthen the hand of that liberal group." Action: $500 approved. (9/21/70)
- "Utah—Request from the Utah State Council to mail the Republican Recession Record to all members in Utah. They will pay the cost of the material and we will pay the postage." Action: $100 in tax-exempt educational funds approved to pay postage. (9/28/70)
- "Report on a luncheon meeting with Senator Ralph Yarborough regarding the establishment of a Committee on Public Information to wind up some non-political expenditures. We have contributed a total of $19,633 to his campaign." Action: $500 in general funds approved. (12/10/70)

1971

- "Request from the Democratic National Committee for $250 for a final IAM contribution on the cost of the campaign caucuses. We had previously contributed $500." Action: $250 approved. (1/11/71)
- "Request from Senator Moss' campaign committee to help on his deficit. This was disapproved on January 22 and there have been subsequent conversations with President Smith." Action: $500 approved. (2/10/71)
- "Request from Gene Therout for the Machinists to pick up the bill for a luncheon with the Democratic Party officials of California. This luncheon was held at our suggestion, but we had not agreed to the financial cost." Action: Payment of bill approved. (2/10/71)
- "Recommendation from President Smith regarding participation in the Democratic fund raising dinner." Action: Three tickets purchased at $500 each. (3/30/71)
- "The table which the Machinists purchased for the Democratic Campaign Dinner amounts to $5,000. Dick Maguire wants to arrange a meeting between President Smith and the Senate and House leadership for the presentation of the

money, the understanding at which we arrived with Dick."
Action: $5,000 authorized. (7/7/71)

• Approved support for Senator Thomas McIntyre (D) of
New Hampshire, of $1,000 in general funds, $1,000 for newsletters and transportation, and a total of $5,000 expected ex-
penditure for his reelection campaign. (7/27/71)

• "Request from Senator Muskie's campaign staff for use of
our sorting equipment on the basis that they will supply the
operator and will be willing to work after 4:30 p.m." Action:
Approved if General Secretary-Treasurer Glover concurs and
subject to same opportunity being available "to other candidates we approve." (9/17/71)

• "Concerned Seniors For a Better Government, headed by
Matt DeMore, has reopened for the 1972 campaign. COPE
has made $5,000 available." Action: $500 approved.
(10/26/71)

1972

• "Request from Brock Adams of Seattle for support of a
dinner meeting in Seattle, Washington, in February, which he
says will be his only fund raiser of the year. Since we are particularly indebted to Brock Adams, Recommend: $1,000 con-
tribution through GVP Meagher." Action: $1,000 approved.
(1/3/72)

• Florida "Anti-Wallace Project—We are participating in
a special anti-Wallace project which has an overall budget of
$10,000. Recommend: We authorize $1,000 and send $500
immediately to Joe Derby, President of the Florida State
Council for payment of initial expenses." Action: Decision
on this recommendation unknown. (2/2/72)

• "The 1972 budget of Frontlash was approved by the
COPE Committee on Frontlash. The goal is $71,000 from
COPE and from national labor organizations. The Steelworkers are contributing $1,000 per month. Recommend: We agree
to contribute $500 a month beginning January through Octo-
ber, for a total of $5,000 toward the $71,000 budget." Action:
Recommendation approved. (2/2/72)

• "Invitation to a reception for Senator Edward Brooke of
Massachusetts, Wednesday, March 22 at the Federal City
Club. Tickets are $50 each. We have projected $1,000 for
Senator Brooke. His 1971 voting record is 5 right, 4 wrong,
2 absent." Action: Invitation rejected. (3/8/72).

• "Invitation from the Reelect Senator Pell Committee—
D.C. for a reception honoring the Senator on Wednesday,
March 15 at the Federal City Club. Tickets are $100 each.
We have projected $5,000 for his race and have already sent

in $1,000. Pell's record in 1971 is 9 right and 1 wrong." Action: $100 approved for one ticket. (3/8/72)

• "The Harris County Central Labor Council has requested assistance from the Machinists for a voter registration drive. They are asking for a black Machinist to be put in the black community to register voters. BR Chuck Bertani would pick the person for the assignment and he has agreed to pay for half of the project from Local Lodge 15 funds. . . ." Action: $300 approved for the project. (3/8/72)

• "There will be a special election in the 27th District of Pennsylvania on April 25. The Democratic candidate is Doug Walgren, who was the guest at a luncheon hosted by the Steelworkers on March 20 here in Washington. If Walgren wins he will be the incumbent Congressman running against Congressman Heinz in November. . . ." Action: $250 contribution approved for Walgren. (3/23/72)

• Purchase of one print of COPE film *Nixon's Broken Promises* for $60. (3/23/72)

• "Request from Lanny Rogers for help in a voter registration drive in the working class precincts of Dallas County. This encompasses the area in which State Senator Mike McKool will be running. We originally were to have responsibility for this congressional district in the marginal district program. However, GLR Bill Wolfe was assigned to another project and we had to go back on our commitment. Now there was a CWA person assigned and they want to conduct a registration drive using college students. The Texas State Council of Machinists, Dallas AFL-CIO, and District 146 are all participating in this program. . . ." Action: $300 approved. (3/23/72)

• "Recommendation for $5,000 to support Rep. Madden in first Congressional District of Indiana, in the primary." Action: $5,000 approved. (4/3/72)

• "Arkansas—Maurer, Fleischer and Zon are doing public relations work for Congressman David Pryor. Part of the project is a political flier to be inserted in *The Machinist* for our Arkansas members. The cost is $360, and we can use dues money for this." Action: Decision on this recommendation unknown.

• "California—GLR Harold Shean has asked that we purchase two tickets for General Vice President Simpson's use to the Democratic State Central Committee's Congressional Ball to honor California Democratic Members of Congress. This money is used to help reelect Democratic incumbents in California. Tickets are $125 each. Recommend: We purchase two tickets and send them to GVP Simpson." Action: Decision on this recommendation unknown. (4/19/72)

- "Hal Shean has also requested 'Nixon's Had ITT' bumper strips. He would like to flood the San Diego and Los Angeles areas with these. They are $60 per thousand. Recommend: We purchase 2,000 and have Shean distribute them." Action: Final decision on this recommendation unknown. (4/19/72)

- "In the Indiana and West Virginia Democratic primaries there are only two candidates—Hubert Humphrey and George Wallace. The Wallace Subcommittee of the COPE Operating Committee recommended that we set up a committee in these two states called 'The Committee for a True Democratic Vote' and use the Wallace film that was produced for COPE on television so that it will have broader coverage than just union membership. The TV budget has been worked at $7,120 for West Virginia and $10,717 for Indiana. Recommend: We contribute $1,000 total to the budget for these two states." Action: Recommendation approved. (4/19/72)

- California—"District Lodge 120 is out in front in the Frontlash program in Riverside and San Bernardino Counties. Machinist is heading up the program. They are requesting assistance to pay his salary. Local Lodge 964 is donating $50 a month. CWA has so far put in $300 and the Steelworkers are also going to put in some money, but no definite amount has been committed. A Frontlash program in this area could help turn the tide to the Democratic nominee for President in 1972. Recommend: We contribute $500 to this program." Action: Recommendation approved. (5/2/72)

- "Connecticut—the 6th Congressional District is our responsibility in the Marginal District Program where Ella Grasso is up for reelection. In 1970, we had two people working in Connecticut in the 2nd and one in the 6th. This year we have no one in the 2nd District. We have been requested by the Connecticut State Council of Machinists to pay ½ of the salary and expenses of a man in the 6th District. According to my figures the total would amount to approximately $6,700 if he were to start full time on May 9 and continue through November 7. Our share would be $3,350. Recommend: We authorize $2,500 for this project now with the understanding that the man will work on a part time basis in the beginning." Action: Decision on this recommendation unknown. (5/2/72)

1972 General Fund Contributions to Democratic Party and Liberal Groups

On April 8, 1972, the Federal Election Campaign Act became effective. As required under the law, MNPL filed periodic reports with the comptroller general of the United States listing its General Fund contributions to political organizations and candidates. Here is a compilation from those periodic reports listing MNPL contributions in 1972 to political organizations:

1972	Organization	Amount Contributed
4/11	Frontlash (N.Y.)	$1,500
4/11	Democratic National Committee	144
4/19	California Democratic State Central Committee	260
4/19	Committee for a True Democratic Vote	1,000
4/19	Young Democratic Clubs of America	100
5/9	Hubert Humphrey Dinner Committee (Calif.)	375
5/9	Independent Voter Committee for Political Education	500
5/24	National COPE	13,383.99
5/25	Frontlash (Calif.)	500
6/1	Democratic National Committee	144
7/13	Frontlash (N.Y.)	500
8/1	Democratic National Committee	2,500
8/4	Democratic National Committee	2,500
8/8	Democratic National Committee	250
8/14	National Labor Committee for McGovern-Shriver	25,000
8/16	Frontlash (N.Y.)	500
8/16	Northern California Labor Committee for McGovern	5,000
8/30	McGovern-for-President Committee	100,000*
9/20	McGovern-for-President Committee	2,500
9/20	Frontlash	500
9/22	McGovern Dinner Committee (Calif.)	1,000
9/25	Southern California Labor Committee for McGovern-Shriver	1,000
9/25	Tennessee Labor Committee for McGovern-Shriver	1,000
9/25	Wisconsin Labor Committee for McGovern-Shriver	5,000
9/25	Indiana Labor Committee for McGovern-Shriver	1,000
9/25	Democratic Study Group	1,000
9/28	Arkansas Labor Committee for McGovern-Shriver	500

* A subsequent MNPL report, on October 10, declared: "This amount forgives loan in September 10 report and is not a repayment."

162

1972	Organization	Amount Contributed
9/28	Kentucky Labor Committee for McGovern-Shriver	1,000
9/28	Massachusetts Labor Committee for McGovern-Shriver	2,000
9/28	McGovern-for-President Committee	1,000
9/28	Ohio Labor Committee for McGovern-Shriver	1,000
9/29	National Labor Committee for McGovern-Shriver	5,000
10/10	Colorado Labor Committee for McGovern-Shriver	1,000
10/10	Connecticut Labor Committee for McGovern-Shriver	1,000
10/10	Utah Labor Committee for McGovern-Shriver	750
10/10	New Jersey Labor Committee for McGovern-Shriver	1,000
10/10	McGovern Dinner Committee (Calif.)	500
10/12	Citizens for McGovern-Shriver (Md.)	100
10/12	Michigan Labor Committee for McGovern-Shriver	1,000
10/12	Nebraska Labor Committee for McGovern-Shriver	500
10/17	Frontlash (N.Y.)	500
10/26	Connecticut Labor Committee for McGovern-Shriver	500
10/26	Illinois Labor Committee for McGovern-Shriver	5,000
10/26	New Jersey Labor Committee for McGovern-Shriver	500
10/27	Connecticut Labor Committee for McGovern-Shriver	1,000
11/1	Massachusetts Labor Committee for McGovern-Shriver	2,000
11/1	Michigan Labor Committee for McGovern-Shriver	2,000
11/1	Missouri Labor Committee for McGovern-Shriver	2,000
11/1	New Jersey Labor Committee for McGovern-Shriver	2,000
11/1	Ohio Labor Committee for McGovern-Shriver	2,000
11/1	Pennsylvania Labor Committee for McGovern-Shriver	4,000

1972	Organization	Amount Contributed
11/1	California Labor Committee for McGovern-Shriver	2,100
11/1	Wisconsin Labor Committee for McGovern-Shriver	3,400
11/1	Texas Labor Committee for McGovern-Shriver	2,000
11/2	California Labor Committee for McGovern-Shriver	2,100
11/2	Northern California Labor Committee McGovern-Shriver	2,000
11/27	Printing of McGovern Pamphlet	900

In summary, the MNPL reports filed with the comptroller general of the United States indicate that in 1972 the MNPL Executive Committee authorized $190,000 to be contributed to the McGovern-for-President Committee and affiliated organizations. No General Fund money was contributed to the Committee for the Reelection of President Nixon or to the Republican National Committee or to any organization affiliated with these two groups.

1972 Educational Fund Political Expenditures

MNPL's Educational Fund, which is made up of tax-exempt compulsory union dues revenue and treasury money, was not immune in 1972 to partisan politics. MNPL records show a $2,000 payment on June 29, 1972, and a $1,000 payment on July 29, 1972, to the Washington, D.C., political public relations firm of Maurer, Fleisher and Zon. The public relations firm pooled this $3,000 with funding from other labor unions to develop public relations programs for a select group of liberal Democratic candidates for the U.S. Senate. On May 24, 1972, a $339.88 payment was made to Phoenix Films for a film of Senator Gale McGee (D) of Wyoming. On August 2, 1972, a $501.94 payment was made to Merkle Press for a flier promoting Congressman David Pryor (D) of Arkansas, who was challenging Senator John McClellan in that state's Democratic senatorial primary. On March 24, 1972, $100 was contributed to Friends of Farenthold for governor of Texas and on April 11, 1972, $200 was given to Wilbur Hobby for governor of North Carolina. Finally, on September 20, 1972, $570.82 was paid to the Sheraton-Palace Hotel in San Francisco to cover a bill for "Lawyers for McGovern." [2]

In analyzing the foregoing 1972 contributions to political

candidates and political organizations, three points should be kept in mind. The first is that 25 percent of the General Fund contributions received by national MNPL is returned to the state, district, and local lodge organizations that raised the money. This 25 percent usually finds its way into the coffers of candidates (mostly Democratic) for federal office also. The second point is that these figures reflect only the financial contributions of IAM-MNPL and do not include the cost of assigned manpower. Finally, there are scores of political committees set up by other labor unions and by the AFL-CIO, and these also contributed funds in 1972. MNPL's contributions are only a small part of the total political spending by labor.

MNPL National Planning Committee

When asked how rank-and-file Machinists influence IAM political policies, union officials and MNPL spokesmen cite the singular functions performed by the National Planning Committee (NPC). This committee acts "in an advisory capacity to the (MNPL) Executive Committee and Director." [3] The National Planning Committee of the MNPL "is unique in its role among trade unions and is composed of the principal leaders of the major districts in the country who assemble in the early part of each year to hammer out policies which are then jointly approved by the IAM Executive Council," MNPL director Don Ellinger once explained. [4]

Members of the National Planning Committee are nominated by their regional GVPs and their nominations are approved by the Executive Committee. Their actual appointment is made by the international president. The result of this selection procedure is that the NPC is composed of local leaders who support the political line laid down by the top IAM leadership. When he served as a GVP from 1961 to 1969 before his election as international president, Floyd Smith made 63 nominations to the NPC and he cannot recall a single instance when one of his nominations was rejected. [5]

Upon his ascendancy to the top post in 1969, Smith—along with his two MNPL co-chairmen—made clear the type of person he expected to be nominated: "While the nominations are completely within the discretion of the General Vice President, we urge that those nominated be the active heads of their respective segments of our union and accept the appointment with the knowledge that they will have special responsibility in carrying out the program they will help design." [6]

Each year, usually in January or February, 70 to 80 members of the NPC assemble in Washington, D.C., to hear political exhortations and to adopt a program of MNPL activities for that year. The IAM Executive Council is in session at the same time and as the year's proposed MNPL program is adopted by the NPC, it is forwarded immediately to the Executive Council for its approval. Occasionally the Executive Council adjourns its own meeting to join the NPC to listen to a prominent political speaker.

Once appointed to the NPC, each member is expected to consider the committee's responsibilities as being part of his own job description. With regard to the NPC annual meeting, "Of course, it goes without saying that the assignment to attend the session comes from your General Vice President, not from us," Ellinger once wrote a group of GLRs, who each held the position of being liaison to the MNPL.[7] Although the NPC meeting deals exclusively with politics, the national league does not pay the expenses of the members who attend. "These expenses should be borne by local, district, or state organizations," Floyd Smith has decreed.[8] Thus, tax-exempt compulsory dues money is used again for a political purpose by the union.

The speakers invited to address the NPC annual meeting are expected to expound a partisan theme. Writing Frank Hoffman of the Democratic National Committee to invite him to address the 1968 NPC, Ellinger implored: "We hope that you will be able to describe the principal Senate contests and your recommendations for the role of the Machinists in each of these races." [9] In a similar letter to Congressman Brock Adams (D) of Washington, Ellinger asked the lawmaker that when addressing the NPC he "discuss the marginal Congressional races and your recommendations on the Machinists role in these contests." [10]

In early 1972 Ellinger was asked whether MNPL would invite the chairman of the Republican National Committee, then Senator Robert Dole of Kansas, to address NPC. Ellinger answered, "He has a hundred percent bad labor record, and we wouldn't invite him any place." [11]

Since 1972 was a national election year, it is worthwhile to take a look at the program of the 1972 NPC to see just which speakers were invited to address the "nonpartisan" organization. The NPC meeting was held January 23–28 and here is a summary of its agenda:

- "The Campaign of 1972"—Senator Henry Jackson (D) Washington
- "The Problems of Modern State Government"—Governor John Gilligan (D) of Ohio
- "Improving the Democratic Process"—Senator Gale McGee (D) of Wyoming

- "The Democratic National Convention of 1972"—Lawrence O'Brien, Chairman, Democratic National Committee
- "The Legal Tax Swindle"—Congressman Charles Vanik (D) of Ohio
- "A Liberal Republican Outlook"—Senator Clifford Case (R) of New Jersey
- "Public Relations Aspects of a Campaign"—Gordon Cole, Editor, *Machinist*
- "The Battle for the Senate and House, 1972"—Frank Hoffman, Executive Director, Democratic Senate Campaign Committee; Congressman Ed Edmondson (D) of Oklahoma, Chairman, Democratic House Campaign Committee
- "The Campaign of 1972"—Senator George McGovern (D) of South Dakota
- "New Rules for Campaign Contributions"—Russ Hemingway, Committee for an Effective Congress
- "Award to Senator Frank Moss (D) of Utah, the only Senator with a 100 percent voting record"
- "On to Victory"—Alexander Barkan, National Director, COPE [12]

International President Smith was the keynoter at the 1973 NPC meeting, which was attended by 83 Machinists. According to the *Machinist* of February 15, 1973, Smith said to those assembled: "Our margin of opposition in Congress is dangerously thin. Certainly it is none too soon to be thinking and planning for the U.S. Senate and House election races of 1974." The article continued:

> With MNPL Vice Chairman George Kourpias presiding, the Planning Committee members heard from a battery of top speakers.
> These included MNPL Co-Chairman Eugene Glover and William Winpisinger, U.S. Sens. Dick Clark of Iowa and Thomas Eagleton of Missouri, Gov. Robert Docking of Kansas, U.S. Reps. Philip Burton of Calif., James Wright and Wright Patman of Texas, Donald Fraser of Minnesota, James O'Hara of Michigan and Andrew Biemiller, AFL-CIO legislative director.

Of the 13 featured speakers at the 1972 NPC meeting, only one was a Republican and his voting record does not differ from that of those many Democrats who benefit from labor's largesse. All of the featured NPC speakers in 1973 were Democrats. NPC members are rarely exposed to the ideas of a middle-of-the-road political leader or of someone even slightly conservative. Perhaps it is this desire not to listen to a different viewpoint that so belies MNPL's assertion that it is nonparti-

167

san. It may well be the reason too why so many young IAM members opt not to get involved in MNPL. About this involvement the NPC once worried aloud:

> The percentage of IAM members under 30 is slowly increasing and now constitutes about 28 percent of the total, 50 percent are under 40 and 25 percent have been members less than 5 years. These members are better educated, more politically oriented and yet many of them do not participate in their union's political programs.[13]

International President Smith strongly promotes the NPC, having served several times as the keynoter at its annual meeting. After the 1971 meeting was held, which Smith keynoted, and its recommendations adopted, the *Machinist* declared:

> Eighty-four of IAM's most savvy leaders came to Washington, heard some of the nation's most respected leaders, worked in committees with some of the Capital's most knowledgeable experts to come up with these recommendations. The recommendations were reviewed and approved by the IAM Executive Council which met in Washington, D.C. at the same time. IAM President Floyd Smith called it a double-barreled program to get America moving again. The twin elements he described as:
> The legislative program for Congress. . . .
> An immediate start on the campaign preparations for 1971 and 1972. They include fund raising, voter registration, aimed particularly at the newly eligible 18-to-20-year olds, and much greater participation by union members in the major political parties with more union representation at the national convention.[14]

Excerpts on MPC Reports

The annual reports and recommendations of the NPC chart the union's political goals and programs for the coming year. These reports and recommendations provide valuable insights as to how union political policy is molded. Here are excerpts from NPC reports and recommendations in recent years:

1970 Report and Recommendations on Campaign Procedure
Early Staff Commitment. The labor movement has divided the 8 Marginal Congressional Districts so that

each of the major unions has accepted special responsibility in certain Congressional Districts. In 16 Senate races, there will be need of special staff help. In so far as Grand Lodge staff is available, we urge the Executive Council members assignment of staff to these strategic areas. The large district lodges should accept responsibility for assigning a full time staff member to these marginal races and where necessary by a combination of MNPL funds, state funds and local or district lodge funds, members should be pulled out of the shop to provide the leadership needed. In some situations it will take 9 months of full time effort to achieve the desired result. In all cases the staff assignment should be at least 3 months.

1971 Report and Recommendations on Labor Participation in Party Affairs

In 1968, the Democratic Party machinery was so divided by the campaign and the convention that it almost ceased to exist as a national force in the early weeks of the Presidential effort. The labor movement then and again in 1970 supplied the organization, the funds, and the skill for the campaign effort. . . .

The IAM now strongly encourages its leaders and staff members to become party officials or delegates. Although we have participated in a minor way in the delegate selection process, the time has come for the labor movement to take its place within the Democratic or Republican Party structure to which its work and funds entitle it. We, therefore, recommend that the IAM, in cooperation with other labor organizations, if possible, seek to influence directly the party committees for the establishment of the broadest type of participation in party organization. We further recommend that we encourage IAM members, officers, and staff to seek to be delegates at the precinct, county, state, and national level in the party of their choice. . . .

We further recommend that the Executive Council mandate to the state councils in every state to set up an education program to educate its members as to the reform that is in process within the Democratic Party and as to how they can participate and help.

1971 Recommendation of the Fund Raising Committee

. . . That the Executive Council explore the possibility of a check off of staff contributions to insure and guarantee 100 percent participation [in the MNPL General Fund drive].

1971 Draft Report of the Fund Raising Committee

In recent years, more states have turned to statewide

drives conducted under the auspices of the state councils of Machinists. Statewide programs have run in Massachusetts, Connecticut, New York, Ohio, Indiana, Wisconsin, Minnesota, Iowa, Illinois, Virginia, Tennessee, California, and Washington. In 1970 new records were set by the big districts. GLRs assisted in promoting the collection of funds on a far more systematic basis than in previous years, through the guidance and instruction of the General Vice Presidents.

1972 Report and Recommendations of the Fund Raising Committee

The intensive rank and file membership solicitation as envisaged by "The Big One" drive successfully reached only about 40,000 members, instead of the hoped-for goal of 100,000. Many individual members, who had never been reached before, were approached, and contributed. Local lodges who followed the recommended procedure and conducted a direct membership solicitation, reported about 25 percent participation. . . .

In order to place the sponsoring membership contributions on a basis of fairness, it is recommended that all sponsoring members drawing a salary or pension of less than $10,000, contribute $25.00; from $10,000 to $15,000—$50.00; $15,000 to $20,000—$100.00; $20,000 to $25,000—$150.00; over $25,000—$200.00. This would apply to all full time local financial officers, Grand Lodge Auditors, Grand Lodge Representatives, Special Representatives, General Chairmen, Business Representatives, Organizers, and all those under the IAM retirement. . . .

All General Funds received by MNPL shall be used for Congressional or Senate races. 25 percent of the total receipts shall be contributed as IAM's share to National COPE; 25 percent returned to the local, district or state body raising the funds, if they so request.

All Presidential contributions shall be used exclusively for the Presidential compaign. One third of the amount raised to be used as direct contribution to the endorsed candidate for President; ⅓ made available for use in the state headquarters in strategic areas for the Presidential campaign; ⅙ made available for travel and hotel expenses of IAM delegates elected to the national convention, and ⅙ to be used for the purchase and distribution of campaign literature

MNPL and the 1976 Elections

The National Planning Committee of the MNPL adopted the following action program at its meeting in February 1975.

The program, formulated by the MNPL Committee on '76 Elections, was published in the *Machinist* of February 13, 1975:

"MNPL ORGANIZING EARLY FOR 1976 U.S. ELECTIONS"

In 1976 we will be electing a President, 33 U.S. Senators, and all 435 U.S. Representatives.

The past six years of Republican administration have caused the working men and women of the United States immeasurable damage and loss of buying power. Instead of the standard of living for workers rising, it has gone down. There is no question that the blame can be laid directly at the feet of the past and present Republican administrations. There is also no doubt in our minds that the only way to change these disastrous policies is to change administrations.

The Democratic Party has numerous good candidates that are either announced or unannounced seekers of their party's nomination. It is our recommendation that every IAM member who is a member of the Democratic Party should take an active interest in helping their chosen candidate win the Democratic nomination. We further recommend that the national MNPL attempt to meet with all candidates who are seeking the Presidential nomination and attempt to determine their qualifications for that office. The national MNPL will then be able to properly advise the IAM membership of the qualifications and abilities of the various candidates.

U.S. SENATE RACES

In 1976, there will be 33 U.S. Senate seats up for election. These 33 seats are presently held by 21 Democrats, 10 Republicans, one Conservative and one Independent. The majority of these seats are held by friendly incumbents who, in some cases, will need early support. A few of the seats are held by out-and-out enemies of organized labor. Perhaps they can be defeated for re-election by a friendly candidate.

It is recommended that in each state, where there is a U.S. Senate race, a committee be set up by the Machinists State Council to determine the situation in that state as regards the race and to communicate that information as soon as possible to the national MNPL.

U.S. HOUSE RACES

Most of the 92 new members were elected by majorities that will place them on the marginal Congressional District list. However, the majority of seats, both Democratic and Republican, will be considered safe. An initial look at all the House seats show that there are 118 that should be considered marginal. These are seats that were won by 55% or less, or changed parties in 1974. These 118 marginal seats are the greatest number in MNPL history.

A look at the list shows some revealing facts. First, 63 of them are Democrats and 58 Republicans. A majority of them (68) are newly elected Representatives. MNPL supported 57 of the Representatives on the marginal list. Of that 57, 50 are newly elected Representatives. Even more startling is the fact that 46 of the newly elected Representatives supported by MNPL on the marginal list were involved in elections that changed the seat from the Republican Party to the Democratic Party. This points out the need for a special effort.

EARLY PREPARATION

We recommend a program to be started early in 1975 immediately following the adjournment of the National Planning Committee meeting. This program is to be aimed at the marginal Senatorial seats and House of Representatives districts.

HELPING INCUMBENT FRIENDS

In those marginal Senate seats and House districts where an incumbent friend will have major opposition and problems getting reelected, we recommend that the state council, IAM district and/or local lodge, whatever the case may be, take the initiative role in seeing that the Senator or Representative in question gets early organizational efforts and financial assistance for the central body COPEs.

A well-organized registration program should be planned using the central body COPEs and other allies such as Frontlash, A. Philip Randolph Institute, Concerned Seniors, the Labor Council for Latin American Advancement and other groups interested in registration drives. We should support efforts this year to enact a Federal postcard registration law.

Early plans should be made to provide full-time and part-time help in the IAM's areas of responsibility in registration, education and get-out-the-vote efforts.

Plans should be made to meet with the Senators and Representatives to advise them of our plans and activities. Plans must be made to carry-out an early fundraising effort to supply the necessary funds for the organizational efforts and financial assistance for the Senators and Representatives involved.

OPPOSING UNFRIENDLY INCUMBENTS

In those seats presently held by unfriendly Senators and Representatives, we recommend that MNPL, with the help and cooperation of state and county central body COPEs, determine if our endorsed candidate from the previous election should be the candidate to challenge the incumbent enemy. If the determination is made that he or she should be our endorsed candidate, then we should take the necessary steps to try to insure that our candidate gets the nomination of his or her party. If this is not the case, we recommend, again with the help and cooperation of the state and county central body COPEs, that a search be made for a qualified candidate to challenge the unfriendly incumbent.

We further recommend that all of these efforts be coordinated through the national MNPL as well as with state and county central body COPEs involved.

Conclusion

An Executive Committee oversees the operations of MNPL. Three of its nine members are the union's chief executive officers. Only MNPL sponsoring members located in the headquarters area and others who happen to attend the election meeting in Washington, D.C., which is held every four years, can vote in the election of members to the Executive Committee.

The minutes of the Executive Committee reveal that a wide variety of political topics is discussed and acted upon. In many cases the recommendations of the two MNPL staff officers are adopted without discussion by the Executive Committee; the result is that these two persons exert the greatest influence on the committee's decisions.

The Executive Committee distributes the General and the Educational funds. Because of the carefully structured way in which Executive Committee members are elected to their positions, the rank and file has little to say how the funds are disbursed. Thus, hundreds of thousands of dollars each election year are distributed for political causes upon the approval of less than a dozen Machinists, most of whom are staff personnel.

In 1970 and 1972 about 99 percent of MNPL contributions went to Democratic Party organizations and candidates.

The National Planning Committee is supposed to act in an advisory capacity to the MNPL Executive Committee. As the NPC members are selectively chosen by the territorial GVPs on the basis of their devotion to political activity, they are in reality little more than a façade of "democracy" under which

173

IAM and MNPL political policies are put into practice. Even the NPC recommendations adopted at its annual meeting must be approved by the IAM Executive Council. The same annual meeting hears outside speakers on political topics; such speakers are invariably Democratic and liberal, seldom Republican, and never conservative.

6

Assignment of the Union's Staff to Political Activity

State councils and district and local lodges are subordinate bodies of IAM. Local MNPL organizations may be created by these subordinate bodies. Because the subordinate bodies are themselves chartered by IAM, the principal officers of the subordinate body "shall be members of the Executive Committee" of the local MNPL although they "need not hold the same office in the league that they hold in the State Council, district or local lodge." [1]

Each state council and district MNPL is authorized and urged to establish a congressional campaign committee made up of delegates from lodges having members in the congressional district, regardless of where the local or district lodge headquarters is located. "If a Congressional Campaign MNPL Committee is established under the authority of the State Council or MNPL, the National League will supply at cost to that Campaign Committee, the names of all IAM members on our computer so they may be checked for registration and organized for campaigning and getting out the vote." [2]

Much of the union's political activity is conducted through the approximately 48 state councils or conferences of Machinists. These councils are not concerned with collective bargaining but specialize in political education, political action, and lobbying.

The obvious political complexion of the Machinist state councils is revealed in this 1971 memorandum from MNPL director William Holayter:

> The Connecticut State Council, in the two-day meeting on January 16 and 17, took some steps forward to make themselves a first-rate political structure. They voted on and passed a new set of MNPL bylaws which would set up a political organization throughout the six Congressional Districts in Connecticut. The organization will be under the direction and leadership of the State Council officers and Executive Board.
>
> The Connecticut State Council of Machinists over the last three years has been one of the most progressive of all the councils in the United States in both organizing

175

politically and fund raising. This is a tribute to the leadership of the Council.[3]

State councils are established voluntarily within a state by local lodges therein. Floyd Smith declares that IAM and MNPL support for candidates is based on recommendations from the state councils and that in the 10 states without state councils the recommendations come from within the membership in the state. Yet Smith admits he has no knowledge of any membership referendums on candidates being conducted in these 10 states.[4]

State councils receive their support through a per capita tax paid by local or district lodges. The amount of the per capita tax is determined within the state and not by the Grand Lodge. For example, in a 1972 notice of the upcoming convention of the Georgia State Council of Machinists it was announced:

> This June Convention is for the purpose of raising funds for the MNPL and discussing support for Statewide and National political candidates.
> The By-Laws of the Georgia State Council provide that affiliation fee to State Council of Machinists and Aerospace Workers shall be per capita tax for one calendar quarter. The dues of this Council shall be $20.00 per year for District Lodges and $.02 (2¢) per member per quarter for Local Lodges and Auxiliaries.[5]

State councils on the whole do not have full-time staff persons. The president and other officers of the council are elected by the delegates from district and local lodges and usually are also officers of these same organizations. The travel expenses of delegates to state council meetings are picked up by the district or local lodges that the delegates represent. Although the purposes of the state council are political, tax-exempt union dues money is used to pay the delegates' expenses.

In some states both a state council and a state MNPL coexist. In such cases endorsement of candidates can be made by either organization, but Holayter has stated that the general practice is to "recess the State Council of Machinists meeting and convene a state MNPL meeting." [6] Don Ellinger has noted that on occasion, when he was meeting with the leadership of the state councils, he found MNPL leaders to be among that leadership.

One of the most politically active state councils is the Ohio State Council of Machinists. Control of Ohio politics has for years been a principal goal of organized labor and the IAM has persistently worked towards that end. The minutes of two educational meetings of the Ohio council in 1968 are illustrative of IAM participation in Buckeye State politics.

At the first meeting, on April 20, 1968, GLR Edward Laucella, "assigned to Political Action in the State of Ohio," reported on Ohio IAM activities in the Democratic primary between conservative incumbent Sen. Frank Lausche and liberal challenger John Gilligan:

In conjunction with the program developed for Ohio, visits were made, action and caucus meetings were held in 19 areas which included Marion, Youngstown, Springfield, Columbus, Columbiana, Newark, Canton, Geneva, Cleveland, Wooster, Orville, and Akron. Caucus for the Machinists Delegates were [sic] held after the Gilligan Dinner meetings. The Machinists attendance at the Gilligan Dinners was outstanding. In Columbus, of an attendance of approximately 1260, there was in excess of 10% Machinists. In Akron, Cincinnati and Cleveland the attendance was in excess of 7%. Concerning the registration situation, irrespective of the obstacles and lack of cooperation from the office of the Secretary of State, a real good job was done. . . . These efforts in some places were in conjunction with the Central Labor Bodies, but in some areas the Machinists had the full burden of doing the job. Our computer at headquarters was utilized through the cooperation of other International Unions sending in the names and addresses of their membership. This was filtered back to the state organizations and fitted in to the registration program. At the conclusion of the registration this information was sent back through the state organization to Washington and is going through the computer again and at this time 565,000 members' names have been processed as to registration on Democrats and Independant [sic]. The processing was delayed due to the riot situation but will be completed about April 25th so it will be in the hands of the Central Bodies so they can get on the "Get out the Vote" program.

The commitment adopted at the Special Convention of the state organization, the Ohio AFL-CIO, has been fulfilled. Due to contributions made by various International Unions more money than the 6¢ per capita tax voted by the Special Convention has been constructively utilized. . . .

Kits were made up and distributed that contained a map of the new congressional districts. A copy of the discription [sic] of the boundaries was procured and reproduced and the Business Representatives were asked

177

to pick up a sufficient supply. The delegates were asked to add them to their kits. Special "register to vote" bulletins were put out to every Machinist member in the State of Ohio and a special register to vote bulletin and manpower letter was sent to all our retired members in the state of Ohio. . . . Leaflets from the Machinists Non-Partisan Political League for plant distribution were passed out to the Business Representatives and Grand Lodge Representatives. These leaflets were for Gilligan for Senate, with his record and the record of Lausche. The week of the 25th of April every "Machinists" family in the State of Ohio will receive a letter asking if they can afford to ignore their rights of citizenship and try to awaken them to the important things of becoming politically educated and understand the issues, the candidates and why they should assert their American Heritage, get out and work and get out and vote. . . . Some of the money raised through the Ohio Machinists Non-Partisan Political League has filtered back to Gilligan. The Machinists was the first International Union to make their contribution to this effort in Ohio. As of this time no one has put in more money than the Machinists Non-Partisan Political League. . . . There have been meetings of the State Democratic Organization, the Gilligan campaign people and the Labor Movement to plan the last three weeks effort and what has to be done. . . . We are going to be in every precinct and polling place and anyone that tries to crossover is going to have to be challenged. We spent money, we did a pretty fair job on registration. So far as we are concerned in the publicity, the literature and everything else we have got the election won. Along with Gilligan we can not overlook other people we have got to elect. We have got to have the manpower to get this job done, we have got to get them out to the polls. . . . In endorsements we made and in endorsements the Democratic Party made, Labor's reputation is at stake in the State of Ohio. Senator Lausche questions Labor's effectiveness in the State of Ohio. We showed them in "48" and in "58", let's show them how effective we can be in 1968.[7]

Organized labor's massive effort for Gilligan in the Democratic primary *was* effective and carried him to victory over Senator Lausche. GLR Laucella appeared at a postprimary educational meeting of the Ohio Council of Machinists "to talk on the legislative program necessary to get John Gilligan elected Senator from Ohio." Laucella candidly observed:

Since the primaries, for the first time in a lot of years,

178

the Democratic party has re-evaluated the situation and a real attempt has been made to put together a real Democratic Party in the State of Ohio. We are supposed to be non-partisan but we speak about the Democratic Party and candidates go out and support the issues favorable to the working people and the Labor Movement, although we have supported numerous Republican Candidates throughout the nation both for Congress and the Senate. On June 15th a meeting was held in Columbus of many Democrat congressional Candidates in Ohio, in addition to Jack Gilligan, in an effort to pull the party together and establieh [sic] a firm and progressive party in the State of Ohio. Labor was invited to the meeting and was represented by Frank King, President of the Ohio AFL-CIO, Warren Smith, Secretary-Treasurer of the Ohio AFL-CIO and Brother Laucella. . . . We are a part of this campaign and we want them to understand that we intend to be a part of it and that without us they cannot operate, we have to operate as a team.[8]

As active politically as its counterpart in Ohio is the California Conference of Machinists. The California conference openly flaunts its support of the Democratic Party. The state leadership's attitude is typified by GVP E. R. White's address to a 1968 meeting of the California conference:

. . . I will work my butt off until we get Humphrey elected . . .
. . . [W]e must work for those people in the political front clear down the line and in the official positions in our trade unions who have shown a willingness and competence to get the job done. . . .
Now we've got tools, I don't know how many of you people have extra people out, and how many of you have circulated the material that has been provided, the special edition of the *Machinist*, every member of this union should have it, every Democrat in the precinct where you live should have it. . . .
. . . and I say to you Districts now, where we have crucial Congressional contests, that are borderline, if you don't get people into these contests, if you don't get people working in those key precincts, if you don't do your job, then you can bear the responsibility of what happens to you, when your anti-labor legislation starts to crack you on butt [sic] that you are sitting on.
Now, I am going to retire, but the greatest gift that you can give me, and you guys that think I am an idiot, you can help too to be sure I don't come back, keep me retired with a Democratic victory. . . .[9]

Should one be led to think that this partisan speech by GVP White was only an aberration, the minutes of another conference meeting held that same year record:

GLR John Snider . . . stated that he and GLR Hal Shean had been assigned to implement the recommendations of the National Planning Committee and in so doing they had visited over half of the lodges in the Southwestern Territory and will visit the others now that most of the strikes are settled. He announced a three pronged program:

1. Registration, which ends in the State of California September 12.
2. Education program takes place between September 12 and election day.
3. On election day a program to "get out the vote."

He announced that there would be a meeting of all Business Representatives and GLR's sometime during this Conference to implement this program. He further pointed out that part of his assignment was to appear in Sacramento to further the interests of the IAMAW in conjunction with the Legislative Committee headed by the Secretary of the Conference. . . .

He spoke on the importance of endorsing Alan Cranston and working to defeat the candidacy of Superintendent of Schools Rafferty in the race for U.S. Senate, and touched on some of the areas in the State where our enemies could be defeated, and our friends elected. In the Visalia area, the incumbent Robert Mathias could be defeated by Harlan Hagen, in the San Bernardino–Ontario areas we have a chance to defeat Wiggins and Pettis. In the San Fernando Valley, a big campaign will be necessary to reelect Congressman Jim Corman in the 22nd District. He pointed out that the State Senate was now made up of 20 Democrats and 20 Republicans and stressed the need for electing a majority of Democrats for the purpose of the formation of Committees. In the Assembly we have excellent chances to increase the 42 to 38 majority we now have. He closed by stating that he and GLR Hal Shean would make appearances in those areas where for various reasons they were unable to meet with them previously, and would assist in any way possible.[10]

Frequently, the California conference and the California MNPL convene a joint meeting. The two organizations share a full-time secretary-treasurer, John Schiavenza. An interesting insight is provided by the resolution that created the secretary-treasurer post, and that was adopted at a meeting of the conference on January 14–17, 1971. The meeting's minutes show that the original resolution was modified shortly after adoption as follows:

> . . . that the second line of the fifth "whereas" where it now reads "would serve as a legislative advocate," should be corrected to read "would serve as liaison" and in the same "whereas" where it says "political action" it should be corrected to read "political education." [11]

Apparently the conference leadership wished to mask the real purpose of the post by using Aesopian language in the resolution creating it. This intertwining of political education and political action was acknowledged by GLR Hal Shean at the same 1971 meeting of the California conference that begot the secretary-treasurer post. Shean reported to those assembled that

> . . . in fact my first assignment was to go back to Washington on one of the first meetings of the new process in the IAM on Education. Each territory has got some guys working in the field today. . . . President Smith spent two days with us and in those two days we found that the educational field was an answer to a lot of our problems including the political field. We had to combine education in our political atmosphere in order to let our people know why we were doing these things in the political field. [12]

The California MNPL makes no pretense of its desire to aid the Democratic Party. One of its meetings included a discussion "[t]hat we work as closely as possible with the Democratic organizations." [13] At still another meeting,

> GLR Hal Shean was then called upon. He stressed the importance of coordination between the Calif. Conf., Grand Lodge and Local Dist. Lodges. He urged more participation in the Demo. Central Committee. [14]

Tax-exempt dues money from California IAM members supports the California MNPL, whether the union's members are sympathetic with the partisan politics of the MNPL or not. As early as 1964 the minutes of the Executive Board of the California MNPL record: "Motion by Ward and seconded by Swisher and carried that the California Conference of Machinists be requested to contribute $400. per month to the C.M.N.P.L. This contribution to be used solely for operating expenses." [15]

The California MNPL receives two of the five cents of the per capita monthly tax levied on the California conference membership. The state's MNPL then uses the tax-exempt funds to aid the Democratic Party. Part of the reasoning behind this overt partisanship was articulated by the IAM director of research, Vernon K. Jirikowic, in a 1970 address to the California conference: ". . . We have to realize that most of the burden will fall on organized labor, because as we have seen the Democratic Party splinter in many states we know that if it is to be done at all, organized labor is going to have to do it." [16]

Assignment of Personnel

The IAM and MNPL have developed a highly sophisticated procedure for assigning the union's staff personnel to political activity. The state councils and conferences play key roles in the procedure.

Prior to 1966, the assignment of personnel was performed only spasmodically. In that year the IAM international president wrote AFL-CIO president George Meany expressing his concern about the upcoming congressional elections, particularly the close contests in New York and New Jersey. He suggested that a special effort be mounted to recruit skilled political organizers from the labor movement for the marginal districts. As a result,

President Meany expanded our initial proposal and called a meeting of all international presidents to develop a program of staff support for all the crucial districts. . . .

The COPE staff has consulted with the state federations and major central bodies throughout the country asking for the names of those whom the local leaders believe to be most effective. President Meany has asked each International to make these people available full time from the first of August until election day.[17]

Accordingly, the IAM international president in June of 1966 wrote five general vice presidents requesting them to make available the full-time services of 12 IAM staff persons to work with COPE in the marginal districts.

Also during 1966 Ellinger wrote the international president: "The Executive Committee believes a wire, similar to the one attached, from you to all GLRs, Auditors, and Business Representatives would be very helpful." [18] The attached proposed wire read:

On next Tuesday, November 8, I will be in Cook County working in a precinct to help turn out the vote. On election day there are no chiefs—just Indians. I believe every member of our staff should be working at the precinct level nearest his present assignment to set an example for our membership to get out and push doorbells, walk precincts, and push cards. Don't call the Grand Lodge on election day, we will all be out working where the votes are.[19]

To reveal the systematic procedure followed by IAM—in many cases in cooperation with COPE—in the assignment of personnel to political activity, examples have been selected over a five-year period, 1968–72. The reader should keep in mind that when full-time IAM staff personnel are assigned to political activity, their salary and expenses continue to be paid by the IAM as if they were performing regular job duties. This means that IAM's tax-exempt treasury, composed of dues income, underwrites political work. On many occasions a member is asked to take time off from his regular employment to handle a political assignment, with his lost time paid by dues money. In this case the tax-exempt MNPL Educational Fund pays the member's salary and expenses. Since the Educational Fund derives from dues revenue and treasury money, once again it is tax-exempt money that is supporting assigned political activity.

1968

INDIANA: Senator Birch Bayh (D) was up for reelection and IAM was intent on seeing that he was successful. Floyd Smith wrote GLR Robert Brown early in the year:

Please accept this letter as an assignment for you to commence cleaning up most of the miscellaneous assignments or items which you have hanging around within your assigned territory so that as soon as is possible and practical full time may be devoted to our MNPL efforts in the State of Indiana. In this connection if we are able to do anything in the third, seventh and eighth Congressional Districts in Indiana, that would be well. However, let me stress upon you that your primary assignments would be in the Senatorial race in Indiana this year in the re-election of U.S. Senator Birch Bayh.[20]

GLR Brown, in turn, wrote Senator Bayh in Washington:

Please be advised that I have been assigned by my

183

Union, the International Association of Machinists & Aerospace Workers, AFL-CIO, to work full-time in the State of Indiana on politics with your re-election receiving top priority. . . . Accordingly, I expect to meet with you and your full time staff in the near future in order to determine how best to approach the over-all project of your re-election. (Will see you March 5 at the Indiana State AFL-CIO Executive Board meeting, Mariott Hotel.)

We are using the computer of the Machinists Union in Washington, D.C. to develop a mailing list of our membership in the State of Indiana. . . .[21]

In mid-1968 Brown wrote Don Ellinger requesting a $5,000 MNPL contribution to Bayh's campaign, declaring: "All labor is completely united in the effort to re-elect Senator Bayh in the State of Indiana. We are completely convinced that we have a winner here providing we have the proper finances and organizational structure to get the job done." [22] A few weeks before the election, Brown reported to Ellinger on two congressional campaigns:

Sister Cora Smolinski of Dist. 113 has for some time been spending full time for Congressman Roush. However the funds are depleted to pay for salaries and expenses we need a minimum of $500.00.

A minimum of $500.00 is also needed to finance the activities (salary & expenses) of Brother William Maikraz District 153 in the 8th Congressional District.

Be advised that the Natl. COPE and the respective Labor Committee have been for sometime bearing full expense of these activities by channeling funds thru our Dist. Lodges.[23]

CALIFORNIA: Joe W. Barnes, Sr., coordinator, Local Lodge 68 in San Francisco, was selected to coordinate MNPL's activity with COPE's in San Francisco and San Mateo counties. Ellinger sent $500 of tax-exempt MNPL funds for use towards the salary and expenses of Barnes under the guise that he "is doing citizenship work for a number of the IAM locals in San Francisco and San Mateo." [24] After the Presidential election, Barnes wrote Ellinger:

On my first rounds of the Democratic Headquarters, I found that they had no election material except for the Local Candidates. . . . I also did not see any Humphrey signs at that time in either San Francisco or San Mateo Counties. I then contacted Brother Crowley of the San Francisco Labor Council who is in charge of COPE in the San Francisco areas and was told about 65 tons of material were to be delivered at the Oakland Airport, to be assigned to all Labor Councils in Northern California. . . .

I delivered campaign materials to all Machinist Lodges, as well as many other Unions in this area who requested same. I also delivered their material to Democratic Headquarters in Redwood City and San Mateo and San Bruno.

I received full and more than full cooperation from all of the Machinists locals and the rest of the Labor Movement. Brother Ray Gabel of 1327, Bill Combs of 1781, as well as Brother Bill Ferguson of Lodge 68 were invaluable aids. . . . Two weeks before the election, the UAW assigned a Brother Harry Fulmer to work with us full time, also the Steelworkers assigned a member. I also had the pleasure of working with International Representative Ralph Mitchell of the Painters and Carpet Layers Union.[25]

FLORIDA: GLR J. George Eichhorn worked with other labor representatives to elect the former governor LeRoy Collins to the U.S. Senate seat being vacated by Senator George Smathers. Eichhorn reported in August that a committee had been formed

as the United Labor Movement to elect Collins, with 1st Vice President of the Florida State Council of AFL-CIO, Art Halgren, being elected Chairman. I was elected 1st Vice Chairman. . . . The facilities of the AFL State machine will be available for all mailings and they are well equipped with the latest mailing equipment.[26]

OREGON: In September GVP Charles West wrote the president of the Oregon AFL-CIO regarding Wayne Morse's Senate campaign. He stated that "[y]our request for Grand Lodge Representative James Blackwell to assist you in the Clackamas County area in the above campaign is herewith honored." [27] After the election COPE area director Walter Gray wrote West:

I would like to express our sincere appreciation for the assignment of Jim Blackwell, Tom Stewart, and Marvin Kelso to the get-out-the-vote operation in Oregon. While the election is still in doubt, it was with their help that we were able to come out of Multnomah County with a lead for Senator Morse of 20,000 votes where he had always trailed in previous elections.[28]

PENNSYLVANIA: The *Philadelphia Inquirer* of March 14, 1968, carried the following article titled "Anti-GOP Fund Drive Begun by Machinists":

A spokesman for the million-member International Association of Machinists and Aerospace Workers said Wednesday night his union is raising a $300,000 national war chest to oust Republican legislators this fall.

Samuel A. Luterotty, a special union representative, outlined the operation—which began January 12—at a meeting of the Philadelphia AFL-CIO. . . .

Luterotty and 33 other union representatives have already been assigned full time work in 100 key congressional races where the margin or loss for Democratic candidates was 5 percent or more.

Democratic Rep. Joshua Eilberg (D.-Phila.) won with only 51.9 percent of the vote in 1966, Luterotty said, and would rate strong union support this fall. He is one of the four key races in the Delaware Valley.

The other three races have Republican incumbents and the union hopes its money and manpower will help retire them.

WASHINGTON STATE: Early in 1968 GVP West assigned special representative James Blackwell

to assist in the forthcoming campaign to re-elect Congressman Foley and Senator Magnuson.

By his copy of this letter, Special Representative Blackwell will be made aware of his assignment to assist in these campaigns to the limit that his daily work responsibilities will permit.[29]

1969

This was an off-election year nationally but special elections were held to fill several vacant congressional seats. These campaigns and others made it an active year for IAM.

NEW JERSEY: A special election was to be held in the state's 8th Congressional District and GVP L. Ross Mathews wrote Don Ellinger:

I agree we must do everything possible to help elect Bob Roe to Congress.

I am assigning GLR Joseph Mastriani to coordinate the IAM activities in the election campaign. In addition, all [9] representatives receiving a copy of this communication are advised by receipt of their copies of this letter that they are assigned to report to Brother Mastriani to help out in the campaign.[30]

MONTANA: John Melcher was the labor-endorsed Democratic candidate in the special election in the 2nd Congressional District. GVP Charles West told GLR Edgar Cozad to "please consider this letter as your assignment to assist Brother Don Ellinger with the Montana Special Election Campaign until June 24, 1969." [31]

WISCONSIN: The executive vice president of the Wisconsin AFL-CIO wrote GVP Gilbert Brunner:

Please accept my profound sincere thanks and appreciation for the manner in which the International Association of Machinists and its affiliated lodges responded to the total effort needed to elect Dale McKenna in the recent special election which was held in the Thirteenth Wisconsin State Senatorial District. . . .

I would be remiss if I did not mention the assistance rendered by John Heidenreich. . . .[32]

TEXAS: Don Ellinger informed a district lodge official in the Lone Star State:

The Bexar Central Labor Committee in San Antonio has written urging that we assist them in making available the services of J. C. Schweigert, a member of District Lodge 100, who has been very helpful in the registration program in San Antonio.

As you know, Senator Yarborough is up for re-election this year and the Machinists are making a special effort to be helpful to him.[33]

MINNESOTA: In 1969 labor leaders began to work for the 1970 election of Hubert Humphrey to the U.S. Senate. They also hoped to pick up additional congressional seats in the North Star State. Union strategists urged that union members should move into positions of party leadership in the Democratic–Farm–Labor Party (DFL) because, as Ellinger wrote COPE director Al Barkan, "success in this effort will pave the way for an effective campaign for registration and with Humphrey as head of the ticket to pick up 2 or 3 congressional seats." [34]

Ellinger believed the project's success would require two three-month drives with an excess of 19 union representatives working full time. He advised Barkan that "[t]he unions from which the first full time staff members should come are Steelworkers (Ray Morrison if possible), IAM (Dale Pommerville) Carpenters, IBEW, Meatcutters, OCAW and CWA." [35]

MASSACHUSETTS: Michael Harrington, a liberal Democrat, was elected to Congress in a special election in the 6th Congressional District. After his election Don Ellinger boasted to International President Smith:

> The performance of our team in the special congressional election in Massachusetts adds credit to the reputation of our union as an efficient and effective political organization.
>
> General Vice President Mathews assigned Grand Lodge Representative William Walsh to coordinate the effort and he worked hard and well. Mathews also assigned . . . [7] Grand Lodge Representatives and Special Representatives to assist and they did an outstanding job. District 38 and the Massachusetts State Council of Machinists recruited . . . [8] workers from outside of the District and they helped on the final election push. [36]

1970

The year 1970 was a crucial national election year. Thirty-five Senate seats and all 435 House seats were up for election. Don Ellinger wrote Floyd Smith describing what was expected from the Machinists:

> We attach a copy of the 8 marginal congressional districts in the country and the 16 marginal Senate races which will be the battleground in 1970. The IAM has been asked to assume the responsibility for special leadership in a number of these races, but we will be active in all of them. The particular request made by Mr. Meany is for early staff help which will become full time staff help at the appropriate time in the campaign. We have special responsibility in the following states:
>
> CALIFORNIA— . . . IAM is especially responsible for the 9th District in San Jose in electing a replacement for Don Edwards, and for directing the reelection campaign of Congressman Dick Hanna in the 34th District in northern Orange County. We will need a staff member either from one of the major districts or the Grand Lodge staff assigned to each of these campaigns as soon as possible to become full time after the June primary.
>
> CONNECTICUT— . . . We will need a full time man for Connecticut who can work both the Senate race and the 6th Congressional District.
>
> INDIANA— . . . We need a full time man as soon

as possible assigned to Hartke's campaign and additional full time help later in the year in the 4th District to help defeat Ross Adair, and in the 8th District to help defeat Congressman Zion.

IOWA—John Culver, in the 2nd District, has been a particular friend of the Machinists. We have been asked to accept major responsibility there. We need a full time staff person assigned to this congressional race later in the year.

KENTUCKY—Our members in Kentucky have been active in the recent Democratic resurgence and with control of both the City Hall in Louisville and the Jefferson County Court House, we are in a position to retire incumbent Congressman Cowger. We need a full time man assigned to this congressional district after the Democratic primary.

MINNESOTA— . . . With Humphrey at the head of the ticket, we should be able to win the 6th and 7th Districts. The IAM has asked to take special responsibility for the 6th District which includes St. Cloud, and we will need a full time man after the Democratic primary in this congressional district.

NEW JERSEY—Senator Pete Williams will have a very tough battle since the Republican sweep this year. We will need a full time man assigned to this campaign as soon as possible to concentrate on the Williams campaign.

NEW MEXICO—Senator Joseph Montoya . . . will have a very difficult race. Although we have only 2,000 members in the state, our people are particularly effective when they are well led. We will need a full time man to work both the Senate race and the northern Congressional district, held by Republican freshman Lujan. . . .

NEW YORK— . . . We have been asked to assume responsibility for Delaney's reelection in New York City. Delaney has been close to the Machinists for years. We need to ask District 15 to make Frank Alexander available full time on this campaign after the June primary.

OHIO—Howard Metzenbaum has been endorsed by our leadership in Ohio. . . . If he wins the May Democratic primary, we should have a full time man assigned to that campaign. This same full time man should assist in organizing the Vanik congressional district in southeastern Cleveland.

TENNESSEE—Senator Albert Gore will be in for the fight of his life. . . . His reelection is among the top priority items. We need a top skilled full time man assigned immediately to work on this campaign through November.

TEXAS—The reelection of Ralph Yarborough now looks better because of the work that has been done in Texas in the registration campaign. We now have Bill Wolfe assigned to this campaign by GVP George Watkins.

WISCONSIN—Senator Bill Proxmire is considered safe, but there is a possibility of winning the 1st Congressional District. We have been asked to give leadership to that campaign which will require close coordination with the UAW.

WYOMING—Senator Gale McGee, who has been a particular friend of the Machinists, faces a very hard reelection effort. The drop in population in Wyoming has reduced the labor movement there to only 7,000 members. . . . Although our membership is small and mainly railroad shopcraft, it is essential that we make every effort in addition to financial support, to assign a full time man into that campaign beginning the first of July.[37]

The IAM under the politically attuned leadership of Smith, wasted little time in implementing Ellinger's strategy for assigning Machinist manpower. Here is a partial record of the campaign work done by the Machinists in 1970.

ILLINOIS: Adlai Stevenson III was the Democratic candidate for the U. S. Senate. GVP GIlbert Brunner wrote GLR Robert Reynolds:

Upon receipt of this letter, I am asking you to make arrangements starting Monday, May 25, 1970, to report to the Adlai Stevenson Headquarters located on the second floor at 18 N. Clark Street, Chicago, Illinois.

Your assignment will require you to be in the office there every day from 12:00 Noon until 9:00 P.M. or longer, as required. This assignment will go on indefinitely until you receive further notice from me or until the date of the election in November of 1970.[38]

The assignment of Reynolds had the apparent blessing of Floyd Smith because a month before Reynolds was notified, Brunner had written Smith: "I have been contacted by the State AFL-CIO requesting the assignment of a full time man to work on the Stevenson campaign. They have requested the assignment of one of our representatives immediately to work in the Stevenson headquarters in Chicago and then to do what else is necessary throughout the state." [39] Brunner then asked Smith to advise him on the assignment of a Machinist.

OHIO: The election of Howard Metzenbaum to the U.S.

Senate was a top Machinist goal in 1970. International President Smith and GVP Fred Purcell co-signed a letter to "All Full Time IAM Staff Members in Ohio" that declared:

> We can put a special friend of our union in the United States Senate from Ohio by putting our full energy behind Howard Metzenbaum. . . .
> The immediate target is to select 1,000 members of the Machinist Union who will be named block captains in the Metzenbaum campaign. This letter is going to the 51 paid staff members in Ohio who know the key people in the local and district lodge you serve. We want you to suggest the best men and women we have who will do the job. . . . Each of them will receive a letter appointing them to this post and will receive a direct communication from Senator-to-be-Metzenbaum. They will be asked to see that campaign materials go out to their neighbors and to assist on the registration and get-out-the-vote effort.[40]

NEW JERSEY: IAM special representative George Almeida was assigned to work on the Senate and House races in the Garden State. He wrote to Don Ellinger two weeks before election day:

> Senator [Harrison] Williams appears to be gaining momentum in his campaign. . . .
> The state is flooded with Williams literature and it has been made available to the Locals in the State at various drops. The District #47 offices were used again as a drop.
> At a meeting of the New Jersey AFL-CIO on Wednesday, October 21, 1970, all labor leaders in the State were urged to keep pushing up to and including Election Day.[41]

VERMONT: Democratic senatorial candidate Philip Hoff wrote GVP L. Ross Mathews in May:

> Assuming all goes well, come next January I shall be working rather closely as a member of the United States Senate with your Political Action Director, Don Ellinger.
> Don may have already told you that Al Barkan has been very helpful to me in my efforts to date and indeed plans to be helpful to me during the coming months. The members of organized labor in the state of Vermont have also been very helpful to me. In fact, a United

Labor Committee for Better Government has been organized and endorsed my candidacy. Several unions have already released employes to work for the United Labor Committee on my behalf. They have organized a rather aggressive voter registration campaign, a petition drive, a schedule for factory visits, and a get-out-the-vote campaign.

. . . I have had several discussions with Carroll Comstock who represents you in Vermont.

If it's at all possible, I would appreciate if you could release Carroll from his present duties so that he could work to assist me in my campaign.[42]

This was one of the few instances where legitimate union business took precedence over a candidate's request, though not completely. GVP Mathews replied to Hoff:

I am in agreement with you that Carroll is an asset to our organization and it is unfortunately precisely for this reason that I find myself in a position where I am unable to release him from his duties during the Summer months.

I have no objection, however, if Carroll can arrange his work schedule to render you his assistance for voter education work from time to time this Summer, as his other duties will permit. In addition, Carroll is in a position to attempt to secure further assistance from other I.A.M. members in the State, which I am certain he will be happy to do.[43]

FLORIDA: Lawton Chiles was the upset winner in the Sunshine State's Democratic senatorial primary. He was opposed in the general election by conservative Republican William Cramer. Organized labor moved quickly to bolster Chiles' campaign. GVP William Winpisinger advised GLR George Brown:

It is obviously extremely important that we do everything in our power to see that Mr. Chiles is victorious in November's general election.

Accordingly, please consider this as your assignment, engage in every lawful way in the campaign to elect Mr. Chiles, as well as the other candidates who have received the endorsement of our organization.

It is my understanding that Grand Lodge Representatives Frank E'Dalgo and George Eichhorn have been similarly assigned by General Vice President George L. Watkins and you are to cooperate and coordinate your work with them.[44]

NEW MEXICO: Senator Joseph Montoya, up for reelection in 1970, sought traditional support from the leaders of organized labor. He wrote International President Smith concerning

> a very critical situation that has arisen in my campaign for re-election to the United States Senate.
>
> I need not emphasize to you my voting record in the Senate in behalf of Labor, nor do I have to remind anyone of the consequences in the loss of another liberal Senator in this year's campaign.[45]

Senator Montoya requested that GLR Herbert Ward be assigned to work in his campaign to register and get out the vote of 8,000 black residents in Bernalillo County. Montoya's letter did not restrict the work of Ward to campaigning among Machinists, but requested that he be assigned to work among a bloc of voters outside the Machinist membership. The full letter is reproduced in Appendix 15.

Montoya's request for campaign assistance was approved. Three weeks after Smith had received the senator's letter, Ellinger was able to inform Smith that "General Vice President Simpson reports that GLR Herb Ward is on duty in Albuquerque working on the campaign as you have suggested."[46]

WYOMING: In June Ellinger wrote territorial GVP Francis Meagher:

> The reelection of Gale McGee is one of the top priority items for the total labor movement including the IAM. Registration in Wyoming does not close until October 19. It would seem to me that if you could make arrangements for Allin Walker to be available to assist in the final drive from Labor Day to October 19 and then through to the election on November 3, that we will have fulfilled our obligation in this campaign.[47]

TENNESSEE: In January GVP Fred Purcell assigned GLR H. A. McClendon to the reelection campaign of Senator Albert Gore. Ellinger, upon being notified of McClendon's pending assignment, wrote Purcell: "If a major primary contest develops, he would need to be in the field by April 1 to develop a registration program for the Machinists and to assist in promoting the campaign activities of the Senator."[48] On March 3, 1970, Ellinger sent McClendon

> our check in the amount of $500 made payable to the Tennessee State Council of Machinists. This check is to establish a revolving fund to assist you in organizing the

193

Labor for Gore structure in the Machinists organization in Tennessee. The Executive Committee has authorized us to replenish this amount as you spend it up to a total of $2,000. . . .

You have also submitted an estimate on the purchase of the bumper stickers. The Executive Committee would like your advice on whether the Gore campaign itself is going to produce such stickers. . . .[49]

The Machinists were not the only labor organization providing early campaign support for Gore. The president of the Memphis AFL-CIO Labor Council informed Floyd Smith in April that in its work to reelect Senator Gore,

The Memphis AFL-CIO Labor Council has checked the membership list of the affiliated locals and has furnished the locals with the names of their unregistered members.

We have distributed over 50,000 pieces of the latest COPE material in the past ninety days.

We have had printed and distributed 20,000 "Gore For Less Taxes" bumper stickers.

We have purchased and made available to local unions the latest COPE films.

We are cooperating with individuals and organizations outside of labor that are supporting the Senator.[50]

The tax-exempt A. Philip Randolph Institute—which organizes voter-registration drives almost exclusively for liberal Democratic candidates—was also hard at work in behalf of Gore. McClendon wrote Ellinger in August that

. . . Brother McCreary did a very outstanding job while working for Senator Gore with the A. Philip Randolph Foundation, known as MOVE.

Request has now been made that lost time and expenses be paid from the MNPL Educational Fund for Brother McCreary to work from now through November 3rd. He would again be working with the A. Philip Randolph Foundation and his efforts would, as before, be centered on the Gore campaign.[51]

INDIANA: GLR Robert Brown was chosen to be chairman of the Indiana Labor Committee for Senator Vance Hartke. In May Brown wrote Ellinger:

The Indiana State Council of Machinists has also embarked upon an idea of sponsoring several "Get-Acquainted Receptions" throughout the state where we have a concentration of membership, aimed at reaching the total leadership and their spouses, Shop-Stewards, Committeemen, Delegates, Local and District Officers, wherein this leadership would have the opportunity to meet the Senator, talk with the Senator, have pictures made with the Senator.[52]

Some weeks later Ellinger sent Brown five checks, writing that "[o]ne is for $500 made payable to the Indiana State Council for your get acquainted receptions. The Committee also authorized an additional $1,000 after August 1."[53] In accord with the common procedure of most state councils, the Indiana State Council of Machinists was used as a surreptitious conduit for IAM support to Senator Hartke's campaign. GLR Brown had suggested MNPL money "be channelled through the State Council (Tony Hodges) Secretary, from which we can pay the bills upon proper receipts of proper expenditures. I will be meeting with Senator Hartke and his staff later this week to work out the date of his receptions."

MAINE: In August Ellinger wrote territorial GVP L. Ross Mathews that "Benjamin Dorsky, President of Maine COPE, has asked National Cope to request the assignment of Roger Hare to the campaigns in Maine."[55] Hare was not the only union representative requested by Dorsky. In a letter to National COPE, Dorsky reported:

I have made the verbal requests for assignment to Maine State COPE for the following persons:
Roger Hare—Machinists
Charles Sherburne—Boot and Shoe Workers
Al Camire—AFL-CIO, Staff Representative Boston Region
Edward Roach—UPP, Local 900, Rumford
Gary Cook—P.S. & P.M.W., Livermore Falls [56]

WISCONSIN: One of the marginal districts assigned by COPE to IAM was the Badger State's 1st Congressional District. Labor's goal was to defeat conservative Republican Henry Schadeberg and to elect Democrat Les Aspin. Special representative Tom Ferguson told of his work for Aspin:

I thought you might like a brief report on my activities as a Special Rep. while so assigned to assist in the election of Les Aspin to Congress in Wisconsin's 1st District.
Les was well aware from the beginning that he needed a big labor vote to win. He got it, as well as token support from disgruntled Republicans and independents. All the polls and people who should know about such things

had Les losing simply because he was not well known. We set out to change that by saturating the district with his name, pictures, materials, plant-gate visits, and personal appearances. We concenrated on areas that normally produced a Democratic vote, in hopes of increasing it enough to offset the other areas. My main duties in this effort were transporting Les and materials between cities, scheduling him for plant gates, appearing with him and for him wherever he could not be. We made Union meetings, social functions, shopping centers, city streets & stores, unemployment lines, bowling alleys, anywhere we could find crowds. He ran very hard and we all put in many long hours, but I am certain that we succeeded in smoking out thousands of votes for him. For the most, we ignored Schadeberg, presented Aspin's views on the issues. We pounded away at the economy and unemployment, which the incumbent refused to discuss. As his 30,000 vote margin indicates, Aspin would have won without my help. But he is well aware of the important part the Machinists played in his election, both in help and money. He is very grateful and I know he will support us in Congress. . . .[57]

IOWA: GLR William Fenton, assigned to the Iowa Congressional campaign, reported six weeks before the election:

In checking with the State Federation of Labor officers and other people working in the 1st District, it looks like Ed Mezvinsky, the Democratic Candidate for Congress, has over a 50 percent chance of winning. . . .

Congressman John Culver I am sure will win in the 2nd, but needs money badly. As you know, this is the District that is the Machinists' responsibility and to which I am assigned. We have the best program that I have ever seen, as all voters in the District have been canvassed. All friends are on computer cards and registration is well under way. . . .

In the 3rd Congressional District [w]e couldn't beat H. R. Gross in the landslide of 1964 so it doesn't look good. . . .

I have been working some in the 4th District, and at this time it is my opinion the Democratic Candidate Roger Blobaum will win and probably by a large margin. Blobaum is also working hard and there are three full time staff people from the AFL-CIO working full time on the campaign. . . .

I am real sure that Congressman Neal Smith will win re-election. If you can send me a check for the $250.00 to replace the $250.00 check I gave back to you in

Minneapolis, Minnesota. Smith is afraid of the check because it comes out of State, but would like for us to pay for some printing for him. . . .[58]

MARYLAND: After the election, which saw Republican J. Glenn Beall, Jr. elected to the Senate, GLR Philip Van Gelder wrote Don Ellinger:

As you know, we lost [Senator Joseph] Tydings in Maryland despite all the hard work of IAM and United Labor (AFL-CIO, UAW, Teamsters and RR) but won the two new Democratic Congressmen, Paul Sarbanes and Parren Mitchell (first black Congressman in history of Maryland). They are both high grade progressives. . . .
IAM Local 186 had a sound truck out operated by President Bielat and myself, and many members of the District 12 locals worked for the labor endorsed candidates before election and at the polls.[59]

CONNECTICUT: Perhaps the best summary of the political work done in the Constitution State by IAM and organized labor is found in an article titled "Internationals, Locals," published in the labor publication *Connecticut Vanguard* in December 1970:

A number of international unions assigned representatives to work with State COPE on a full or part-time basis during the fall election campaign.
State COPE Chairman John J. Driscoll praised their work on voter registration and on informing union members and their families of the crucial issues in the election. He also lauded the work of more than 400 local COPE workers who played a major role in the campaign.
The United Steelworkers assigned Frank Meehan of Bridgeport, who worked full-time in the Fourth Congressional District race.
The Machinists Union, in cooperation with the State Council of Machinists, assigned two representatives, Stephen Favreau of New Britain and Hank Zuilkowski of Middletown. Steve worked full time in the Sixth District while Hank was supposed to cover the Second District East of the Connecticut River. . . .
George Poulin, representing the Machinists Non-Partisan Political League, was in charge of Sixth District COPE campaigns and IAM Grand Lodge Representative Justin Ostro coordinated COPE work in the First District through the Greater Hartford Labor Council. Ostro has strong support from Bill Kuehnel and Ron Croke, both State Executive Board members.

The Third District campaign was coordinated by Vin Sirabella, president of the Greater New Haven AFL-CIO Council, and the Fifth by Ray Mengacci, president of the Naugatuck Valley Labor Council.

Meatcutters Local 371 lent the services of Ron Petronella, who helped on scheduling the statewide candidates.

The Fire Fighters assigned International Representative James King of New York, who worked in several locations around the state, including the Hartford primaries and the Fourth District general campaign.

"Corky" O'Connor of New Britain, president of the State Association of Uniformed Fire Fighters, was also assigned to work part-time with State COPE. He concentrated on the Sixth District.

The Textile Workers Union of America assigned Teddy Misiaszek, a staff organizer, who assisted in the COPE operation in the Sixth District. TWUA Eastern Joint Board manager Frank Gencarella and his aide, Dick Macfadyen, gave considerable help in the Second District.

The various city central labor councils assigned a large number of members for the final job of canvassing the voters and getting out the vote on Election Day.

The 400-plus COPE workers were engaged in hundreds of voting precincts, checking on union members whose names appeared on the voter-identification computer lists made available by National COPE. . . .

The grass-roots work of local unionists was a big factor in the Democrats' being able to salvage a majority in both Houses of the State Legislature, since the COPE workers reminded everyone they called to vote for the COPE endorsed candidates.[60]

1971

Although this was an off year as far as national elections were concerned, MNPL began its preparations for the 1972 congressional races. In November Don Ellinger informed the IAM Executive Council:

At the Marginal District Subcommittee meeting of AFL-CIO COPE, the Machinists were asked to accept the responsibility for 8 congressional districts, marking the special effort labor is making in a total of perhaps 50 districts in the country. The request is that each of the major international unions accept the responsibility in a congressional district to assign a staff member or to free a rank and file member beginning the first of January,

1972 to work in that district in cooperation with the AFL-CIO state and city central bodies and the COPE areas directors.[61]

In late December Ellinger sent a memorandum to six IAM staff members assigned by their GVPs to marginal congressional districts. The six and their assigned districts were GLR Charles Beyer, Connecticut 6th; GLR William Wolfe, new Texas district; GLR Harold Shean, California 34th; business representative John Heidenreich, Wisconsin 1st; GLR William Fenton and business representative Russell Fisher, Iowa 2nd.[62] Ellinger's memorandum also contained a statement of what was expected from each:

1. To consult with the state AFL-CIO and to inform those officers that he has been designated by the IAM to assist in the congressional district.
2. To meet with local central body officers and get their suggestion on how you can be most useful to them.
3. To get acquainted with the candidate and his campaign staff and discuss the strategy of reaching all labor unions in the district.
4. To make an assessment of the chances in the district and pinpoint the problems and send a report to us for transmittal to COPE, and to your state AFL-CIO or city central body.
5. To review the registration program in the area and to assist the state or local central body in improving registration.[63]

1972

In addition to throwing its support behind the Democratic Presidential ticket of McGovern-Shriver, the IAM was active in its assigned congressional districts and other key races.

TEXAS: Ralph Yarborough, who was defeated in the 1970 Democratic primary in his bid for reelection to the U.S. Senate, was making another attempt to capture the Democratic nomination, this time to oppose incumbent Republican Senator John Tower. Yarborough wrote Don Ellinger in January:

It is encouraging to know that Grand Lodge Representative William Wolfe will be assigned full time to my campaign. Where will he be? I have inquired of this in the State headquarters in 1970 and all of those whom I have been able to find over the telephone the last few days say that they do not know him and never saw him there. I only make that comment as you say that he "will

199

again be assigned." It is very important to me to know where he will be stationed and where I might reach him when he is so assigned. When will his assignment begin? . . . .

We hope he will work out of our State Headquarters here in Austin. We will need him beginning next week.[64]

NEW MEXICO: GLR Gilbert Padilla was appointed New Mexico labor coordinator for Hubert Humphrey for President. To get support for Humphrey so that he might win the state's Presidential primary, Padilla wrote MNPL director William Holayter:

We feel we can whip McGovern. I have named County Chairmen throughout the state that are real hustlers and political pros. Because of lack of funds and materials I am requesting that M.N.P.P.L. through the Merkil Press or whatever other means you may have, send me at least 50,000 Humphrey bumper stickers. Also a monetary contribution to the Humphrey Campaign of at least $2,000. . . .[65]

CONNECTICUT: The Nutmeg State's 6th Congressional District was a target marginal seat assigned to IAM. In May the president of the Connecticut State Council of Machinists wrote Holayter:

I am happy to hear that the Executive Council has authorized up to $2,500.00 for the Lost Time and expenses of Joseph Maksim to work in the Sixth Congressional District in Connecticut.

We have estimated that the cost of this project will be about $5,000.00 which will be shared by both of us.

Brother Maksim is to work on a part time basis up until August 1, 1972, and then on that date begin full time.

He will work with the Sixth Congressional District COPE and State AFL-CIO.[66]

WASHINGTON STATE: The IAM was also assigned responsibility for Washington's 4th Congressional District. International representative L. H. Thornton of the United Steelworkers of America wrote Holayter early in June:

You may know that I have been asked to coordinate our efforts in the marginal congressional districts in the western part of the U. S. in the Fall elections.

My listing indicates that your union is charged with

200

the responsibility of providing one of your members in this effort in the 4th congressional district of Washington. The list also indicated that Walter Berg has been assigned. I would appreciate it if you would confirm this appointment or give me the name of your appointee, together with address so that I might communicate directly with him.

I will be asked for periodic reports and will be visiting the area sometime early this Fall.[67]

Holayter reaffirmed to Thornton that Machinist Walter Berg had been assigned to Washington's 4th Congressional District.[68]

MASSACHUSETTS: GLR William Walsh had been assigned to coordinate the political activity of IAM with that of the United Automobile Workers in regard to the Massachusetts Labor Committee for McGovern-Shriver. He reported to Holayter:

Brother Olerio has advised me that UAW has assigned one full-time field representative and as of Monday, Sept. 25th 3 additional Representatives will be assigned to the Committee for the purpose of coordinating Local Lodge activities. In addition, UAW has donated a check in the amount of Fifteen Hundred Dollars ($1,500). . . .

In view of the foregoing, I request a donation of Two Thousand Dollars ($2,000) for the above subject committee. . . .[69]

KENTUCKY: Holayter responded to Joseph Rourke, assistant director or national COPE, in September:

Re: Manpower—Kentucky

In regard to your request for the services of Floyd Connors in Kentucky to work statewide in the Senate race. Floyd is a full time employee of District Lodge 53, Bowling Green, and as such is free to do whatever he can in the political race being restricted only by his local activities.[70]

What Is the Value of Assigned Services?

Can a dollar value be attached to the amount of time spent on political activities by IAM Grand Lodge and special representatives? The Washington, D.C., accounting firm of Yates & Ross attempted to do so for the plaintiffs in the *Seay* case. A team of the firms's accountants examined the weekly activity reports and expense vouchers submitted by IAM

GLRs and special representatives who receive salaries, employee benefits and expense reimbursement from the Grand Lodge. Yates & Ross concluded that the reports and vouchers were

> unable to develop complete schedules reflecting the political activities and expenditures of these Representatives. In addition, we were not able to determine the amount of political expenditures associated with the bulk of the approximately 750 IAM staff personnel who, as indicated by IAM correspondence and other documents, are engaged extensively in political activity for substantial portions of each year, but not required to report such activities.[72]

Despite this hindrance, Yates & Ross was able to develop, based on the material and documents that were available, partial schedules of expenditures associated with the political activities of IAM Grand Lodge and special representatives for the years 1968–72. Total yearly expenditures are found in Table VIII.

Table VIII*
Expenditures on Political Activities of IAM
Grand Lodge and Special Representatives
1968–1972

1968	$176,577.06
1969	80,825.75
1970	227,286.24
1971	57,317.38
1972	147,533.79

* Yates & Ross commented on its schedules:

> Political days were determined by evaluating the activities noted on "International Association of Machinists and Aerospace Workers Grand Lodge Representatives Weekly Activity Reports." To a limited extent other I.A.M. documents and correspondence were also used in determining political days. This was necessary because some reports contained vague, incomplete and misleading information. Considering the contents of other IAM documents reviewed and the aforementioned vague and misleading information, we do not believe that our schedules contain a complete listing of politically related days.
> Politically related days were scheduled when a Representative's time was spent propagating political doctrine,

concepts, ideologies and/or legislative programs. Whenever political activities were noted a minimum of one-half day was scheduled.[71]

The following schedule for 1972—a national election year —was compiled by Yates & Ross and shows IAM expenditures on political activities of Grand Lodge and special representatives:

Political Expenditures Associated
With the Activities of I.A.M.
Grand Lodge and Special Representatives
Calendar Year 1972

| Representative | Days of Political Activity | Politically Related Expenditures | | | Total Expenditures |
		Salary	Benefits	Expense	
Adams, A. T.	.5	$ 33.57	$ 10.59	$ *	$ 44.16
Almeida, George S.	13	823.55	264.11	332.10	1,419.76
Anderson, Dale	4	254.56	81.54	*	336.10
Aycock, T. B.	2	150.34	46.03	*	196.37
Barrett, Jr., Harold F.	9.5	637.74	204.27	336.38	1,178.39
Barstad, Elton P.	10.5	710.96	223.81	205.00	1,139.77
Berg, Walter E.	35.5	2,242.89	719.71	663.23	3,625.83
Berta, Dominic F.	3	201.39	63.54		264.93
Beyer, Charles E.	38	2,550.94	804.82	843.75	4,199.51
Blue, Daniel G.	10	671.30	211.80	339.99	1,223.09
Bourgeois, Valerie E.	1	57.95	19.08	*	77.03
Bowles, George E.	2.5	167.83	52.95	*	220.78
Brackin, Robert J.	6.5	436.35	137.67	229.70	803.72
Braden, Alton D.	2	134.26	42.36	*	176.62
Brandon, Forrest C.	.5	33.57	10.59	*	44.16
Brown, George M.	16	1,074.08	338.87	345.21	1,758.16
Brown, Robert H.	33	2,215.29	698.92	1,343.87	4,258.08
Buckholtz, George O.	1	67.13	21.18	*	88.31

204

Burnett, Jerome L.	4	268.52	84.72	*	353.24
Carrig, Edwin J.	7.5	503.48	158.85	165.00	827.33
Chatten, John D.	1	67.13	21.18	*	88.31
Christian, Harvey	2.5	167.83	52.95	*	220.78
Ciampolillo, Anthony F.	2	130.76	41.56	*	172.32
Cohen, Sidney	1	67.13	21.18	*	88.31
Comstock, Jr, Carroll P.	12.5	751.13	244.64	252.13	1,247.90
Courtney, John	.5	33.57	10.59	*	44.16
Cozad, Edgar E.	2.5	167.83	52.95	*	220.78
Cremona, Frank	.5	24.53	8.52	*	33.05
Daniels, John F.	1	67.13	21.18	*	88.31
Davis, Richard C.	35.5	2,383.12	751.87	992.05	4,127.04
Deckard, John M.	3.5	234.96	74.13	*	309.09
Donath, William J.	1	67.13	21.18	*	88.31
Downs, Donald E.	.5	33.57	10.59	*	44.16
Drennan, George	.5	30.22	9.82	*	40.04
Duff, Allen J.	1	67.13	21.18	*	88.31
Dunlap, Charles	1	67.13	21.18	*	88.31
E'Dalgo, Frank A.	25	1,678.25	529.49	585.19	2,792.93
Eichhorn, J. George	9.5	637.74	201.21	282.97	1,121.92
Faircloth, L. T.	5.5	369.22	116.49	199.20	684.91
Fairow, John E.	10	671.30	211.80	137.20	1,020.30
Fenton, William F.	11	738.43	232.97	175.20	1,146.60
Fitzgerald Woodrow W.	1	67.13	21.18	*	88.31
Foote, John D.	13	872.69	275.33	186.99	1,335.01
Friters, Theodore	.5	27.30	9.16	*	36.46

Subscribe Now To
UNIONS AND PUBLIC POLICY
A Report on Organized Labor

This confidential report, for readers who are leaders, goes behind the scenes into today's union movement. It provides up-to-date commentary on organized labor's economic and political plans and activities.

With organized labor the single most powerful influence in our government, no student of public affairs nor citizen interested in politics can afford not to read this important publication, the only one of its kind in the U.S.

Among the many topics covered in **UNIONS AND PUBLIC POLICY** are:

- Labor Bosses' plans for the 1976 elections

- Unions' legislative agenda for Congress in 1977

- How our election laws have been twisted to help the unions and their candidates.

- Management of union pensions—a national scandal?

- Drive to unionize all government employees

- Unions—Washington's most powerful lobby (the most powerful in state capitals also)

- How the union leaders use dues money to finance radical political, social and consumer groups

- Growing split between conservative and moderate rank-and-file and radical union leaders

- Why the Justice Department treats the union bosses with kid gloves

- Which members of Congress are union controlled

- Why the union movement will swing even further Left after Meany

. . . and scores of other topics dealing with contemporary union affairs.

UNIONS AND PUBLIC POLICY is investigatory reporting at its best. Edited by Douglas Caddy, Washington attorney and author of *The Hundred Million Dollar Payoff*, it is written in an objective, non-partisan style and employs facts, evidence and accurate analysis.

America has needed a report such as **UNIONS AND PUBLIC POLICY** for a long time. Many union leaders today are playing a key, perhaps *the* key, role in pushing our country to the Left, towards totalitarianism. **UNIONS AND PUBLIC POLICY** can awaken John Q. Public, including the rank-and-file union members who are politically moderate and conservative, to what is really happening and why.

Representative	Days of Political Activity	Politically Related Expenditures			Expenditures Total
		Salary	Benefits	Expense	
Gallagher, John L.	2	134.26	42.36	*	176.62
Gill, Cecil	1	67.13	21.18	*	88.31
Hammond, William A.	1.5	100.70	31.77	*	132.47
Harbron, Donald	6	392.28	124.67	160.40	677.35
Hare, Roger C.	42	2,819.46	889.54	1,133.94	4,842.94
Harrison, George W.	4	268.52	84.72	*	353.24
Harrison, O. C.	2	113.54	35.82	*	149.36
Hindle, Harold J.	.5	33.57	10.59	*	44.16
Hinman, Robert L.	2	134.26	42.36	*	176.62
Holly, William S.	1.5	100.70	31.77	*	132.47
House, Edgar M.	21.5	1,443.30	455.36	704.36	2,603.02
Hutto, Robert	.5	33.57	10.59	*	44.16
Johns, Allen F.	1	67.13	21.18	*	88.31
Johnsen, Robert E.	6.5	436.35	137.67	57.90	631.92
Johnson, Carl R.	6.5	436.35	137.67	102.60	676.62
Joly, Jean J.	1	67.13	21.18	*	88.31
Keele, William G.	1	67.55	21.27	*	88.82
Landers, Thomas A.	32.5	2,181.73	688.34	815.63	3,685.70
Long, O. R.	1	67.13	21.18	*	88.31
Luterotty, Samuel A.	1.5	100.70	31.77	*	132.47
Maddin, T. F.	3.5	234.96	74.13	*	309.09
Meacham, George E.	2.5	167.83	52.95	*	220.78
Mellott, Orr W.	.5	33.57	10.59	*	44.16

206

Yes, please enter my one year subscription to **UN-IONS AND PUBLIC POLICY,** edited by Douglas Caddy and published by the Public Policy Research Corporation. Subscription rate: $100 per year, for 24 issues.

☐ bill me
☐ bill my organization
☐ check enclosed (please make check payable to **UNIONS AND PUBLIC POLICY)**

Name _____

Organization _____

Street _____

_____

City _____ State _____ Zip _____

Postage
Will Be Paid
by
Addressee

Business Reply Mail

First Class Permit No. 72531   Washington, D.C.

Public Policy Research Corporation

1721 De Sales Street, N.W.

Washington, D.C. 20036

No
Postage Stamp
Necessary
If Mailed in the
United States

Merrill, Merritt J.	.5	32.69	10.39	*	43.08
Molen, Jarrett W.	1.5	98.07	30.94	*	129.01
McClendon, H. A.	3.5	234.96	74.13	*	309.09
McEvoy, George B.	1	67.13	21.18	*	88.31
McKimmey, Vernon E.	28.5	2,142.35	655.99	827.44	3,625.78
Norbeck, Walter F. J.	25.5	1,711.82	540.08	716.12	2,968.02
Ostro, Justin J.	81.5	5,288.54	1,684.40	1,002.76	7,975.70
Padilla, Gilbert	1	67.13	21.18	*	88.31
Page, Gerald D.	19	1,428.23	437.32	829.55	2,695.10
Paulson, C. Lowell	14	939.82	296.51	558.70	1,795.03
Peralta, Nep P.	10.5	657.30	214.74	392.04	1,264.08
Petrone, Peter	1	67.13	21.18	*	88.31
Pollard, John E.	.5	33.57	10.59	*	44.16
Pommerville, Dale S.	58	3,893.54	1,228.41	2,081.16	7,203.11
Popp, Peter	2	134.26	42.36	*	176.62
Poulin, George J.	31.5	2,114.60	667.16	1,034.10	3,815.86
Pryor, Jr., Merle E.	7	469.91	148.26	218.60	836.77
Quick, Houston B.	.5	33.57	10.59	*	44.16
Raines, Robert A.	3.5	234.96	74.13	*	309.09
Rogers, Coney E.	.5	33.57	10.59	*	44.16
Russell, Richard M.	3	201.39	63.54	*	264.93
Russell, Verle W.	6	402.78	127.08	153.64	683.50
Ryan, John M.	4	268.52	84.72	*	353.24
Sammon, Leo C.	1	67.13	21.18	*	88.31
Schenck, Billy E.	1.5	100.70	31.77	*	132.47
Scott, Loren D.	41	2,752.33	868.36	1,551.66	5,172.35

Representative	Days of Political Activity	Politically Related Expenditures			Total Expenditures
		Salary	Benefits	Expense	
Shaw, John K.	1	67.13	21.18	*	88.31
Shean, Harold	67	4,497.71	1,419.03	2,356.77	8,273.51
Smith, Thomas J.	8.5	570.61	180.03	330.67	1,081.31
Spencer, Roe	2	134.26	42.36	*	176.62
Stenzinger, Robert E.	21.5	1,443.30	455.36	427.00	2,325.66
Sullivan, J. W.	1	67.13	21.18	*	88.31
Summers, H. C.	6.5	436.35	137.67	151.80	725.82
Temple, Charles C.	21.5	1,443.30	455.36	196.60	2,095.26
Thayer, Harold E.	39.5	2,651.64	836.59	1,030.40	4,518.63
Tosti, Abraham L.	2.5	167.83	52.95	*	220.78
Van Gelder, Philip H.	21.5	1,443.30	455.36	366.60	2,265.26
Vogel, George	2	134.26	42.36	*	176.62
Waggoner, Fred L.	3	201.39	63.54	*	264.93
Wagoner, Jim D.	9	604.17	190.62	218.95	1,013.74
Walker, Alexander	4	268.52	84.72	*	353.24
Walker, Allin K.	1	69.81	21.79	*	91.60
Walsh, William E.	17	1,141.21	360.05	435.29	1,936.55
Ward, Herbert C.	148.5	9,968.81	3,145.16	4,128.26	17,242.23
Webb, Edward M.	1.5	100.70	31.77	*	132.47
Wharton, Donald E.	12	902.04	276.20	437.50	1,615.74
Williams, Clyde	1	67.13	21.18	*	88.31
Williams, Steven E.	1	67.13	21.18	*	88.31

208

		4,967.62	1,567.28	2,538.70	9,073.60
Wolfe, William S.	74				
Wright, Lloyd A.	2	126.70	40.63	*	167.33
Wright, Walter T.	3	201.39	63.54	*	264.93
TOTAL		$87,379.22	$27,580.27	$32,574.30	$147,533.79

* Politically related expenses were not determined for Representatives with less than five (5) days activity.

To provide the reader with a sampling of the multitude of political activities engaged in by IAM staff personnel, the summarized activity report of a single Grand Lodge representative for the year 1971 follows:

209

Representative—Justin Ostro
Annual Salary—$18,150.00

Year—1971
Daily Rate—$63.46

			Political Expense			Total
Week Ending	Description	Political Days	Per Diem	Incidental Allowance	Other	Political Expense
1/9	Met "various senators and representatives"	5	$ —	$ 4.00	$ 1.00	$ 5.00
1/16	State Labor Council Legislative committee Meeting-State Council of Machinists Political meeting	2.5	36.00	8.00	20.60	64.60
1/23	Met various State Senators & Reps. Re: AFL-CIO Leg. Program	1.5	24.00	4.00	3.00	31.00

1/30	Met various State Legislators, Cong. Cotter, and labor Leg. Groups	2.5	—	16.00	5.00	21.00
2/6	Meetings Sen. Muskie, State Demo. Chairman & various State Senators & Representatives	3	—	20.00	8.34	28.34
2/13	Met Senator Dinielli & Hartford Labor Council Re: Labor's Leg. Prog.	1.5	—	12.00	3.00	15.00
2/20	Met Nat'l COPE Rep. & Senator Smith	.5	—	4.00	1.00	5.00
3/13	AFL-CIO Leg. Meeting	.5	—	4.00	1.00	5.00
3/20	Legislative Hearing	.5	—	4.00	1.00	5.00
3/27	Legislative Activity—met Senate Majority Leader Ed. Caldwell	1	—	8.00	2.00	10.00
4/3	Met State Reps. & Senators	.5	—	4.00	1.00	5.00
4/10	Met Labor Reps. Re: "Labor's Candidate for City Council"	1	—	8.00	2.00	10.00
4/17	Met Labor Reps: Re: "Labor's Candidate for City Council & State Democratic Chairman"	1	—	8.00	2.00	10.00
4/24	Met various State Democratic Officials. Re: Legislation	1	—	8.00	2.00	10.00

5/1	Meetings concerning Governors appointments and politics	1	—		8.00	2.00	10.00
5/8	Met various State Democratic Officials	1.5	—		12.00	3.00	15.00
5/15	Democratic Caucus Re: Labor Candidate	.5	—		4.00	1.00	5.00
5/22	Meetings with State Legislators— A. Philip Randolph Meeting	3.5	—		28.00	7.00	35.00
5/29	Meetings State Democratic Officials Re: Legislative Programs	2	—		16.00	4.00	20.00
6/5	Labor Legislative Activity and MNPL function	1.5	—		12.00	9.60	21.60
6/12	COPE Conference—met Conn. Legislators	1.5	—		12.00	27.48	39.48
6/19	MNPL Activity	.5	—		4.00	1.00	5.00
6/26	A. Philip Randolph—met Senators & Labor Representatives Re: Legislation	1	—		8.00	7.64	15.64
7/3	COPE Conference	.5	—		4.00	7.64	11.64
7/10	MNPL & COPE Election preparation activity	.5	—		4.00	1.00	5.00
7/17	Met Senator Bayh's Assistant	.5	—		4.00	1.00	5.00
7/24	Congressman Cotter Re: Legislation	.5	—		4.00	1.00	5.00
7/31	Met city and union officials Re: Elections and A. Philip Randolph Programs	1.5	—		12.00	3.00	15.00
9/4	Met Hartford Mayoral Candidate	.5	—		4.00	1.00	5.00

9/11	Hartford pre-election activity with union & Democratic Officials	3	—	24.00	16.58	40.58
9/25	Meetings with Democratic Officials Re: Elections	1	—	8.00	2.00	10.00
10/9	COPE and Connecticut Democratic Meetings	1	—	8.00	2.00	10.00
10/23	COPE & Democratic Party meetings Re: Elections	.5	—	4.00	1.00	5.00
10/30	COPE Activity	1.5	—	12.00	14.28	26.28
11/6	COPE—Get-Out-The-Vote	.5	—	4.00	1.00	5.00
11/20	Met COPE Director	.5	—	—	1.00	1.00
12/4	West Hartford Democratic Function	.5	—	4.00	1.00	5.00
12/11	Meetings Re: Democratic Nat'l Convention	1	—	8.00	1.00	9.00
12/18	Meetings Re: Democratic Nat'l Convention and City Political Activity	1	—	8.00	2.00	10.00
	Expense totals	$60.00		$328.00	$172.16	$560.16

Salary   45 x $63.46/Day   2,855.70
Benefits   851.28

Total Politically Related $4,267.14

Conclusion

Much of IAM's political activity is conducted through approximately 48 state councils and conferences. These chartered subordinate bodies are subject to the administrative control of the national union.

The *raison d'etre* of the state councils and conferences is to carry out the union's legislative and political programs. Despite the obviously political nature of their activities, the councils and conferences are supported by per capita taxes levied on affiliated district and local lodges. This results in compulsory tax-free dues money being used to finance the partisan political activities of the councils and conferences.

Frequently the state MNPL is also subsidized by the state council or conferences. Thus compulsory tax-free dues money may be siphoned out of the district and local lodge treasuries to finance two Machinist political organizations operating within the state.

There is intimate cooperation between IAM and COPE, the political action arm of the AFL-CIO, in developing staff support in scores of crucial marginal congressional districts and other key congressional races. IAM Grand Lodge and special representatives have been assigned to the campaigns of these labor-backed candidates.

Candidates to whom Machinist staff personnal and union members are assigned are invariably Democrats. In many instances the candidates themselves directly approach the union to request that manpower be assigned to their campaigns.

Weekly activity reports filed by the Grand Lodge and special representatives, while vague and incomplete, reflect an average of hundreds of thousands of tax-free dollars spent annually on the salaries and expenses of these IAM staff personnel while they are assigned to political activity. Some of the Grand Lodge and special representatives spend from as much as one quarter to one half of the working year on political activity.

Voter-Registration and
Get-out-the-Vote Campaigns

One key to organized labor's success in electing its candidates on election day lies in its massive and sophisticated voter registration and get-out-the-vote campaigns. Hundreds of thousands of union staff personnel and members are mobilized to conduct these programs, which frequently provide the margin of victory for labor candidates.

IAM-MNPL places heavy emphasis on registering sympathetic voters, an emphasis that is highly selective. As Don Ellinger has admitted, MNPL does not encourage its workers to go into conservative voting areas to register voters.[1] Instead, the effort is directed at union members and their families, and at liberal voting blocs such as blacks and Chicanos. The net effect of this strategy is to register a vastly disporportionate percentage of voters who will vote for liberal and Democratic candidates.

Here is a sampling of the union's "nonpartisan" voter-registration and get-out-the-vote drives in recent years, drives that were financed primarily through tax-exempt dues revenue.

1968

GEORGIA: IAM's international president received the following telegram from the state coordinator of the Labor Committee for Humphrey-Muskie:

> Urgent. Urgent. All signs point to great opportunity to pick up Weltner Georgia Fifth District and Mackay Fourth District, and greatly improve our chances for a Humphrey victory provided we can get out the vote on November 5. This will take funds which we presently do not have. Please help in any way you can. Nonpartisan Get Out the Vote efforts are being handled by the Non-Partisan Get Out the Vote Committee, Suite 1422, 40 Marietta Street, N.W., Atlanta, Georgia 30303, and funds should be sent there.[2]

MNPL responded the day it received the telegram by sending a check for $200 payable to Georgia Get Out the Vote

214

Non-Partisan Committee.[3] Three weeks earlier MNPL had sent the same committee $250 as well as a $200 check payable to the Weltner for Congress Committee.[4]

CALIFORNIA: Territorial GVP E. R. White in August wrote all directing business representatives in California:

> For more years than I care to recall, I have warned that the right-wing movement would slowly strangle organized labor unless we were active in the political area 365 days a year. . . .
>
> Today, with the nomination of Richard Nixon for President, we face the grim reality that the knife will be twisted a little deeper in our backs. . . .
>
> I request that every Business Representative spend at least ten days between now and September 12th in a hard-hitting, comprehensive registration drive.[5]

HAWAII AND CALIFORNIA: GLR John Snider reported:

> I discussed the situation in Hawaii with Grand Lodge Representative George Bowles twice and he has advised me that the Congressional races have become complicated by the entrance into the campaign of Mayor Blaisdell of Honolulu, a Republican. Prior to his entrance into the campaign we had considered both Congresswoman Mink and Congressman Matsunaga as easy winners. However, Brother Bowles after conferring with our own representatives and representatives of the two candidates that we are supporting, advised me that he, in conjunction with other Labor representatives, are planning an all-out campaign. . . .
>
> One of the bright spots . . . was the highly successful registration drive of the Southeast part of Los Angeles County, which is predominantly colored and where Sam McAllister, of the Negro Labor Community Council, and our own Trudy Slaughter, registered with their crew more than 26,000 votes, 90 percent of whom were Democrat.[6]

VIRGINIA: Much of the Machinists' effort went into promoting the registration of blocs of liberal voters not connected with the union membership. An example of this partisan strategy shows in the following memorandum, which Don Ellinger sent to the MNPL Executive Committee. The committee approved this proposed recommendation:

> Walter Davis of the Seafarers' Union has called to ask if

we can help on the get-out-the-vote operation in Norfolk-Portsmouth, second district of Virginia. Barkan has put in $2,000. UAW has put in $400 and they are asking us for $400 of dues money to be used primarily in the Negro neighborhood under the supervision of COPE. I recommend that we do this.[7]

1969

WYOMING: Senator Gale McGee rated all-out union support in his reelection bid. Ellinger won the Executive Committee's approval of this recommendation:

Al Barkan has called to ask if we would help Gale McGee to the extent of paying for the key punching of 5,000 names of registered Democrats in Wyoming, and to put them in our machine as a service to him for mailings, registration, etc. The cost of key punching is 5.7¢ per name and can be done within a week for a total cost of $3,705. Machine time would be in addition and would run in the neighborhood of $500. In my opinion, this would all have to be general fund money and would be considered as a contribution toward the Gale McGee campaign, and is at his request.

Recommend: Since he is one of the top priority Senators we approve this expenditure to the limit of $4,500.[8]

Subsequently, MNPL contributed $500 to the Wyoming AFL-CIO for use in the organization's voter-registration program in behalf of the McGee campaign.[9] When the expenses were finally paid by MNPL for the McGee computer operation, they amounted to over $9,000 and were paid from the tax-exempt educational funds.

MINNESOTA: In September the Minneapolis-based political public relations firm of Valentine, Sherman and Associates submitted a written voter-registration proposal to the Minnesota Democratic–Farmer–Labor Party (DFL). The firm proposed, for a fee, to "have available on computer tape the names, addresses, party identification, and registration status of all persons in the state of Minnesota who have a telephone in their home." [10] The firm agreed to supervise and train volunteers for the information-gathering project. However,

The Democratic Party or the candidates will have to supply the volunteers and phones if the canvas is to be done by phone. We will travel to outstate areas to help organize this effort in cooperation with district or legislative district organizations, candidates, and the Democratic Party field men. . . .[11]

Norman Sherman wrote Ellinger that he "had hoped to 'tap' the Machinists for $10,000 for the project, in two payments, one in January or February, another, if we produce what we think we can, in the spring or early summer." [12]

Hubert Humphrey, who was running for the U. S. Senate in 1970, was extremely anxious that the Valentine, Sherman project be funded. He approached Ellinger, saying:

> I understand that you have received from Norman Sherman some material about a voter survey and registration project in Minnesota. I am deeply interested in this project and getting it started as soon as possible. I hope when Norman contacts you shortly that the Machinists will be able to participate in its financing.
>
> The project, by the way, has the support and cooperation of Senator Mondale, all the incumbent congressmen, and the state DFL office.[13]

There is ample evidence that other unions supported the Valentine, Sherman proposal even though it was designed to aid only one political party. James Cuff O'Brien, political action director of the Steelworkers, informed one of his union's officers:

> After the exchange of correspondence between Mr. Abel's office and the Vice President as well as the letters exchanged with you and my conversations in Pittsburgh on December 30th, I met with Norman Sherman. He provided me with materials and a complete review of the project recommended by Vice President Humphrey.
>
> It is worthwhile and I find that the Teamsters, the Machinists, and two or three other unions have so far pledged participation. It fits into our Voter Registration Program and relates well to other Minnesota matters that Mr. Abel has discussed with all of us. It would be expected that the cost we would be billed for by Valentine, Sherman and Associates would total $5,000 in February and $5,000 in May. I do, having examined the excellent preparations and highly professional approach, advocate as I had discussed with you on the phone that we proceed with this.[14]

MNPL subsequently did write at least one check for $1,000 payable to Valentine, Sherman and Associates for the Minnesota project. However, MNPL records are not clear whether the money was ever put toward the project. Nevertheless, the correspondence surrounding the proposal provides an illustration as to how union funds are used to underwrite a partisan voter-registration project.

1970

TEXAS: Because the Steelworkers is a strong union in the Lone Star State, James Cuff O'Brien was asked to go to Texas in January 1970 by COPE director Al Barkan, Frontlash executive director Charlotte Roe, Texas AFL-CIO president Hank Brown, and Ellinger. O'Brien's assignment was to survey the political scene and then propose what could be done by labor to help Senator Yarborough's reelection campaign. In his subsequent report to the Steelworkers Political Action Committee and to Barkan, O'Brien stated:

Nillson, who recorded the music for Midnight Cowboy, has a song that is titled "I Guess The Lord Must Be In New York City." It is hard to imagine that a God conceived in terms of grandeur and omnipotence would not look at Texas as more to his taste than New York City. A film like Easy Rider with its magnificent photography that synthesizes space and time into a feeling of limitlessness prepared you for what is there but only partially. It is just so damned big and so damned complicated.

On Wednesday, January 7, I went to Houston and met with Director Ward and Representative Ed Ball through a whole afternoon through which frequently we were joined by local union officers from various locals. Registration, which would end on the 31st of January, was the focal point. The Steelworkers would, it was agreed through Ed Ball, who was transferred back to Texas from Arkansas, maintain continued communication with the Texas Voter Registration Committee, the State AFL-CIO and the newly formed Mexican-American Registration Committee through the final and intensive effort on registration for the balance of January.

Maclovio Barraza, now with the Steelworkers Political Action Department, would be assigned to Texas for the balance of January and Chano Merino, formerly with the Steelworkers and now National COPE, would also move from New Mexico to Texas for full-time duty until registration was closed.

In addition, an agreement was reached that the

218

Steelworkers, through Director Ward's good offices, would absorb a sizeable portion of the Mexican-American Registration budget. Barraza and Merino are members of the Committee. . . .

On Thursday evening, we met again. This time with Ben Musselwhite and Ty Fain of Senator Yarborough's staff, Charlotte Roe of Frontlash, Maclovio Barraza and Chano Merino, Alfred Montoya and a number of other people concerned with registration . . . .

The following morning we met again for breakfast and then Chano Merino and I left for Corpus Christi. During the afternoon I met with Bob Harris, the counsel of the Senate Labor Committee, and other staff members preparing for hearings that Senator Gaylord Nelson would hold on Friday, January 9th. In the evening there was a registration rally and fishfry . . . . Senator Yarborough was in excellent form and his own morale was greatly buoyed by the event.

After our return to the hotel, I met at length with Senator Nelson who had arrived there and discussed the techniques he had used in his 1968 model campaign in Wisconsin hoping we could find ways of applying them to the Yarborough contest. However, the size and complexity of Texas plus lack of large sums of money were bound to contribute to the limits of what could be done along Nelson's lines . . . .

The attendance at the hearings in Corpus Christi in the county courthouse was massive—300 or more. More than size though what was exciting was the composition of the audience. The two most important elements were the Chicanos with their sun-leathered faces, faded denims and Western-style hats sitting side by side with mini-skirted students recruited by Frontlash for the Registration Drive. Television and radio and press coverage was excellent which was important because Senator Yarborough gets the highest percentage of votes here of any urban area in the State of Texas. I could not close this report without a special tribute to the young people. Mobilized through Frontlash, they had been in action weeks before I witnessed the operation. With magnificent efficiency, they were doing block by block canvassing and registration in the Mexican-American and working class areas. In teams with 30 or 40 involved on weekday nights and 75 to 100 on weekends, they were setting records for percentage of voters registered in seemingly impossible areas where previous history had shown a very low yield.

If through organized labor support we can multiply Frontlash-type youth projects around the country, we will be tapping a source of strength that has unlimited potential . . . .

The book would probably show that by any scientific measurement, we could not expect to win with Yarborough. Enthusiasm, heart and soul though may do in Texas what the politics of John Mitchell and Kevin Phillips can't.[15]

WYOMING: The IAM computer was used to prepare a list of the Equality State's 68,000 Democrats for Senator Gale McGee's reelection campaign. An official of the Wyoming State AFL-CIO informed the Machinists:

> When the printout came from the computer, the variety was staggering (red and green bordered cards in state and alpha order, print-out sheets in state alpha and alpha and county order), nevertheless the usefulness of all types of the printouts became apparent.
>
> The street order lists and street order cards were most useful for precinct canvass, voter registration and voter registration turnout on election day. Lists were also used to generate mailings to all unregistered Democrats and Independents from Senator McGee. Print-out cards were key in our election day procedures and we feel that they account in large part for the efficiency of our election day procedures. . .
>
> I cannot say enough for the help the Machinists have given us in this election. Not only with the computer system, but with your fine assistance in Gillette, Wyoming which, in my opinion, is the "Hell hole of Wyoming." [16]

Senator McGee and his campaign staff were equally pleased with the computer work performed by the IAM. Rod Crowlie, associate staff director of the Senate Post Office and Civil Service Committee, whose chairman is McGee, wrote Don Ellinger, "At the risk of being effusive in my thanks, I need to say how much both the Senator and I appreciate the help you have given us." [17] Crowlie submitted for Ellinger's perusal a McGee campaign document titled "A Brief Report Concerning Wyoming's Registration Drive with Particular Emphasis on the Role of the Computer." In some aspects the document provides a classic blueprint for the development of a voter-registration and voter-turnout strategy. For this reason portions of the report are reproduced in Appendix 16.

---

* See also Appendix 17 for "The Computer's Role in Getting out the Vote," from the *Federationist*, September 1973.

MARYLAND: Because of the strong support by organized labor, Senator Joseph Tydings (D) survived a challenge in the state's Democratic primary. Ten weeks before the primary, business representative Patrick O'Brien informed Ellinger of labor's political strategy to boost the Tydings vote:

> The unions in the Baltimore area of the Maryland AFL-CIO have adopted a program to get out the vote for Senator Joseph Tydings, with a minimum budget of $30,000. This budget is designed to provide 30 sound cars, 30 drivers, telephone banks to be located in 6 offices in Baltimore City and the surrounding area. It is my opinion that this is the minimal effort that Labor can make in the forthcoming primary so far as Senator Tydings and other Labor-endorsed candidates are concerned within the area cited.
>   . . . [U]nless an all out effort is made both with money and manpower in behlaf of Senator Tydings in the forthcoming primary, it appears without argument that Senator Tydings will not survive the primary.[18]

Shortly after receipt of O'Brien's letter, MNPL sent him $500 to be used in getting out the vote for Tydings.[19]

ARIZONA: When organized labor does cooperate, on those few occasions, in truly nonpartisan voter-registration drives, it usually does so because it is convinced that the increased registration will help its own candidates. Herbert Ely, the state chairman of the Democratic Party in the Grand Canyon State, solicited IAM financial support for just such a drive:

> . . . We would have a Republican co-chairman . . . and it would be a genuine non-partisan registration drive; there would be no hanky-panky about that . . . .
>   We would conduct the drive the last two weeks prior to the close of registration. Registration closes September 14th; therefore the drive would be conducted from September 1, to September 14th. As you can see your immediate attention is necessary if we are to get this off the ground. I'm sending a copy of this letter to Darwin Aycock, Secretary Treasurer of the Arizona AFL-CIO because I assume Al Barkan would be interested in helping if he could be convinced that the registration drive would be, not only important, but perhaps crucial to Orren Beaty and the senatorial candidate. Let me direct the rest of this letter as to just how crucial this registration drive can be. John Burke, myself, the Grossman people and all other knowledgeable politicians of Arizona believe an intense non-partisan registration

drive will add thousands of Democrats to the rolls for the general election. Most Republicans that are going to register have registered. Since 1966 approximately 97,000 registrants in Maricopa County (Phoenix) had their registrations cancelled and have not registered. About two-thirds of these are Democrats.

In our 85 key Democratic precincts approximately 40,000 have not registered since 1966. It is obvious that a two week registration drive will not put all these people back on the books but 30,000 Democrats is a projected figure. For the first time in history in this County, Republicans outnumber Democrats, but the difference is only about 5,000. We can easily overcome this difference with the type of drive we are talking about. Part of this drive would be directed to our Indian population and while it is difficult to estimate a precise figure as to how many new Democrats we can register, we believe that with a well directed drive we could have 5,000 to 10,000 from among the Indians.

What I am saying is simply this, a major registration effort could make the difference between winning or losing our senatorial and third congressional race and possibly gubernatorial race. If you are able to get this organized, I hope that we can implement this forthwith because time is of the essence.[20]

A few days after he received the Arizona Democratic chairman's letter, Ellinger replied:

I have just read your excellent letter on your proposed September 1 to September 14 registration effort. This will be placed before our Executive Committee which will meet the first part of next week and we will be able to give you a definite figure of what the Machinists can do toward your budget.

I am forwarding a copy of this letter and yours to James O'Brien of the Steelworkers, Alexander Barkan of COPE, and Bernard Rapoport of the American Income Life Insurance Company.[21]

INDIANA: William Holayter has described the A. Philip Randolph Institute as "a group with whom we are working closely." [22] The relationship between the tax-exempt institute and organized labor's political activities is elaborated upon by GLR Robert Brown:

The A. Philip Randolph Institute has begun a nonpartisan registration drive in the black wards and precincts in Indianapolis. The black vote could well determine if Andy Jacobs is returned to Congress.

Labor has furnished seven full time people to assist the Randolph Institute and has provided some funds to hire a receptionist and two sound trucks. However, if they are to accomplish the job of registration as well as getting out the vote, the Institute will need additional funds.[23]

The A. Philip Randolph Institute, like organized labor, conducts its voter-registration drives in a rigidly partisan manner. Norman Hill, associate director of the institute, describes it this way:

> Trade unionists and civil rights activists have good reason to be concerned about the outcome of the 1972 elections. It is essential that liberals elect a President and Congress that will respond to the needs of workers, the poor and minorities. If we are to elect a pro-Negro and pro-labor Congress we must continue to organize now to insure a heavy liberal vote.[24]

1972

ILLINOIS: GLR Loren Scott, in requesting certain lodge membership lists for registration purposes, told Ellinger:

> As a result of a series of meetings and conversations I have worked out a cooperative voter registration and get-out-the-vote effort with, National Farmers Union, Illinois Education Association, Am. Fed. of State, County, and Municipal Employees Union, and several student groups. Rather than overlap in our effort we plan to assign specific precincts to different organizations for registration. National Farmers Union and AFSCME each have a full time person already working on the program covering about one-half of down state Illinois, and they are being tremendously effective . . . .
>
> All these Lodges are in the new 22nd Congressional District in which George Shipley will be our candidate. They will also be critical to the success of Gubernatorial candidate Paul Simon, and Senatorial candidate Roman Pucinski.[25]

VIRGINIA: In October William Holayter was alerted by the president of the Virginia State Machinists Council that

> we have received a request from the Democratic Com-

223

mittee for cars on Election Day. We have also received a request from the Chesapeake Forward, a black civic league, to furnish cars and drivers to take people to and from the polls.

We are trying to turn out the largest vote ever for McGovern and Spong and we want to furnish cars for Norfolk, Portsmouth, Chesapeake, and Virginia Beach. We will need about thirty-two cars for the four cities. The last time we used this sytem was for the Howell campaign which was very successful.

The last election, we coordinated this from my office and we paid each driver $25. for twelve hours driving, from the time the polls opened to the time they closed.[26]

Within a week MNPL responded: "As per your request, the Executive Committee of MNPL voted to contribute $750 for the expenses of 32 cars to be used to get-out-the-vote. Each driver is to receive $25 for the day . . ." [27]

IAM's consistent practice of funding voter-registration and get-out-the-vote drives to aid candidates of only one of the major political parties is a misuse of the organization's tax-exempt status and could violate other federal statutes. But the union persists, despite this legal warning from its own general counsel: "It is my personal opinion after examining Section 313 of the Federal Corrupt Practices Act that where we use our own dues monies for the purpose of getting out a vote against one candidate or another, that that constitutes an expenditure in violation of Section 313 of the Corrupt Practices Act." [28]

Conclusion

Union voter-registration and get-out-the-vote drives, financed by tax-exempt Machinist dues money, aim only at blocs of voters that will support liberal and Democratic candidates.

IAM's computer provides voter-registration information to labor-backed candidates.

MNPL's tax-exempt Educational Fund has paid for get-out-the-vote drives, during which cars, drivers, sound trucks, and telephone banks are used to ensure a maximum turnout of voters sympathetic to union-backed candidates.

The Grand Lodge tax-exempt treasury pays the salaries, employee benefits, and expenses of union personnel assigned to voter-registration and voter-turnout projects.

8

IAM-MNPL's Cooperation With Political Groups, Liberal Candidates, and the Democratic Party

In national election years, IAM frequently sponsors schools for teaching campaign techniques and strategies to its staff personnel and members. Three such institutes on political techniques, under IAM auspices, were held in 1968: at Rutgers University in New Jersey, at the University of Wisconsin, and at the University of California (Berkeley). In April 1968 Don Ellinger informed the IAM Executive Council that 115 congressional races had been designated as marginal congressional districts and many of these "are the battleground for 1968." He continued:

> As part of the Action Program we have set up 3 training schools at which we hope to give the latest political techniques and information to key leaders in each of these Congressional Districts or other districts which later become essential. . . .
> These institutes are designed as a post graduate course for those who will take a leading role in a Congressional District race.[1]

It is useful to study the institutes in order to apprehend what IAM is attempting to accomplish by sponsoring such meetings. The IAM Institute of Political Techniques at the University of Wisconsin was held July 7–12, 1968. A month before the meeting Ellinger wrote the president of the Wisconsin State AFL-CIO:

> . . . Attending this conference will be full-time staff members of our union who will be assigned to political activity in various key congressional districts in your State and throughout the nation. . . .
> We would like to invite you to speak to our institute, . . . Specifically, we would like you to discuss the political role of the State Federation and Local Central Bodies and the need for cooperation among the various unions in the particular locality. This is a practical program designed to field a better prepared political staff than we have done before. . . .[2]

225

In still another letter that month Ellinger told the COPE area director about the Wisconsin conference: "We will have from 30 to 40 of the best political operators we can get together in the country. We hope that this program will produce a more efficient and effective campaign in 1968." [3]

Thirty-six Machinists did attend the Wisconsin institute. Five of these were GLRs and the rest were representatives of various districts and local lodges. The institute's staff comprised six members of the university's faculty, four IAM officials, the president of the Wisconsin State AFL–CIO, Ohio Democratic senatorial candidate John Gilligan, COPE director Al Barkan, COPE area director Richard Fallow, Robert Maurer of the labor political public relations firm of Maurer, Fleisher and Zon, and a representative from each of the following organizations: NAACP, Wisconsin Rural Electric Co-op, the Humphrey for President campaign, and the National Council of Senior Citizens.

The institute's agenda included workshops on voter registration, opinion polling, mass media, campaigning, and use of the IAM computer.

The makeup of the institute's staff, attendees, and agenda gains added significance when one recognizes that this conference, as with other IAM political schools, is regarded as educational by the union and paid for with tax-exempt union treasury money. Yet there is little doubt that the schools actually are used to spawn union workers for partisan political campaigning in all sections of the country.

In 1970, three similar political conferences were sponsored by IAM, this time being called (more appropriately) campaign caucuses. MNPL co-chairmen Floyd Smith, Eugene Glover, and Charles West issued in January 1970 a memo to "All Local and District Lodges in the United States" that declared:

> The three campaign training caucuses have been planned by the IAM Education Department and the MNPL for IAM leaders who will be working in a campaign this year. They are designed to put a keen edge on the political skills and knowledge that you already possess by professional advice and workshops in polling, mass media, working with other groups, spending money efficiently, and planning a campaign from start to election day.
>
> Checks covering the tuition. . . should be made payable to the MNPL Educational Fund. [4]

Don Ellinger authored several additional letters also in January 1970 about the campaign caucuses. The contents of these missives further flesh out the purposes and motives behind IAM's sponsorship. In the first, to GVP William Winpisinger, he stated:

> We have asked the territorial General Vice Presidents to assign Grand Lodge Representatives to assist in getting Business Representatives or outstanding rank and file leaders to participate in these 3 conferences. Hopefully all the participants will be made available full time for at least the last 3 months of the campaign in which we will have major responsibility.[5]

From GVP Gilbert Brunner, Ellinger requested:

> In your territory we would greatly appreciate the assignment of Loren Scott, Walter Norbeck, William Fenton, Dale Pommerville, Kenneth Holland, and James Malott. We are fully aware of the other demands on your staff's time, but we have to, if possible, elect Adlai Stevenson and Hubert Humphrey, and to reelect Quentin Burdick, Bill Proxmire, and Stuart Symington.[6]

In the third letter, to the president of Local Lodge 1487 in Des Plaines, Illinois, Ellinger suggested:

> In view of the importance of the Stevenson campaign and one of the few places in America where we can pick up a Senator, we believe that Local Lodge 1487 should select an outstanding officer or rank-and-file member to participate in the Campaign Caucus at the University of Missouri at St. Louis, April 19–24, with the expectation that this person will be made available full time for at least the last 3 months of the campaign.[7]

If IAM sticks to its tradition, it will continue to sponsor future political training schools for the purpose of turning out skilled workers for the campaigns of labor-endorsed candidates. Unless IAM alters its practice, the expenses of these schools will be borne by the tax-exempt IAM treasury and by the tax-exempt treasuries of the local and district lodges that send representatives to attend. These biennial political schools have become an important pipeline through which IAM provides trained manpower for political campaigns.

The overriding political strategy of IAM is to aid and supplement Democratic Party organizations, on the national, state, and local levels. Evidence of this has been cited in earlier chapters, which showed how the union's financial and manpower resources are mobilized for political action. This concluding part of the study of IAM-MNPL deals with specific striking examples of how the union, despite giving lip service to being nonpartisan, has in the past and is at present working to aid solely liberal candidates and the Democratic Party. Again we shall confine our study to the years of 1968–72.

1968

IAM's leadership was an early and strong supporter of Hubert Humphrey for President once Lyndon Johnson had announced his intention not to run for reelection. A delegation of 12 IAM officials, including almost the entire IAM Executive Council, visited the Democratic National Convention in Chicago. Afterwards, these leaders committed the union's resources to Humphrey's campaign. Humphrey himself was deeply appreciative of the union's support and did not hesitate to express his gratitude. He wrote the president of the California Conference of Machinists soon after his nomination:

> I want you and all of the leadership and members of the Western States Conference of Machinists to know how much I appreciate your fine support at the National Convention, and also to learn how ably Norman Paul presented our case at the conference in Las Vegas which I unfortunately could not attend.
> We now face an uphill fight, but this will keep us on our toes. With the help of good people like yourself and the working support of organizations like the Machinists, I know we will win! [8]

The IAM organization sprang to life in all sections of the country to aid Humphrey. GVP Gilbert Brunner assigned two staff persons to attend the founding of the New York State Labor Committee for Humphrey. Don Ellinger wrote Mary Zon, who had temporarily switched from COPE to work at the labor desk of the Democratic National Committee, asking for a speaker to address the New England Council of Machinists. An article in a California Machinist publication reported that "IAM Vice President Ernie White this week charged representatives of 160,000 California Machinists to lead the membership to a Democratic victory Nov. 5 that 'will save the economic and social programs which have made this country' a great nation." [9]

In October the MNPL Executive Committee received the following:

We have a telephone request from Mel Fish, AFL-CIO Maritime Committee, for financial assistance to pay a bill for $2,600 incurred by "tools for victory committee" for flashing type lapel badges for Humphrey-Muskie. This order has been placed at the request of Nordy Hoffman, Democratic Senate Campaign Committee. . . .[10]

The MNPL Executive Committee promptly authorized $500 toward paying the bill.

Another MNPL check was sent in response to the following letter from Eric Schmidt, boycott coordinator, United Farm Workers, AFL-CIO:

With the up-coming election being so vitally important to the farm workers, we would like to do our part. Our Philadelphia office at this time has the manpower but lacks the finances. We would like to ask for one hundred dollars for the partial payment of anti-Nixon buttons we have ordered.

We are looking forward to any help we can receive from you in our efforts to elect Humphrey and to boycott grapes.[11]

Still the IAM headquarters continued to receive troubling reports of discontent among the rank and file. GLR H. A. McClendon reported from Tennessee after the election:

A member of another union hand-billed our largest plant and the Business Representative was elsewhere. We, through the cooperation of the local Lodge President, managed to keep Wallace supporters from having a straw vote at the Avco Plant in Nashville. Lodge 1501 managed to keep Wallace people from making a local endorsement of Wallace but his supporters tried on three consecutive meetings. During our strike at Combustion Engineering in Chattanooga, we saw at least 2,000 Boilermaker members cross our picket lines with Wallace bumper stickers, still our members who were on strike in the main voted for Wallace.[12]

The recording secretary of a local lodge in South Carolina sent a letter that had been signed by 87 lodge members protesting the Machinist leadership's support of the national Democratic ticket:

Having duly read and considered the proposals in your memorandum of October 18, 1968, the undersigned

229

members of Local No. 1002 of the International Paper Co. of Georgetown, S.C. wish to respectfully submit that:

1. We feel the request for a blanket support of the Humphrey-Muskie ticket is asking us to sacrifice the privilege of voting for our individual choice for President and Vice President of U.S.A.

2. We are not in accord with the plan to use union funds in any manner in an effort to influence an individual to vote other than for his personal choice for highest offices in the nation.

3. We feel that the pending elevation in union dues would not be necessary if treasury funds had not been committed for partisan political purposes.[13]

Yet the IAM hierarchy pressed forward determinedly for Humphrey's election. As election day approached, it became obvious that the gap between Nixon and Humphrey was being closed. This led the three IAM executive officers to send the following telegram to key Machinists assigned to the campaign:

We have secured advance information usually reliable that final polls will show the election so close that the results cannot be predicted. What is done over the weekend and on election day can make the difference. Humphrey and Muskie now lead in Maine, Massachusetts, Rhode Island, New York, D.C., West Virginia, Michigan, Minnesota, New Mexico, Washington and Hawaii for a total of 123 electoral votes. The nine (9) states that are considered even are: Connecticut, Pennsylvania, Ohio, Tennessee, Florida, Wisconsin, Texas, Missouri and California with a total of 177. If we can win eight (8) of these nine (9) states, we have a friend in the White House. Urge all possible effort in all states, but we need superhuman effort in these nine (9).[14]

IAM political activity in 1968 was concentrated not solely on the Presidential campaign. Support was provided in these key congressional races also:

OKLAHOMA: George Nelson, IAM legislative representative on Capitol Hill, reminded GLR G. W. Flinn in July:

You will recall that at our last MNPL Executive meeting, Tuesday, July 16, a donation of $500.00 was authorized to assist House Majority Leader Carl Albert in his primary campaign.

I attended a meeting of labor groups which had been

called for the Congressional Hotel that afternoon and due to the fact that Carl Albert comes from a 95-percent rural area and also because his opponent is charging him with being "a tool of the labor bosses," it was unanimously agreed that Richard Dell, Washington representative for the National Rural Electric Cooperatives, would act as treasurer of the Carl Albert Campaign Committee.

Also, under state law, Carl Albert does not have to report any donations of less than $500.00 until after the primary; therefore, would you please draw a check in the amount of $499.00 made out to the "Carl Albert for Congress Committee" and send to Richard Dell, P. O. Box 19066, Washington, D.C.[15]

Within a week after the above memorandum was written, MNPL sent a check to Richard Dell "for $499 payable to the Carl Albert for Congress Committee, of which you are Treasurer." [16]

Today Carl Albert is Speaker of the House of Representatives and is second in line to become President if that post becomes vacant.

INDIANA: GLR Robert Brown in March reported to Floyd Smith:

. . . U.S. Senator Birch Bayh: I have met with the Senator and his Indiana and Washington Staff and completed programing the forthcoming election drive, which of course will change from time to time; the Senator is very happy about the efforts of yourself and the Executive Council on his behalf. He wants me to act as his Contact man with the rest of the Labor movement in Indiana. . . .[17]

OREGON: For years IAM has been a power in Oregon politics. It has backed the campaigns there of a number of successful candidates for federal offices. In 1968 the union again attempted to perpetuate its influence by backing Robert Duncan for U.S. senator. The strategy to get Duncan elected actually began in 1967, when the union asked Bardsley and Haslacher, Inc., a public opinion polling firm, to take a poll to sound out Duncan's strength with the voters. The firm completed its poll and sent to the IAM "a billing for $6,000 for political research on behalf of Bob Duncan." [18] The bill was paid with tax-exempt monies from the MNPL Educational Fund despite the partisan purpose of the poll.

Later, Duncan was invited to address the National Planning Committee in January 1968. His remarks were reprinted by

MNPL—which used (once again) tax-exempt monies from the Educational Fund to pay the bill—under the title "A Senator for the 1970s." According to this brochure, Duncan concluded his remarks before the NPC by saying: "I am delighted that a part of Machinists planning for the political future includes Duncan and the Senate race in Oregon. You will be helping in a major way in that race. We are going to win this election." [19]

Although the MNPL poured more than $12,000 into Duncan's 1968 race and additional manpower support, he was not victorious. When four years later Duncan made another attempt to run for U.S. Senate, MNPL again helped to finance a public opinion poll to gauge his public support.

1969

INDIANA: Senator Birch Bayh, who had been victorious in his reelection effort in 1968, continued to receive tax-exempt union contributions for his campaign deficit during 1969. The senator's administrative assistant wrote Don Ellinger four months after the election:

As you know, Senator Bayh won re-election last fall. The campaign was an expensive one, and, frankly, we ended with a deficit. I know how difficult the 1968 campaign was for all national candidates and I realize that the voluntary dollars of yours and all other unions were exhausted in the effort.

Several unions have been able to be extremely helpful in using dues money to purchase copies of the Senator's book, *One Heartbeat Away*, for use in their individual education programs. We are making available a special edition, which will be individually autographed by the Senator, at a cost of $10.00 per copy. I would hope that you could find it possible to purchase a number of these educational books for your union's program.

A few days later Ellinger responded: "Attached is our check for $600 for 60 copies of the book of Senator Birch Bayh, 'One Heartbeat Away.'" [21]

VIRGINIA: The Old Dominion allows compulsory dues money to be spent in campaigns for state offices. In 1969, as in 1973, labor's candidate for governor was Henry Howell, a liberal who also projected a populist image to the voters. The total of all contributions from labor organizations to the 1969 Howell gubernatorial campaign exceeded $50,000, most of which was union dues money. Even though Howell was not running for federal office, MNPL contributed $500 to his campaign, after Ellinger had written two officials of the Virginia Machinists Council:

> We have received a request for financial support for the Governor's race in Virginia. The Virginia State AFL-CIO has endorsed and is supporting Henry Howell. Contributions for a Governor's race may be made from local or district lodge treasuries and the National League does not normally become involved in Governor's races unless there is a direct bearing on a Congressional or Senate race. . . .
> Senator Howell is a proven friend of labor and we would like your recommendation on what you think the National League should do.[22]

TEXAS AND WYOMING: Up for reelection in 1970, several senators from these states began receiving Machinist help in 1969 in the form of transportation back home. In March 1969 Ellinger wrote Senator Yarborough:

> We were able to get the tickets that we discussed on the telephone yesterday, but I would like to clarify our procedure. We have instructed our office to clear with your designee Gene Godley on all transportation matters concerning travel to and from Texas to meet with our leadership. . . .[23]

In April Ellinger reported to territorial GVP Charles West:

> We met yesterday with Senator Gale McGee of Wyoming to plan his campaign for re-election. Fred Harris, Democratic National Committee Chairman, and Al Barkan participated along with representatives of a number of unions. In accordance with the action of the Executive Committee, I have notified Senator McGee that we would make available 2 round trip airplane tickets back to his state upon his request. . . .[24]

MNPL tapped tax-exempt monies from its Educational Fund to pay for the candidates' transportation.

WASHINGTON STATE: Congressman Lloyd Meeds (D) is frequently a recipient of IAM dues money for his political activities. For example, in July 1969 Ellinger wrote his Executive Committee:

> Lloyd Meeds, Congressman of the 2nd District of

Washington, still has a campaign deficit. He is on the Education and Labor Committee and many organizations in the city, if given the opportunity, would participate in helping him raise the $3,000 or $4,000 he needs.

Walter Mason of the Building Trades Department, Al Chesser of the United Transportation Union and I have discussed this matter and would like to jointly sponsor a reception inviting the participation of all labor unions in the city and other interested organizations. The cost would be approximately $100 each. The proposed date would be July 30, and I would hope we could do it in our auditorium to minimize costs. The 3 sponsoring organizations would pay the cost of light hors d'oeuvres and drinks and issuing of invitations. Al Barkan agreed with this procedure.

Recommend: The MNPL share the cost of the reception for Lloyd Meeds at the Machinists auditorium, 5:30 P.M., July 30. Tickets are $25 each and we would purchase 10 tickets.[25]

The fund-raising event for Meeds took place as scheduled, on July 30, and $1,600 in contributions was collected from 10 union representatives and presented to Meeds.

On August 1, 1969, Ellinger wrote Al Chesser, who had been a co-host:

The total costs of the other evening were $113.40 for liquor, and $225.90 for food, bartenders, ice and mixers.

One half of this amount is $168.65. We will pay the bills and you can reimburse us. We are using dues money to pay these expenses.[26]

ILLINOIS: In July Ellinger wrote Senator Fred Harris, chairman of the Democratic National Committee, of his hope for a Democratic victory in the special election in Illinois' 13th Congressional District. The seat had been vacated by Donald Rumsfeld when he joined the Nixon administration. Harris responded appreciatively to Ellinger's letter:

Thank you so much for your recent letter on the 13th Congressional District in Illinois.

I agree whole-heartedly with you that a Democratic victory in this District would be a truly remarkable and satisfying achievement.

Furthermore, I want to thank you for your indispensable help in the previous elections as well as for your wise counsel to both Mark Shields and myself.[27]

CALIFORNIA: In November Ellinger visited California and reported to the MNPL Executive Committee:

In recent weeks, I have attended the California Conference of Machinists and the Project 70 statewide meeting of the Democratic Party. At both of these meetings I visited at length with IAM and party leaders regarding the situation in California. My conclusions are:
. . . There will be at least 3 Congressional vacancies in 1970 because George Brown and John Tunney are running for the Senate and Don Edwards has announced his retirement. Both of these seats will take substantial effort to be held. In addition, Dick Hanna and Glenn Anderson are in very marginal districts and will require special effort. These 5 races should be priority targets for the IAM in 1970.
The control of the Legislature is so close that a switch of 2 Senators or 4 Legislators will give either house to the Democrats. Because the 1970 census will give California 6 New Congressmen, it is vitally important that at least one house of the Legislature be controlled by the Democrats. Therefore, the National League should urge concentration in California on 4 Senate seats that can be taken and 8 possible legislative seats.
The coalition which can spell victory for the Democratic party must include labor, Negroes, Mexican-Americans, students, individual liberals of the Democratic club variety and organizational court house politicians. At the present time, the spokesmen for these groups are so bitterly divided that I see little prospect of them being put back together on a statewide basis particularly after bitter primary elections.[28]

1970

CALIFORNIA: Despite Ellinger's pessimism about forging an alliance among the warring factions of the state's Democratic Party, IAM-MNPL showed no hesitation in committing its resources to the election of John Tunney (D) and the defeat of Senator George Murphy (R). MNPL published a brochure whose contents clearly reflected a pro-Tunney bias. Thousands of copies of the brochure were sent by MNPL to California for distribution and these, in turn, engendered requests for more copies. The business representative of District Lodge 1578 in California wrote Ellinger, "We would appreciate it if you could send our district 10,000 or 15,000 so we can blanket certain areas for support of Tunney." [29] The brochure cost the

IAM $2,506.77. The California MNPL paid $390.35 and the national MNPL paid the balance—$1,740.75 from its tax-exempt Educational Fund and $375.67 from its General Fund.[30]

As Democratic candidate for the congressional seat being vacated by John Tunney in his bid for the Senate, Dave Tunno requested Machinist help in his campaign. He wrote Ellinger that "Floyd Melton is a man who knows this district like the back of his hand. He can be of great help not only to my campaign, but to John Tunney's campaign." [31] Subsequently, IAM "assigned one of its B.A.'s full time from now to the election to Tunno's campaign." [32]

Machinists were assigned to other congressional races as well. GVP Robert Simpson wrote directing business representative Virgil Pergram of District 1578: "As of this writing it is our understanding that besides yourself, Business Representative Loomis, C. Hester and Mercy Lizarraga will be active in the campaigns" in the 17th, 34th, and 38th Congressional Districts.[33] The District Lodge 94 business manager informed Simpson: "I will assign Business Representative Thomas R. Burniston to work in any capacity and for the time needed to re-elect our friend, Congressman R. Hanna." [34]

Congressman Richard Hanna (D) is another frequent recipient of IAM support, and his 1970 campaign offers several examples of this. On June 1, 1970, Hanna wrote Ellinger of a proposed voter-registration program that Hanna deemed vital to his election: "With the intensive registration drive we plan to wage we hope to raise the district to at least 53.5 percent Democratic. We feel this can be accomplished because most of the unregistered voters are Democrats." [35] The voter-registration project was three-pronged; Hanna noted:

The third part of the program is directed at unregistered Union Members. Through the coordination of your IAM locals, COPE and our office we hope to have a list of each unregistered union member by local. By June 30, we will have a resources survey completed and know exactly to what extent each union can register its own members. We are arranging to have at least one deputy registrar at each hall and shop. By June 30, we will know the union resources, and the requirements and will fill in the gaps with both paid and volunteer Party registrars.

In addition to the above program, we are running a separate, but coordinated, intensive registration effort in the fairly large Mexican-American barrio in the 34th District. We are not including this effort as part of the budget we are submitting to you because of the strong

236

support we anticipate (and have always had in the past) from the Laborers' Local in Santa Ana. The registration effort in Santa Ana will be largely under their auspices with the broad leadership of the Mexican-American community participating. . . .

Hanna then requested that the IAM "arrange for financial support" amounting to $6,000 to meet the costs of the voter-registration drive. MNPL responded, sending a check for $500.[36] Later, Machinist manpower was assigned to work in the Hanna campaign.

After his reelection, the successful Hanna expressed his gratitude for IAM support:

My warm appreciation and strong thanks goes to you and your organization for the support and assistance rendered in our recent campaign. I hope you will take an appropriate supply of my abundant satisfaction in our victory. Jim Quick, Bernie Swisher and George Spear were really great on the campaign trail and we used their good offices in an effective manner. We send a special thanks to these gentlemen and will recall fondly the productive relationship we had with them.[37]

Hanna was not the only Democratic Congressman in California receiving IAM help. The secretary-treasurer of District 720 reported:

Two years ago we elected Glenn Anderson to Congress from the 17th District and we intend to re-elect him in November. When I say we, I mean a group including men from the Maritime Unions, myself from the Machinists, and others from various unions in this area. Anderson has this solid backing from true unionists and he works with us in a personal hardhitting campaign.[38]

Subsequently a Machinist worker in the Anderson campaign was advised by Ellinger:

You can get, through the State AFL-CIO, a run of all the registered voters on the list there. Since their computer list will be used as walking list and for getting out the vote, it is important that you correct the errors so that the names now on your registered list can be put back where they belong. Bill Holayter will be coming to California about the 1st of September to be of what assistance he can in your absolutely vital job of registration.[39]

ILLINOIS: On November 3, 1970, business representative Guy Stubblefield reported to International President Smith on the Senate race in his state:

> During the week of October 26th, both Brother Name and I organized our political activity in behalf of Adlai Stevenson III. All Lodge No. 1553 plants were hand-billed on either Thursday or Friday and leadership in the plants was encouraged to work in their own respective neighborhoods.
>
> Approximately 4,000 copies of the Adlai material furnished by the Machinists were distributed to and by I.A.M. members. Additionally, 3,000 copies of the Adlai material were furnished to other labor unions through the Central Body. Our members distributed over 2,000 copies of the Stevenson material supplied by State AFL-CIO.[40]

NORTH DAKOTA: MNPL educational funds had been used to publish and distribute brochures praising the public records of Senators Albert Gore (D) Tennessee and Ralph Yarborough (D) of Texas. In April William Holayter wrote Senator Quentin Burdick (D) of North Dakota: "Enclosed is a copy of the pamphlet we did for Senator Gore and Senator Yarborough that you and I discussed on the airplane returning from Minnesota. If we can be of any service to you along these lines, let me know and I will look into it." [41]

NEW MEXICO: In September, MNPL published another campaign brochure, this time for Senator Joseph Montoya (D) of New Mexico. The Machinists offered to make the printing plates available to other unions that might want to print more copies of the pamphlet for distribution in Montoya's campaign.

DEMOCRATIC NATIONAL COMMITTEE: Floyd Smith, openly discarding the nominal nonpartisan label worn by the union, appeared on a nation-wide closed-circuit television campaign program sponsored by the Democratic National Committee. The *Machinist* of September 17, 1970, in an article titled "IAM Leaders to Aid Campaign Caucus," reported:

> IAM President Floyd Smith is urging IAM representatives to take part in the Democratic Party campaign caucuses Saturday, Sept. 26th. The meeting, scheduled in 18 cities across the country, will be linked to Washington, D.C. by closed-circuit television.
>
> The Democratic Campaign Caucus '70 is a massive attempt by the Democratic National Committee to bring

together labor, farmers, youth and party workers for a three-hour session on campaign tactics. In addition to the closed-circuit TV program originating in Washington, the meetings will feature a question and answer telephone hook-up.

With Senator Harrison Williams (D) of New Jersey, Joseph Keenan of IBEW, and I. W. Abel of the Steelworkers, Smith appeared on the program in a panel discussion of labor political action.

1971

INDIANA: Senator Vance Hartke's reelection in 1970 did not stop his campaign organization from continuing to solicit union funds the following year to cover the Democrat's deficit. In April Don Ellinger replied to an official of Volunteers for Hartke:

In reviewing our contributions to Senator Hartke during his recent campaign, we find that the Machinists Non-Partisan Political League contributed $10,000 directly to the campaign effort, spent $1,500 for auxiliary services, and supplied the full-time services of a representative.

Our Committee feels that our contribution is more than our fair share now. We, therefore, will not contribute to the fund for his deficit.[42]

GLR Robert Brown had been assigned full time to Senator Hartke's campaign. After the election he provided Ellinger with a report on his political activities:

As you know we started in April, 1970 working on this race and with good reason, since the polls indicated at that time we had a loser in Senator Hartke. . . .

Our early start was necessary and beneficial. We first formed an "Indiana labor committee for the Re-Election of Senator Hartke." The U.A.W. did not join with this committee even though they were invited. Yours truly, was elected as Chairman of this Committee, with the State Director of the Teamsters as Vice-Chairman.

The Indiana Democratic Convention was held June 16, 1970. During May and June we were engaged in a fight to beat down the efforts of two (2) ambitious congressmen. Namely, Andy Jacobs and Lee Hamilton, who sought the Senate nomination against Senator Hartke, we were successful . . . .

On about September 15, we printed and made available a voting record comparison between Senator Hartke and his opponent which was passed out at Plant gates, 500,000 copies, paid for again by the Machinists and Steelworkers . . . .

It is an understatement to say that the Machinists Union and the Steelworkers Union did the main job for Senator Hartke. We won by 4,383 votes less than one vote per precinct as there is 4,442 precincts in the state. Thus our efforts were of an absolute necessity in order to re-elect Senator Hartke.[43]

SOUTH CAROLINA: A special election was held in early 1971 to fill the seat of Congressman Mendel Rivers (D) who had died. Mendel Davis, a relative of Rivers, was the Democratic nominee and was liberal enough to win the support of MNPL, and other labor groups. Ellinger wrote a South Carolina IAM official: "Attached is our check for $250 to assist in the Davis campaign. In addition we have ordered 5,000 buttons saying 'Navy Yard wants Mendel Davis in Congress.' "[44]

Later, after Davis's victory, the South Carolina Labor Council began planning its campaign to defeat Senator Strom Thurmond (R). Ellinger wrote a council official: "We regard the coming epic fight to retire Strom Thurmond to be one of the most important in the country and although we will not be at your convention, count on us when we get down to making campaign plans and budgets."[45]

CALIFORNIA, KANSAS, AND KENTUCKY: MNPL was host at three events in Washington attended by labor leaders for prominent Democratic politicians. On March 1, its guests were Charles T. (Chuck) Manatt, the chairman of the Democratic Central Committee in California, and four other California Democratic Party officials.

On August 30, 1971, the MNPL sponsored a dinner for Democratic governor Robert Docking of Kansas "to discuss his future plans."[46] Twenty-three of labor's political strategists, representing 17 unions, attended.

Kentucky gubernatorial candidate Wendell Ford (D) was MNPL's guest the next day at a luncheon attended by 28 labor representatives from 21 unions.

In another California development, an MNPL official reported to GVP Robert Simpson on his talk with Congressman John McFall (D):

I have had an opportunity to talk with McFall about his last campaign and what his plans are to keep his political organization intact for the next election. He stated the same thing that GLR Shean had reported to us as far as there being no Democratic Party organiza-

240

tion to speak of. The Organization that was set up was McFall's own and labor. He had high praise for labor in general and Harry Warner and Mike Manfredo in particular for his reelection. We discussed keeping the campaign organization intact and he was in full agreement. I feel that perhaps there should be periodic meetings of leaders in that Congressional District and not let it fall apart only to be rebuilt every two years . . . .[47]

Later, Don Ellinger advised Howard Samuel of the Amalgamated Clothing Workers Union that

Grand Lodge Representative Harold Shean . . . has been designated by General Vice President Robert Simpson to handle the 34th Congressional District of California. Hal has the territorial political assignment and will be trying to locate the staff representative who will be assigned to this district as soon as the outcome of the aerospace wage negotiations and pay board case are known. . . .[48]

UTAH: The luncheons and dinners in Washington, D.C. sponsored by unions for prominent Democratic candidates played an important role in mobilizing labor support behind the candidates. That this is true is evident in this memorandum of June 1971 that Ellinger wrote to the MNPL Executive Council about Wayne Owens of Utah, who the next year was elected to Congress (and who was a senatorial aspirant in 1974):

I met today with Wayne Owens, Administrative Assistant to Senator Ted Moss of Utah. Wayne is almost certainly going to run for Congress in the 2nd District. He is well known in party circles in Utah, but does not have much of a public image. . . .

He reports that he has talked with Brothers Inskeep and Roe and with other labor leaders in the state. They are tentatively planning a fund raiser to launch the campaign sometime in November. If our Utah leaders are in agreement we will ask the Steelworkers to join us in a small luncheon here in Washington for Wayne to meet the other political directors. This district, with an unknown running in 1970, was 52–48, and should probably be on the marginal list of COPE in 1972.[49]

SENATE: On June 28, 1971, Ellinger prepared a memorandum for his Executive Committee titled "Early Commitment in Senate Races." Here are excerpts:

There are a few races for the United States Senate in which our position is clear and it is practical to make an early commitment for initial contribution. These races are:

Iowa Congressman John Culver will run against Senator Jack Miller in what will be an up hill fight against an incumbent. A Republican split in the Governors race should help Democratic prospects. Our leadership is in complete support of Culver.

Kansas Governor Robert Docking will run against James Pearson and will have unanimous labor support. This will be a very close race but one that can be won.

Maine Our Maine leadership have endorsed Congressman William Hathaway against Margaret Chase Smith. Hathaway has a perfect record and Smith's record has become progressively worse in recent years. This will be an up hill fight.

Minnesota We will be supporting Fritz Mondale for re-election. This should be a relatively easy contest. Clark McGregor who ran against Humphrey last time and got 42% of the vote will undoubtedly be the Republican candidate.

Montana Lee Metcalf has expressed some doubt about running for re-election because of personal reasons. But the labor movement is unanimous in encouraging him to make the race. Would like early commitment to him to encourage him to run. We should make our commitment as soon as possible contingent on his decision.

New Hampshire Thomas McIntyre is running for re-election. The law of New Hampshire prohibits contributions from out of state organizations. At least one of our New Hampshire lodges is part of District 38 and this qualifies District 38 as an in state organization. This will be a very difficult race since McIntyre is the only Democrat office holder there. We should make an early commitment through District 38 for the campaign.

Rhode Island Claiborne Pell is in for a very tough battle with former Governor Chaffee. He is slightly behind on the Machinists sample poll there. Our leadership is in support of Pell. We should make an early commitment.[50]

NEW HAMPSHIRE: Senator Thomas McIntyre was one of those who, Ellinger felt, deserved early commitment from IAM. Later in 1971 Ellinger wrote Senator McIntyre:

242

This is to confirm the arrangements we discussed for you to meet with the key leaders of our organization in New Hampshire on Saturday, November 13. . . . Two principal officers from each of our local lodges in New Hampshire will attend plus key members of their organizations they wish to bring . . . .

It is our expectation the meeting will take an hour or an hour and one-half and we will be able to discuss thoroughly the kinds of help we can give you in your campaign for deserved reelection.[51]

DEMOCRATIC PARTY: Money flowed from MNPL coffers into the Democratic Party treasury in this off-election year. Nothing, of course, went to the Republican Party. In June Ellinger wrote Richard Maguire of the Democratic Congressional Dinner Committee that the Executive Committee had voted to contribute $5,000 to the Dinner Committee. Later Ellinger responded to Senator Ernest Hollings (D) of South Carolina, who was chairman of the Democratic Senate Campaign Committee:

The Machinists Non-Partisan Political League is prepared to make a $5,000.00 contribution to the Democratic Dinner Committee based on the same understanding we arrived at with Dick Maguire, prior to the dinner last summer.

We repeat the understanding that:

1. These funds will be used for campaign contributions to Democratic nominees to the House and Senate at the direction of the MNPL.

2. The check written for the candidate by the Senate or House Campaign Committee shall be delivered to the MNPL who, in turn, will deliver it to the candidate for Congress or Senate through our local representative.

I will be in contact with Nordy Hoffman to work out the details.[52]

In October MNPL contributed $1,000 to be patron at the Democratic Study Group's 12th Anniversary Dinner; in December it contributed another $1,000 to the Democratic National Committee to help towards the printing of a brochure on delegate selection to the party's national convention. In addition, MNPL received the following request from the Democratic National Committee:

Areas where we could use some financial help.

1. Consultant work by Professor Al Stern, Wayne State, on reapportionment strategy (2 months) $2,000.

243

2. $3,000 DNC share of Democratic Fact Book 1970 outstanding to Senate Campaign Committee. 600 copies of the book at $5.00.

3. Informal labor commitments on Campaign Caucus to cover twenty percent of tickets: broken down by Union, still would leave balance as follows:

UAW	$ 300
Steel	$1,000
ILGW	$ 500
Machinists	$ 250
Retail Clerks	$ 750
Transportation	$ 450
Laborers	$ 750
CWA	$ 500
IBEW	$ 750 [53]

Many of the congressional candidates supported by IAM-MNPL can be classified as liberal to New Left. Because of their Leftist political persuasion, these Democratic members of Congress at times vote against the union's position on what are bread-and-butter issues to the IAM rank and file. This causes grave embarrassment to the Machinists' leadership; but because it is also of the same liberal persuasion, it is wary of causing unrest among the rank and file. Occasionally a truly crucial issue does arise that causes discontent among the rank and file and presents a dilemma to the leadership. Such an issue was the building of the supersonic transport. Had Congress approved the SST legislation, its construction would have provided employment for many Machinists. Yet many of those congressmen who voted against SST had previously received union campaign support. This prompted one irate California Machinist to write the editor of the *Machinist*:

Why don't you put the blame where it belongs? The blame I'm referring to is the defeat of support for the SST.

I blame G. Meany and the Editors of the *Machinist* Magazine and the left-wing creeps operating COPE. They supported those bastards Cranston, Tunney, Hartke, etc. who voted against the interests of the aircraft workers and the country.

They used my dues and the newspaper my dues goes to [to] support these left-wing freaks.

These S.O.B.'s don't want workers who think and vote for themselves. They want welfarers who vote in blocs for the jerks who sweeten the pot for them.

You and these other freaks are leading this country down the road to socialism and ruin. . . .[54]

244

Because the IAM leadership broke with George Meany and supported the McGovern-Shriver ticket, IAM personnel were active in the Democratic Presidential campaign. Among these was GLR Charles Beyer, who became vice chairman of the Connecticut Labor Committee for McGovern. Beyer also helped to develop a committee campaign budget of $10,000 of which IAM's pro-rata share was set at $3,075.

John Heidenreich, the directing business representative of District 10 in Wisconsin, was another Machinist active in the McGovern campaign. In September he wrote Holayter:

. . . We here in the State of Wisconsin have established a Wisconsin Labor for McGovern-Shriver Committee, which I became a co-chairman of. This Committee was established for the purpose of working independently of but in cooperation with the McGovern-Shriver National Campaign Committee . . . .

Other co-chairmen of this committee are Gilbert Jewell, International President of the Allied Industrial Workers, and Ray Majerus, Regional Director for the UAW. . . . Both Brother Jewell and Majerus have pledged a substantial financial contribution to support this committee's activities, and, of course, they are expecting a substantial contribution from the Machinist Non-Partisan Political League. I would suggest and recommend that the Executive Officers of our National MNPL allocate $10,000 out of the Big One to Wisconsin and in behalf of McGovern's campaign. . . .[55]

An official of District Lodge 720 in California was working actively to denigrate President Nixon. William Holayter wrote him:

. . . We would be glad to have you act as a distribution center for the "Dump Nixon" button, and we are having an order for 10,000 shipped directly to you.

Would you please let us know if you would like us to bill you for the entire shipment or send us the names of local lodges to whom bills should be sent.[56]

IAM was, of course, active in congressional campaigns as well as in the Presidential race. Here are some highlights of the work the union did in 1972 for liberal and Democratic Congressional candidates.

COLORADO: In a letter in January to a Colorado resident, Ellinger declared: "We have no optimism for the defeat of

Gordon Allott. However, if a candidate presents himself and if we think there is a remote prayer of winning, we will be of assistance." [57]

Allott, the Republican senator, was challenged in the general election by Democrat Floyd Haskell. Haskell won by a narrow margin, a victory due in large part to labor's tax-exempt money and manpower, which were poured into his campaign.

UTAH: Wayne Owens, the Democratic nominee for Congress in the 2nd Congressional District, had begun campaigning early. In February Ellinger wrote to a Utah Machinist official:

> Attached is our check for $500.00 for Wayne Owens for Congress in response to an appeal made by Senator Moss and Senator Kennedy at a widely attended luncheon in Washington, D.C.
>
> We recommend that you use this check to negotiate with other labor organizations to come up with early money for Owens. [58]

NEBRASKA, TEXAS, AND IOWA: Again, in 1972, MNPL hosted a number of luncheons in the nation's capital for prominent Democratic candidates. These get-togethers were attended by many of labor's political strategists. For example, in February William Holayter wrote his Executive Committee:

> Governor J. J. Exon of Nebraska will be in town on the 25th of February. Don had been asked if we could co-host a luncheon for the Governor along with CWA. The purpose of the luncheon would be to hear from the Governor on the political situation in Nebraska, especially the Senate race, and to evaluate any chances of defeating Senator Curtis. This cost would be approximately $200. [59]

The MNPL Executive Committee approved the expenditure for the Exon luncheon.

Also in February, Holayter—along with James Cuff O'Brien of the Steelworkers and Bill Dodds of UAW—sent the following invitation to key labor political strategists:

> Texas State Senators Mike McKool of Dallas, Barbara Jordan of Houston, and Charlie Wilson of east Texas will be in Washington at the end of the month preparing their campaigns for the Democratic nomination for Congress in their respective areas.
>
> The Steelworkers, CWA and the Machinists will host

a luncheon on Monday, February 28 . . . . We would very much like you to join us for lunch to meet and talk with these Senators.[60]

In the November election, Jordan and Wilson were elected to Congress.

In March MNPL co-chairmen Floyd Smith, Eugene Glover, and Charles West sent the following invitation to other union representatives:

> On April 4, 1972 the MNPL is sponsoring a luncheon for Dick Clark, a candidate for the U. S. Senate from Iowa . . . .
>
> Dick Clark, since 1964, has been the Administrative Assistant to Congressman John Culver of Iowa's Second District. We feel that Senator Miller can be defeated in 1972. We would appreciate very much your attendance at this luncheon so that you may have the opportunity to meet Dick and visit with him concerning the Iowa Senatorial race.[61]

Thirty labor leaders representing 24 unions attended the Clark luncheon. In November Clark defeated Republican Senator Miller.

NEW HAMPSHIRE: The MNPL continued to make good on its promise to help reelect the Democratic Senator Thomas McIntyre. Holayter informed his Executive Committee in April:

> I met yesterday with political directors of several other unions. We discussed the situation of Senator McIntyre of New Hampshire. According to New Hampshire law, we cannot donate any money directly to the Senator. Donations must go through a D.C. Committee because of the strictness of the New Hampshire law. In the past we have used the Democratic Senatorial Campaign Committee which did not have to report to the Secretary of the Senate. However, on April 8 a new campaign law will go into effect which will require that Committee to report its contributions. It will be, after that date, therefore difficult, if not impossible, to contribute to Senator McInyre's campaign.
>
> We had projected $5,000 for his campaign and have already donated $2,000. It is my recommendation that we donate the other $3,000 now, and funnel it through Nordy Hoffman at the Democratic Senatorial Campaign Committee.

247

Since April 7 is the deadline, and only two days away, a quick answer would be appreciated.[62]

CALIFORNIA: The performance of Congressman Richard Hanna (D) of the 34th Congressional District was the subject of critical comment by local IAM leaders, even though he was the beneficiary of the union's tax-exempt political money and manpower. Holayter requested that GLR Hal Shean look into the situation. Shean reported back that the union leaders with whom he had spoken

> stated that Hanna's problem was his staff and he himself, in how he handled his last campaign. They stated he was rarely present in his area during his term of office and during the campaign. Another point they made was that he failed to attend the victory party of all his workers, and instead went to a dinner and cocktail party for the elite of the area. . . .[63]

VIRGINIA: MNPL director William Holayter accepted the campaign post of liaison to organized labor for the congressional campaign of Democrat Harold Miller in Virginia's 10th Congressional District, a seat held by veteran Republican legislator Joel Broyhill. At a strategy meeting of Miller, Holayter, and officials of the Greater Washington (D.C.) Central Labor Council, "It was agreed that all National and International requests for contributions would go through William Holayter's office, with a copy in the Greater Washington Central Labor Council office. Also, all Local Union contributions will be managed through the COPE Headquarters of the Central Labor Council." [64]

IAM was not the only organization actively supporting Miller. A Miller campaign official informed Holayter in June:

> For example, Harold has now been endorsed by the National Committee For An Effective Congress and received a contribution of $1,000. Two weeks ago the American Federation of State, County and Municipal Employees gave their endorsement and a check for $500. And, the National Education Association has arranged for us to receive a $1,500 discount from Valentine-Sherman for our computer service (please treat this confidentially for the moment) . . . .
>
> The NEA has a project going that provides discounts on the costs of the Valentine-Sherman computer service that we and other campaigns are using. We have been allocated a $1,500 discount. There is a certain sensitivity about discussing this too publicly, as it was not voted on

by Virginia people yet. The national people, however, know it was important to do something now and went ahead on their own. Our contact at NEA has been Jean Parlette. . . .[65]

On July 6, 1972, Holayter sponsored a meeting for other labor political leaders to meet candidate Miller. The meeting took place in room 1002 of the IAM headquarters building. This is another example of how the union uses its tax-exempt resources for partisan politics.

OREGON: Radical activist Charles O. Porter won the Democratic nomination for Congress in the 4th Congressional District. After his victory he wrote MNPL: "I believe that I can win this Fall, but I'll need help. If you can send some of that important Early Money, also called Seed Corn, and perhaps suggest other sources and ideas for the campaign please do it now." [66] IAM rendered campaign help to Porter by commissioning a public opinion poll in his behalf, paid for by the MNPL Educational Fund. The request for the poll was made in July by an official of the Oregon MNPL who wrote Holayter: "We are requesting $500.00 to take an in depth poll in the 4th District on Charles Porter." [67]

NEW JERSEY: Labor is constantly attempting to tighten its political grip on the Garden State. In its debt are the state's two U. S. senators and a large number of congressmen. So MNPL responded agreeably with a $500 contribution when it received the following letter from district business manager Charles Bennett: "Due to the fact of the change in chairman of the Democratic Party of Union County, who will cooperate with all labor organizations within the County, we are requesting some financial aid because they are in dire need of funds." [68]

WASHINGTON STATE: IAM paid for the campaign signs of Congressman Mike McCormack (D). Shortly before McCormack was reelected, GVP Francis Meagher wrote an official of the Washington Machinists Council: "Enclosed you will find two (2) checks from the Machinists Non-Partisan Political League—one for $1,400 which is the check I mentioned would reimburse the Council for the signs made for Mike McCormack's campaign and one for $500 which is to be sent to Mike McCormack as a contribution." [69]

SENATE RACES: The Washington political public relations firm of Maurer, Fleisher and Zon is an integral part of labor's program to assist Democratic candidates. The firm is retained by unions to provide special campaign services for key Democrats.

In July William Holayter wrote Robert Maurer of the firm:

According to our records the $1,000 payment enclosed for newsletter materials and legislative materials for Senator Pell of Rhode Island completes our original commitment to the project, which contained help for Senators McIntyre, Metcalf and Pell and Senatorial candidates Edmondson, Pryor, Abourezk, Norvell and Johnston.

In addition to this, I understand the original project will include Senatorial candidate Dick Clark of Iowa. If this does become the case, please let us know. With the exception of Clark this should complete our commitment to this project.[70]

Two months later MNPL sent the firm an additional $5,000 check "as our part of the cost of your new project for the various political studies." [71]

DSG: The Democratic Study Group, composed of the most liberal and radical Democratic members of the House of Representatives, is a frequent recipient of labor's financial support.

On August 18, 1972 DSG chairman Philip Burton, a congressman from California, wrote International President Floyd Smith:

The Democratic Party faces a critical fight for control of the House in 1972. A loss of 40 seats will make the Republicans the majority party in Congress. In order to help incumbents and non-incumbents in a very tough year, I hope your organization will consider contributing directly to the DSG Campaign Fund, so that we can elect the maximum number of pro-labor Democrats to the House of Representatives.

DSG has 165 members, who comprise the backbone of labor strength in the House. The DSG Campaign Fund gives only to pro-labor incumbents and non-incumbents in marginal races, so that all of its money is targeted where it is most needed.[72]

On September 27, 1972 MNPL sent DSG a check for $1,000.

Conclusion

In national election years IAM sponsors schools on campaign techniques for its staff personnel and members. The curricula "are designed as a post graduate course for those who will take a lead in a Congressional District race." Despite the obvious political overtones of these schools, expenses are paid by tax-exempt monies from the union's general treasury, the MNPL Educational Fund, and local lodge treasuries.

IAM works with COPE and other labor organizations in developing and funding political front groups. In many instances tax-exempt union monies are used to finance the political activities of these outside groups.

The primary political strategy of IAM-MNPL has provided tax-exempt funds and manpower for liberal candidates and the Democratic Party. The union's extensive resources were made available to the Dmocratic Party during the Humphrey campaign in 1968 and McGovern's in 1972.

In addition to funds, campaign aid is provided in the form of transportation, brochures, signs, and mailing lists. IAM's international president has actively participated in a national school on campaign techniques that was sponsored by the Democratic National Committee, and key IAM leaders have attended the campaign planning sessions of liberal Democratic candidates.

IAM sponsors luncheons and dinners in the nations's capital to which Democratic candidates are invited in order to discuss their political aspirations and campaign needs with labor's leading strategists. The IAM-MNPL also contributes to the Democratic National Committee, Democratic Senate Campaign Committee, Democratic Study Group, and other Democratic Party organizations. It does not contribute to Republican Party organizations.

PART III

Available Remedies: Executive,
Legislative, and Judicial

Correcting an Imbalance in Our Political System

The questions are: (1) Shall a union, under a compulsory dues agreement, be permitted to use compulsory-membership dues money, even in part, to finance political parties and political candidates so as to impose political conformity upon the workers who are required to pay the dues?

(2) Is an individual worker deprived of his freedom of association, freedom of conscience, freedom of political thought—and thereby deprived of liberty and property without due process of law—when he is required to make a choice between forfeiting his job and paying compulsory union dues to support candidates and causes he would not willingly support?

These issues have been explored before, although the growing political boldness of organized labor in recent years brought them into sharper focus. Supreme Court Justice William O. Douglas, concurring in *International Association of Machinists* v. *Street* (367 U.S. 740 [1961]), observed:

> Membership in a group cannot be conditioned on the individual's acceptance of the group's philosophy. Otherwise, First Amendment rights are required to be exchanged for the group's attitude, philosophy or politics. I do not see how that is constitutionally permissible under the Constitution. . . .
> The collection of dues for paying the costs of collective bargaining of which each member is a beneficiary is one thing. If, however, dues are used, or assessments are made, to promote or oppose birth control, to repeal or increase the taxes on cosmetics, to promote or oppose the admission of Red China into the United Nations, and the like, then the group compels an individual to support with his money causes beyond what gave rise to the need for group action.
> I think the same must be said when union dues or assessments are used to elect a Governor, a Congressman, a Senator or a President. It may be said that the election of a Franklin D. Roosevelt rather than a Calvin Coolidge might be the best possible way to serve the cause of collective bargaining. But even such a selective use of union funds for political purposes subordinates the individual's First Amendment rights to the views

of the majority. I do not see how that can be done, even though the objector retains his rights to campaign, to speak, to vote as he chooses. For when union funds are used for that purpose, the individual is required to finance political projects against which he may be in rebellion.

Justice Hugo Black, in his dissent in the *Street* case, also pointed out: "There can be no doubt that the federally sanctioned union-shop contract here, as it actually works, takes a part of the earnings of some men and turns it over to others, who spend a substantial part of the funds so received in efforts to thwart the political, economic and ideological hopes of those whose money has been forced from them under authority of law. . . ."

In *Street*, the Court backed away from granting a blanket injunction against all expenditures of funds by the union for political purposes, but indicated that union members have two available remedies: (1) members may seek to enjoin such amount of their contributions as would have been devoted to political purposes; or (2) members may seek restitution to each individual member of that portion of his money that the union expended, despite his notification, for political causes to which he advised the union he was opposed. The intervening years since *Street* reveal these remedies to be illusory, more apparent than real. They have had no effect in preventing a union from political spending of compulsory dues money, and the average member still finds himself powerless when he wishes to protest against the institutional abuses represented by the union.

It may be asked: If these issues have been grappled with before, why are they still with us today? The answer is that because of temporizing the issues never were resolved. The condition continues to worsen, and we now have an imbalance in our political system that threatens to impose on America a labor government, under which the elected representatives will be responsible no longer to the American people but to the labor bosses.

Evidence of this imbalance is seen today in Congress, where a lop-sided majority of members in both the House and the Senate owes its election to organized labor. This majority of union-controlled legislators is bound to increase unless a balance is struck, since labor is now using its funds and resources to support incumbents it controls and to defeat challengers.

The time has come for the American people to call upon all three branches of our federal government to fashion remedies to protect the constitutional rights of the individual worker, who sees his dues money unwillingly being used for political purposes he does not support, and to protect the general taxpayer against a discriminatory and greater tax burden because of tax-exempt union treasury money that is being devoted to political activities.

Executive Branch Remedies

• A special prosecutor, as in the Watergate case, should be appointed. The courts should convene grand juries so that he could subpoena union leaders and union political directors, to question them about the use of tax-exempt dues money for partisan politics. To trace these expenditures, subpoena *duces tecum* should be served to obtain the accounting books, records, correspondence, and files of these unions and their leaders. These are normal investigatory procedures and were used by the Watergate special prosecutor against corporations and corporate officers suspected of having broken campaign finance laws.

The Nixon administration, when it took power in 1968, knew of illegal campaign spending by labor unions. But for reasons that can only be surmised, it took no steps to end the violations of the law. According to the *New York Times* of September 20, 1968, in its article "Agnew Questions Humphrey's Aid; Says AFL-CIO Staff Loan May Be Illegal":

Mr. Agnew told a press conference. . . "I believe he [Mr. Meany] said he was going to call upon many of his staff workers to work full time for Mr. Humphrey. I submit that this is just as bad a situation as some of his workers going automatically to Mr. Wallace."

Mr. Agnew, a former labor lawyer, said there was a "Federal prohibition against utilizing the workingman's money for political purposes without his consent," and he added, "I think the AFL-CIO is getting dangerously close to this in this election."

Mr. Agnew noted that union staff workers are paid by union dues and then asserted that if those staff workers are allowed to work for a political candidate without the consent of the union rank and file it would be a violation of "at least the spirit and intent of the Federal prohibitions."

• The proposed special prosecutor should consider investigating and prosecuting candidates and public officeholders who had knowledge that they were receiving tax-exempt union treasury money in their campaigns. There is precedent for such prosecutions. The *Washington Post*, in a December 1973 article, "Phillips Oil Official Fined for Nixon Gift," reported:

> Assistant Special [Watergate] prosecutor Thomas F. McBride also disclosed that Phillips had contributed up to $60,000 to "a substantial number" of candidates for Congress in 1970 and 1972.
>
> McBride said the oil company would not be prosecuted for those donations but that the candidates for Congress who received them are under "active investigation" by the special prosecutor's office.
>
> He said these candidates, none of whom he would identify, must have known that the money came from corporate funds before they can be prosecuted successfully.

Applying the same legal principle to political contributions from union treasuries, which are also violations of the law, it would seem that a large number of members of Congress could be put under "active investigation" since they have not only received such funds but also, as the evidence in this book discloses, had knowledge of the source of the funds and, in many instances, openly solicited them.

• The Department of Labor should consider intervening to support a suit when brought by a protesting union member to force his union's officials responsible for the disbursement of tax-exempt treasury funds for political activities to reimburse the union from their own pockets, a procedure which is authorized by the Landrum-Griffin Act. Another remedy akin to this was instituted by U.S. District Court Judge Charles Richey in 1973, when he ordered former United Mine Workers' head Tony Boyle to reimburse his union treasury in the amount of $49,250. This represented the sum he had taken from the union treasury, mostly to contribute to Hubert Humphrey's Presidential campaign in 1968.

Legislative Branch Remedies

There is great ferment in Congress to corect the ills afflicting campaign spending practices. But are there enough men of courage and rectitude in Congress to enact meaningful reform legislation? There are those who doubt that this can be done. Aleksandr Solzhenitsyn, the Russian writer, has made observations about our political system that reveal him to be as perceptive about American politics as about life under the Soviet leaders. In an article, "Solzhenitsyn Attacks Democratic Party," in the August 12, 1973, *Washington Post* the famed author accuses the West of a double standard in judging recent events in the Soviet Union and in the West: "This deep hypocrisy is characteristic even of today's American political life, of the Senate leaders with their distorted view of the sensational Watergate scandal."

After accusing the Democrats of "affected, loudmouthed wrath," Solzhenitsyn asks: "Has American politics not been full of mutual deceit and misuse already in earlier election campaigns, maybe only with the difference that it happened without electronics and was fortunately not discovered?"

One of those most fervently condemning the Watergate scandal is Senator Joseph Montoya of New Mexico. Yet, perhaps typically, the New Mexico Democrat's own skirts are far from clean. An article in the *Wall Street Journal* of June 28, 1973, was titled "Backers 'Laundered' '70 Campaign Gifts to Watergate Prober; Montoya Donations by Unions and Other Interest Groups Were Routed to Hide Source." It reported:

Like Mr. Nixon's collectors in 1972, Mr. Montoya's in 1970 "laundered" large sums—as much as $100,000—through phony committees to hide the sources. And after narrowly winning re-election the Senator himself filed a sworn financial statement that failed to acknowledge the receipt of money channeled through the dummy committees or the sources of contributions to those committees . . . .

Through the dummy committes, Montoya fund raisers routed contributions that might have generated political problems for the Senator had they been disclosed. In this way they laundered $57,000 from various political-action arms of labor unions which would have tended to support Republican campaign charges that the Senator was in hock to organized labor—as well as $45,000 or so from other special-interest groups . . . .

In enacting the Federal Election Campaign Act of 1971, Congress voted to continue the prohibition that is found in title 18, section 610 of the United States Code. This prohibition forbids banks, corporations, and labor organizations making contributions or paying expenses out of their own funds in connection with any federal election or primary. However, attached to the act was a provision that allows union leaders to use compulsory dues money to pay for the soliciting of campaign contributions. The net effect of the provision is that it allows union treasury money to pay the overhead costs of raising "voluntary" funds that can legally be contributed to candidates for federal offices.

The story of how the provision got tacked into the 1971 legislation is a textbook example of the hypocrisy that Solzhenitsyn observed in American politics. The purported author of the amendment was Congressman Orval Hansen (R-Idaho), but it is more likely that the AFL-CIO had a hand in its drafting. AFL-CIO lobbyist Kenneth Young has denied this. However, the *Wall Street Journal* of January 18, 1972, reported:

> Still, an unusual mix-up on the House floor involving Rep. [Frank] Thompson suggests that lobbyist Young isn't telling all he knows.
>
> The mix-up occured on the day of the House vote, right after Mr. Hansen explained his amendment. When he sat down, Rep. Thompson got up "to commend the distinguished gentleman from Idaho for the development and for the offering of this amendment." Mr. Thompson spoke some more off-the-cuff, then gained permission to "revise and extend"—that is, edit—his remarks before publication in the *Congressional Record*. In so doing, he inadvertently inserted a copy of the canned explanatory speech that had also been supplied to Mr. Hansen.
>
> The consequence of Mr. Thompson's slipup appears in the *Congressional Record* of Nov. 30. Diligent readers of that day's proceedings will find Mr. Hansen and Mr. Thompson giving almost the same speech, back to back. Except for minor editing ("Analytically, my proposal has three component parts," Mr. Hansen intoned; "Analytically, the proposal has three component parts," Mr. Thompson echoed) the two successive explanations coincide word for word for 18 paragraphs.
>
> Mr. Thompson attributed this embarrassing overlap not to a common authorship but to "interchangability of staff and identity of legislative intent."

As Congress undertakes again to study and implement campaign reform legislation, undoubtedly more illustrations will surface that will lay bare the hypocrisy permeating the debate. In fact, already come to public light is the proposed legislation to provide for a national system of registering to vote using a postcard form. The proposal originated with the AFL-CIO and was endorsed at its 1973 convention. Senator Sam Ervin predicted that if it passes "there is going to be a general resurrection of the dead on every election day." Senator Hiram Fong of Hawaii warned: "If this bill is passed, we will be registering cemetery lists, we will be registering tombstones, we will be registering vacant places, and we will be registering fictitious people."

Public financing of congressional campaigns is a key item on the agenda of Congress, spurred on by the disclosures of Watergate. Senator Walter Mondale (D-Minn.), a proponent of public financing, admitted: "Despite the incredible tales of Mr. Nixon's 1972 fund-raising activities now unfolding, no one can pretend that they represent a problem unique to Republicans. My own party's fund-raising record—while never in Mr. Nixon's league—has not always been as open and as forthright as I would like it to have been."

David S. Broder, ace political analyst of the *Washington Post,* observed:

> If access to large sums is eliminated for one candidate or party by the provision of equal public subsidies for all, then the election outcome will likely be determined by the ability to mobilize other forces.
>
> The most important of these other factors are probably manpower and publicity. . . .
>
> That immediately conjures up for Republicans and conservatives a picture of the union boss, the newspaper editor and the television anchor-man—three individuals to whom they are rather reluctant to entrust their fate— electing the next President.[1]

Information compiled by the Senate Watergate Committee on union political spending in the 1972 Presidential election may prove helpful to Congress in fashioning reform legislation, although it is unfortunate that its inquiry was limited solely to labor spending on the Presidential campaign. The committee's questionnaire was sent to union officials in October 1973. Columnist Victor Riesel once again hit the target dead center, when in commenting on the questionnaire he observed:

> What seems to me most significant in this communication is the opportunity to count more than cash contributions. The really vital political information will be in the replies to questions 10 and 11. They go to the crunch—what does labor contribute in imponderables, in services and in things of value as well as money? How do you "cost out" the value of 75,000 door-to-door political activists or 95,000 Election Day car pool drivers and baby-sitters such as labor turned out in '68? Or Joe Beirne's Communication Workers of America (AFL-CIO) rounding up 10,000 telephone operators to volunteer to take contribution calls during the recent Democratic telethon?
>
> In effect, Question 10 asks: Did the union provide

services to any candidate? Question 11 queries: Did the union pay any bills or obligations or salaries to or for any candidate? [2]

The AFL-CIO favors public financing of Presidential and congressional campaigns. When one looks behind the federation's reasons in support of its position, it is easy to see why it does. Testifying in September 1973 before the Senate Subcommittee on Privileges and Elections in support of public financing, AFL-CIO legislative director Andrew Biemiller declared:

> We want the Congress to put the AFL-CIO out of the business of making campaign contributions. We would be delighted if the AFL-CIO never had to raise another dime for a candidate.
> Without fund-raising headaches, we would be able to better fill our members' needs for registration assistance, providing them information about candidates and issues, and finally getting our members out to vote their consciences on Election Day.

What Mr. Biemiller is really saying is that organized labor prefers not to have to spend compulsory dues money on the costs of raising "voluntary" funds to be used as campaign contributions. Freed from the costs of fund raising, labor leaders then could spend more compulsory dues money on partisan registration and voter-turnout drives, on publicity and propaganda, and on manpower to work in campaigns.

When Congress undertakes to legislate new campaign spending laws, it should analyze carefully the effects of the Hansen Amendment. This amendment carved out three exceptions to its prohibition, as incorporated into section 610 of title 18, on the use of dues money by unions for political purposes:

(1) communications to union members for political purposes;
(2) non-partisan registration and get-out-the-vote drives aimed at members and their families; and
(3) the establishment, administration, and solicitation of contributions to separate segregated political funds.

Congress should study the concept of union communications to union members for political purposes since these communications invade the protected rights of free speech of the individual member. Since a union's right to speak on political issues must surely come from its relationship to its members, how can it claim a protected right of free speech when its political positions may represent the minority viewpoint of its membership? The individual members have First Amendment rights of freedom of speech, of association, and of political thought and action. The First Amendment rights of union workers are violated when their dues are utilized by the union's leadership to support political programs and campaigns that they, the workers, would not willingly support or, indeed, might strenuously oppose.

For this reason the first exception of section 610 should be narrowed by Congress to prohibit the use of compulsory union dues for communications supporting or opposing candidates for federal office.

The second exception of section 610 raises the problem of enforcement rather than the need for new legislation. Clearly the evidence proves beyond a reasonable doubt that labor's voter-registration drives are not nonpartisan but, instead, designed to aid a particular political party. Labor's get-out-the-vote drives consistently favor only certain candidates. The present law requiring that these voter programs be conducted in a nonpartisan fashion is being violated. Congress should protest the failure to enforce the law.

The third exception allows unions to use tax-exempt treasury money to pay the overhead costs of raising "voluntary" funds for the purpose of contributing directly to federal candidates. If the total amount of tax-exempt treasury money spent by all unions and labor organizations to raise these "voluntary" funds were calculated, it would exceed several million dollars. The effect of this exception is to operate as an indirect tax subsidy of partisan political activities. The National Right to Work Committee, in testimony submitted on December 14, 1973, to the Subcommittee on Elections of the Committee on House Administration, suggested an amendment to section 610 that might be considered by Congress in remedying the defects created by the Hansen provision.

The proposed amendment to section 610 would add the following at the end of the second paragraph:

Provided further, That it shall be unlawful for money or anything of value secured by physical force, job discrimination, or financial reprisal, or by dues, fees, or other monies required as a condition of employment, to be used to pay the costs of: (1) communications by a corporation to its stockholders and their families or by a labor organization to its members and their families supporting or opposing any candidate for the offices referred to in this section, or support or opposing any political party or political committee, or (2) establishing, administering, and soliciting contributions to a separate segregated fund to be utilized for political purposes by a corporation or labor organization.

Enactment of this amendment or of language of similar intent would go a long way toward curbing the abuse of compulsory union dues by labor leaders who are using the dues for political purposes.

Congress is also tinkering with the idea of tax reform. When it does undertake to consider new tax legislation it would be an appropriate time for it also to make clear that only that union income shall be regarded as tax-exempt that is devoted to defraying costs germane to collective bargaining. Any portion of union income diverted to the support of political and ideological causes should be subject to a 100 percent tax in the same manner as are unauthorized expenditures of charitable foundations under those amendments to the Internal Revenue Code that implemented the Tax Reform Act of 1969.

An amendment to the Internal Revenue Code that would remove the tax exemption of treasury money used by unions for political purposes might contain this language:

PROHIBITION OF CERTAIN POLITICAL ACTIVITIES

Section 501 of the Internal Revenue Code of 1954 (relating to exemption from tax) is amended by redesignating subsection (f) as (g) and by inserting after subsection e) the following new subsection:

(f) Prohibition on Certain Political Activities—No organization described in subsection (c) or (d) shall be exempt from taxation under subsection (a) for any taxable year in which any part of its income, or of the amounts received for its support, from dues, fees, or other monies required as a condition of employment is used, directly or indirectly—

(1) to support or opose any candidate for nomination for election, or for election to public office, or

(2) to support or oppose any political party, organization, or committee,

(3) to make communications supporting or opposing any candidate for nomination for election, or for election, to public office,

(4) to carry on partisan voter registration and get-out-the-vote campaigns, or

(5) to establish, administer, or solicit contributions to a separate segregated fund to be utilized for political purposes."

(b) The amendment made by this section shall apply with respect to taxable years beginning after the date of enactment of this Act.

Finally, while discussing legislative remedies that could be fashioned to end union abuse of campaign spending laws, it should be noted that the one positive effect of the Watergate scandal is that 38 states have enacted new legislation to close spending loopholes. Others may do so in coming months. Unfortunately, the strongest pressure group at the state level is organized labor, which can be expected to fight meaningful campaign spending reform. The AFL-CIO Executive Committee in its 1973 report boasted: "Since the last convention of the AFL-CIO, every state legislature has been in session. As the Kansas State Federation of Labor, AFL-CIO, reports, the one lobby covering state legislative sessions on bills affecting the general public are the state affiliates of the AFL-CIO."

Nevertheless, Arizona, Missouri, North Carolina, Texas, and Wyoming have since 1972 enacted laws that prohibit unions from using treasury funds to contribute to political candidates.

Judicial Remedies

In what is likely to be a landmark labor case, a federal judge on January 20, 1976, banned the use of compulsory union dues for any political purposes or other non-collective-bargaining activities.

The class-action summary judgment was issued in a case involving a group of Western Airline employees, all of whom were forced to pay dues to the Brotherhood of Railway, Airline and Steamship Clerks (AFL-CIO). They had filed suit in 1973 protesting the use of their "agency-fee" dues for political and ideological purposes.

The consolidated case is *Ellis-Fails, et al.* v. *Brotherhood of Railway, Airline and Steamship Clerks, et al.* (civil cases Nos. 73–113–N and 73–118–N), filed in the U.S. District Court for the Southern District of California.

U. S. District Court Judge Leland C. Nielsen ruled that the use by the union, BRAC, of "dues and fees of protesting employees for noncollective bargaining activities and purposes constitutes a breach of fiduciary duty of fair representation

BRAC owes each plaintiff." He added, "The Railway Labor Act prohibits the use of fees and dues for noncollective bargaining purposes and activities, over protest from a represented employee."

Judge Nielsen listed a wide range of current BRAC activities for which the union must stop spending dues and fees. These include "organizing and recruiting"; "support for or opposition to proposed, pending or existing legislative measures"; "publications in which substantial coverage is devoted to general news, recreational and social activities, political and legislative matters, and cartoons"; "contributions to charities and individuals"; "conducting and attending conventions of BRAC and other organizations and/or labor unions"; and recreational, social and entertainment expenses.

The Western Airlines employees alleged that BRAC spends compulsory dues and fees extracted from them over their written objections for political, legislative, and various other non-collective-bargaining purposes. They stated that these expenditures deprived them of their rights under the NRLA and the First, Fifth, and Ninth amendments of the Constitution and, further, constituted a breach by defendant BRAC of its duty of fair representation owed to them.

The workers also alleged that the so-called rebate procedure set up by BRAC was unavailable to them and that, even if available, was arbitrary and discriminatory because it violated their political and ideological beliefs.

In Washington, Tom Harris, chairman of the board of the National Right to Work Legal Defense Foundation, praised the decision:

> This was a major victory for American working people, one that is a giant step toward providing meaningful political freedom for employees. The decision is sure to give pause to union officials—in this Presidential election year—as they prepare to spend millions and millions of forced union dues dollars for a wide range of "in-kind" political activities.
>
> The victory is, without question, a major step down the road toward ending one of the most flagrant abuses of compulsory unionism—the use of members' dues for political spending.

The issue first came to national prominence in 1961 in the *International Association of Machinists* v. *Street* (BRAC was also involved in the *Street* case) when the Supreme Court expressed sharp disapproval of this practice but provided no meaningful way for individual workers to apply that ruling to their own situation. The case was remanded to the Court of Appeals and, interestingly, the defendant unions, rather than open their books so that the Court could determine how much of the members' dues were being spent for politics, agreed to exempt the plaintiffs from the compulsory union shop contract.

The current case is a class action and it will be interesting to see if the union in this case will be willing to exempt its entire membership from the requirement that they pay dues or lose their jobs!

It is heartening that after all these years the words of the late Supreme Court Justice Hugo Black are beginning to have some meaning. Justice Black said in the *Street* case, "The stark fact is that this Act of Congress [National Railway Labor Act] is being used as a means to exact money from these employees to help get votes and win elections for parties and candidates and to support doctrines they are against. If this is constitutional, the First Amendment is not the charter of political and religious liberty its sponsors believed it to be."

Harris pointed out that Justice Black foresaw these developments when in his *Street* opinion he wrote: "The constitutional question raised in this case . . . is bound to come back here soon with a record so meticulously perfect that the Court cannot escape deciding it."

The full text of Judge Nielsen's decision granting interlocutory summary judgment can be found in Appendix 18.

Regarding judicial remedy, Judge Nielsen's decision in the *Ellis-Fails* case is perhaps the most equitable, fair-minded, and forthright that can be fashioned under present circumstances. It constitutes a major legal victory for millions of American working people and takes without doubt a long step toward providing rank-and-file employees with meaningful political freedom. It places a cloud—in this national election year—over the indiscriminate use by union officials of compulsory union dues for any "in-kind" political purposes whatsoever.

Conclusion

A number of remedies are available to curb union campaign financing abuses and to correct the existing imbalance in our political system. Each of the three branches of government—the executive, the legislative, and the judiciary—possesses the necessary powers to fashion appropriate and equitable remedies. What is first needed to bring this about is an aroused citizenry that will demand implementation, abetted by persons of courage within government who will steadfastly press forward until corrective measures are instituted.

Appendices

Appendix 1

(Note: The following study by Common Cause released on April 11, 1975, is based on cash contributions to congressional candidates. The author of this book, while praising this compilation of election information by Common Cause, must nevertheless point out that in this study, as in past studies by Common Cause, no attempt is made to tabulate and disclose the in-kind contributions of goods and services by organized labor to the candidates it supports, primarily Democrats. These in-kind contributions by unions are ten times the amount of its cash contributions; hence, studies such as this one by Common Cause are not definitive.)

Common Cause Study Reveals
$74 Million Spent by Congressional Candidates
Who Ran in 1974 General Elections

Almost $74 million was reported spent by the 1161 candidates for Congress who ran in the 1974 general elections, according to a Common Cause study released today. Democrats outspent Republicans, $38.4 million to $32.5 million, in House and Senate races with candidates from both major parties, the study revealed.

An additional $1.7 million in total expenditures was reported by incumbents (62 Democrats, 1 Republican) who did not have major party challengers in the general election. Minor party and independent candidates who ran in the general election reported total spending of some $1.3 million. (See attached Appendix A.)

Democratic incumbents outspent their Republican challengers by an average of more than two to one. Republican incumbents outspent their Democratic challengers by a margin of three to two.

The study conducted by the Common Cause Campaign Finance Monitoring Project covered general election candidates for the period from September 1, 1973 through December 31, 1974. It included 468 Democratic candidates, 407 Republicans and 286 minor party and independent candidates.

House Races

Some $45.1 million was reported spent by candidates in the 435 House races. The top House spenders included winners Robert Krueger (D-Tx), $312,000 (included a primary runoff); James Scheuer (D-NY), $301,000; Abner Mikva (D-

Ill), $286,000; and defeated Representatives Samuel Young (R-Ill), $251,000, and Joel Broyhill (R-Va), $249,000. (See attached Appendix B for list of top 25 House spenders.)

Of the 810 major party House candidates, only 22 had total expenditures higher than $168,000. This amount represents the combined overall spending limit ($84,000 in a primary and $84,000 in a general election) imposed on future House candidates by the newly enacted campaign finance law. The 22 largest House spenders included 10 incumbents and nine major party candidates in races not involving an incumbent. Only three of the 40 challengers who defeated House incumbents in the 1974 general elections, had total expenditures higher than the $168,000 combined overall limit. The highest total amount spent by the 248 minor party and independent candidates who ran in the general election was $85,680 by Don Elliot (Lib-NY). Elliot, after losing in the Democratic primary, ran as a Liberal in the general election.

Incumbents outspent their major party challengers in almost 80 percent of the 323 House races involving an incumbent and major party challenger. Approximately 70 percent of the 323 major party challengers to incumbents spent less than $50,000.

Senate Races

Some $28.9 million was spent in the 34 Senate races. Seven Senate candidates, including five incumbents, spent more than $1 million during their election. Their states ranged in size from South Dakota to California. The top spenders were incumbents Alan Cranston (D-Ca), $1,336,000; George McGovern (D-SD), $1,173,000; challenger John Glenn (D-Ohio), $1,149,000; incumbents Robert Dole (R-Ks), $1,110,000; Jacob Javits (R-NY), $1,090,000; Birch Bayh (D-In), $1,024,000; and challenger Wendell Ford (D-Ky), $1,007,000. (See attached Appendix C for list of top 10 Senate spenders.)

Of the 65 major party Senate candidates, only 16 had total expenditures higher than the combined overall spending limits to be imposed for future Senate races by the new law. The 16 candidates included eight incumbents, four challengers and four contestants running in a race with no incumbent. Only two of the 38 minor party and independent candidates reported spending more than $100,000. Barbara A. Keating, the Conservative Party candidate in New York, reported spending $192,000 and John Grady, the American Party candidate in Florida, reported spending $148,000.

Incumbents outspent their major party challengers in 24 of

the 25 Senate races involving an incumbent and major party challenger. Only two challengers beat Senate incumbents: Wendell Ford (D-Ky) who outspent Senator Marlow Cook $1,007,000 to $525,000; and Gary Hart (D-Col.) who spent $353,000 and was outspent by Senator Peter Dominick's $502,000.

The almost $74 million total reported as spent in 1974 by general election Congressional candidates compares with $66.4 million reported as spent in 1972. The 1972 figures covered the period from April 7, 1972, the effective date of the Federal Election Campaign Act of 1971, to December 31, 1972.

In contrast with the $6 million spending margin for Democrats over their Republican opponents in 1974, Republicans outspent Democratic opponents in 1972 by $4.6 million. The party totals in 1972 were $34.2 million for Republicans and $29.6 million for Democrats.

The Common Cause study was based on thousands of disclosure reports filed by 1974 Congressional general election candidates under the 1971 campaign finance law. Common Cause obtained copies of each one of these disclosure reports from the Secretary of the Senate and the Clerk of the House, the federal supervisory officers under the 1971 law for Congressional races.

Campaign finances for each candidate were determined by combining the candidates' reports with the reports of all of the political committees supporting the candidate. House and Senate candidates have been given the opportunity to review the findings and to offer any corrections they felt should be made.

The number of reports, candidates, political committees, and entries covered by these reports make it impossible to guarantee absolute accuracy. The General Accounting Office made this point clear with respect to the studies it released on Presidential finances in the 1972 elections. Common Cause has taken all possible steps to assure the accuracy of its findings.

Appendix A

Expenditures Reported by General Election Candidates in 1974 Congressional Races

	HOUSE		SENATE		OVERALL TOTALS	
	No. of Candidates	Expenditures	No. of Candidates	Expenditures	No. of Candidates	Expenditures
Democrats	(434)	23,615,780	(34)	16,585,840	(468)	40,201,620
Republicans	(376)	20,609,762	(31)	11,842,625	(407)	32,452,387
Minor Party/Independents	(248)	826,882	(38)	458,726	(286)	1,285,608
Totals	(1,058)	45,052,424	(103)	28,887,191	(1,161)	73,939,615

	HOUSE		SENATE	
	No. of Candidates	Expenditures	No. of Candidates	Expenditures
Incumbents with Major Party Challengers	(323)	20,463,731	(22)	13,153,649
Major Party Challengers to Incumbents	(323)	12,892,599	(22)	7,316,731
Races with No Incumbents in General Election				
Democrats	(52)	5,644,054	(9)	4,794,221
Republicans	(52)	4,185,069	(9)	2,422,497

Appendix B

House General Election Candidates

Expenditures Reported by Top 25 Spenders
in 1974 House Races

		(state-cong. dist.)	
***	1. Robert Krueger (D)	†† TX-21	311,953
***	2. James H. Scheuer (D)	NY-11	301,135
**	3. Abner J. Mikva (D)	IL-10	286,225
*	4. Samuel H. Young (R)	IL-10	251,249
*	5. Joel T. Broyhill (R)	VA-10	248,709
***	6. F. W. Richmond (D)	NY-14	245,533
**	7. Charles J. Horne (D)	VA-09	232,341
****	8. Jeff LaCaze (D)	†† LA-06	229,335
***	9. Paul Simon (D)	IL-24	223,163
*	10. Sam Steiger (R)	AZ-03	203,899
*	11. William H. Hudnut (R)	IN-11	201,673
*	12. James M. Collins (R)	TX-03	192,058
*	13. David C. Treen (R)	LA-03	190,135
*	14. Robin L. Beard (R)	TN-06	189,216
****	15. Lawrence P. McDonald (D)	GA-07	188,093
***	16. Norman Y. Mineta (D)	CA-13	185,236
**	17. Bill Clinton (D)	†† AR-03	180,882
*	18. J. J. Pickle (D)	TX-10	180,294
*	19. Robert F. Drinan (D)	MA-04	178,871
***	20. Butler C. Derrick, Jr. (D)	SC-03	176,022
***	21. Henry J. Hyde (R)	IL-06	175,087
*	22. Alan Steelman (R)	TX-05	168,457
*	23. Floyd Spence (R)	SC-02	167,188
*	24. Paul N. McCloskey (R)	CA-12	166,441
**	25. Charles Grisbaum, Jr. (D)	LA-03	166,203

Fourteen Democrats and eleven Republicans are listed above.

```
   * Incumbent
  ** Challenger to Incumbent
 *** Races with No Incumbent in General Election
**** Races with No Incumbent in General Election, where Candidate
     Listed defeated an Incumbent in the Primary
  †† Primary Run-Off
```

Appendix C

Senate General Election Candidates

Expenditures Reported by Top 10 Spenders in 1974 Senate Races

*	1. Alan Cranston (D)	CA	$1,336,202
*	2. George McGovern (D)	SD	1,172,831
***	3. John Glenn (D)	OH	1,149,130
*	4. Robert Dole (R)	KS	1,110,024
*	5. Jacob Javits (R)	NY	1,090,437
*	6. Birch Bayh (D)	IN	1,024,486
**	7. Wendell Ford (D)	KY	1,006,670
***	8. Richard Stone (D)	†† FL	919,787
**	9. Ramsey Clark (D)	NY	855,576
**10.	William Roy (D)	KS	836,927

Eight Democrats and two Republicans are listed above.
Two incumbents who lost in the primary also spent substantial sums: Senator Howard Metzenbaum (D-OH), defeated by John Glenn (listed third above), spent $921,462 and Senator William Fulbright (D-AR) spent $837,481.

* Incumbent
** Challenger to Incumbent
*** Races with No Incumbent in General Election
†† Primary Run-Off

CAMPAIGN EXPENDITURES IN 1974 HOUSES RACES COMPILED BY THE COMMON CAUSE CAMPAIGN MONITORING PROJECT

This list includes the total campaign expenditure figures for all major party candidates and significantly financed minor party or independent candidates in the 1974 general election.

The source of the information on campaign expenditures is the reports filed under the Federal Election Campaign Act of 1971. The totals cover the period between September 1, 1973 and December 31, 1974. Expenditures for each candidate were determined by combining the reports filed by each candidate with those filed by political committees exclusively supporting that candidate. Expenditures include all money spent by the campaign including debts outstanding (except loans outstanding) as of December 31, 1974. Expenditures do not include funds which have been invested in government bonds or certificates of deposit, or funds which have been used to repay loans made to the campaign. Adjustments have also been made to eliminate all transfers of funds within a campaign.

On the list, winning candidates are listed first. Incumbents are indicated by an asterisk (*). The races printed in *italics* are those in which there was no incumbent in the general election. Candidates indicated by a double asterisk (**) won their primary after a runoff election. The primary vote percentage listed for those candidates is for the runoff. *Congressional Quarterly* is the source of all data on vote percentages.

Expenditures for All November 1974 House Races

Con. Dist.	Source: Common Cause Campaign Monitoring Project	Primary Vote %	General Election Vote %	Expenditures
	ALABAMA			
1	Jack Edwards* (R)	No Opp.	59.5	$ 69,347
	Augusta E. Wilson (D)	No Opp.	37.0	57,288
2	William L. Dickinson* (R)	No Opp.	66.1	33,071
	Clair Chisler (D)	No Opp.	33.9	6,134
3	Bill Nichols* (D)	No Opp.	95.9	2,538
4	Tom Bevill* (D)	No Opp.	99.8	5,174
5	Robert E. Jones* (D)	No Opp.	No Opp.	1,262
6	John Buchanan* (R)	No Opp.	56.6	65,235
	Nina Miglionico (D)	64.6	41.0	71,291
7	Walter Flowers* (D)	66.3	91.0	26,604
	ALASKA			
1	Donald E. Young* (R)	No Opp.	53.8	140,729
	William L. Hensley (D)	50.2	46.2	136,112
	ARIZONA			
1	John J. Rhodes* (R)	No Opp.	51.1	136,038
	Patricia M. Fullinwider (D)	69.1	42.3	20,136
2	Morris K. Udall* (D)	No Opp.	62.0	66,130
	Keith Dolgaard (R)	65.7	38.0	100,581
3	Sam Steiger* (R)	No Opp.	51.1	203,899
	Pat Bosch (D)	50.5	48.9	68,203
4	John B. Conlan* (R)	No Opp.	55.3	97,922
	Byron T. Brown (D)	No Opp.	44.7	55,126
	ARKANSAS			
1	Bill Alexander* (D)	No Opp.	90.6	19,691

* Incumbent
** Primary Run-Off Winner

Con. Dist.	Source: Common Cause Campaign Monitoring Project	Primary Vote %	General Election Vote %	Expenditures
	James L. Dauer (R)	No Opp.	9.3	1,060
2	Wilbur D. Mills* (D)	No Opp.	58.9	71,338
	Judy Petty (R)	No Opp.	41.1	55,573
3	J. P. Hammerschmidt* (R)	No Opp.	51.8	101,709
	Bill Clinton (D)**	69.0	48.2	180,882
4	Ray Thornton* (D)	No Opp.	No Opp.	1,567
	CALIFORNIA			
1	Harold Johnson* (D)	80.1	85.8	30,467
2	Don H. Clausen* (R)	82.9	53.0	75,641
	Oscar Klee (D)	28.8	42.7	53,942
3	John Moss* (D)	No Opp.	72.3	23,145
	Ivaldo Lenci (R)	No Opp.	27.7	2,267
4	Robert Leggett* (D)	No Opp.	No Opp.	11,977
5	John L. Burton* (D)	70.5	59.6	25,457
	Thomas Caylor (R)	61.3	37.7	37,712
6	Philip Burton* (D)	No Opp.	71.3	32,038
	Tom Spinosa (R)	No Opp.	21.8	10,749
7	*George Miller (D)*	*36.1*	*55.6*	*95,000*
	Gary Fernandez (R)	*No Opp.*	*44.4*	*76,829*
8	Ronald V. Dellums* (D)	69.6	56.6	78,339
	Jack Redden (R)	47.6	39.6	19,878
9	Fortney Stark* (D)	81.1	70.6	60,642
	Edson Adams (R)	No Opp.	29.4	23,778
10	Don Edwards* (D)	77.8	77.0	17,948
	John Enright (R)	51.9	23.0	425
11	Leo Ryan* (D)	83.5	75.8	22,778
	Brainard Merdinger (R)	No Opp.	21.3	2,074
12	Paul N. McCloskey* (R)	49.8	69.1	166,441
	Gary Gillmor (D)	31.9	30.9	37,128
13	*Norman Y. Mineta (D)*	*77.8*	*52.6*	*185,236*
	George W. Milias (R)	*46.3*	*42.4*	*122,239*
14	John McFall* (D)	80.6	70.9	52,268
	Charles Gibson (R)	55.6	24.1	4,154
15	B. F. Sisk* (D)	No Opp.	72.0	55,723
	Carol Harner (R)	No Opp.	28.0	5,303
16	Burt L. Talcott* (R)	No Opp.	49.2	152,455
	Julian Camacho (D)	61.7	47.8	156,084
17	John Krebs (D)	61.5	51.9	130,193
	Robert B. Mathias* (R)	82.2	48.1	136,407
18	William Ketchum* (R)	71.7	52.7	69,806
	George Seielstad (D)	51.4	47.3	48,604

Con. Dist.	Source: Common Cause Campaign Monitoring Project	Primary Vote %	General Election Vote %	Expenditures
19	Robert J. Lagomersino* (R)	91.0	56.3	74,832
	James Loebl (D)	60.0	43.7	90,337
20	Barry M. Goldwater, Jr.* (R)	91.3	61.2	80,385
	Arline Mathews (D)	42.8	38.8	21,212
21	James C. Corman* (D)	No Opp.	73.5	77,204 [1]
	Mel Nadell (R)	No Opp.	26.5	3,603
22	Carlos Moorhead* (R)	86.2	55.8	51,841
	Richard Hallin (D)	66.6	44.2	68,449
23	Thomas M. Rees* (D)	93.1	71.4	80,318
	Jack Roberts (R)	No Opp.	28.6	5,520
24	*Henry A. Waxman (D)*	*74.2*	*64.0*	*95,151*
	Elliott Graham (R)	*30.5*	*33.0*	*22,411*
25	Edward R. Roybal* (D)	No Opp.	No Opp.	24,630
26	John Rousselot* (R)	No Opp.	58.9	66,043
	Paul Conforti (D)	48.9	41.1	8,235
27	Alphonzo Bell* (R)	81.6	63.9	32,270
	John Dalessio (D)	36.1	32.5	29,025
28	Yvonne Burke* (D)	89.8	80.1	29,739
	Tom Neddy (R)	No Opp.	19.9	0
29	Augustus Hawkins* (D)	87.0	No Opp.	6,268
30	George Danielson* (D)	53.6	74.2	64,413
	John Perez (R)	37.7	25.8	5,953
31	Charles H. Wilson* (D)	56.2	70.4	70,813
	Norman Hodges (R)	No Opp.	26.8	38,954
32	Glenn Anderson* (D)	No Opp.	87.7	44,232
33	Del Clawson* (R)	No Opp.	53.4	80,347
	Robert White (D)	21.2	43.1	56,364
34	*Mark W. Hannaford (D)*	*24.1*	*49.8*	*86,981*
	Bill Bond (R)	*44.9*	*46.3*	*82,917*
35	Jim Lloyd (D)	23.4	50.3	153,087
	Victor V. Veysey* (R)	75.5	49.7	147,861
36	George Brown* (D)	75.7	62.6	43,635
	Jim Osgood (R)	81.8	32.3	21,412
37	Jerry Pettis* (R)	No Opp.	63.2	33,818
	Bobby Ray Vincent (D)	39.9	32.9	9,732
38	*Jerry M. Patterson (D)*	*46.6*	*54.0*	*165,696*
	David Rehmann (R)	*46.1*	*41.3*	*120,744*
39	Charles Wiggins* (R)	74.4	55.3	53,292
	William Farris (D)	38.6	40.4	26,533

(1) According to the office of Rep. James Croman (D-Cal), the total expenditure listed includes Congressional office expenses and therefore is not exclusively campaign expenditures.

Con. Dist.	Source: Common Cause Campaign Monitoring Project	Primary Vote %	General Election Vote %	Expenditures
40	Andrew J. Hinshaw* (R)	69.5	63.4	72,022
	Roderick Wilson (D)	49.0	30.9	11,781
41	Bob Wilson* (R)	No Opp.	54.5	149,467
	Colleen O'Connor (D)	29.9	43.0	51,980
42	Lionel Van Deerlin* (D)	No Opp.	69.9	38,462
	Wes Marden (R)	No Opp.	30.1	10,555
43	Clair Burgener* (R)	No Opp.	60.4	64,022
	Bill Bandes (D)	49.1	39.6	22,055
	COLORADO			
1	Patricia Schroeder* (D)	No Opp.	58.5	104,126
	Frank K. Southworth (R)	No Opp.	40.8	105,532
2	Timothy E. Wirth (D)	No Opp.	51.9	134,103
	Donald G. Brotzman* (R)	No Opp.	48.0	165,911
3	Frank Evans* (D)	62.1	67.9	30,855
	E. Keith Records (R)	No Opp.	32.1	5,120
4	James P. Johnson* (R)	No Opp.	52.0	53,940
	John S. Carroll (D)	No Opp.	48.0	62,704
5	William L. Armstrong* (R)	No Opp.	57.7	108,701
	Ben Galloway (D)	No Opp.	38.5	32,446
	CONNECTICUT			
1	William Cotter* (D)	No Opp.	62.7	52,604
	F. Mac Buckley (R)	No Opp.	35.9	28,045
2	*Christopher J. Dodd (D)*	*No Opp.*	*59.0*	*102,209*
	Samuel B. Hellier (R)	*No Opp.*	*39.2*	*87,844*
3	Robert Giaimo* (D)	No Opp.	65.1	40,079
	James Altham, Jr. (R)	No Opp.	31.4	6,556
4	Stewart B. McKinney* (R)	No Opp.	53.2	94,365
	James Kellis (D)	No Opp.	45.2	51,034
5	Ronald A. Sarasin* (R)	No Opp.	50.4	134,440
	William R. Ratchford (D)	61.2	48.0	86,808
6	*Anthony J. Moffett (D)*	*58.0*	*63.4*	*144,806*
	Patsy J. Piscopo (R)	*No Opp.*	*36.1*	*89,328*
	DELAWARE			
1	Pierre DuPont* (R)	No Opp.	58.5	92,246
	James Soles (D)	No Opp.	39.6	68,839
	FLORIDA			
1	Robert Sikes* (D)	No Opp.	No Opp.	5,740
2	Don Fuqua* (D)	85.7	No Opp.	32,316

Con. Dist.	Source: Common Cause Campaign Monitoring Project	Primary Vote %	General Election Vote %	Expenditures
3	Charles Bennett* (D)	86.4	No Opp.	2,728
4	Bill Chappell, Jr.* (D)	No Opp.	68.2	63,817
	Warren Hauser (R)	No Opp.	31.8	17,116
5	*Richard Kelly (R)*	*52.9*	*52.8*	*111,194*
	JoAnn Saunders (D)**	*55.9*	*44.8*	*62,119*
6	C. W. Bill Young* (R)	No Opp.	75.8	32,105
	Herbert Monrose (D)	No Opp.	24.2	4,771
7	Sam Gibbons* (D)	No Opp.	No Opp.	6,228
8	James Haley* (D)	74.8	56.7	15,879
	Joe Lovingood (R)**	64.7	43.3	45,650
9	Louis Frey, Jr.* (R)	No Opp.	76.7	53,787
	William Rowland (D)	52.9	23.3	5,044
10	Skip Bafalis* (R)	No Opp.	73.7	32,735
	Evelyn Tucker (D)	No Opp.	26.3	4,360
11	Paul Rogers* (D)	85.6	No. Opp.	15,517
12	J. Herbert Burke* (R)	74.5	51.0	30,554
	Charles Friedman (D)**	51.1	49.0	32,038
13	William Lehman* (D)**	67.7	No Opp.	81,915
14	Claude Pepper* (D)	No Opp.	69.1	26,393
	Michael Carricarte (R)	56.8	30.9	18,631
15	Dante Fascell* (D)	No Opp.	70.5	41,957
	S. Peter Capua (R)	No Opp.	29.5	47,775
	GEORGIA			
1	Ronald B. Ginn* (D)	No Opp.	86.1	27,277
	Bill Gowan (R)	No Opp.	13.9	1,627
2	Dawson Mathis* (D)	No Opp.	No Opp.	16,201
3	Jack Brinkley* (D)	No Opp.	87.7	26,824
	Carl Savage (R)	No Opp.	12.3	12,520
4	Elliott H. Levitas (D)	62.7	55.1	121,724
	Ben B. Blackburn* (R)	No Opp.	44.9	160,151
5	Andrew Young* (D)	No Opp.	71.6	83,481
	Wyman Lowe (R)	No Opp.	28.3	7,713
6	John Flynt, Jr.* (D)	No Opp.	51.5	33,035
	Newt Gingrich (R)	No Opp.	48.5	85,505
7	*Lawrence P. McDonald (D)*	*51.7*	*50.3*	*188,093*
	Quincy Collins (R)	*73.1*	*49.7*	*66,827*
8	Bill Stuckey, Jr.* (D)	59.5	No Opp.	34,674
9	Phil Landrum* (D)	66.6	74.8	17,710
	Ronald Reeves (R)	No Opp.	25.2	2,140
10	Robert Stephens, Jr.* (D)	No Opp.	68.4	17,410
	Gary Pleger (R)	62.5	31.6	18,788

Con. Dist.	Source: Common Cause Campaign Monitoring Project	Primary Vote %	General Election Vote %*	Expenditures
	HAWAII			
1	Spark Matsunaga* (D)	No Opp.	59.3	165,469
	William Paul (R)	No Opp.	40.7	29,799
2	Patsy T. Mink* (D)	70.0	62.6	97,104
	Carla Coray (R)	No Opp.	37.4	34,089
	IDAHO			
1	Steven D. Symms* (R)	No Opp.	58.3	125,268
	J. Ray Cox (D)	50.1	41.7	43,784
2	*George V. Hansen (R)*	*53.3*	*55.7*	*120,923*
	Max Hanson (D)	*76.2*	*44.3*	*20,982*
	ILLINOIS			
1	Ralph Metcalfe* (D)	No Opp.	93.7	37,900
	Oscar Haynes (R)	No Opp.	5.5	833
2	Morgan Murphy* (D)	79.2	87.5	12,299
	James Ginderske (R)	No Opp.	12.5	350
3	Martin A. Russo (D)	No Opp.	52.6	79,420
	Robert Hanrahan* (R)	81.2	47.4	40,912
4	Edward Derwinski* (R)	No Opp.	59.2	41,646
	Ronald Rodger (D)	53.3	40.8	18,301
5	John Kluczynski* (D)	No Opp.	86.0	22,269
	William Toms (R)	No Opp.	14.0	503
6	*Henry J. Hyde (R)*	*48.1*	*53.4*	*175,087*
	Edward V. Hanrahan (D)	*56.1*	*46.6*	*66,284*
7	Cardiss Collins* (D)	No Opp.	87.9	7,292
	Donald Metzger (R)	No Opp.	12.1	16,207
8	Dan Rostenkowski* (D)	No Opp.	86.5	25,720
	Salvatore Oddo (R)	No Opp.	13.5	0
9	Sidney Yates* (D)	No Opp.	No Opp.	11,226
10	Abner J. Mikva (D)	No Opp.	50.9	286,225
	Samuel H. Young* (R)	No Opp.	49.1	251,249
11	Frank Annunzio* (D)	89.0	72.4	58,239
	Mitchell Zadrozny (R)	No Opp.	27.6	33,362
12	Philip Crane* (R)	No Opp.	61.1	60,122
	Betty Spence (D)	No Opp.	38.9	51,594
13	Robert McClory* (R)	71.0	54.5	38,921
	Stanley Beetham (D)	66.3	45.5	39,642
14	John Erlenborn* (R)	No Opp.	66.6	34,214
	Robert Renshaw (D)	47.0	33.4	3,474
15	*Tim L. Hall (D)*	*44.8*	*52.0*	*29,398*
	Clifford D. Carlson (R)	*24.1*	*45.6*	*110,540*

Con. Dist.	Source: Common Cause Campaign Monitoring Project	Primary Vote %	General Election Vote %	Expenditures
16	John B. Anderson* (R)	No Opp.	55.5	74,346
	Marshall Hungness (D)	No Opp.	28.7	4,587
17	George M. O'Brien* (R)	No Opp.	51.5	80,053
	John Houlihan (D)	73.3	48.5	24,863
18	Robert Michel* (R)	No Opp.	54.8	33,851
	Stephen Nordvall (D)	72.6	45.2	10,776
19	Tom Railsback* (R)	No Opp.	65.3	61,789
	Jim Gende (D)	50.3	34.7	43,533
20	Paul Findley* (R)	No Opp.	54.8	118,162
	Peter Mack (D)	52.7	45.2	53,369
21	Edward Madigan* (R)	No Opp.	65.8	68,372
	Richard Small (D)	52.2	34.2	21,431
22	George Shipley* (D)	No Opp.	59.8	50,328
	William A. Young (R)	71.3	40.2	91,781
23	Melvin Price* (D)	90.3	80.5	27,847
	Scott Randolph (R)	No Opp.	19.5	670
24	*Paul Simon (D)*	*68.4*	*59.6*	*223,163*
	Val Oshel (R)	*57.7*	*40.4*	*50,566*
	INDIANA			
1	Ray Madden* (D)	74.5	68.6	20,416
	Joseph Harkin (R)	57.4	31.4	10,369
2	Floyd J. Fithian (D)	No Opp.	61.1	155,580
	Earl O. Landgrebe* (R)	No Opp.	38.9	73,909
3	John Brademas* (D)	79.6	64.1	145,733
	Virginia Black (R)	No Opp.	35.9	16,184
4	J. Edward Roush* (D)	89.8	51.9	57,615
	Walter P. Helmke (R)	68.0	46.5	77,576
5	Elwood Hillis* (R)	No Opp.	56.6	55,490
	William Sebree (D)	27.6	43.4	18,758
6	David Evans (D)	55.4	52.4	15,846
	William Bray* (R)	88.5	47.6	45,434
7	John Myers* (R)	No Opp.	57.1	44,556
	Eldon Tipton (D)	32.9	42.1	13,916
8	Philip Hayes (D)	48.4	53.4	67,429
	Roger H. Zion* (R)	87.0	46.6	122,329
9	Lee Hamilton* (D)	No Opp.	71.1	69,375
	Delson Cox, Jr. (R)	39.5	28.9	7,553
10	Philip R. Sharp (D)	68.5	54.4	74,199
	David W. Dennis* (R)	88.4	45.6	79,840
11	Andrew Jacobs, Jr. (D)	86.4	52.5	47,336
	William H. Hudnut* (R)	94.0	47.5	201,673

Con. Dist.	Source: Common Cause Campaign Monitoring Project	Primary Vote %	General Election Vote %	Expenditures
	IOWA			
1	Edward Mezvinsky* (D)	No Opp.	54.4	81,166
	James A. Leach (R)	No Opp.	45.6	89,786
2	*Michael T. Blouin (D)*	*45.4*	*51.1*	*137,750*
	Tom Riley (R)	*69.0*	*48.1*	*107,884*
3	*Charles E. Grassley (R)*	*41.9*	*50.8*	*107,102*
	Stephen J. Rapp (D)	*35.8*	*49.2*	*100,007*
4	Neal Smith* (D)	No Opp.	63.9	0
	Chuck Dick (R)	No Opp.	35.5	55,231
5	Tom Harkin (D)	No Opp.	51.1	120,544
	William J. Scherle* (R)	No Opp.	48.9	103,582
6	Berkley Bedell (D)	No Opp.	54.6	130,742
	Wiley Mayne* (R)	No Opp.	45.4	96,085
	KANSAS			
1	Keith Sibelius* (R)	No Opp.	58.4	60,893
	Donald Smith (D)	46.0	33.0	64,428
2	*Martha Keys (D)*	*38.4*	*55.0*	*88,959*
	John C. Peterson (R)	*57.6*	*43.9*	*114,214*
3	Larry Winn, Jr.* (R)	No Opp.	62.9	77,681
	Samuel Wells (D)	50.6	35.0	26,318
4	Garner Shriver* (R)	No Opp.	48.8	67,446
	Bert Chaney (D)	43.1	42.5	24,467
	John S. Stevens (A)		8.7	2,922
5	Joe Skubitz* (R)	86.9	55.2	63,968
	Franklin D. Gaines (D)	57.6	44.8	99,553
	KENTUCKY			
1	*Carroll Hubbard, Jr. (D)*	*50.5*	*78.2*	*64,599*
	Charles Banken, Jr. (R)	*41.0*	*18.7*	*1,350*
2	William Natcher* (D)	74.9	73.0	14,505
	Art Eddleman (R)	No Opp.	23.7	21
3	Romano Mazzoli* (D)	90.9	69.7	28,353
	Vincent Barclay (R)	No Opp.	26.6	2,446
4	Gene Snyder* (R)	No Opp.	51.7	86,973
	Kyle Hubbard (D)	52.0	48.3	82,150
5	Tim Lee Carter* (R)	No Opp.	68.2	18,763
	Lyle Willis (D)	45.9	29.3	228
6	John Breckinridge* (D)	83.0	72.1	20,932
	Thomas Rogers III (R)	60.6	24.1	2,217
7	Carl Perkins* (D)	No Opp.	75.6	2,100
	Granville Thomas (R)	No Opp.	24.4	104

Con. Dist.	Source: Common Cause Campaign Monitoring Project	Primary Vote %	General Election Vote %	Expenditures
	LOUISIANA			
1	F. Edward Hebert* (D)	80.1	No Opp.	4,712
2	Corinne Boggs* (D)	87.2	81.8	49,846
	Diane Morphos (R)	No Opp.	14.6	7,192
3	David C. Treen* (R)	No Opp.	58.5	190,135
	Charles Grisbaum, Jr. (D)	No Opp.	41.5	166,203
4.	J. D. Waggonner, Jr.* (D)	No Opp.	No Opp.	3,459
5	Otto E. Passman* (D)	73.6	No Opp.	23,902
6	*Henson Moore III (R)*	*No Opp.*	*54.1*	*158,971*
	Jeff LaCaze (D)	*51.6*	*45.9*	*229,335*
7	John Greaux* (D)	87.7	89.3	29,991
8	Gillis W. Long* (D)	No Opp.	No Opp.	36,325
	MAINE			
1	David Emery (R)	No Opp.	50.2	68,040
	Peter Kyros* (D)	69.1	49.8	68,094
2	William S. Cohen* (R)	No Opp.	71.4	91,548
	Markham Gartley (D)	65.8	28.6	30,412
	MARYLAND			
1	Robert E. Bauman* (R)	No Opp.	53.0	137,046
	Thomas Hatem (D)	56.2	47.0	48,043
2	Clarence D. Long* (D)	No Opp.	77.1	33,181
	John Seney (R)	No Opp.	22.9	6,234
3	Paul Sarbanes* (D)	No Opp.	83.8	8,765
	William Matthews (R)	No Opp.	16.2	193
4	Marjorie S. Holt (R)	No Opp.	58.1	99,717
	Fred L. Wineland (D)	54.9	41.9	134,323
5	*Gladys N. Spellman (D)*	*67.1*	*52.6*	*90,144*
	John B. Burcham, Jr. (R)	*74.0*	*47.4*	*39,038*
6	Goodloe Byron* (D)	75.1	73.7	31,308
	Elton Wampler (R)	No Opp.	26.3	11,556
7	Parren J. Mitchell* (D)	No Opp.	No Opp.	22,376
8	Gilbert Gude* (R)	85.0	65.9	48,063
	Sidney Kramer (D)	44.8	34.1	43,889
	MASSACHUSETTS			
1	Silvio O. Conte* (R)	No Opp.	71.1	47,736
	Thomas R. Manning (D)	55.1	28.9	8,067
2	Edward P. Boland* (D)	No Opp.	No Opp.	56
3	*Joseph D. Early (D)*	*31.8*	*49.5*	*120,584*
	David J. Lionett (R)	*83.2*	*38.4*	*127,978*

Con. Dist.	Source: Common Cause Campaign Monitoring Project	Primary Vote %	General Election Vote %	Expenditures
	Douglas J. Rowe (Ind)		*12.0*	*69,267*
4	Robert F. Drinan* (D)	No Opp.	50.8	178,871
	Jon Rotenberg (Ind)	No Opp.	34.7	76,576
	Alvin Mandell (R)	No Opp.	14.4	14,322
5	Paul E. Tsongas (D)	72.5	60.6	105,267
	Paul W. Cronin* (R)	No Opp.	39.4	124,049
6	Michael J. Harrington*(D)	74.4	No Opp.	29,810
7	Torbert MacDonald*(D)	No Opp.	79.8	15,596
8	Thomas P. O'Neill, Jr.* (D)	No Opp.	87.9	1,414
9	John Joseph Moakley*(D)	No Opp.	89.3	74,237
10	Margaret Heckler* (R)	No Opp.	64.2	71,100
	Barry Monahan (D)	No Opp.	35.8	34,012
11	James A. Burke* (D)	73.1	No Opp.	39,707
12	Gerry Studds* (D)	No Opp.	74.8	103,350
	J. Alan MacKay (R)	No Opp.	25.2	37,505
	MICHIGAN			
1	John Conyers, Jr.* (D)	No Opp.	90.7	20,292
	Walter Girardot (R)	No Opp.	8.7	85
2	Marvin L. Esch* (R)	No Opp.	52.3	106,747
	John S. Reuther (D)	31.5	45.4	112,860
3	Garry Brown* (R)	No Opp.	51.2	52,305
	Paul Todd, Jr. (D)	No Opp.	47.6	42,961
4	Edward Hutchinson* (R)	No Opp.	53.1	8,254
	Richard Daugherty (D)	No Opp.	45.5	7,606
5	Richard Vander Veen*(D)	No Opp.	52.6	143,603
	Paul G. Goebel (R)	54.5	43.4	158,891
	Dwight W. Johnson (AIP)		3.7	11,255
6	*Bob Carr (D)*	*72.4*	*49.3*	*157,478*
	Clifford W. Taylor (R)	*42.2*	*48.9*	*119,329*
7	Donald Riegle, Jr.* (D)	81.0	64.7	46,731
	Robert Eastman (R)	No Opp.	33.2	8,902
8	Bob Traxler* (D)	No Opp.	54.8	76,856
	James M. Sparling (R)	89.9	43.4	82,879
9	Guy Vander Jagt* (R)	No Opp.	56.6	51,196
	Norman Halbower (D)	No Opp.	42.1	21,382
10	Elford Cederberg* (R)	77.1	53.7	38,876
	Samuel Marble (D)	No Opp.	45.9	19,974
11	Philip Ruppe* (R)	No Opp.	50.9	45,240
	Francis Brouillette (D)	53.2	48.8	62,656

Con. Dist.	Source: Common Cause Campaign Monitoring Project	Primary Vote %	General Election Vote %	Expenditures
12	James G. O'Hara* (D)	No Opp.	72.2	22,289
	Eugene Tyza (R)	No Opp.	27.6	997
13	Charles Diggs, Jr.* (D)	No Opp.	87.4	400
	George McCall (R)	No Opp.	11.1	194
14	Lucien Nedzi* (D)	73.8	71.2	14,717
	Herbert Steiger (R)	No Opp.	27.1	0
15	William D. Ford* (D)	No Opp.	78.1	43,458
	Jack Underwood (R)	73.2	20.8	79
16	John Dingell* (D)	No Opp.	77.7	25,410
	Wallace English (R)	56.4	20.5	1,345
17	*William Brodhead (D)*	*27.4*	*69.5*	*55,180*
	Kenneth Gallagher (R)	*62.9*	*29.4*	*97*
18	James J. Blanchard (D)	33.8	58.7	133,021
	Robert J. Huber* (R)	No Opp.	40.2	120,426
19	William Broomfield* (R)	No Opp.	62.9	34,439
	George Montgomery (D)	No Opp.	36.9	6,357

MINNESOTA

1	Albert Quie* (R)	No Opp.	62.6	67,101
	Uric Scott (D)	63.3	37.4	54,539
2	*Tom Hagedorn (R)*	*72.8*	*53.1*	*148,833*
	Steve Babcock (D)	*51.8*	*46.9*	*142,812*
3	Bill Frenzel* (R)	No Opp.	60.4	104,815
	Bob Riggs (D)	71.9	39.6	33,486
4	Joseph Karth* (D)	No Opp.	76.0	58,551
	Joseph Rheinberger (R)	68.0	24.0	5,740
5	Donald Fraser* (R)	No Opp.	73.8	63,397
	Phil Ratte (D)	No Opp.	24.7	13,340
6	*Richard Nolan (D)*	*69.9*	*55.4*	*139,342*
	Jon Grunseth (R)	*78.4*	*44.6*	*121,048*
7	Bob Bergland* (D)	No Opp.	75.0	92,608
	Dan Reber (R)	No Opp.	25.0	15,082
8	*James Oberstar (D)*	*50.3*	*62.0*	*106,186*
	Jerome Arnold (R)	*68.1*	*26.1*	*38,435*

MISSISSIPPI

1	Jamie L. Whitten* (D)	No Opp.	88.2	3,209
2	David R. Bowen* (D)	81.9	66.1	60,735
	Ben F. Hilburn (R)	No Opp.	27.7	27,000
3	G. V. Montgomery* (D)	No Opp.	No Opp.	0
4	Thad Cochran* (R)	98.5	70.2	83,884
	Kenneth L. Dean (D) **	50.9	28.8	11,360

Con. Dist.	Source: Common Cause Campaign Monitoring Project	Primary Vote %	General Election Vote %	Expenditures
5	Trent Lott* (R)	No Opp.	73.0	31,464
	Walter W. Murphey (D)	50.1	14.4	2,163
	MISSOURI			
1	William Clay* (D)	67.8	68.3	43,810
	Arthur Martin (R)	53.9	31.7	1,881
2	James W. Symington* (D)	71.6	61.0	74,762
	Howard C. Ohlendorf (R)	No Opp.	39.0	43,330
3	Leonor K. Sullivan* (D)	89.5	74.3	27,800
	Jo Ann P. Raisch (R)	67.4	24.3	2,254
4	William J. Randall* (D)	86.7	67.9	19,596
	Claude Patterson (R)	No Opp.	32.1	12,771
5	Richard Bolling* (D)	86.6	69.1	20,590
	John J. McDonough (R)	55.3	29.9	9,247
6	Jerry Litton* (D)	No Opp.	78.9	52,896
	Grover Speers (R)	No Opp.	21.1	745
7	Gene Taylor* (R)	76.0	52.3	96,782
	Richard L. Franks (D)	70.4	47.7	94,173
8	Richard H. Ichord* (D)	84.6	69.9	50,156
	James A. Noland, Jr. (R)	No Opp.	30.1	195
9	William L. Hungate* (D)	No Opp.	66.4	30,091
	Milton Bischof, Jr. (R)	No Opp.	33.6	13,369
10	Bill D. Burlison* (D)	80.1	72.8	28,021
	Truman Farrow (R)	59.6	27.2	2,063
	MONTANA			
1	Max S. Baucus (D)	43.6	54.8	111,096
	Richard G. Shoup* (R)	No Opp.	45.2	101,118
2	John Melcher* (D)	No Opp.	63.0	57,016
	John K. McDonald (R)	63.6	37.0	32,341
	NEBRASKA			
1	Charles Thone* (R)	No Opp.	53.3	98,307
	Hess Dyas (D)	No Opp.	46.7	133,261
2	John Y. McCollister* (R)	No Opp.	55.2	92,834
	Daniel C. Lynch (D)	64.2	44.8	87,691
3	*Virginia Smith (R)*	*21.7*	*50.2*	*102,820*
	Wayne W. Ziebarth (D)	*68.9*	*49.8*	*90,123*
	NEVADA			
1	James Santini (D)	53.8	55.8	122,199
	David Towell* (R)	87.1	36.4	111,697

Con. Dist.	Source: Common Cause Campaign Monitoring Project	Primary Vote %	General Election Vote %	Expenditures
	NEW HAMPSHIRE			
1	Norman E. D'Amours (D)	49.8	52.1	75,128
	David A. Banks (R)	39.5	47.9	108,163
2	James C. Cleveland* (R)	86.1	64.2	27,102
	Helen L. Bliss (D)	56.5	35.8	15,835
	NEW JERSEY			
1	James J. Florio (D)	82.8	57.5	97,679
	John E. Hunt* (R)	No Opp.	38.5	57,787
2	William J. Hughes (D)	54.7	57.3	119,864
	Chas. W. Sandman,Jr.*(R)	No Opp.	41.3	98,734
3	James J. Howard* (D)	No Opp.	68.9	52,474
	Kenneth W. Clark (R)	No Opp.	29.8	15,231
4	Frank W. Thompson* (D)	64.9	66.8	44,542
	Henry J. Keller (R)	No Opp.	33.2	11,891
5	Millicent Fenwick (R)	47.9	53.4	131,861
	Frederick Bohen (D)	57.4	43.5	117,033
6	Edwin B. Forsythe* (R)	93.3	52.5	46,521
	Charles B. Yates (D)	34.0	45.5	66,501
7	Andrew Maguire (D)	50.9	49.7	137,280
	William B. Widnall* (R)	63.4	44.4	49,575
	Milton Gralla (Ind)		5.9	26,404
8	Robert A. Roe* (D)	92.7	73.9	36,496
	Herman Schmidt (R)	No Opp.	24.6	415
9	Henry Helstoski* (D)	91.4	64.5	35,192
	Harold A. Pareti (R)	No Opp.	32.9	23,813
10	Peter W. Rodino, Jr.* (D)	89.0	81.0	26,286
	John R. Taliaferro (R)	No Opp.	15.2	0
11	Joseph G. Minish* (D)	No Opp.	69.2	47,606
	William B. Grant (R)	No Opp.	29.4	29,292
12	Matthew J. Rinaldo* (R)	92.6	65.0	128,915
	Adam K. Levin (D)	82.4	32.4	143,895
13	Helen S. Meyner (D)	47.2	57.3	129,289
	Joseph J. Maraziti* (R)	No Opp.	42.7	68,838
14	Dominick V. Daniels* (D)	94.3	79.9	80,556
	Claire J. Sheridan (R)	73.8	16.1	0
15	Edward J. Patten* (D)	No Opp.	71.0	38,113
	E. J. Hammesfahr (R)	No Opp.	27.5	11,165
	NEW MEXICO			
1	Manuel Lujan, Jr.* (R)	No Opp.	58.6	150,825
	R. A. Mondragon (D)	No Opp.	39.7	113,847

Con. Dist.	Source: Common Cause Campaign Monitoring Project	Primary Vote %	General Election Vote %	Expenditures
2	Harold Runnels* (D)	No Opp.	66.7	59,733
	Donald W. Trubey (R)	No Opp.	31.9	22,131
	NEW YORK			
1	Otis G. Pike* (D)	No Opp.	65.0	26,907
	Donald R. Sallah (R)	No Opp.	28.6	4,999
2	Thomas J. Downey (D)	No Opp.	48.8	44,423
	James R. Grover, Jr.* (R)	No Opp.	44.7	11,258
3	Jerome A. Ambro, Jr. (D)	No Opp.	51.8	77,140
	Angelo D. Roncallo* (R)	No Opp.	46.1	68,716
4	Norman F. Lent* (R)	No Opp.	53.6	53,568
	Franklin Ornstein (D)	No Opp.	46.4	70,256
5	John Wydler* (R)	No Opp.	54.2	68,115
	Allard K. Lowenstein (D)	No Opp.	45.8	112,369
6	Lester L. Wolff* (D)	No Opp.	66.7	54,012
	Edythe Layne (R)	No Opp.	33.3	17,919
7	Joseph P. Addabo* (D)	No Opp.	No Opp.	19,841
8	B. S. Rosenthal* (D)	No Opp.	79.0	14,100
	Albert Lemishow (R)	No Opp.	21.0	880
9	James J. Delaney* (D)	No Opp.	93.0	29,698
10	Mario Biaggi* (D)	No Opp.	82.4	16,524
11	*James H. Scheuer (D)*	*53.4*	*72.2*	*301,135*
	E. G. Desborough (R)	*No Opp.*	*14.2*	*809*
12	Shirley Chisholm* (D)	69.4	80.2	8,947
	Francis J. Voyticky (R)	No Opp.	13.9	–0–
13	*Stephen J. Solarz (D)*	*43.8*	*81.8*	*67,334*
	Jack N. Dobosh (R)	*No Opp.*	*18.2*	*623*
14	*F. W. Richmond (D)*	*42.1*	*71.3*	*245,533*
	Michael Carbajal, Jr. (R)	*No Opp.*	*11.5*	*1,000*
	Donald Elliott (Lib)	*27.1[2]*	*13.5*	*85,680*
15	*Leo C. Zeferetti (D)*	*50.1*	*58.4*	*53,775*
	Austen Canade (R)	*No Opp.*	*37.9*	*39,133*
16	Elizabeth Holtzman* (D)	No Opp.	78.9	31,746
	Joseph Gentilli (R)	No Opp.	21.1	1,249
17	John M. Murphy* (D)	51.1	57.7	75,272
	Frank J. Biondolillo (R)	No Opp.	25.6	6,760
18	Edward I. Koch* (D)	No Opp.	76.7	57,530
	John Boogaerts, Jr. (R)	No Opp.	18.8	14,156
19	Charles B. Rangel* (D)	No Opp.	96.9	15,536

(1) Primary results are for Democratic primary in which Elliott lost to Richmond.

Con. Dist.	Source: Common Cause Campaign Monitoring Project	Primary Vote %	General Election Vote %	Expenditures
20	Bella S. Abzug* (D)	No Opp.	78.7	12,655
	Stephen Posner (R)	No Opp.	15.6	224
21	Herman Badillo* (D)	No Opp.	96.7	7,476
22	Jonathan B. Bingham* (D)	No Opp.	85.1	6,545
	Robert Black (R)	No Opp.	9.0	–0–
23	Peter A. Peyser* (R)	78.4	57.6	73,506
	W. S. Greenawalt (D)	No Opp.	42.4	53,111
24	*Richard L. Ottinger (D)*	*No Opp.*	*57.8*	*120,896*
	C. J. Stephens (R)	*No Opp.*	*42.2*	*60,458*
25	Hamilton Fish, Jr.* (R)	No Opp.	65.3	56,398
	Nicholas B. Angell (D)	No Opp.	33.6	105,404
26	Benjamin A. Gilman* (R)	No Opp.	54.0	91,812
	John G. Dow (D)	No Opp.	38.5	44,465
27	*Matthew F. McHugh (D)*	*50.0*	*52.8*	*56,361*
	Alfred J. Libous (R)	*43.9*	*43.1*	*62,196*
	Franklin B. Resseguie (Con)		*4.1*	*31,904*
28	Samuel S. Stratton* (D)	89.7	80.6	26,618
	Wayne E. Wagner (R)	61.5	17.3	12,232
29	Edward W. Pattison (D)	43.0	54.5	36,227
	Carleton J. King* (R)	59.8	45.5	35,962
30	Robert C. McEwen* (R)	No Opp.	55.0	15,710
	Roger W. Tubby (D)	No Opp.	45.0	25.944
31	Donald J. Mitchell* (R)	No Opp.	59.6	71,642
	Donald J. Reile (D)	51.8	37.7	30,820
32	James M. Hanley* (D)	No Opp.	59.1	70,820
	William E. Bush (R)	No Opp.	40.9	24,942
33	William F. Walsh* (R)	No Opp.	65.3	39,085
	Robert H. Bockman (D)	No Opp.	30.2	4,857
34	Frank Horton* (R)	No Opp.	67.5	68,207
	Irene Gossin (D)	No Opp.	29.0	26,379
35	Barber B. Conable,Jr.*(R)	No Opp.	56.8	75,157
	Margaret Costanza (D)	46.8	39.6	79,560
36	*John J. La Falce (D)*	*69.2*	*59.6*	*65,761*
	Russell A. Rourke (R)	*No Opp.*	*40.4*	*95,249*
37	*Henry J. Nowak (D)*	*No Opp.*	*75.0*	*14,841*
	Joseph R. Bala (R)	*No Opp.*	*24.6*	*22,118*
38	Jack F. Kemp* (R)	No Opp.	72.1	111,609
	Barbara C. Wicks (D)	No Opp.	27.9	11,038
39	James F. Hastings* (R)	No Opp.	60.2	39,974
	W. L. Parment (D)	No Opp.	37.1	7,857

Con. Dist.	Source: Common Cause Campaign Monitoring Project	Primary Vote %	General Election Vote %	Expenditures
	NORTH CAROLINA			
1	Walter B. Jones* (D)	90.0	77.5	14,958
	Harry McMullan (R)	No Opp.	22.5	23,729
2	L. H. Fountain* (D)	No Opp.	No Opp.	923
3	David N. Henderson* (D)	No Opp.	No Opp.	560
4	Ike F. Andrews* (D)	63.7	64.7	111,307
	Ward Purrington (R)	No Opp.	34.6	95,418
5	Stephen L. Neal (D)	83.4	52.0	61,107
	Wilmer Mizell* (R)	No Opp.	47.6	62,930
6	Richardson Preyer* (D)	No Opp.	63.7	66,534
	R. S. Ritchie (R)	No Opp.	35.9	85,604
7	Charles C. Rose III* (D)	60.4	No Opp.	39,315
8	W. G. Hefner (D)	No Opp.	57.0	71,793
	Earl B. Ruth* (R)	No Opp.	43.0	35,603
9	James G. Martin* (R)	No Opp.	54.4	128,937
	Milton Short (D)	53.4	44.1	54,071
10	James T. Broyhill* (R)	No Opp.	54.4	78,850
	Jack L. Rhyne (D)	72.4	45.6	19,607
11	Roy A. Taylor* (D)	No Opp.	66.0	18,796
	Albert F. Gilman (R)	No Opp.	34.0	5,999
	NORTH DAKOTA			
1	Mark Andrews* (R)	78.4	55.7	86,855
	Byron Dorgan (D)	No Opp.	44.3	50,990
	OHIO			
1	Willis D. Gradison, Jr. (R)	52.1	50.9	126,407
	Thomas Luken* (D)	No Opp.	49.1	79,500
2	Donald D. Clancy* (R)	No Opp.	53.4	33,369
	E. W. Wolterman (D)	50.4	46.6	13,089
3	Chas. W. Whalen, Jr.* (R)	No Opp.	No Opp.	2,545
4	Tennyson Guyer* (R)	No Opp.	61.5	26,471
	J. L. Gehrlich (D)	54.0	38.5	8,704
5	Delbert L. Latta* (R)	No Opp.	62.5	26,183
	Bruce Edwards (D)	No Opp.	37.5	7,790
6	William H. Harsha* (R)	No Opp.	68.2	14,306
	Lloyd A. Wood (D)	No Opp.	31.2	9,085
7	Clarence J. Brown Jr.* (R)	No Opp.	60.5	94,367
	Patrick L. Nelson (D)	62.7	28.7	27,676
8	*Thomas N. Kindness (R)*	*37.0*	*42.4*	*75,516*
	T. Edward Strinko (D)	*34.8*	*38.0*	*72,951*
	Don Gingerich (Ind.)		*19.6*	*36,039*

Con. Dist.	Source: Common Cause Campaign Monitoring Project	Primary Vote %	General Election Vote %	Expenditures
9	Thomas L. Ashley* (D)	78.9	52.8	24,409
	C. S. Finkbeiner, Jr. (R)	51.5	47.2	33,472
10	Clarence E. Miller* (R)	No Opp.	70.4	20,052
	H. Kent Bumpass (D)	No Opp.	29.6	2,423
11	J. William Stanton* (R)	No Opp.	60.5	25,834
	Michael D. Coffey (D)	60.0	39.5	35,009
12	Samuel L. Devine* (R)	No Opp.	50.9	73,858
	Fran Ryan (D)	No Opp.	49.1	94,243
13	Charles A. Mosher* (R)	No Opp.	57.5	17,254
	Fred M. Ritenauer (D)	60.7	42.5	14,889
14	John F. Sieberling, Jr.* (D)	No Opp.	75.4	16,666
	Mark Figetakis (R)	No Opp.	24.6	13,840
15	Chalmers P. Wylie* (R)	No Opp.	61.5	61,241
	Mike McGee (D)	68.9	38.5	21,960
16	Ralph S. Regula* (R)	No Opp.	65.6	61,552
	John G. Freedom (D)	42.9	34.4	15,985
17	John M. Ashbrook* (R)	65.3	52.7	90,357
	David D. Noble (D)	No Opp.	47.3	57,646
18	Wayne L. Hays* (D)	79.5	65.6	32,285
	Ralph Romig (R)	No Opp.	34.4	2,347
19	Charles J. Carney* (D)	76.8	72.7	15,133
	James L. Ripple (R)	No Opp.	27.3	794
20	James V. Stanton* (D)	86.8	86.9	26,109
	Robert A. Frantz (R)	No Opp.	13.1	1,757
21	Louis Stokes* (D)	70.7	82.0	42,214
	Bill Mack (R)	No Opp.	18.0	–0–
22	Charles A. Vanik* (D)	89.1	78.7	649
	William J. Franz (R)	No Opp.	21.3	4,190
23	*Ronald M. Mottl (D)*	*42.7*	*34.8*	*63,671*
	George E. Mastics (R)	*66.8*	*30.5*	*78,348*
	Dennis J. Kucinich (Ind.)		*29.4*	*18,195*

OKLAHOMA

Con. Dist.		Primary Vote %	General Election Vote %	Expenditures
1	James Jones* (D)	81.4	67.9	60,686
	George A. Mizer, Jr. (R)	68.4	32.1	17,878
2	*T. M. Risenhoover (D)***	*52.0*	*59.1*	*79,791*
	Ralph F. Keen (R)	*53.8*	*40.9*	*19,395*
3	Carl Albert* (D)	81.7	No Opp.	18,034
4	Tom Steed* (D)	No Opp.	No Opp.	7,451
5	John Jarman* (D)	61.0	51.7	46,295
	M. H. Edwards (R)	No Opp.	48.3	31,255

293

Con. Dist.	Source: Common Cause Campaign Monitoring Project	Primary Vote %	General Election Vote %	Expendi- tures
6	Glenn L. English, Jr.(D)**	56.4	53.2	78,411
	John N. Camp* (R)	58.1	44.4	53,532

OREGON

1	Les AuCoin (D)	48.9	56.0	95,168
	Diarmuid O'Scannlain (R)	38.8	43.9	83,659
2	Al Ullman* (D)	81.2	78.1	49,496
	Kenneth Brown (R)	No Opp.	21.9	629
3	Robert Duncan (D)	34.4	70.4	84,124
	John Piacentini (R)	66.3	29.5	54,285
4	James Weaver (D)	35.5	52.9	42,271
	John Dellenback* (R)	No Opp.	47.1	52,614

PENNSYLVANIA

1	William A. Barrett* (D)	No Opp.	75.8	14,729
	Russell M. Nigro (R)	No Opp.	23.3	7,841
2	Robert N. C. Nix* (D)	55.7	74.0	12,122
	Jesse W. Woods, Jr. (R)	No Opp.	26.0	15,833
3	William J. Green* (D)	No Opp.	75.4	51,066
	Richard P. Colbert (R)	No Opp.	24.6	3,082
4	Joshua Eilberg* (D)	76.3	71.0	45,286
	Isadore Einhorn (R)	No Opp.	29.0	4,059
5	Richard T. Schulze (R)	43.5	59.6	29,965
	Leo D. McDermott (D)	53.4	40.4	39,922
6	Gus Yatron* (D)	No Opp.	74.6	42,670
	Stephen Postupack (R)	No Opp.	24.0	9,326
7	Robert W. Edgar (D)	65.5	55.3	38,819
	S. J. McEwen, Jr. (R)	50.4	43.7	110,075
8	Edward G. Biester, Jr.* (R)	67.1	56.3	9,660
	William B. Moyer (D)	76.3	40.9	24,343
9	E. G. Shuster* (R)	No Opp.	56.5	60,691
	Robert D. Ford (D)	51.6	43.5	32,281
10	Joseph M. McDade* (R)	No Opp.	64.9	34,512
	Thomas J. Hanlon (D)	54.4	35.1	11,146
11	Daniel J. Flood* (D)	No Opp.	74.5	40,699
	Richard A. Muzyka (R)	No Opp.	25.5	3,369
12	John P. Murtha* (D)	85.2	58.1	58,192
	Harry M. Fox (R)	69.2	41.9	42,598
13	R. Lawrence Coughlin*(R)	No Opp.	62.5	62,677
	Lawrence H. Curry (D)	60.0	37.5	22,039
14	William S. Moorhead* (D)	No Opp.	77.4	23,929
	Zachary Taylor Davis (R)	No Opp.	22.5	1,129

Con. Dist.	Source: Common Cause Campaign Monitoring Project	Primary Vote %	General Election Vote %	Expenditures
15	Fred B. Rooney* (D)	No Opp.	No Opp.	12,261
16	Edwin D. Eshleman* (R)	84.0	63.5	6,996
	Michael J. Minney (D)	No Opp.	35.0	4,507
17	Herman T.Schneebeli*(R)	No Opp.	52.1	47,611
	Peter C. Wambach (D)	50.3	47.9	38,899
18	H. John Heinz III* (R)	No Opp.	72.1	89,449
	Francis J. McArdle (D)	57.7	27.9	23,727
19	*William F. Goodling (R)*	*39.8*	*51.4*	*42,944*
	Arthur L. Berger (D)	*25.5*	*47.6*	*67,162*
20	Joseph M. Gaydos* (D)	No Opp.	81.7	24,778
	Joseph J. Anderko (R)	No Opp.	18.3	101
21	John H. Dent* (D)	No Opp.	69.9	26,636
	C. L. Sconing (R)	57.4	30.1	5,324
22	Thomas E. Morgan* (D)	31.8	63.6	64,572
	J. R. Montgomery (R)	93.4	31.7	173
23	Albert W. Johnson* (R)	54.4	52.7	50,758
	Yates Mast (D)	28.2	47.3	10,870
24	Joseph P. Vigorito* (D)	68.7	58.6	16,327
	Clement R. Scalzitti (R)	No Opp.	41.4	3,619
25	Gary A. Myers (R)	30.9	53.8	33,064
	Frank M. Clark* (D)	56.2	46.2	88,588

RHODE ISLAND

1	F. J. St. Germain* (D)	No Opp.	72.9	59,244
	Ernest Barone (R)	No Opp.	27.1	3,556
2	*Edward Beard (D)*	*51.8*	*78.2*	*20,583*
	Vincent J. Rotondo (R)	*No Opp.*	*21.8*	*41,113*

SOUTH CAROLINA

1	Mendel J. Davis* (D)	No Opp.	72.7	40,729
	George B. Rast (R)	No Opp.	25.9	–0–
2	Floyd Spence* (R)	No Opp.	56.1	167,188
	Matthew J. Perry (D)	57.1	43.0	92,813
3	*Butler C. Derrick Jr. (D)*	*65.2*	*61.8*	*176,022*
	Marshall J. Parker (R)	*No Opp.*	*38.2*	*105,897*
4	James R. Mann* (D)	No Opp.	63.3	26,536
	Robert L. Watkins (R)	No Opp.	36.7	13,994
5	*Kenneth L. Holland (D)***	*53.3*	*61.4*	*96,834*
	Len Phillips (R)	*No Opp.*	*37.8*	*44,759*
6	John W. Jenrette, Jr. (D)	No Opp.	52.0	150,887
	Edward L. Young* (R)	No Opp.	48.0	145,823

Con. Dist.	Source: Common Cause Campaign Monitoring Project	Primary Vote %	General Election Vote %	Expenditures
	SOUTH DAKOTA			
1	Larry Pressler (R)	51.3	55.3	58,106
	Frank E. Denholm* (D)	No Opp.	44.7	20,583
2	James Abdnor* (R)	No Opp.	67.8	66,250
	Jack M. Weiland (D)	No Opp.	32.2	58,907
	TENNESSEE			
1	James H. Quillen* (R)	No Opp.	64.2	10,683
	Lloyd Blevins (D)	No Opp.	35.8	2,013
2	John J. Duncan* (R)	95.6	70.9	28,825
	Jesse James Brown (D)	65.8	29.1	–0–
3	Marilyn Lloyd (D)	(1)	51.1	44,920
	LaMar Baker* (R)	No Opp.	45.9	96,717
4	Joe L. Evins* (D)	No Opp.	99.9	4,776
5	Richard Fulton* (D)	76.2	99.2	34,502
6	Robin L. Beard* (R)	No Opp.	56.7	189,216
	Tim Schaeffer (D)	48.9	43.3	96,288
7	Ed Jones* (D)	70.7	No Opp.	74,880
8	Harold E. Ford (D)	54.7	49.9	146,940
	Dan Kuykendall* (R)	81.9	49.4	132,411
	TEXAS			
1	Wright Patman* (D)	53.4	68.6	141,936
	J. W. Farris (R)	No Opp.	31.4	111,902
2	Charles Wilson* (D)	No Opp.	No Opp.	18,405
3	James M. Collins* (R)	82.4	64.7	192,058
	Harold Collum (D)	58.9	35.3	79,372
4	Ray Roberts* (D)	No Opp.	74.9	16,337
	Dick LeTourneau (R)	No Opp.	25.1	28,765
5	Alan Steelman* (R)	No Opp.	52.1	168,457
	Mike McKool (D)	51.4	47.9	122,086
6	Olin E. Teague* (D)	No Opp.	83.0	7,249
	Carl A. Nigliazzo (R)	No Opp.	17.0	1,203
7	Bill Archer* (R)	No Opp.	79.2	80,941
	Jim Brady (D)	76.8	20.8	10,827
8	Bob Eckhardt* (D)	76.3	72.2	12,841
	Donald D. Whitefield (R)	No Opp.	27.8	10,008
9	Jack Brooks* (D)	No Opp.	61.9	79,023
	Coleman R. Ferguson (R)	No Opp.	38.1	12,805
10	J. J. Pickle* (D)	67.7	80.4	180,294

(1) Mrs. Lloyd replaced her husband who is deceased as the nominee.

Con. Dist.	Source: Common Cause Campaign Monitoring Project	Primary Vote %	General Election Vote %	Expenditures
	Paul A. Weiss (R)	No Opp.	19.6	500
11	W. R. Poage* (D)	80.5	81.6	8,606
	Don Clements (R)	No Opp.	17.2	190
12	Jim Wright* (D)	No Opp.	78.7	118,839
	James S. Garvey (R)	No Opp.	21.3	65,161
13	John Hightower (D)	64.2	57.6	124,132
	Robert Price* (R)	No Opp.	42.4	157,697
14	John D. Young* (D)	No Opp.	No Opp.	2,861
15	Eligio de la Garza* (D)	No Opp.	No Opp.	1,562
16	Richard White* (D)	No Opp.	No Opp.	11,373
17	Omar Burleson* (D)	No Opp.	No Opp.	9,200
18	Barbara Jordan* (D)	No Opp.	84.8	19,825
	Robbins Mitchell (R)	No Opp.	14.0	4
19	George Mahon* (D)	No Opp.	No Opp.	2,044
20	Henry B. Gonzalez* (D)	No Opp.	No Opp.	8,993
21	*Robert Krueger (D)***	*51.5*	*52.6*	*311,953*
	Douglas Harlon (R)	*60.8*	*45.2*	*164,675*
	Ed Gallion (A)		*2.2*	*9,260*
22	Bob Casey* (D)	68.4	69.5	133,623
	Ron Paul (R)	No Opp.	28.4	16,206
23	Abraham Kazen, Jr.* (D)	71.4	No Opp.	44,737
24	Dale Milford* (D)	58.0	76.1	63,103
	Joseph Beaman, Jr. (R)	No Opp.	20.4	1,285

UTAH

Con. Dist.		Primary Vote %	General Election Vote %	Expenditures
1	K. Gunn McKay* (D)	No Opp.	62.6	25,611
	Ronald Inkley (R)	52.7	31.5	10,938
2	*Allan T. Howe (D)*	*55.8*	*49.5*	*95,540*
	Stephen M. Harmsen (R)	*59.7*	*46.9*	*103,717*

VERMONT

Con. Dist.		Primary Vote %	General Election Vote %	Expenditures
1	*James Jeffords (R)*	*39.5*	*52.9*	*55,883*
	Francis Cain (D)	*42.8*	*40.0*	*47,037*

VIRGINIA

Con. Dist.		Primary Vote %	General Election Vote %	Expenditures
1	Thomas Downing* (D)	No Opp.	99.8	2,897
2	G. Wm. Whitehurst* (R)	No Opp.	60.0	83,545
	Robert R. Richards (D)	No Opp.	40.0	44,418
3	David Satterfield III* (D)	No Opp.	88.5	4,406
4	Robert W. Daniel Jr.* (R)	No Opp.	47.2	79,134
	Lester E. Schlitz (D)	No Opp.	35.9	79,837
5	W. C. Daniel* (D)	No Opp.	99.4	1,165

Con. Dist.	Source: Common Cause Campaign Monitoring Project	Primary Vote %	General Election Vote %	Expenditures
6	M. Caldwell Butler* (R)	No Opp.	45.1	63,622
	Paul J. Puckett (D)	No Opp.	27.0	25,933
	Warren D. Saunders (A)	No Opp.	26.1	57,819
7	J. Kenneth Robinson* (R)	No Opp.	52.6	96,443
	George H. Gilliam (D)	No Opp.	47.1	62,839
8	Herbert Harris (D)	52.5	57.6	101,299
	Stanford E. Parris* (R)	No Opp.	42.4	149,450
9	William C. Wampler* (R)	No Opp.	50.9	116,944
	Charles J. Horne (D)	No Opp.	49.1	232,341
10	Joseph L. Fisher (D)	42.2	53.6	144,751
	Joel T. Broyhill* (R)	No Opp.	45.2	248,709

WASHINGTON

Con. Dist.		Primary Vote %	General Election Vote %	Expenditures
1	Joel Pritchard* (R)	No Opp.	69.5	84,093
	Will Knedlick (D)	37.3	28.6	7,108
2	Floyd Meeds* (D)	No Opp.	59.7	65,954
	Ronald Reed (R)	63.3	38.9	14,317
3	*Don Bonker (D)*	*36.0*	*60.9*	*81,853*
	A. Ludlow Kramer (R)	*No Opp.*	*38.1*	*136,810*
4	Mike McCormack* (D)	78.4	58.9	52,217
	Floyd S. Paxton (R)	77.4	41.1	106,726
5	Thomas S. Foley* (D)	84.9	64.3	48,059
	Gary Gage (R)	64.0	35.7	12,228
6	Floyd Hicks* (D)	72.3	71.8	10,357
	George M. Nalley (R)	No Opp.	28.2	8,185
7	Brock Adams* (D)	No Opp.	71.1	46,122
	Raymond Pritchard (R)	56.9	28.9	2,309

WEST VIRGINIA

Con. Dist.		Primary Vote %	General Election Vote %	Expenditures
1	Robert H. Mollohan* (D)	87.1	59.7	62,952
	Joe A. Laurita Jr. (R)	57.2	40.3	105,927
2	Harley O. Staggers* (D)	No Opp.	64.4	15,484
	William H. Loy (R)	No Opp.	35.6	30,995
3	John M. Slack, Jr.* (D)	59.6	68.5	54,008
	William L. Larcamp (R)	No Opp.	31.5	8,123
4	Ken Hechler* (D)	No Opp.	No Opp.	449

WISCONSIN

Con. Dist.		Primary Vote %	General Election Vote %	Expenditures
1	Les Aspin* (D)	No Opp.	70.5	30,443
	Leonard W. Smith (R)	No Opp.	29.5	7,629
2	Robt. W. Kastenmeier*(D)	No Opp.	64.8	17,663
	Elizabeth T. Miller (R)	No Opp.	35.2	16,658

Con. Dist.	Source: Common Cause Campaign Monitoring Project	Primary Vote %	General Election Vote %	Expenditures
3	Alvin J. Baldus (D)	39.7	51.1	72,958
	Vernon W. Thomson* (R)	No Opp.	47.4	87,902
4	Clement J. Zablocki* (D)	No Opp.	72.5	9,852
	Lewis H. Collison (R)	No Opp.	23.8	5,986
5	Henry S. Reuss* (D)	No Opp.	80.0	2,073
	Mildred A. Morries (R)	No Opp.	20.0	459
6	William A. Steiger* (R)	No Opp.	59.5	51,495
	Nancy J. Simenz (D)	No Opp.	35.4	6,128
7	David R. Obey* (D)	No Opp.	70.5	25,807
	Josef Burger (R)	No Opp.	29.4	12,683
8	Robert J. Cornell (D)	56.6	54.4	63,736
	Harold V. Froelich* (R)	No Opp.	45.6	93,272
9	*Robert W. Kasten (R)*	*56.9*	*52.9*	*91,770*
	Lynn S. Adelman (D)	*59.4*	*45.0*	*104,934*
	WYOMING			
1	Teno Roncalio* (D)	No Opp.	54.7	52,860
	Tom Stroock (R)	76.8	45.3	98,581

CAMPAIGN EXPENDITURES IN 1974 SENATE RACES COMPILED BY THE COMMON CAUSE CAMPAIGN MONITORING PROJECT

This list includes the total campaign expenditure figures for all major party candidates and significantly financed minor party or independent candidates in the 1974 general election.

The source of the information on campaign expenditures is the reports filed under the Federal Election Campaign Act of 1971. The totals cover the period between September 1, 1973 and December 31, 1974. Expenditures for each candidate were determined by combining the reports filed by each candidate with those filed by political committees exclusively supporting that candidate. Expenditures include all money spent by the campaign including debts outstanding (except loans outstanding) as of December 31, 1974. Expenditures do not include funds which have been invested in government bonds or certificates of deposit, or funds which have been used to repay loans made to the the campaign. Adjustments have also been made to eliminate all transfers of funds within a campaign.

On the list, winning candidates are listed first. Incumbents are indicated by an asterisk (*). The races printed in *italics* are those in which there was no incumbent in the general election. Candidates indicated by a double asterisk (**) won their primary after a runoff election. The primary vote percentage listed for those candidates is for the runoff. *Congressional Quarterly* is the source of all data on vote percentages.

Expenditures for All November 1974 Senate Races

(The winning candidate is listed first. The contests printed in *italic* are those in which there was no incumbent; those printed in roman had an incumbent candidate. —in Primary Vote % column means candidate was nominated by state convention.)

Source: Common Cause Campaign Monitoring Project	Primary Vote %	General Election Vote %	Expenditures
ALABAMA			
James Allen (D)*	82.6	95.8	37,328
ALASKA			
Mike Gravel (D)*	53.2	58.3	469,300
C. R. Lewis (R)	53.0	41.7	353,701
ARIZONA			
Barry Goldwater (R)*	No Opp.	58.3	394,042
Jonathan Marshall (D)	53.7	41.7	129,260
ARKANSAS			
Dale Bumpers (D)	*65.2*	*84.9*	*335,874*
John Jones (R)	*No Opp.*	*15.1*	*18,651*
CALIFORNIA			
Alan Cranston (D)*	83.4	60.5	1,336,202
H. L. (Bill) Richardson (R)	64.5	36.2	702,767
COLORADO			
Gary Hart (D)	39.3	57.2	352,557
Peter Dominick (R)*	No Opp.	39.5	502,343
CONNECTICUT			
Abraham Ribicoff (D)*	—	63.7	435,985
James H. Brannen (R)	—	34.3	66,162

* Indicates Incumbent
**Indicates Primary Runoff Winner

FLORIDA
Richard Stone (D)**	51.0	43.4	919,787
Jack Eckerd (R)	67.3	40.9	421,169
John Grady (A)		15.7	148,495

GEORGIA
Herman Talmadge (D)*	81.2	71.7	65,207
Jerry Johnson (R)	No Opp.	28.2	12,856

HAWAII
Daniel Inouye (D)*	No Opp.	82.9	205,265

IDAHO
Frank Church (D)*	85.6	56.1	300,300
Robert Smith (R)	72.0	42.1	127,926

ILLINOIS
Adlai E. Stevenson III (D)*	82.6	62.2	757,329
George M. Burditt (R)	82.7	37.2	488,556

INDIANA
Birch Bayh (D)*	—	50.7	1,024,486
Richard G. Lugar (R)	—	46.4	619,678 [1]
Don L. Lee (A)		2.8	19,194

IOWA
John Culver (D)	No Opp.	52.0	470,970
David Stanley (R)	66.6	47.3	336,067

KANSAS
Robert Dole (R)*	No Opp.	50.9	1,110,024
William R. Roy (D)	84.7	49.1	836,927

KENTUCKY
Wendell H. Ford (D)	84.9	53.5	1,006,670
Marlow Cook (R)*	87.1	44.1	524,569

LOUISIANA
Russell Long (D)*	74.5	No Opp.	498,774

MARYLAND
Charles Mathias (R)	75.7	57.3	329,845
Barbara Mikulski (D)	40.4	42.7	74,311

(1) According to Lugar, the Indiana Republican State Central Committee expended an additional $418,000 on behalf of the Lugar for U. S. Senate Committee.

MISSOURI
Thomas F. Eagleton (D)*	87.3	60.1	647,143
Thomas Curtis (R)	81.8	39.3	362,804

NEVADA
Paul Laxalt (R)	*81.3*	*47.0*	*385,861*
Harry Reid (D)	*59.9*	*46.6*	*410,553*

NEW HAMPSHIRE
John H. Durkin (D)	*50.0*	*49.7*	*128,389*
Louis Wyman (R)	*83.2*	*49.7*	*138,605*

NEW YORK
Jacob K. Javits (R)*	No Opp.	45.3	1,090,437
Ramsey Clark (D)	47.8	38.2	855,576
Barbara A. Keating (C)		15.9	192,462

NORTH CAROLINA
Robert B. Morgan (D)	*50.6*	*62.1*	*781,201*
William E. Stevens (R)	*65.5*	*37.0*	*385,527*

NORTH DAKOTA
Milton Young (R)*	No Opp.	48.4	300,121
William Guy (D)	82.9	48.3	115,561
James R. Jungroth (Ind)		2.9	13,187

OHIO
John H. Glenn (D)	*54.5*	*64.6*	*1,149,130*
Ralph Perk (R)	*63.7*	*30.7*	*292,838*

OKLAHOMA
Henry Bellmon (R)*	86.9	49.4	622,480
Ed Edmondson (D)	58.5	48.9	195,429

OREGON
Robert Packwood (R)*	No Opp.	54.9	333,004
Betty Roberts (D)	—	44.2	80,193

PENNSYLVANIA
Richard S. Schweiker (R)*	No Opp.	53.0	799,499
Peter Flaherty (D)	46.1	45.9	256,483

SOUTH CAROLINA
Ernest F. Hollings (D)*	No Opp.	69.5	227,835
Gwenyfred Bush (R)	No Opp.	28.6	6,754

SOUTH DAKOTA
George McGovern (D)*   No Opp.   53.0   1,172,831
Leo K. Thorsness (R)   52.2   47.0   528,817

UTAH
E. J. Garn (R)   —   *50.0*   *363,162*
Wayne Owens (D)   —   *44.1*   *445,500*

VERMONT
Patrick Leahy (D)   *76.3*   *49.5*   *152,817*
Richard Mallary (R)   *59.7*   *46.4*   *90,617*

WASHINGTON
Warren Magnuson (D)*   92.5   60.7   463,116
Jack Metcalf (R)   59.9   36.1   63,153

WISCONSIN
Gaylord Nelson (D)*   No Opp.   61.8   247,551
Thomas Petri (R)   84.8   35.8   80,590

Appendix 2

Speech by Rep. Robert Michel (R.-Ill.)
Exposing Union "In-Kind" Contributions in Four
Special Congressional Elections in 1974*

One final point I would like to make in transgressing upon the Member's time in general debate here is what I see is left out of the bill and which I would like to have seen offered in the form of an amendment to appropriately treat the in-kind services and goods, for the special interest groups often make substantial contributions by providing in-kind services and goods, such as telephones, cars, airplanes, computer time, staff "volunteers," and the like.

The committee bill would exempt these contributions from both the limitation and in some cases the disclosure requirements.

To prevent this type of campaign abuse, the amendment I had intended to offer before adoption of the closed rule would have prevented or prohibited such in-kind contributions in excess of $100.

I might say that in the four particular special elections for seats in the House of Representatives that were held earlier in the year it has been estimated with pretty good justification, and I will insert with my remarks, when I have asked for permission to revise and extend, some documents that will lead us to believe in just those four special elections the in-kind services provided actually approached or exceeded the amount of hard contributions.

Current law defines the word "contribution" to exclude "services provided without compensation by individuals volunteering a portion or all of their time on behalf of a candidate or political committee," and the committee bill further exempts certain other limited personal services, so my amendment would have had no effect on truly voluntary efforts by individuals on behalf of a candidate.

The amendment would, however, have curbed the type of "in-kind" contributions of special interest groups that have resulted in millions of dollars worth of what are, in effect, unreported campaign contributions.

Such contributions have been extensively documented in past campaigns, and represent a serious violation of the spirit, if not the actual letter, of our campaign law.

* *Congressional Record,* August 7, 1974.

While several legislative methods of dealing with this problem have been suggested, a flat prohibition of "in-kind" contributions in excess of $100 is by far the most effective since it would eliminate, beyond the $100 level, the inevitable questions that arise over the worth or dollar value of such services to a candidate.

It seems to me if we hope to maintain any measure of credibility in our efforts at campaign reform, we must certainly take the steps necessary to curb abuses such as this.

Mr. Chairman, I am inserting in the RECORD the material I referred to earlier.

Pennsylvania's 12th District

The documented record of the race between Democrat John Murtha and Republican Harry Fox reveals that literally tens of thousands of union dollars were poured into the campaign by Murtha for former Representative John Saylor's (R-Pa) seat in the 12th District.

Contributions were of two types:

1. "Hard" contributions, in the form of cash donations, from thirty-two different union political action committees in the amount of $25,450.00 that were made to the Citizens for Murtha Committee.

2. "Soft" contributions, in the form of full time union staff personnel from national COPE, state COPE, the Pennsylvania state AFL-CIO and various other unions, the mailing by unions in behalf of Murtha, organizational activity at Indiana University that was clearly coordinated with Frontlash and supervised by a union "volunteer," last minute get-out-the-vote activities, polls conducted by the state AFL-CIO, and other such "soft" contributions. The amount identified in this area—by no means a full tally since the record for most of these hidden contributions remains in the hands of private organizations—comes to over $40,000—or nearly double the amount of hard contributions made by union officials.

STAFF TIME

It is clear that at least 20 union officials contributed time and effort during the campaign. They were:

1. Alexander Barkan, Director, COPE, $32,274.00 annual salary and $6,727.23 expenses.

2. Joseph Ferguson, Business Agent, International Ladies Garment Workers, $11,388.00 in annual salary, and $1,274.46 expenses.

3. Douglas Allen, Pennsylvania State AFL-CIO, salary unknown.

4. Mike Trbovich, Vice President, United Mine Workers, $31,100.57 annual salary and $3,049.04 expenses.

5. John Vento, Pennsylvania State AFL-CIO, salary unknown.

6. Carl Stellmack, Pennsylvania State AFL-CIO, salary unknown.

7. Harry Boyer, Pennsylvania State AFL-CIO, salary unknown.

8. Bernard Lurye, Assistant Manager, Garment Workers, $12,855.00 salary and $938.25 expenses.

9. James Myers, Organizer, AFSCME, $8,793 salary and $8,563.05 expenses.

10. Andrew Koban, District 15, Steelworkers, $17,314.59 salary and $4,179.56 expenses.

11. Edward Monborne, District 2, and International Exec. Board Member UMW, $22,491.73 salary and $4,600.61 expenses.

12. Frank Kulish, District 2 President, UMW, $15,314.17 salary and $87.22 expenses.

13. Mike Johnson, Vice President, Pennsylvania State AFL-CIO, salary unknown.

14. Robert Spence, International Representative, COM-PAC, salary unknown.

15. Walter Carmo, Pennsylvania Education Assoc., salary unknown.

16. Chuck Krawetz, UMW, salary unknown.

17. Arnold Miller, President, UMW, $36,283.79 salary and $3,966.71 expenses.

18. Irwin Aronson, staff Pennsylvania State AFL-CIO, salary unknown.

19. Tom Reddinger, President, Indiana Labor Council (IAM), union salary, if any, unknown.

20. Dana Henry, member, IAM, no union salary.

Each of these individuals were identified—either through newspaper accounts, internal memos or union newsletters and papers—as having spent from one day to as much as five weeks promoting the Murtha candidacy.

One unionist, Tom Reddinger, identified by the *Johnstown Tribune-Democrat* as President of the Indiana County Central Labor Council, admitted in a personal interview, that he took five weeks of unpaid leave time from his job at Fisher-Scientific Company, Indiana, Pa., to work in the Murtha campaign. He further stated that all his expenses during this time were paid for by the Pennsylvania State AFL-CIO, including the cost for four telephones at headquarters, that, according to a General Telephone Company spokesman in Johnstown, would cost $126.80 during the five week period. Based on Reddinger's rate of pay with Fisher, his "in-kind" contribution in salary during the five week period would come to approximately $1000.

Where salaries are available, the union official involved was pro-rated at the actual salary (plus identifiable expenses), for the period of time he was involved; where no salary was available, a reasonable figure of $15,000 per annum was assigned (a low figure in light of the bulk of identified salaries of union officials).

On this basis, it was determined that salaries involved amounted to $5,902.78 and expenses to $2,317.73, for a total of $8,220.51.

Printing

There were four mailings to the 66,000 union members in the district and 6,500 active and retired teacher union members by the Pennsylvania AFL-CIO COPE and the Political Action Committee for Education (PACE), political arm of the state teachers union (Penn. State Education Association).

The two mailed under Permit #1, Harrisburg (the permit is held by Speed Mail, Inc.) were costed out by reputable printers at the following rates:

1. Mailing of January 18, 1974 to 1,000 retirees only:

Printing, $10 and postage, $80 (mailed first class); totals $90.

Mailing of January 25, 1974 to 6,500 active and retired educators:

Printing at $10/m, $650 and postage, $520 (mailed first class) totals $1,170.

Two additional mailings were sent out at the non-profit organization rate (1.7 cents per piece) under permit #668 at Pittsburgh, Pa., a permit registered to the Pennsylvania State. . . . Costs of these two mailings, were as follows:

Mailing to 66,000 union members in District by United Labor Committee:

Printing at $27/m, $1,782; postage at 1.7¢, $112; and postage $191, totals $2,025.

The second quoted postage cost is the difference between a non-profit mailing rate of 1.7¢ and what the candidate would have had to pay if the mailing had gone out regular bulk mail rates.

Mailing to same members in district of flyer with four halftones:

Printing at $40/m, $2,640; postage at 1.7¢, $112; and postage, $191; totals $2,943.

Thus, the total value of mailings by unions in behalf of the Murtha candidacy came to $6,288.00.

Other Contributions

Other "soft" contributions by unions to the Murtha race included:

1. At least 15,000 telephone calls by the Indiana County Central Labor Committee to members of the union in the county. (Source—interview with Tom Reddinger.)

2. "At least $12,000 is expected to go into the district from labor for last minute campaign expenses and election day activities." (*Philadelphia Bulletin*, February 3, 1974.)

3. "$14,000 which . . . the state and national AFL-CIO and COPE committees spent to house and feed staff members at a downtown Johnstown motel during the election campaign." (*Johnstown Tribune-Democrat*, January 30, 1974.)

4. The AFL-CIO was "operating out of 15 rooms at the Sheraton Inn, on Market Street." (*Johnstown Tribune-Democrat*, December 18, 1973.)

5. The state AFL-CIO conducted a telephone poll for Murtha in the 12th District. (*Johnstown Tribune-Democrat*, December 18, 1973.)

6. Democratic telephone bank workers use facilities of Gautier Hall, which is owned by the Steelworkers Union. (Photo in the *Johnstown Tribune-Democrat*, February 5, 1974.)

Summary

By category, identifiable soft contributions by unions to the Murtha campaign are as follows:

Staff time, salaries and expenses deferred .....$ 8,220.51
Printing and postage for mailings 6,288.00
Student activities 369.53
Other:
  Last minute get-out-the-vote 12,000.00
  Costs at the Sheraton 14,000.00

              Subtotal................$40,878.04

When one includes the "hard" (reported) contributions of $28,450.00, it can be seen that the value of the total union effort in the district is at least $66,328.04, or nearly as much as Murtha reported for his entire campaign.

There is very little doubt that, both in and off the record, union officials and their political organizations had a tremendous impact on the race between the Democrat, Tom Luken, and the Republican, Bill Gradison, on March 5th.

Direct contributions by union political organizations to the Luken for Congress Committee were made by thirty-three separate union organizations in the amount of $30,875.00.

The scope and significance of the indirect contributions by union officials is captured in the February 8, 1974 edition of the *Chronicler*, a bimonthly publication of the Cincinnati AFL-CIO Labor Council, which is distributed to 2,000 labor officials in the Cincinnati area.

In it, an announcement is made of the "most important business meeting for all union stewards and committeemen geared to their vital part in labor's effort to insure the election of Tom Luken to Congress." It goes on to note that "materials will be furnished and *definite assignments outlined* for the action required to build a Luken victory . . ." (emphasis supplied).

The cost of the space devoted in the *Chronicler* to Luken over the January 8–March 25 period represents an indirect cost of $360 alone.

In addition, William Sheehan, head of the Labor Council, disclosed that at least 4 national and state staffers were in for the election—or as George Meany put it on "Face the Nation" on March 3rd concerning the race, "We're putting in the usual—we're sending in outsiders. Some of our COPE men . . ."

Among those in Cincinnati were Ray Alverez, Area Director of COPE ($2,085.46 contribution in salary and expenses under previous formula); Ruth Colombo, COPE ($1,977.19 pro rated salary and expenses for one month); Jane Adams Ely, Ohio State AFL-CIO (salary unknown); W. C. Young, National Field Director, COPE (salary $20,373.50, expenses $8,659.84). Ely and Young were in for an undisclosed period of time, but the bare minimum of salary and expenses for even one day's stay could reasonably be put at $500.00.

Thus, identifiable staff time and expenses for union officials came to $4,562.65.

Moreover, Alverez stated in an interview that at least 84,000 telephone calls were made from the phone banks at the Central Labor Council to union members in the District. If the cost of those calls were projected at the same 4½ cents per call rate used in Michigan, that would place their value at $3,780.00.

As in other districts, there were many mailings to union members:

1. At least two—one dated February 18, 1974 and another February 28, 1974 were sent out to members of District 30, United Steelworkers of America.

2. Another mailer dated February 28, 1974 was sent to all members of Local 863, UAW.

3. Yet another mailer dated February 18, 1974 was sent to members of the Amalgamated Clothing Workers.

4. Space was devoted in local union papers to promoting the candidacy of Luken.

In all at least $8,342.65 in paid staff time and telephone costs on a projected basis were pumped into the Luken's campaign.

Michigan's Eighth District

As in the case with other special, off-year elections, the race between Democrat Robert Traxler and Republican Jim Sparling was significantly influenced by the infusion of "hard" and "soft" contributions made by union officials to the Traxler campaign.

Hard contributions amounted to nearly $29,000.00 with the United Auto Workers—an independent union based in the state—contributing nearly half the "hard" labor money, as reported by the Traxler for Congress Volunteer Committee

Some 22 labor political action groups contributed $28,880. in "hard" money to the campaign, a figure that even cursory research shows does not realistically measure the contribution on the part of the union hierarchy in behalf of the Traxler campaign.

Staff

A minimum of eight national, state and local union officials contributed their salaried staff time (plus expenses) to the project of getting Traxler elected.

Those officials were:

James George, United Auto Workers (UAW), Detroit, annual salary $17,093.80, expenses $4,285.06.

Sam Fishman, UAW, salary $23,088.10, expenses $6,219.25.

Ray Alvarez, Area Director, AFL-CIO COPE, salary $19,772.50, expenses $6,868.17.

Ernest Dillard, UAW, Detroit, salary, $18,294.65, expenses $6,246.37.

W. C. Young, National Field Director, COPE, salary $20,373.60, expenses $8,659.84.

John Dewan, UAW, Madison Heights, Michigan, salary $16,943.80, expenses, $3,992.16.

Ruth Colombo, Assistant Area Director, Women's Activities Program (COPE), salary $20,360.50, expenses $3,365.90.

In addition, Wallace J. "Butch" Warner, 2575 N. Orr Rd., Hemlock, Michigan, was off his job (unpaid) from January 14, 1974 through the election (April 16, 1974) to work as coordinator on the campaign for the "Traxler for Congress Labor Coordinator."

An employee of Michigan Bell and a paid staffer as President of Communications Workers of America Local No. 4108, Warner's worth to the campaign (he is a cable splicer and earns $235 per week under terms of the union contract) comes to $3,202.50.

Warner disclosed in an interview that he had indeed worked with COPE and UAW personnel, identifying Sam Fishman as having been on the scene for at least one week, W. C. Young for 10 days, Ruth Colombo as having supervised for "at least 10 days" the phone banks used to contact the 43,000 active UAW members, 5,000 retirees and 25,000 AFL-CIO members in the district.

For various reasons—such as an unlisted number, personnel moving, etc.—some 50% of the 73,000 union members, according to Warner, were not contacted. Thus, some 43,800 calls were made, many of them twice, once they were identified as in the Traxler camp. Assuming 1/2 of those contacted were in this category, that means approximately 65,200 phone calls to union members alone at the rate of 4½ cents per call (as billed in Michigan) for a net cost of $2,922.

In terms of paid staff time, we must weigh in the appropriate pro rata share of Ray Alvarez' salary and expenses. Alvarez candidly admits he was assigned to work in three congressional districts (Ohio 1, Michigan 5 and Michigan 8) from January 3 through April 16—or 28% of his annual time.

Thus, in all three races, his "in-kind" contribution was $6,256.40, a third of which ($2,085.46) is allocated to the race in Michigan 8.

Applying the same pro rata formula, the "in-kind" contributions for other COPE and UAW operatives are as follows:

W. C. Young had salary of $738.00 and expenses of $309. which total $1,047.

Ruth Colombo had salary of $738.00 and expenses of $309. which total $1,047.

Sam Fishman had salary of $444.00 and expenses of $120. which totals $564.

In summary, a cursory glance will establish at least $7,945.96 in "soft" contributions of paid staff time to the Traxler campaign.

Printing

In addition to the identifiable staff time and expenses involved, a substantial "soft" contribution came in the form of four separate mailings, three of which were sent "To all UAW members in Michigan's 8th Congressional District." Copies of those mailings are attached as "A."

Two different mailing permits were used at the non-profit organization rate, with permit #3333, which belongs to American Mailers and Binders of Detroit, on two mailings, and the UAW's own permit #8000 being used for the third.

In terms of cost, as estimated by a Michigan printer, here is what each of the mailings would cost:

Mailing of March 30, 1974 to 43,000 UAW members:

Printing at $28.80/m, $1,238.40; postage at 1.7¢, $73.10; and postage, $124.70, totals $1,436.20.

Mailing of April 2, 1974 to 43,000 UAW members (it is noteworthy that this mailing made from Detroit under permit #3333, contained as an insert a six panel brochure allegedly paid for by the Traxler for Congress Volunteer Committee):

Printing a two page letter at $38.30/m, $1,668.40; postage at 1.7¢, $73.10; and postage at 2.9¢, $124.70, totals $1,866.20.

Mailing of April 6, 1974 to 43,000 UAW members:

Printing, $1,688.40; postages at 1.7¢, $73.10; and postage at 2.9¢, $124.70, totals $1,866.20.

Mailing of "8th Congressional District Special Election Edition" of Michigan *AFL-CIO News* (Vol. 35, No. 37, April 16, 1974) to UAW members in the 8th District.

(In this 8 page tabloid, five pages are devoted unabashedly to promoting the candidacy of Traxler. Taking 1/8th of the costs the "in-kind" contribution is shown below.)

Printing, $2,750.00; and postage $200.00, totals $2,950.00.

Thus, total soft printing costs contributed by the UAW and Michigan State AFL-CIO to the candidacy of Traxler came to a total of $8,118.60.

Summary

It is therefore reasonable to state that many thousands of dollars in soft contributions were funneled into the Michigan 8 race by the unions and union officials.

The contributions break down as follows:

"Hard" contributions from labor sources, $28,880.
"Soft" contributions:

Staff time and expenses $7,945.96
Printing 8,118.60
Telephone costs 2,922.00

Total $18,986.56

This "investment" is over and above the reported money, for a grand total union contribution of $47,866.00.

Additionally, three union officials were identified as being on the scene, whether as paid or unpaid is not clear. The three were: James George, UAW, Detroit (annual salary of $17,093.80); Ernest Dillard, UAW, Detroit (annual salary of $18,294.64); and John Dewan, UAW, Madison Heights (annual salary $16,943.80).

Michigan's Fifth District

The race for Vice President Gerald Ford's former seat in Congress was somewhat different from the other three special elections, in that a professional firm—headed by John Martilla—took over direction and management of the Vander Veen campaign.

Nevertheless, the union influence directing the campaign was exercised in both a direct and indirect fashion, much as it was in all other special elections.

1. Direct contributions as filed by the treasurer of the Vander Veen for Congress Committee lists some 12 separate union political action groups contributed a total of $18,711.00 to the Vander Veen campaign—or approximately 38% of the total direct reported contributions of $49,588.70.

2. Indirect contributions. Perhaps because a professional consulting firm was retained to direct the Vander Veen campaign, the "high profile" maintained by union officials while working in other special elections was not as evident. However, Ray Alvarez, area Director of the AFL-CIO's Committee on political education (COPE) admitted to having been in Michigan's 5th District. Under the same formula developed for the Michigan's 8th District some $2,085.46 of Alvarez' annual salary and expenses of $26,590.67 could be considered an indirect campaign contribution.

The printing area was one that afforded a good deal of "in-kind" support for the Democrat. Curiously, the same format, type face, halftones, paper, three of the pages are exactly the same and appeared in a tabloid-type mailer that went out under *both* the permit number of the candidate (#552) and the permit of the Western American mailers (#1), which mailed the piece in behalf of Region 1-D, United Auto Workers, Box H, Grand Rapids, Mich.

In terms of specific mailings and costs, the following were sent during the course of the campaign:

Two page letter, enclosing a xeroxed "fact sheet" on Vander Veen plus a postage paid return card under Permit #4721 addressed to Region 1-D, UAW, soliciting workers for the Vander Veen campaign.

Printing, $1,151.70; postage at 1.7¢, $374.00; and postage at 29¢, $683.00, totals $2,163.70

Tabloid mailer (mentioned previously) sent to all UAW members in the district.

Printing, $2,373.00; postage at 1.7¢, $374.00; and postage at 2.9¢, $638.00, totals $3,385.00

In addition a separate tabloid mailer was also prepared that is, once again, similar and identical in places to the other two tabloids. The difference is that this is printed on offset stock instead of newsprint and in all likelihood mailed at an estimated cost of $3,315.00 to all UAW members in the district.

Thus total "in-kind" printing and contributions to the Vander Veen Campaign came to $8,863.70; combined with the salary for just one member of the COPE staff, Ray Alvarez, the total in-kind contributions in their quietest of the districts comes to at least $10,949.30

Obviously, not all "soft" contributions are covered in the report on this district—telephones, etc.—but the low profile maintained by union officials during the race makes them almost impossible to detect.

Appendix 3

ADA and ACU Ratings of Members of Congress Endorsed and Supported by COPE*

(• = COPE Endorsement)

ALABAMA

Senators	ADA Rating LQ	ACU Rating
• John J. Sparkman (D)	6	46
James B. Allen (D)	6	84
Representatives		
1 Jack Edwards (R)	5	83
2 William L. Dickinson (R)	5	81
3 Bill Nichols (D)	5	72
•4 Tom Bevill (D)	16	67
•5 Robert E. Jones, Jr. (D)	37	29
6 John H. Buchanan (R)	21	75
7 Walter Flowers (D)	5	58

ALASKA

Senators		
Ted Stevens (R)	33	39
• Mike Gravel (D)	78	23
Representative (At Large)		
Don Young (R)	5	74

ARIZONA

Senators		
Paul J. Fannin (R)	11	97
Barry Goldwater (R)	6	100
Representatives		
1 John J. Rhodes (R)	11	86
•2 Morris K. Udall (D)	47	0
3 Sam Steiger (R)	0	100
4 John B. Conlan (R)	0	100

ARKANSAS

Senators		
John L. McClellan (D)	6	65

* The ratings of Members of Congress by the Americans for Democratic Action and the American Conservative Union are based on their voting record in 1975. ADA LQ refers to Liberal Quotient.

		ADA Rating LQ	ACU Rating
• Dale Bumpers (D)		56	11

Representatives

		ADA Rating LQ	ACU Rating
•1	Bill Alexander (D)	21	56
•2	Wilbur D. Mills (D)	11	53
3	John P. Hammerschmidt (R)	5	86
4	Ray Thornton (D)	26	53

CALIFORNIA

Senators

		ADA Rating LQ	ACU Rating
•	Alan Cranston (D)	89	6
•	John V. Tunney (D)	83	19

Representatives

		ADA Rating LQ	ACU Rating
•1	Harold T. Johnson (D)	58	19
2	Don H. Clausen (R)	5	74
•3	John E. Moss (D)	89	3
•4	Robert L. Leggett (D)	95	3
•5	John L. Burton (D)	95	6
•6	Phillip Burton (D)	89	0
•7	George Miller (D)	100	6
•8	Ronald V. Dellums (D)	100	3
•9	Fortney H. (Pete) Stark (D)	89	0
•10	Don Edwards (D)	100	0
•11	Leo J. Ryan (D)	89	11
•12	Paul N. McCloskey, Jr. (R)	68	32
•13	Norman V. Mineta (D)	95	8
•14	John J. McFall (D)	68	14
•15	B. F. Sisk (D)	42	29
16	Burt L. Talcott (R)	5	88
•17	John Krebs (D)	89	19
18	William M. Ketchum (R)	0	97
19	Robert J. Lagomarsino (R)	11	86
20	Barry Goldwater, Jr. (R)	0	89
•21	James C. Corman (D)	95	3
22	Carlos J. Moorhead (D)	5	94
•23	Thomas M. Rees (D)	74	7
•24	Henry A. Waxman (D)	89	4
•25	Edward R. Roybal (D)	95	3
26	John H. Rousselot (R)	0	97
•27	Alphonzo Bell (R)	17	21
•28	Yvonne Braithwaite Burke (D)	89	0
•29	Augustus F. Hawkins (D)	84	12
•30	George E. Danielson (D)	68	22
•31	Charles H. Wilson (D)	63	20

	ADA Rating LQ	ACU Rating
•32 Glenn M. Anderson (D)	58	33
33 Del Clawson (R)	0	97
•34 Mark W. Hannaford (D)	79	10
•35 Jim Lloyd (D)	68	25
•36 George E. Brown, Jr. (D)	89	0
37 Shirley N. Pettis	12	86
•38 Jerry M. Patterson (D)	79	22
•39 Charles E. Wiggins (R)	11	75
40 Andrew J. Hinshaw (R)	5	74
41 Bob Wilson (R)	11	82
•42 Lionel Van Deerlin (D)	79	20
43 Clair W. Burgener (R)	0	89

COLORADO

Senators

• Floyd K. Haskell (D)	89	9
• Gary Hart (D)	94	11

Representatives

•1 Patricia Schroeder (D)	84	17
•2 Timothy E. Wirth (D)	79	12
•3 Frank E. Evans (D)	79	11
4 James T. Johnson (R)	21	75
5 William L. Armstrong (R)	16	94

CONNECTICUT

Senators

• Abraham A. Ribicoff (D)	78	3
Lowell P. Weicker, Jr. (R)	72	35

Representatives

•1 William R. Cotter (D)	89	9
•2 Christopher J. Dodd (D)	79	9
•3 Robert N. Giaimo (D)	89	15
4 Stewart B. McKinney (R)	72	34
5 Ronald A. Sarasin (R)	58	42
•6 Anthony Toby Moffett (D)	100	8

DELAWARE

Senators

William V. Roth, Jr. (R)	33	71
• Joseph R. Biden, Jr. (D)	78	19

Representative (At Large)

Pierre S. duPont IV (R)	53	64

FLORIDA

	ADA Rating LQ	ACU Rating
Senators		
• Lawton Chiles (D)	39	49
• Richard Stone (D)	22	50
Representatives		
•1 Robert L. F. Sikes (D)	11	67
•2 Don Fuqua (D)	37	56
•3 Charles E. Bennett (D)	37	67
•4 Bill Chappell, Jr. (D)	5	75
5 Richard Kelly (R)	0	97
6 C. W. Bill Young (R)	16	94
•7 Sam Gibbons (D)	68	40
•8 James A. Haley (D)	16	78
9 Louis Frey, Jr. (R)	5	86
10 L. A. (Skip) Batalis (R)	5	83
11 Paul G. Rogers (D)	26	64
12 J. Herbert Burke (R)	21	81
•13 William Lehman (D)	95	0
•14 Claude Pepper (D)	58	15
•15 Dante B. Fascell (D)	89	6

GEORGIA

	ADA Rating LQ	ACU Rating
Senators		
• Herman E. Talmadge (D)	6	63
• Sam Nunn (D)	11	67
Representatives		
•1 Bo Ginn (D)	11	75
2 Dawson Mathis (D)	0	76
•3 Jack Brinkley (D)	11	78
•4 Elliott Levitas (D)	32	58
•5 Andrew Young (D)	95	3
6 John J. Flynt, Jr. (D)	5	91
7 Larry McDonald (D)	0	100
8 W. S. (Bill) Stuckey, Jr. (D)	16	78
9 Phil M. Landrum (D)	0	85
•10 Robert G. Stephens, Jr. (D)	0	67

HAWAII

	ADA Rating LQ	ACU Rating
Senators		
Hiram L. Fong (R)	22	48
• Daniel K. Inouye (D)	56	12
Representatives		
•1 Spark M. Matsunaga (D)	68	9
•2 Patsy T. Mink (D)	95	3

	ADA Rating LQ	ACU Rating

IDAHO

Senators
- Frank Church (D) — 78, 18
  James A. McClure (R) — 6, 91

Representatives
1 Steven D. Symms (R) — 0, 100
2 George Hansen (R) — 0, 97

ILLINOIS

Senators
Charles H. Percy (R) — 56, 17
- Adlai E. Stevenson III (D) — 72, 0

Representatives
- 1 Ralph H. Metcalfe (D) — 84, 3
- 2 Morgan F. Murphy (D) — 74, 8
- 3 Martin A. Russo (D) — 79, 26
4 Edward J. Derwinski (R) — 0, 85
- 5 John Fary (D) — 45, 0
6 Henry J. Hyde (R) — 5, 86
- 7 Cardiss Collins (D) — 100, 7
- 8 Dan D. Rostenkowski (D) — 58, 6
- 9 Sidney R. Yates (D) — 100, 3
- 10 Abner J. Mikva (D) — 89, 3
- 11 Frank Annunzio (D) — 47, 23
12 Philip M. Crane (R) — 0, 100
13 Robert McClory (R) — 32, 53
14 John N. Erlenborn (R) — 11, 78
- 15 Tim L. Hall (D) — 84, 11
16 John B. Anderson (R) — 58, 48
17 George M. O'Brien (R) — 11, 79
18 Robert H. Michel (R) — 16, 88
19 Tom Railsback (R) — 42, 50
20 Paul Findley (R) — 37, 63
21 Edward R. Madigan (R) — 21, 63
- 22 George E. Shipley (D) — 42, 36
- 23 Melvin Price (D) — 58, 14
- 24 Paul Simon (D) — 89, 6

INDIANA

Senators
- Vance Hartke (D) — 72, 9
- Birch Bayh (D) — 72, 4

Representatives
- 1 Ray J. Madden (D) — 89, 9

	ADA Rating LQ	ACU Rating
•2 Floyd J. Fithian (D)	68	31
•3 John Brademas (D)	95	3
•4 J. Edward Roush (D)	94	22
5 Elwood Hillis (R)	26	53
•6 David W. Evans (D)	68	43
7 John T. Myers (R)	0	89
•8 Philip H. Hayes (D)	89	11
•9 Lee H. Hamilton (D)	68	31
•10 Philip R. Sharp (D)	89	11
•11 Andrew Jacobs, Jr. (D)	74	34

IOWA

Senators

• Dick Clark (D)	100	3
• John C. Culver (D)	100	0

Representatives

•1 Edward Mezinsky (D)	84	0
•2 Michael T. Blouin (D)	95	8
3 Charles E. Grassley (R)	21	75
4 Neal Smith (D)	63	8
5 Tom Harkin (D)	95	21
6 Berkley Bedell (D)	89	21

KANSAS

Senators

• James B. Pearson (R)	33	32
Robert Dole (R)	17	53

Representatives

1 Keith G. Sebelius (R)	16	87
•2 Martha Keys (D)	89	11
3 Larry Winn, Jr. (R)	16	74
4 Garner E. Shriver (R)	5	82
5 Joe Skubitz (R)	16	79

KENTUCKY

Senators

• Walter Huddleston (D)	50	17
• Wendell H. Ford (D)	56	26

Representatives

•1 Carroll Hubbard, Jr. (D)	37	51
•2 William N. Natcher (D)	42	42
•3 Romano L. Mazzoli (D)	63	25
4 Gene Snyder (R)	5	83
5 Tim Lee Carter (R)	11	72

	ADA Rating LQ	ACU Rating
•6 John B. Breckinridge (D)	42	34
•7 Carl D. Perkins (D)	58	20

LOUISIANA

Senators

• Russell B. Long (D)	22	56
J. Bennett Johnston, Jr. (D)	28	49

Representatives

•1 F. Edward Hebert (D)	5	42
•2 Lindy (Mrs. Hale) Boggs (D)	47	19
3 David C. Treen (R)	0	94
4 Joe D. Waggonner, Jr. (D)	0	81
5 Otto E. Passman (D)	11	64
6 W. Henson Moore (R)	0	97
•7 John B. Breaux (D)	11	57
•8 Gillis W. Long (D)	47	25

MAINE

Senators

• Edmund S. Muskie (D)	89	9
• William D. Hathaway (D)	94	11

Representatives

1 David F. Emery (R)	68	56
2 William S. Cohen (R)	74	32

MARYLAND

Senators

• Charles McC. Mathias, Jr. (R)	83	10
J. Glenn Beall, Jr. (R)	44	36

Representatives

1 Robert E. Bauman (R)	0	100
•2 Clarence D. Long (D)	53	39
•3 Paul S. Sarbanes (D)	100	13
4 Marjorie S. Holt (R)	5	92
•5 Gladys Noon Spellman (D)	95	14
6 Goodloe E. Byron (D)	5	79
•7 Parren J. Mitchell (D)	79	9
•8 Gilbert Gude (R)	89	9

MASSACHUSETTS

Senators

• Edward M. Kennedy (D)	89	0
• Edward W. Brooke (D)	89	0

	ADA Rating LQ	ACU Rating
Representatives		
1 Silvio O. Conte (R)	74	20
•2 Edward P. Boland (D)	79	15
•3 Joseph D. Early (D)	89	14
•4 Robert F. Drinan (D)	100	3
5 Paul E. Tsongas (D)	100	3
•6 Michael J. Harrington (D)	100	11
•7 Torbert H. Macdonald (D)	68	15
•8 Thomas P. O'Neill, Jr. (D)	74	9
•9 Joe Moakley (D)	100	3
•10 Margaret M. Heckler (R)	74	27
•11 James A. Burke (D)	84	14
•12 Gerry E. Studds (D)	100	6

MICHIGAN

	ADA Rating LQ	ACU Rating
Senators		
• Philip A. Hart (D)	61	0
Robert P. Griffin (R)	6	67
Representatives		
•1 John Conyers, Jr. (D)	79	4
2 Marvin L. Esch (R)	26	69
3 Garry Brown (R)	11	74
4 Edward Hutchinson (R)	5	94
•5 Richard F. Vander Veen (D)	84	6
•6 Bob Carr (D)	89	17
•7 Donald W. Riegle, Jr. (D)	74	11
•8 Bob Traxler (D)	89	14
9 Guy Vander Jagt (R)	16	82
10 Elford A. Cederberg (R)	5	94
11 Philip E. Ruppe (R)	42	48
•12 James G. O'Hara (D)	74	14
•13 Charles C. Diggs, Jr. (D)	79	0
•14 Lucien N. Nedzi (D)	84	9
•15 William D. Ford (D)	89	9
•16 John D. Dingell (D)	63	14
•17 William M. Brodhead (D)	100	8
•18 James J. Blanchard (D)	95	14
19 William S. Broomfield (R)	11	72

MINNESOTA

	ADA Rating LQ	ACU Rating
Senators		
• Walter F. Mondale (D)	94	5
• Hubert H. Humphrey (D)	94	2

	ADA Rating LQ	ACU Rating
Representatives		
1 Albert H. Quie (R)	37	58
2 Tom Hagedorn (R)	16	88
3 Bill Frenzel (R)	53	56
•4 Joseph E. Karth (D)	79	4
•5 Donald M. Fraser (D)	74	4
•6 Richard Nolan (D)	100	3
•7 Bob Bergland (D)	95	6
•8 James L. Oberstar (D)	100	3

MISSISSIPPI

	ADA Rating LQ	ACU Rating
Senators		
James O. Eastland (D)	0	70
John C. Stennis (D)	0	63
Representatives		
1 Jamie L. Whitten (D)	16	65
•2 David R. Bowen (D)	16	69
3 G. V. (Sonny) Montgomery (D)	0	94
4 Thad Cochran (R)	5	86
5 Trent Lott (R)	0	86

MISSOURI

	ADA Rating LQ	ACU Rating
Senators		
• Stuart Symington (D)	72	29
• Thomas F. Eagleton (D)	72	13
Representatives		
•1 William Clay (D)	100	3
•2 James W. Symington (D)	79	12
•3 Leonor K. (Mrs. J. B.) Sullivan (D)	58	21
•4 William J. Randall (D)	26	57
•5 Richard Bolling (D)	79	8
•6 Jerry Litton (D)	68	10
7 Gene Taylor (R)	0	94
•8 Richard H. Ichord (D)	0	77
•9 William L. Hungate (D)	74	27
•10 Bill D. Burlison (D)	53	46

MONTANA

	ADA Rating LQ	ACU Rating
Senators		
• Mike Mansfield (D)	83	15
• Lee Metcalf (D)	89	10
Representatives		
•1 Max S. Baucus (D)	74	11
•2 John Melcher (D)	74	20

	ADA Rating LQ	ACU Rating
NEBRASKA		
Senators		
Roman L. Hruska (R)	6	100
Carl T. Curtis (R)	0	100
Representatives		
1 Charles Thone (R)	26	72
2 John Y. McCollister (R)	0	91
3 Virginia Smith (R)	5	86
NEVADA		
Senators		
• Howard W. Cannon (D)	28	38
Paul Laxalt (R)	22	88
Representative (At Large)		
• Jim Santini (D)	26	47
NEW HAMPSHIRE		
Senators		
• Thomas J. McIntyre (D)	78	3
• John Durkin (D)	100	0
Representatives		
•1 Norman E. D'Amours (D)	63	36
2 James C. Cleveland (R)	16	76
NEW JERSEY		
Senators		
• Clifford P. Case (R)	83	3
• Harrison A. Williams, Jr. (D)	89	6
Representatives		
•1 James J. Florio (D)	68	25
•2 William J. Hughes (D)	79	25
•3 James J. Howard (D)	89	3
•4 Frank Thompson, Jr. (D)	89	3
5 Millicent Fenwick (R)	58	32
6 Edwin B. Forsythe (R)	47	61
•7 Andrew Maguire (D)	100	6
•8 Robert A. Roe (D)	79	22
•9 Henry Helstoski (D)	79	7
•10 Peter W. Rodino, Jr. (D)	84	3
•11 Joseph G. Minish (D)	79	15
•12 Matthew J. Rinaldo (R)	79	31
•13 Helen S. Meyner (D)	95	9
•14 Dominick V. Daniels (D)	74	15
•15 Edward J. Patten (D)	74	22

	ADA Rating LQ	ACU Rating
NEW MEXICO		

NEW MEXICO

Senators
	ADA Rating LQ	ACU Rating
• Joseph M. Montoya (D)	44	38
Pete V. Domenici (R)	22	56

Representatives
1 Manuel Lujan, Jr. (R)	5	90
•2 Harold Runnels (D)	0	85

NEW YORK

Senators
• Jacob K. Javits (R)	72	9
James L. Buckley (C)	0	81

Representatives
•1 Otis G. Pike (D)	84	14
•2 Thomas J. Downey (D)	100	8
•3 Jerome Ambro, Jr. (D)	89	17
4 Norman F. Lent (R)	26	63
5 John W. Wydler (R)	26	77
•6 Lester L. Wolff (D)	79	15
•7 Joseph P. Addabbo (D)	95	6
•8 Benjamin S. Rosenthal (D)	89	3
•9 James J. Delaney (D)	53	31
•10 Mario Biaggi (D)	47	27
•11 James H. Scheuer (D)	95	8
•12 Shirley Chisholm (D)	95	0
•13 Stephen J. Solarz (D)	100	3
•14 Frederick W. Richmond (D)	95	3
•15 Leo C. Zeferetti (D)	47	36
•16 Elizabeth Holtzman (D)	95	6
•17 John M. Murphy (D)	47	22
•18 Edward I. Koch (D)	100	3
•19 Charles B. Rangel (D)	89	0
•20 Bella S. Abzug (D)	95	3
•21 Herman Badillo (D)	100	0
•22 Jonathan B. Bingham (D)	100	3
•23 Peter A. Peyser (R)	53	24
•24 Richard L. Ottinger (D)	89	3
25 Hamilton Fish, Jr. (R)	37	57
26 Benjamin A. Gilman (R)	63	42
•27 Matthew F. McHugh (D)	95	9
•28 Samuel S. Stratton (D)	42	43
•29 Edward W. Pattison (D)	89	12
30 Robert C. McEwen (R)	11	84
31 Donald J. Mitchell (R)	26	58

		ADA Rating LQ	ACU Rating
•32	James M. Hanley (D)	58	29
•33	William F. Walsh (R)	37	58
•34	Frank Horton (R)	63	35
35	Barber B. Conable, Jr. (R)	26	81
•36	John L. LaFalce (D)	84	11
•37	Henry J. Nowak (D)	89	8
38	Jack F. Kemp (R)	5	97
39	James F. Hastings (R)	16	77

NORTH CAROLINA

Senators

	Jesse A. Helms (R)	0	100
•	Robert Morgan (D)	17	66

Representatives

1	Walter B. Jones (D)	21	60
2	L. H. Fountain (D)	5	72
3	David N. Henderson (D)	16	66
•4	Ike F. Andrews (D)	26	73
•5	Stephen L. Neal (D)	68	31
•6	Richardson Preyer (D)	37	33
•7	Charles G. Rose (D)	16	39
•8	W. G. Hefner (D)	32	60
9	James G. Martin (R)	5	90
10	James T. Broyhill (R)	5	88
•11	Roy A. Taylor (D)	21	69

NORTH DAKOTA

Senators

	Milton R. Young (R)	0	69
•	Quentin N. Burdick (D)	67	11

Representative (At Large)

	Mark Andrews (R)	32	71

OHIO

Senators

	Robert Taft, Jr. (R)	22	54
•	John Glenn (D)	50	12

Representatives

1	Willis D. Gradison, Jr. (R)	21	83
2	Donald D. Clancy (R)	0	92
•3	Charles W. Whalen, Jr. (R)	84	11
4	Tennyson Guyer (R)	11	85
5	Delbert L. Latta (R)	5	94
6	William H. Harsha (R)	16	76

	ADA Rating LQ	ACU Rating
7 Clarence J. Brown (R)	16	77
8 Thomas N. Kindness (R)	0	92
•9 Thomas L. Ashley (D)	74	15
10 Clarence E. Miller (R)	5	92
11 J. William Stanton (R)	26	63
12 Samuel L. Devine (R)	0	94
13 Charles A. Mosher (R)	68	37
•14 John F. Seiberling, Jr. (D)	95	0
15 Chalmers P. Wylie (R)	21	86
16 Ralph S. Regula (R)	21	67
17 John M. Ashbrook (R)	5	97
•18 Wayne L. Hays (D)	53	27
•19 Charles J. Carney (D)	84	14
•20 James V. Stanton (D)	79	18
•21 Louis Stokes (D)	89	0
•22 Charles A. Vanik (D)	95	13
•23 Ronald M. Mottl (D)	74	39

OKLAHOMA

Senators
Henry Bellmon (R)	17	71
Dewey F. Bartlett (R)	6	95

Representatives
•1 James R. Jones (D)	16	67
•2 Theodore M. Risenhoover (D)	26	41
•3 Carl Albert (D)	0	0
•4 Tom Steed (D)	26	50
•5 John Jarman (R)	0	88
•6 Glenn English (D)	16	71

OREGON

Senators
Mark O. Hatfield (R)	83	33
Bob Packwood (R)	72	41

Representatives
•1 Les AuCoin (D)	74	12
•2 Al Ullman (D)	79	11
•3 Robert Duncan (D)	53	24
•4 James Weaver (D)	100	6

PENNSYLVANIA

Senators
Hugh Scott (R)	39	26
• Richard S. Schweiker (R)	89	9

	ADA Rating LQ	ACU Rating
Representatives		
●1 William A. Barrett (D)	42	19
●2 Robert N. C. Nix (D)	68	6
●3 William J. Green (D)	95	10
●4 Joshua Eilberg (D)	74	9
5 Richard T. Schulze (R)	16	86
●6 Gus Yatron (D)	47	38
●7 Robert W. Edgar (D)	100	6
●8 Edward G. Biester, Jr. (R)	89	23
9 Bud Shuster (R)	0	89
●10 Joseph M. McDade (R)	58	39
●11 Daniel J. Flood (D)	58	19
●12 John P. Murtha (D)	42	50
13 Lawrence Coughlin (R)	53	51
●14 William S. Moorhead (D)	84	3
●15 Fred B. Rooney (D)	68	23
16 Edwin D. Eshleman (R)	0	93
17 Herman T. Schneebeli (R)	16	91
●18 H. John Heinz III (R)	68	44
●19 William F. Goodling (R)	16	83
●20 Joseph M. Gaydos (D)	58	26
●21 John H. Dent (D)	32	33
●22 Thomas F. Morgan (D)	63	13
23 Albert W. Johnson (R)	11	69
●24 Joseph P. Vigorito (D)	58	24
25 Gary A. Myers (R)	42	67

RHODE ISLAND

Senators		
● John O. Pastore (D)	67	11
● Claiborne Pell (D)	89	6
Representatives		
●1 Fernand J. St. Germain (D)	95	15
●2 Edward P. Beard (D)	95	15

SOUTH CAROLINA

Senators		
Strom Thurman (R)	0	97
● Ernest F. Hollings (D)	44	44
Representatives		
●1 Mendel J. Davis (D)	26	55
2 Floyd Spence (R)	11	86
●3 Butler Derrick (D)	26	58

		ADA Rating LQ	ACU Rating
•4	James R. Mann (D)	5	77
•5	Kenneth L. Holland (D)	47	39
•6	John W. Jenrette, Jr. (D)	37	50

SOUTH DAKOTA

Senators

•	George McGovern (D)	89	6
•	James Abourezk (D)	94	6

Representatives

1	Larry Pressler (R)	58	54
2	James Abdnor (R)	16	16

TENNESSEE

Senators

	Howard H. Baker, Jr. (R)	11	63
	Bill Brock (R)	22	77

Representatives

1	James H. Quillen (R)	0	94
2	John J. Duncan (R)	5	89
•3	Marilyn Lloyd (D)	32	47
•4	Joe L. Evins (D)	42	30
5	Richard Fulton (D)	100	0
6	Robin L. Beard (R)	100	97
•7	Ed Jones (D)	0	53
•8	Harold E. Ford (D)	79	17

TEXAS

Senators

	John G. Tower (R)	11	89
	Lloyd M. Bentsen (D)	39	33

Representatives

•1	Wright Patman (D)	42	37
•2	Charles Wilson (D)	42	35
3	James M. Collins (R)	0	97
4	Ray Roberts (D)	5	63
5	Alan Steelman (R)	26	85
6	Olin E. Teague (D)	5	80
7	Bill Archer (R)	0	97
•8	Bob Eckhardt (D)	84	3
•9	Jack Brooks (D)	32	24
10	J. J. Pickle (D)	26	49
11	W. R. Poage (D)	0	85
12	Jim Wright (D)	32	43

	ADA Rating LQ	ACU Rating
•13 Jack Hightower (D)	11	63
14 John Young (D)	26	53
15 E. de la Garza (D)	11	59
16 Richard C. White (D)	11	58
•17 Omar Burleson (D)	0	89
•18 Barbara Jordan (D)	89	3
19 George H. Mahon (D)	11	64
20 Henry B. Gonzalez (D)	42	34
•21 Robert Krueger (D)	32	63
22 Bob Casey (D)	11	70
•23 Abraham Kazen, Jr. (D)	16	64
24 Dale Milford (D)	5	74

UTAH

Senators

• Frank E. Moss (D)	61	12
Jake Garn (R)	11	83

Representatives

•1 Gunn McKay (D)	42	39
•2 Allan T. Howe (D)	63	28

VERMONT

Senators

Robert T. Stafford (R)	72	15
• Patrick J. Leahy (D)	94	3

Representative (At Large)

James M. Jeffords (R)	68	37

VIRGINIA

Senators

Harry F. Byrd, Jr. (I)	0	89
William L. Scott (R)	22	91

Representatives

1 Thomas N. Downing (D)	5	86
2 G. William Whitehurst (R)	5	92
3 David E. Satterfield III (D)	0	100
4 Robert W. Daniel, Jr. (R)	0	97
5 Dan Daniel (D)	0	100
6 M. Caldwell Butler (R)	0	97
7 J. Kenneth Robinson (R)	0	97
•8 Herbert E. Harris II (D)	89	11
9 William C. Wampler (R)	5	89
•10 Joseph L. Fisher (D)	95	3

	ADA **Rating LQ**	**ACU** **Rating**

WASHINGTON

Senators

• Warren G. Magnuson (D)	55	17
• Henry M. Jackson (D)	61	17

Representatives

•1 Joel Pritchard (R)	47	42
•2 Lloyd Meeds (D)	95	6
•3 Don Bonker (D)	95	11
•4 Mike McCormack (D)	79	9
•5 Thomas S. Foley (D)	63	8
•6 Floyd V. Hicks (D)	58	17
•7 Brock Adams (D)	89	3

WEST VIRGINIA

Senators

• Jennings Randolph (D)	67	23
Robert C. Byrd (D)	28	44

Representatives

•1 Robert H. Mollohan (D)	32	23
•2 Harley O. Staggers (D)	53	24
•3 John M. Slack (D)	37	37
•4 Ken Hechler (D)	74	31

WISCONSIN

Senators

• William Proxmire (D)	78	22
• Gaylord Nelson (R)	89	3

Representatives

•1 Lee Aspin (D)	95	9
•2 Robert W. Kastenmeier (D)	100	6
•3 Alvin Baldus (D)	89	14
•4 Clement J. Zablocki (D)	58	31
•5 Henry W. Reuss (D)	95	8
6 William A. Steiger (R)	26	66
•7 David R. Obey (D)	100	6
•8 Robert J. Cornell (D)	95	6
9 Robert W. Kasten, Jr. (R)	21	83

WYOMING

Senators

• Gale W. McGee (D)	39	37
Clifford P. Hansen (R)	0	94

Representative (At Large)

• Teno Roncalio (D)	68	22

Appendix 4

Affidavit of Jerry Wurf, President, AFSCME,
July 26, 1973

SUPERIOR COURT OF THE DISTRICT OF COLUMBIA
MAMIE ADAMS, et al.,
                        Plaintiffs,
            v.   Misc. No. 56-72
CITY OF DETROIT, AFSCME
COUNCIL 77, et al.,
                        Defendants.

The undersigned, Jerry Wurf, as President of the American Federation of State, County and Municipal Employees, AFL-CIO, being duly sworn, makes the following statement:

1. The American Federation of State, County and Municipal Employees, AFL-CIO (hereinafter AFSCME) receives revenues in the form of per capita tax payments of $1.50 per member per month from its local unions, as set forth in Article IX, Section 7 of the International Constitution currently in effect. Per capita tax revenues so received are co-mingled in the general fund of AFSCME and used for its programs and activities, including political action and legislative action programs.

2. The per capita payments required by the AFSCME Constitution to be transmitted to AFSCME by its affiliated local unions also include payment in the same amount, $1.50 per month, for each non-member agency fee payer, and all such payments are co-mingled and used as described in the foregoing paragraph.

3. In carrying on its political action programs and activities AFSCME utilizes its officers and salaried staff personnel. A portion of the salaried time and reimbursed expenses of staff personnel and of the costs of office space, office supplies, telephone and telegraph, printing and general overhead and administration expenses of AFSCME are either directly related to its political action programs and activities or provide administrative support for such programs and activities.

4. In recent years, the political programs and activities of AFSCME have been closely related to one of the two major political parties, particularly at the national level. Some AFSCME officers and staff personnel hold official positions in that party at the national, state or local level, and participate in the election campaigns of candidates of that party.

Through coordination with other international unions and their state and local representatives AFSCME and its PEOPLE Committee assist in providing financial, organizational and manpower resources for voter registration drives, preparation and dissemination of campaign literature, and get-out-the-vote activities in support of candidate campaigns. These activities are at times coordinated with those of other organizations with similar objectives.

5. The cost of publication of the *Public Employee,* which is the official newspaper of AFSCME, is paid for out of AFSCME general funds.

6. One of the departments of AFSCME, the Department of Legislation and Political Action, consists of a staff of professional and clerical employees engaged in political training and education programs and in dealing with legislative developments of interest to AFSCME. All salaries and expenses including office overhead and administration of such Department are paid for out of the general funds of AFSCME.

7. Contributions are made from the general funds of AFSCME to candidates for state and local offices where such contributions are not prohibited by law and where AFSCME has determined that such support it in the interest of public employees. For the purposes set forth in Article VIII, Section 5 of its Constitution, AFSCME has established a PEOPLE Committee (Public Employees Organized to Promote Legislative Equality) which is administered by its officers. This Committee received voluntary financial contributions from AFSCME members. The constitutional provision directs that these voluntary contributions are to be used for the achievement of the legislative goals of AFSCME. For this purpose the PEOPLE Committee furnished financial assistance to some candidates for federal office. The expenses of voluntary fund-raising activities of the PEOPLE Committee including staff salaries and expenses and use of physical facilities, are to the extent legally permissible, paid for from the general funds of AFSCME.

8. The Department of Education has assisted in training of the Legislation and Political Action staff in use of educational techniques and has assisted in the presentation of its programs. The salaries and expenses of staff personnel and the cost of operation is paid for out of AFSCME general funds.

/s/ Jerry Wurf
International President
American Federation of State, County
and Municipal Employees, AFL-CIO

Appendix 5

ACA Study of Union Contributions to Members of Congress Who Voted for Common Site Picketing Bill

WASHINGTON, D.C.—The Americans for Constitutional Action on January 28, 1976, released a study of contributions by organized labor to Members of Congress who voted for the Construction Site Picketing Bill which was later vetoed by President Gerald R. Ford.

Miss J. Charlene Baker, Chairman of the conservative political action group, stated, "The total of $5,758,780.64 represents the minimum amounts reported to the proper recording agencies for the 1974 campaign (or last election). These figures do not include 'contributions-in-kind' which are generally not reported.

"In the Senate, 41 Democrats voted for the bill and received $2,871,992.44. Eleven Republicans voted for it and received $350,162.69. Of the eleven, to our knowledge, Senators Robert Stafford, Robert Taft, and Lowell Weicker did not receive union contributions in 1970 but have received labor money towards their 1976 campaigns.

Miss Baker continued, "On the House side, 206 Democrats received $2,368,675.51 from the unions while 23 Republicans received $80,495.00. Seven House Members 'paired' for the bill; six Democrats and one Republican received a total of $87,455. Union contributions to 212 Democrats and 24 Republicans in the House totaled $2,536,625.51.

"ACA will be issuing additional studies on labor union contributions for the 1976 elections," Miss Baker concluded.

The following figures represent a study issued January 28, 1976, by Americans for Constitutional Action showing the amount of money contributed by organized labor to Members of Congress who voted for the Construction Site Picketing Bill.

These figures represent the minimum amounts reported for the 1974 campaign (or last election) year.

SENATE

MEMBER	STATE	DEMOCRAT	REPUBLICAN
John Durkin	New Hampshire	172,065.93*	
Birch Bayh	Indiana	170,949.53	
Mike Gravel	Alaska	170,701.78	
Harrison Williams	New Jersey	153,466.30	
Thomas Eagleton	Missouri	120,000.00	
John Culver	Iowa	110,688.12	
Richard Schweiker	Pennsylvania		107,266.61
John Tunney	California	105,850.00	
Stuart Symington	Missouri	103,060.50	
Warren Magnuson	Washington	94,560.00	
Vance Hartke	Indiana	93,531.85	
Jacob Javits	New York		86,871.08
Claiborne Pell	Rhode Island	86,746.15	
Wendell Ford	Kentucky	86,436.45	
Walter Mondale	Minnesota	85,025.00	
Lee Metcalf	Montana	84,824.00	
Alan Cranston	California	83,967.51	
Philip Hart	Michigan	81,521.25	
Dick Clark	Iowa	78,595.70	
James Abourezk	South Dakota	76,830.00	
Adlai Stevenson	Illinois	74,350.00	
Frank Moss	Utah	70,421.95	
George McGovern	South Dakota	65,375.69	

335

Hubert Humphrey	Minnesota	63,000.00	
Gary Hart	Colorado	62,610.53	
Charles Mathias	Maryland	58,351.00	58,675.00
Joseph Biden	Delaware	49,847.80	
Patrick Leahy	Vermont	46,381.00	
William Proxmire	Wisconsin	45,940.00	
Gale McGee	Wyoming	45,000.00	
Frank Church	Idaho	44,781.00	
Quentin Burdick	North Dakota		39,900
Clifford Case	New Jersey		
Edmund Muskie	Maine	39,350.00	
William Hathaway	Maine	36,913.00	
Floyd Haskell	Colorado	33,135.00	
Russell Long	Louisiana	32,800.00	
Edward Kennedy	Massachusetts	30,965.00	
Daniel Inouye	Hawaii	30,500.00	
Ted Stevens	Alaska		20,300.00
Jennings Randolph	West Virginia	17,475.00	
Abraham Ribicoff	Connecticut	16,850.00	
John Pastore	Rhode Island	16,100.00	
Bob Packwood	Oregon		14,300.00
Henry Jackson	Washington	13,825.00	
Charles Percy	Illinois		13,700.00
Mike Mansfield	Montana	12,050.00	
Edward Brooke	Massachusetts		9,150.00

Member	State	Democrat	Republican
Robert Byrd	West Virginia	7,150.00	
Robert Stafford	Vermont		—0—
Robert Taft	Ohio		—0—
Lowell Weicker	Connectict		—0—
	SUB-TOTALS	$2,871,992.44	$350,162.69
	TOTAL	$3,222,155.13	

*The amount of contributions to John Durkin represents both the General and Special Elections.

HOUSE

Member	District & State	Democrat	Republican
Robert Traxler	8—Michigan	88,355.00*	
Robert Carr	6—Michigan	57,093.00	
Richard Vander Veen	5—Michigan	50,852.00	
James Blanchard	18—Michigan	48,211.99	
John Burton	5—California	37,430.00	
Thomas O'Neill	8—Massachusetts	35,750.00	
Les Au Coin	1—Oregon	35,508.43	
Mike Blouin	2—Iowa	35,200.00	
Allan Howe	2—Utah	32,550.00	

Member	District & State	Democrat	Republican
Edward Mezvinsky	1—Iowa	31,525.00	
Richard Nolan	6—Mississippi	30,775.00	
Pat Schroeder	1—Colorado	30,715.00	
John Dent	21—Pennsylvania	29,275.00	
Alvin Baldus	3—Wisconsin	28,650.00	
John Murphy	17—New York	28,450.00	
Robert Cornell	8—Wisconsin	28,415.00	
Paul Simon	24—Illinois	28,075.00	
James Santini	At Lg—Nevada	28,050.00	
James Florio	1—New Jersey	26,600.82	
Frank Thompson	4—New Jersey	26,300.00	
Philip Sharp	10—Indiana	26,250.00	
Tim Wirth	2—Colorado	24,894.74	
Norman Mineta	13—California	24,636.50	
Martha Keys	2—Kansas	24,063.57	
John LaFalce	36—New York	23,739.30	
William Brodhead	17—Michigan	23,674.50	
Herb Harris	8—Virginia	23,595.00	
Mark Hannaford	34—California	23,430.00	
Lloyd Meeds	2—Washington	22,500.00	
Floyd Fithian	2—Indiana	22,425.00	
Philip Hayes	8—Indiana	22,100.00	
Don Bonker	3—Washington	22,050.00	

338

			21,555.00
Peter Peyser	23—New York	21,290.00
Lester Wolff	6—New York	20,750.00
Jerry Patterson	38—California	20,570.00
Joshua Eilberg	4—Pennsylvania	19,750.00
William Roush	4—Indiana	18,850.00
William Clay	1—Missouri	18,850.00
James Oberstar	8—Minnesota	18,700.00
John Brademas	3—Indiana	18,650.00
Andrew Jacobs	11—Indiana	18,550.00
William Lehman	13—Florida	18,525.00
Martin Russo	3—Illinois	18,160.00
Gladys Spellman	5—Maryland	17,916.62
Toby Moffett	6—Connecticut	17,737.50
Chris Dodd	2—Connecticut	17,700.00
Claude Pepper	14—Florida	17,150.00
Joseph Karth	4—Minnesota	16,900.00
Ronald Mottl	23—Ohio	16,900.00
Ted Risenhoover	2—Oklahoma	16,750.00
Brock Adams	7—Washington	16,700.00
Lenore Sullivan	3—Missouri	16,600.00
James Hanley	32—New York	16,525.00
John Melcher	2—Montana	16,468.82
Gerry Studds	12—Massachusetts	16,050.00
James Lloyd	35—California	15,900.00
Wayne Hays	18—Ohio	15,500.00
Andrew Maguire	7—New Jersey	

339

Member	District & State	Democrat	Republican
Joe Minish	11—New Jersey	15,400.00	
Robert Duncan	3—Oregon	15,100.00	
George Shipley	22—Illinois	15,100.00	
Leo Zefferetti	15—New York	14,762.96	
Helen Meyner	13—New Jersey	14,700.00	
James O'Hara	12—Michigan	14,300.00	
John Murtha	12—Pennsylvania	14,150.00	
George Miller	7—California	13,950.00	
Frank Annunzio	11—Illinois	13,600.00	
Gus Yatron	6—Pennsylvania	13,600.00	
James Symington	2—Missouri	13,380.00	
Phillip Burton	6—California	13,300.00	
Henry Waxman	24—California	13,000.00	
Bob Mollohan	1—West Virginia	12,950.00	
Max Baucus	1—Montana	12,737.30	
Andrew Young	5—Georgia	12,635.00	
James Stanton	20—Ohio	12,575.00	
Dominick Daniels	14—New Jersey	12,550.00	
Frederick Richmond	14—New York	12,550.00	
Teno Roncalio	At Lg—Wyoming	12,500.00	
Fortney Stark	9—California	12,290.00	
Thomas Downey	2—New York	11,772.00	
Robert Edgar	7—Pennsylvania	11,500.00	

340

Name	District—State	Amount
Edward Patten	15—New Jersey	11,450.00
Mike McCormack	4—Washington	11,282.62
Les Aspin	1—Wisconsin	11,262.00
James Burke	11—Massachusetts	10,950.00
Matthew Rinaldo	12—New Jersey	10,840.00
William Ford	15—Michigan	10,650.00
James Howard	3—New Jersey	10,500.00
Fernand St. Germain	1—Rhode Island	10,300.00
Robert Bergland	7—Minnesota	10,250.00
James Ambro	3—New York	10,178.55
Ray Madden	1—Indiana	10,100.00
Donald Riegle	7—Michigan	9,750.00
James Weaver	4—Oregon	9,668.27
John Joseph Moakley	9—Massachusetts	9,650.00
Joseph Early	3—Massachusetts	9,550.00
Doc Morgan	22—Pennsylvania	9,350.00
Robert Giaimo	3—Connecticut	9,100.00
Charles Carney	19—Ohio	8,900.00
John Dingell	16—Michigan	8,750.00
Tim Hall	15—Illinois	8,650.00
Harold Ford	8—Tennessee	8,650.00
Charles Wilson	31—California	8,500.00
John Moss	3—California	8,450.00
Clifford Allen	5—Tennessee	8,400.00
John Slack	3—West Virginia	8,350.00
Frank Horton	34—New York	8,280.00

341

MEMBER	DISTRICT & STATE	DEMOCRAT	Republican
Margaret Heckler	10—Massachusetts		8,120.00
Torbert Macdonald	7—Massachusetts	8,100.00	
William Cotter	1—Connecticut	7,500.00	
Mario Biaggi	10—New York	7,450.00	
Matthew McHugh	27—New York	7,300.00	
Louis Stokes	21—Ohio	7,300.00	
Ralph Metcalfe	1—Illinois	7,250.00	
James Scheuer	11—New York	7,250.00	
James Delaney	9—New York	7,250.00	
George Danielson	30—California	7,200.00	
Thomas Foley	5—Washington	7,150.00	
Bob Eckhardt	8—Texas	7,150.00	
Lindy Boggs	2—Louisiana	6,850.00	
Peter Rodino	10—New Jersey	6,600.00	
George Brown	36—California	6,350.00	
John McFall	14—California	6,275.00	
Daniel Flood	11—Pennsylvania	6,100.00	
Robert Leggett	4—California	6,050.00	
Dan Rostenkowski	8—Illinois	6,000.00	
David Obey	7—Wisconsin	5,950.00	
Glenn Anderson	32—California	5,900.00	
Otis Pike	1—New York	5,900.00	
Joel Pritchard	1—Washington		5,850.00

342

Joseph Addabbo	7—New York	5,800.00	
Gillis Long	8—Louisiana	5,650.00	
Donald Fraser	5—Minnesota	5,550.00	
Richard Bolling	5—Missouri	5,510.00	
Joseph Fisher	10—Virginia	5,423.64	
Bill Hungate	9—Missouri	5,350.00	
Edward Beard	2—Rhode Island	5,350.00	
Morgan Murphy	2—Illinois	5,150.00	
Paul Tsongas	5—Massachusetts	4,953.08	
Robert Drinan	4—Massachusetts	4,900.00	
David Evans	6—Indiana	4,860.00	
Bella Abzug	20—New York	4,850.00	
Stephen Solarz	13—New York	4,650.00	
Joseph McDade	10—Pennsylvania		4,600.00
John Conyers	1—Michigan	4,550.00	
Spark Matsunaga	1—Hawaii	4,550.00	
Samuel Stratton	28—New York	4,500.00	
Morris Udall	2—Arizona	4,400.00	
Paul McCloskey	12—California		4,150.00
Romano Mazzoli	3—Kentucky	4,050.00	
Clement Zablocki	4—Wisconsin	4,050.00	
Leo Ryan	11—California	4,000.00	
Henry Nowak	37—New York	3,975.00	
Barbara Jordan	18—Texas	3,875.00	
Edward Roybal	25—California	3,750.00	
William Barrett	1—Pennsylvania	3,600.00	

343

Member	District & State	Democrat	Republican
Patsy Mink	2—Hawaii	3,560.00	
Floyd Hicks	6—Washington	3,500.00	
William Walsh	33—New York		3,500.00
Ronald Dellums	8—California	3,460.00	
Lucien Nedzi	14—Michigan	3,450.00	
Charles Rangel	19—New York	3,450.00	
Richard Ottinger	24—New York	3,400.00	
Lionel Van Deerlin	41—California	3,350.00	
Al Ullman	2—Oregon	3,210.00	
John Seiberling	14—Ohio	3,200.00	
Yvonne Burke	28—California	3,150.00	
Don Edwards	10—California	3,000.00	
Cardiss Collins	7—Illinois	2,950.00	
Jerry Litton	6—Missouri	2,950.00	
James Corman	21—California	2,860.00	
Melvin Price	23—Illinois	2,800.00	
Henry Reuss	5—Wisconsin	2,750.00	
Thomas Ashley	9—Ohio	2,650.00	
John Fary	5—Illinois	2,600.00	
Silvio Conte	1—Massachusetts		2,600.00
Robert Roe	8—New Jersey	2,597.30	
Benjamin Rosenthal	8—New York	2,550.00	
Charles Wilson	2—Texas	2,500.00	

344

Name	District—State		
Parren Mitchell	7—Maryland	2,450.00	
Ronald Sarasin	5—Connecticut		2,350.00
Robert Kastenmeier	2—Wisconsin	2,300.00	
William Moorhead	14—Pennsylvania	2,250.00	
Jack Brooks	9—Texas	2,200.00	
Shirley Chisholm	12—New York	2,125.00	
Dante Fascell	15—Florida	2,100.00	
Bill Burlison	10—Missouri	2,100.00	
Edward Koch	18—New York	2,075.00	
William Randall	4—Missouri	2,050.00	
Al Quie	1—Minnesota		2,000.00
Fred Rooney	15—Pennsylvania	2,000.00	
Lee Hamilton	9—Indiana	1,950.00	
Michael Harrington	6—Massachusetts	1,950.00	
Harold Johnson	1—California	1,950.00	
Alphonzo Bell	27—California		1,900.00
Thomas Rees	23—California	1,700.00	
Benjamin Gilman	26—New York		1,600.00
Richard Ichord	8—Missouri	1,600.00	
Augustus Hawkins	29—California	1,450.00	
B. F. Sisk	15—California	1,350.00	
Elizabeth Holtzman	16—New York	1,250.00	
Charles Diggs	13—Michigan	1,050.00	
Don Clausen	2—California		1,000.00
Hamilton Fish	25—New York		800.00
Elwood Hillis	5—Indiana		800.00

Member	District & State	Democrat	Republican
Paul Sarbanes	3—Maryland	800.00	
Jonathan Bingham	22—New York	750.00	
Robert Jones	5—Alabama	650.00	
Ken Hechler	4—West Virginia	550.00	
Carl Perkins	7—Kentucky	500.00	
Edward Biester	8—Pennsylvania		300.00
Henry Gonzalez	20—Texas	300.00	
Sidney Yates	9—Illinois	250.00	
Robert Lagomarsino	19—California		250.00
Herman Badillo	21—New York	240.00	
Charles Bennett	3—Florida	–0–	
Edward Boland	2—Massachusetts	–0–	
John Breaux	7—Louisiana	–0–	
Joe Evins	4—Tennessee	–0–	
Barry Goldwater, Jr.	20—California		–0–
Gilbert Gude	8—Maryland		–0–
Stewart McKinney	4—Connecticut		–0–
William Natcher	2—Kentucky	–0–	
Robert Nix	2—Pennsylvania	–0–	
Neal Smith	4—Iowa	–0–	
Burt Talcott	16—California		–0–
Charles Vanik	22—Ohio	–0–	
Joseph Vigorito	24—Pennsylvania	–0–	

Charles Whalen, Jr.   3—Ohio

| | SUB-TOTALS | $2,368,675.51 | —0— |
| | TOTAL | $2,449,170.51 | $80,495.00 |

*The amount of contribution to Robert Traxler represents both the Special and General Elections.

"PAIRED" HOUSE MEMBERS

MEMBER	DISTRICT & STATE	DEMOCRAT	REPUBLICAN
Abner Mikva	10—Illinois	36,325.00	
John Jenrette	6—South Carolina	15,600.00	
Henry Helstoski	9—New Jersey	13,350.00	
Mendel Davis	1—South Carolina	8,600.00	
John Heinz	18—Pennsylvania		5,850.00
William Green	3—Pennsylvania	5,180.00	
Harley Staggers	2—West Virginia	2,550.00	
	SUB-TOTALS	$81,605.00	$5,850.00
	TOTAL	$87,455.00	

TOTALS

Senate:	$3,222,155.13
House:	2,449,170.51
"Paired Members":	87,455.00

GRAND TOTAL $5,758,780.64

Appendix 6

Excerpts from "Preliminary Report AFL-CIO Register and Vote Program, November 14, 1968," Prepared by COPE

Complete and accurate financial and manpower reports associated with our AFL-CIO registration and get-out-the-vote programs are presently being compiled in the field. This is a time consuming process, and pending receipt of the final data within the next few weeks, we are attaching a brief and necessarily incomplete, summarization of the results of our effort in 46 states and in the District of Columbia. As of November 15, data is still not available from the following states: Alabama, Hawaii, Louisiana and Mississippi.

Discounting any inflation, the result of a very natural tendency to "brag" a bit, the record is an impressive one. However, from our personal knowledge, we honestly believe that the figures, while incomplete, are on the conservative side.

By actual count, prior to and on Election Day there were telephone banks in operation in 638 locations, with a total of 8,055 telephones manned by 24,611 labor recruited workers, for the most part, volunteers.

In addition, in many states, a separate house to house canvass was conducted in connection with getting out the vote, particularly in selective labor areas and in minority areas where there are comparably few telephones. The number of people involved in these operations, an adjunct to Election Day activity, totaled 72,225.

Again, on Election Day there were 94,457 trade-unionists doing the necessary "knitty gritty," acting as baby sitters, car drivers, poll watchers, material distributors, etc.

In summary, Labor mobilized a total of 191,293 paid workers and mostly union volunteers in the week prior to and on Election Day.

Accurate registration data is not as yet available, but an estimated total of 4,611,660 potential voters were placed on the registration rolls as a result of AFL-CIO effort. The estimate not only indicates trade union member registration, but also the results of labor initiated activity in the Negro, Puerto Rican and Spanish American communities. In several states, including Florida and Idaho, a complete re-registration was necessary because of purged lists.

From the compiled data, three general observations can be made. First, in a majority of states, Labor did the job alone,

349

meeting the challenge with its own financial resources and manpower for the Democratic Party was either unable or unwilling to mount an effective effort to meet its political responsibility. For the most part, what assistance was available came from the Humphrey organization.

Second, while AFL-CIO effort was able to surmount and turn around an indicated swing of trade union votes to Wallace, there were still several closely contested states (Florida, Illinois, New Jersey, Ohio, Oklahoma, Virginia and Wisconsin) where Humphrey might possibly have won had the American Independent Party not been on the ballot.

Third, with the exception of Iowa, in those states where the Democratic Party had an effective operation, the state carried for Humphrey.

The results speak for themselves.

Appendix 7

Committee on Political Education

September 23, 1968

Memorandum
To: International Union Presidents and Secretaries
From: Alexander E. Barkan, Director
Subjec: The Wallace Threat

The presidential candidacy of George Wallace is making alarming inroads. Polls among the public at-large show him securing 20 percent, or more, of the total vote. Our own polls among union members show equal, and in some cases higher, percentages of support.

The Wallace threat, I feel, must be met head-on. Members must be educated on his record. They must be made aware that he threatens their contract, their wages and working conditions—that a vote for Wallace is a vote against their own best interests.

To achieve this, we will need your full cooperation. Every effort should be made to involve regional representatives, local union leaders and stewards. These are the persons in constant contact with members. Unless we can make them aware of and concerned about the Wallace threat, we cannot adequately reach the membership.

In addition, I enclose a sample of a leaflet produced and distributed to its members by the Communications Workers. I urge your union to prepare a similar printed piece for distribution to your members. It has far more impact than one distributed under the signature of National COPE or National AFL-CIO.

You could, if you wish, use this same leaflet, substituting your union's signature for CWA's. The art-work is in Washington, and we could make printing arrangements for you.

If you wish help in the preparation of a new piece, or in reprinting the enclosed, my staff will work with you in every way possible. Please let me know.

Appendix 8

Machinists Non-Partisan Political League

October 27, 1964

Memorandum
To: A. J. Hayes, Chairman
From: Jack O'Brien, Coordinator
Subject: Trouble in Texas

A short time ago we received a wire from John Heath, President of the Texas MNPL, requesting $5,000.00 to help Ralph Yarborough on television in a last-minute desperate effort to bolster his sagging fortunes in Texas. This wire was actually the result of "needling" by Bill Sewall to get District 776 working more aggressively to prevent Yarborough's defeat at the polls.

The big issue however, which is confirmed by reports of Steve Williams to Ross Mathews and by my own checking with Texas Machinists and with Al Barkan, is the fact that the "fix is in" to defeat Ralph Yarborough and to replace him with a Republican, Bush, the son of Prescott Bush of Connecticut. The only question at issue is whether this "fix" is a product of Governor Connally alone or is the product of a joint effort between Connally and President Johnson.

However, there is general agreement that Johnson has done nothing to aid the Yarborough campaign, with the most recent illustration of this fact being the absence of Mrs. Yarborough from the campaign plane of Mrs. Johnson which has just completed a trip through Texas.

Al Barkan reports that Walter Reuther called Lyndon Johnson to express his concern with the failure to invite Mrs. Yarborough to accompany the plane through Texas. Johnson reportedly told Walter Reuther that Mrs. Yarborough was traveling with Mrs. Johnson, but this is not true. Mrs. Yarborough was only invited to meet her at one of the stops in Texas. She was not on the plane. Therefore Walter Reuther was misinformed.

Johnson is scheduled to go to Texas for the wind-up of the campaign on Monday; and according to Barkan, it is reported that he is willing to make a Statewide campaign with Yarborough, but that Yarborough apparently does not reciprocate in this cooperative effort. Hank Brown reports to Barkan that this is not true and that the tape for the Monday broadcast has already been cut, that Yarborough was not invited to participate in the broadcast and that therefore there is no part for Yarborough in this tape recording. Yarborough, according to Hank Brown, would be delighted to make a TV broadcast with the President if he is given the opportunity.

Barkan reports that $26,000.00 is required to pay for this broadcast and he is seeking a meeting with Richard McGuire, Treasurer of the Democratic Committee, to get a commitment to pay for this broadcast in Texas, on the grounds that Labor has already contributed handsomely to the Committee and that this money should be used for the Yarborough and Johnson broadcast. Meanwhile, there ia an apparent stalling on the whole proposition of helping Yarborough win reelection. Barkan reports that George Meany is aware of this problem and that Joe Keenan, traveling with the President, is committed to bring this problem to Johnson's attention on the plane and to seek his affirmative support for Yarborough's reelection.

Hank Brown also reported to Al Barkan that the Houston Chronicle poll coming out today will show Yarborough running behind Bush. Many people in Texas consider that the polls have been doctored to show a steady attrition in Yarborough's strength at the polls, with a steady rise in the candidacy of Bush.

Al Barkan asked that I call this problem to your attention for whatever assistance you could give to get a Johnson forthright endorsement of Yarborough for reelection. This is more important, in the opinion of Al Barkan than any last-minute contribution to buy TV time for Ralph Yarborough, such as has been requested by John Heath.

Ralph Yarborough is the last stand-up Democratic liberal we have in the South, and his defeat would be a major loss for Organized Labor and for the liberal elements in the Democratic Party.

Appendix 9

The COPE Conference for the northeastern Region covered
Vermont, New Hampshire, New York and New Jersey. The
format consisted of meetings with individual State leadership,
one general session and the presentation of aid offered by
COPE for 1969–70.

The 1969–70 COPE Aid Program to States

COPE offered the following programs to the states interested
in pursuing a more effective political action course in 1969 and
1970:

1. *Special COPE Committee on Marginal Congressional
   Districts*—
   A special national committee to meet with state labor
   officials to determine the number of marginal seats at
   stake in 1970, if any within each state. Approximately
   80 congressional seats nationwide are involved. Where
   agreement is reached that a Congressional seat is marginal, an International Union will be assigned to head up
   the campaign, furnishing manpower and even funds.
   The International Union will work with the state COPE
   organization. An estimated 10 to 15 such districts will
   be assigned to IAM.
2. *Special COPE Committee on Marginal State Assembly
   Districts*—
   Again, a special national committee is prepared to work
   with the states to determine which legislative seats in the
   State Assemblies are considered marginal and should
   be given special attention. The concern is that a failure
   to elect friendly state legislators will result in gerry-
   mandering in re-apportionment following the 1970 census. Pooch Maile of the Rubber Workers will head up
   this effort for National COPE.
3. *Voter Registration Program*—
   AFL-CIO Executive Council has agreed that registration of voters should be an annual effort. Some
   $600,000 is available for this purpose in 1969. Although
   the initiative for developing this program rests with the

state organizations, Joe Rourke will work on this program. National COPE will contribute $2.00 for each $1.00 put in by the states when a budget has been agreed upon by both parties. The registration program, with a few exceptions, is to be conducted on a statewide basis. Data processing utilizing IAM's computer will be used in some states.

4. *Minority Workers Program—*
COPE has established a black trade union program through the A. Philip Randolph Institute to register blacks, to educate them on issues and candidates and to get out the black vote on election day in cities where there are a large number of blacks. Personnel used in this effort will be black union members from local unions in the area. Norm Hill, Bayard Rustin and W. C. Young are largely responsible for this program. They will recruit black union members to work in the program with the assistance of Central Labor Bodies and State organizations.

Appendix 10

**List of Union Political Leaders Present
at the December 1, 1971, Strategy Meeting to Defeat
Senator John McClellan**

John J. Hauck, ST
Operative Plasterers' & Cement Mason's Intl. Assn.

Joseph Cribben
United Assn. of Plumbers & Pipe Fitters

John Pecoraro
Intl. Brotherhood of Painters

John Joyce, Treas.
Intl. Union of Bricklayers, Masons & Plasters

Joseph Miller, Rep.
Marine Engineers Beneficial Assn.

Walter Mason
Building & Construction Trades Dept.

Hoyt Haddock
National Maritime Union of America

William McClennan, Pres.
Intl. Assn. of Fire Fighters

Anthony Mazzocchi, Leg. Rep.
Oil, Chemical & Atomic Workers Intl. Union

Helmuth Kern, COPE Director
Amalgamated Meat Cutters

Angelo Georgian, ST
United Shoe Workers of America

David Selden, Pres.
American Federation of Teachers

Dean Clowes
United Steelworkers of America

Joseph D. Kennan, Sec.
Intl. Brotherhood of Electrical Workers

Mel Boyle
Intl. Brotherhood of Electrical Workers

Evelyn Dubrow
ILGWU Political Committee

Jane O'Grady
Amalgamated Clothing Workers

O. William Moody, Jr.
Maritime Trades Dept.

Richard Murphy, COPE Dir.
Service Employees Intl. Union

Girard P. Clark, Dir.
Dept. of Leg. & Community Affairs, AFSCME

James Kennedy
Brotherhood of Railway,
Airline and Steamship
Clerks

Page Groton, Asst. to Pres.
Intl. Brotherhood of Boilermakers

James Huntley
Retail Clerks Intl. Assn.

J. William Webb
Communication Workers of
America

A. M. Lampley, Vice Pres.
United Transportation Union
William Dodds
United Auto Workers

David Sweeney
Intl. Brotherhood of Teamsters

Charles Caldwell
United Mine Workers

Joseph Malloney
Intl. Assn. of Iron Workers,
Bridge & Structural

James C. O'Brien
United Steelworkers of
America

William DuChessi, COPE
Dir.
Textile Workers Union of
America

James F. Bailey, Leg. Rep.
United Brotherhood of
Carpenters

J. C. Turner
Intl. Union of Operating
Engineers

Jack Curran, Leg. Director
Laborers' Intl. Union of
N.A.

Appendix 11

Senator Frank Moss Campaign Document
Utah Senate Campaign 1969 Activities

Since the election of 1968, several discussion and planning meetings have been held by Senator Moss, both in Utah and in Washington, with members of his staff and political advisors. Based on these deliberations, the following list has been prepared. It includes the minimum 1969 requirements for an effective Moss campaign.

I.   Public Relations Activities

Funds are needed for expansion of the regular information and news-dispensing activities of the Senator's office. Such expansion should include:

A. TV films (3 copies) to be sent weekly to Utah stations

B. Radio tapes to supplement the present spot-news coverage with a regular coverage of Utah radio stations

C. Mats to be sent twice monthly to weekly newspapers

D. Additional newsletters and mailing which will require paper beyond office allotment

II.   Travel

The number of trips allotted by the Senate is insufficient for the year before a campaign. This is the year that the Senator should get a considerable amount of visiting done in the smaller population counties. A considerable increase in travel is required, principally for the Senator, but some for staff and Mrs. Moss.

III.   Polling

A current assessment of voter sentiment on potential candidates and issues is considered essential to the formation of campaign plans. A poll should be taken within the next 90 days. Follow-ups would be considered for the end of this year and the beginning of next.

IV.   Public Relations Counsel

The advice of seasoned, nationally experienced public

relations counsel would be helpful. It is also believed desirable to name a Utah advertising agency soon so that its advice may be utilized in campaign planning. In addition, consideration is being given to working with a Utah commercial art firm for preparation of an overall campaign design and color scheme.

V. Filming

Effective television commercials are an essential of a successful 1970 campaign. To produce such commercials—and to produce a documentary film should one be decided on—a considerable footage of color movie film must be shot this year.

VI. Newspaper Tab

The decision has been made to use a tabloid newspaper special section to be carried by the five Utah daily newspapers on a Sunday near election. This was done in 1964 and was most effective. Following the procedure of the last campaign, the tab will be produced (art work, copy, and layout) this year, and printed early next.

VII. Christmas Card

It is anticipated that a color Christmas post card showing Senator and Mrs. Moss and their two grandchildren will be mailed for Christmas 1969 to about half the households in Utah.

VIII. Position Papers

A considerable increase is needed in the number of Moss Senate statements, statements for mailing, and speeches—both in and out of Washington. For the preparation of these, additional research and writing help is needed. Particularly someone informed in the economic area would be helpful. Much of what is needed could be done by the Senator's staff, but cannot be handled in addition to the regular work load.

IX. Pre-Campaign Activities

A. Expansion of the Senator's mailing list is essential. This is now being done by staff assistants.
B. Meetings of the Senator with special groups in

Utah should be arranged. Some of this has already been done, and more is in the preparation stage.

C. Activities should begin this year to build the Senator's relationship with, and enlist the support of, the members of certain groups. The most important of these are:
1. Housewives
2. Young Voters and Youth
3. Organized Labor
4. Rural Voters
5. Federal Employees
6. Educators

Appendix 12

November 24, 1969

Memorandum
To: United Steelworkers Executive Board Members of
          Political Action Committee
From: James Cuff O'Brien, Political Action Director
          Dean Clowes, Deputy Political Action Director
Subject: Utah Senate Race and Related Matters

Introductory Comments

Utah has consumed perhaps a greater number of our combined man-hours in meetings in Washington, Salt Lake City, Los Angeles, and elsewhere than almost any other single project we have been continually involved in. It certainly merits the attention for there is scarcely a finer human being, as well as first-rate senator, then Ted Moss. He is deserving of our support and, of course, the Race is critical with serious and deep-rooted obstacles to be overcome and a real shortage of funds, manpower and professionalism available. Some of the work that we have done is better not discussed, in detail. Suffice it to say there were deep internal divisions in the Democratic Party in the state, disturbing difficulties encountered with the Utah AFL-CIO leadership and problems of personnel and factions among our own Steelworkers. We have tried successfully in some instances and, alas, inadequately in others to act as mediators and bring about a measure of cohesiveness and unity to achieve the absolute solidarity that is essential to victory in so marginal an enterprise.

The United Steelworkers constitutes by far the largest segment of the labor movement in Utah but we hope to work effectively, not only with all those affiliated with the AFL-CIO, but with whatever organized units of the UAW, Teamsters, Railroad Brotherhoods, etc., will join with us. At the end of this report of our activities in connection with Utah-'70, we will attach a political profile of the state.

Initial Preparations

On March 5, 1969, a meeting was held at the headquarters of the Democratic National Committee. The planning for the 1970 elections in Utah was initiated. In attendance were:

Fred R. Harris, Chairman,   Geri Joseph, Vice Chairman,
   DNC   DNC

Bill Welsh, DNC
George Bristol, DNC
Al Spivak, DNC
Cong. Ed Edmondson, House Campaign Committee
Ken Harding, House Campaign Committee
Ted Henshaw, House Campaign Committee
Al Barkan, COPE Director
Mary Zon, COPE Research Director
Don Ellinger, IAM
Walt Davis, SIU
Norma Thomas, Demo. State Vice Chairman
Phil Cowley, Moss Campaign Mgr.
Don Holbrook, Governor's Campaign Manager
William DuChessi, TWU
Roy Purdy, CWA

Dean Clowes, USWA
Jim O'Brien, USWA
Reuben Johnson, Natl. Farmers Union
Senator Daniel Inouye, Senate Campaign Committee
Nordy Hoffman, Senate Campaign Committee
Wayne L. Black, Natl. Committeeman, Utah Demo. Party
Jean Westwood, Natl. Committeewoman, Utah Demo. Party
John Klas, Demo. State Chairman
Brent Cameron, Moss's State Off.
Desmond Kunkel, Sec.-Treas. Utah State AFL-CIO
Kermit Overby, NRECA

The meeting was lively with a great many blunt statements made and facts brought to light that showed the immensity of the task to be grappled with. National level people and people from the field were quite frank in indicating to each other their differences and gripes. This was all valuable because by early exposure of areas of concern it enabled people to pledge themselves to steps to correct and notify situations that serve to endanger the security of a campaign operation. There were eight areas of protracted review, only one of which we will address ourselves to. They are:

1. Public Relations Activities
2. Travel
3. Polling
4. In-State Professional Help
5. Filming
6. Newspaper Tabloid
7. Position Papers
8. *Pre-Campaign Activities*

The labor movement was our first cause of concern with all agreeing that steps had to be taken on a personal basis to resolve a breakdown in communication between some elements of the trade union movement and Senator Moss and his associates. It was agreed that LaMar Gulbransen, with such help as could be rendered by Dean Clowes and Jim O'Brien, would try to launch a series of discussions at which the tremendous stakes would be spelled out and people asked to subordinate their individual differences on behalf of a cause which was more significant than day to day rivalry and competition.

On the senior front, it was agreed that an organizer from the National Council of Senior Citizens would spend sufficient time in Utah to set up a nucleus for a Senior Citizens for Moss structure that could be built up for real momentum in the last months of the campaign. On the minorities as well as the Senior Citizen portion of the program it was established that Jim O'Brien would take responsibility for seeing to it that both of these areas received special attention as the principal minority to be dealt with is the Mexican-American population and the Steelworkers already have several active clubs of senior Steelworkers with good leadership in several locations in Utah.

It was also established that as soon as LaMar and Dean Clowes could schedule mutually satisfactory dates that they would personally participate in Utah meetings.

Congressional Candidates

The elections in Utah in 1970 do not offer particularly promising opportunities for election of labor candidates to either of the two seats. In all likelihood, the candidate in the First District will be Merrill Jenkins. In the Second District, the likely candidate is Milton Weilemnann. He ran a very effective race for the Senate in 1968, has a strong following and is an able, convincing and impressive person. He deserves any extra help that we can achieve for him even though it is hard to, on a mathematical basis, give marginal district and, therefore, priority status to this jurisdiction.

Implementation and Follow-Through

April 10, 1969

Dean traveled to Salt Lake City and held meetings with John Klas, the Democratic State Chairman; Ev Burger, Pres. of the Utah State AFL-CIO; George Wilde, United Steelworkers Staff Representative and Utah Political Action Coordinator; Milton Saathoff, Steelworkers L & E Chairman and others. These meetings tried to open a new dialogue and obtain acquiescence and pledges of cooperation from people nominally allies though, alas, frequently feuding.

All participants agreed they were going to support Senator Moss but there were varying degrees of accord as to how well they would cooperate with one another.

363

September 15, 1969

Dean again visited Utah and after traveling to several cities with Union strength in the state held a wind-up meeting in Salt Lake City. He had, as part of his scheduled program, arranged to have Senator Moss attend and address Steelworkers Subdistrict COPE meeting in Provo. This proved to be a very satisfactory event and did much to solidify and activate Steelworkers plans for participation right through until November 1970.

At the meeting that terminated Dean's activities in Utah on this trip, Kenny McTavish, the Steelworkers Subdistrict Director; George Wilde, the PAC Coordinator; Lenny Neilson, Steelworkers Staff Representative; a Farmers, Mine and Mill International Representative; and Tommy Consiglio of Los Angeles, Steelworkers COPE coordinator for District 38 were all in attendance. In a separate session Dean met with Senator Moss, Wayne Owens, Brent Cameron, John Klas, and Tommy Consiglio to outline what had been accomplished and to obtain their agreement to certain steps they would take to demonstrate their spirit of cooperation and to help resolve some disputed difficulties.

October 21, 1969

Jim O'Brien spent October 20 and 21 in Utah. The principal result of his visit was to provide a final resolution of the problem of a labor coordinator for the Voter Education and Registration Program acceptable to all groups. It was universally concurred that Bill Hayda, Vice President of the Garfield Local of Kennecott Copper, had an outstanding reputation, was looked upon with respect by all elements and would provide a first rate performance both because of his experience and background and his qualities as a person of tact and sensitivity.

In a meeting with John Klas; Brent Cameron, the Senator's Field AA; and Wayne Owens, now of Senator Kennedy's staff but occasionally available on an adhoc basis; all of the outstanding matters that had taken so many months to resolve were once more thoroughly scrutinized. It is hoped that as a result of what had been outlined here as well as a number of other factors, including conferences not described, that the situation is as nearly put together as could be expected and that a solid foundation has been laid for progress along the lines previously achieved in Wyoming, Montana and other contested territories not covered in this report.

Appendix 13

Representatives of Labor
Within Democratic Party Leadership

Meany Loyalists	Others
Democratic National Committee	

John J. Driscoll, AFL-CIO, Connecticut state president	William Lucy, American Federation of State, County & Municipal Employees (AFSCME), Int'l sec.-treas.
Michael Johnson, AFL-CIO, Pennsylvania state exec. vice president	
Victor Bussie, AFL-CIO, Louisiana state president	Sam Fishman, United Auto Workers, Coordinator, Michigan UAW Community Action Program
George Hardy, Service Employees Int'l Union, AFL-CIO, president	
Frank W. King, AFL-CIO, Ohio state president	Floyd E. Smith, Machinists Union, president
William C. Marshall, AFL-CIO, Michigan state president	
Joseph P. Molony, United Steel Workers, retired regional director	
Frank Raftery, AFL-CIO, Brotherhood of Painters & Allied Trade, president	
David K. Roe, AFL-CIO, Minnesota state president	
John Schmitt, AFL-CIO, Wisconsin state president	

Meany Loyalists	Others
Democratic Charter Commission	

Charles Walker, Int'l Brotherhood of Electrical Workers, Ass't to Int'l. Secretary	Mildred Jeffrey, UAW, coordinator, Consumer Affairs
Jacob Clayman, AFL-CIO, administration director, Industrial Union Dept.	Michael W. Kerwin, UAW, coordinator, SE Michigan Consumer Affairs Project
	Charles Hughes, AFSCME,

Dean Clowes, United Steel Workers, director, Political Action Committee

Richard Murphy, Service Employees Int'l Union, AFL-CIO, political director

Helmuth Kern, Amalgamated Meat Cutters Union, political director

Victor Bussie, AFL-CIO, Louisiana state president

Gary Cook, Maine State-Federated Labor Council, exec. board member

Helen O'Donnell, Retail Clerks Union, retired President, Local 711, Boston

Evelyn Dubrow, Int'l Ladies Garment Workers Union (ILGWU), Leg. rep. and exec. sec., Political Dept.

Julie Maieatta, AFL-CIO, Field Services Coordinator, Pennsylvania state COPE

Joe Davis, AFL-CIO, Washington State Labor Council, president

Patty Sleath, AFL-CIO, Director, Women's Activities Dept., COPE, West Virginia Labor Federation

president, Local 372, New York

Howard Samuel, Amalgamated Clothing Workers of America, vice president

William B. Welsh, AFSCME, Ass't. to the President for Political, Legislative Affairs

Meany Loyalists
Others
Delegate Selection Committee

Hugh Clark, AFL-CIO, Iowa state president

William DuChessi, Textile Workers Union, sec.-treas.

Gladys Harsin, AFL-CIO, Women's Activities Director, Florida State

Edward Donahue, Graphic Arts Int'l. Union, vice president

Victor Gotbaum, AFSCME, exec. dir., Council 37, New York

Anthony Zivilich, Teamsters Union, recording secretary

Michael Johnson, AFL-CIO,
   Pennsylvania State Exec.
   V-P
Ernest Post, AFL-CIO,
   Montana State COPE
   director

& business agent, Local
528, Atlanta

(The Democratic National Committee has a total membership of 298, the Charter Commission 165, and the Delegate Selection Commission 72.)

Appendix 14

The 70s Left
Socialists Come out of the Closet *
by Alice Widener

A major new move of deepest political significance to the entire nation is under way within the Democratic Party. In a split with aging George Meany's concealed socialism called "industrial democracy," the two most influential intellectual leaders of the Democratic Left—economist John Kenneth Galbraith, author of "The Affluent Society," and Michael Harrington, author of "The Other America"—decided to come out of the closet as avowed socialists. As such, they intend to lead a "70's Left" movement within the Democratic Party as the best vehicle for turning our country into a socialist nation.

What authors Galbraith and Harrington want is a nonviolent revolution in America, Asia, Africa and Latin America. The kind of revolution they want is described in Michael Harrington's pamphlet "American Power in the Twentieth Century" (published by the League for Industrial Democracy, New York, 1967). Mr. Harrington wrote:

"It requires, to use John Kenneth Galbraith's symbolic language, a revolution that would be less than a 'Russian' and yet more profound than a 'French' revolution . . . .

"To make a democratic revolution here and now, it is necessary to go beyond the French model—to institute extensive economic planning, and to ignore the allocation of resources made by the market."

No matter how it is put, what Messrs. Galbraith and Harrington want is what all socialists want: abolition of the free market and the collectivization of our entire society.

The scenario for the "70's Left" movement within the Democratic Party led by avowed socialists is as follows:

In June 1973, Michael Harrington, chairman during 1968–72 of the old Socialist Party founded by Eugene Debs and Norman Thomas, resigned from its successor organization, the Social Democrats, U.S.A. Mr. Harrington and other long-time socialists—including David Selden, president, American Federation of Teachers, and Victor Reuther, brother of the late Walter Reuther of U.A.W.—clashed with George Meany's AFL-CIO over the latter's support of the Vietnam War, their

---

*U.S.A. (530 E. 72 St., New York, N.Y. 10021), October 1973.

"neutrality" in the 1972 presidential election and their "obsessive anti-Communism."

On September 10, the *New York Times* reported "Socialists Plan Founding Parley—Harrington and 45 Others in New Group Issue Call." The call is for "a new American socialist organization" and its aim is "to set up a socialist caucus within the Democratic Party."

On September18, Leonard Silk, economics editor of the *New York Times*, reviewed John Kenneth Galbraith's new book "Economics and the Public Purpose" (Houghton Mifflin Company, Boston, 1973). Mr. Galbraith reveals in it that he is a socialist and he describes socialism as "indispensable" for our country. Leonard Silk commented, "So Mr. Galbraith has at last come out of the closet as a socialist." Mr. Silk opined that Mr. Galbraith's coming out "is publicly useful; it will add clarity and realism to the debate."

It will and it already has.

On October 12, the new Democratic Socialists held a preconvention public meeting at Loeb Student Center, New York University. The main speaker was socialist David Lewis, head of the Canadian New Democratic Party. Introduced to the New York audience by Victor Reuther, Mr. Lewis said, "We don't need supporters; what we need is people's confidence." He described past socialist experience in the Province of Saskatchewan and boasted that today his New Democratic Party holds the balance of power in Canada.

Next morning at the McAlpin Hotel in Manhattan, Michael Harrington delivered the opening address to the new Democratic Socialists, setting the political tone and strategy. "There are socialists in every sector of the Democratic Party," he said. "What we are doing here today is building the 70's Left." Mr. Harrington said it is time to bury the differences among members of the 60's Left, including "the veterans of SDS [Students for a Democratic Society] and those who argued with them."

Taking his cue from John Kenneth Galbraith, Mr. Harrington said socialists must come out openly as socialists in their political work. "It is time to come out of the closet," he declared. "The victory we seek is the victory that radicalizes people."

To grasp the full meaning of what Mr. Harrington, Prof. Galbraith and their associates mean by "coming out of the closet," it is necessary to know where and why the so-called democratic socialist movement in our country was in the closet. What happened, briefly, is that in 1905, Upton Sinclair, Jack London and Clarence Darrow founded the Intercollegiate Socialist Society to propagate Fabian socialism in the United

369

States. For 16 years, the society conducted pioneering educational work in our colleges, in conferences, summer training courses, lectures and debates. In 1921 there was a wave of public resentment in our nation over the activities of Leftist radicals, anarchists and Communists. The adjective "socialist" became so repugnant to the vast majority of Americans that the Intercollegiate Socialist Society deemed it prudent and expedient to change its name to the League for Industrial Democracy. What the socialists did was to assume an alias and hide behind it to conduct their activities in, as it were, a closet. At the League's 40th anniversary in 1945, Dr. Harry A. Overstreet recounted:

> . . . I can remember the time when this organization was just starting meeting with a number of teachers of the University of California, very apprehensively and timidly making an effort to study this terrible thing called socialism.
> We studied socialism and we didn't want anybody to know we were doing it.

Among the nationally prominent people who belonged to the League for Industrial Democracy but who didn't want anybody to identify them as socialists were, for example, Walter Lippmann, Walter and Victor Reuther, and John Dewey, father of "progressive" education.

In 1962, the student branch of the League for Industrial Democracy broke away from it to become Students for a Democratic Society but still avoiding the name "socialist." By that time, Michael Harrington was board chairman of the League. He still is a board member. Both the League and SDS remained in the closet by not publicly describing themselves as socialists. But that is what they were and are—though their factionalism is expressed in all variations, from palest weakest mildest pink to bloody dark red.

On October 13, 1973, at the new Democratic Socialist convention, Michael Harrington called for a socialist united front "not as a vanguard" [that is how the Communist Party invariably describes itself] but as a kind of prod pushing liberals further and further to the Left. He said the new Democratic Socialist organization will "back the Kennedy-Griffiths National Health Security bill as a step to socialized medicine, and will back tax reform as a step to total income redistribution."

The Democratic Socialists' attention will be focussed on "workers, students, intellectuals, blacks and other minorities." The new group does not want a large number of supporters or contributors; what the new Democratic Socialists seek is what David Lewis said, "the people's confidence" and they mean to get it by acting as a caucus within the Democratic Party, pushing and pushing to the Left and bringing their intellectual influence to bear on prominent Democrats. Mr. Harrington told his group to "let George Wallace and his followers alone." The members of the group want to plant their socialism in more hospitable ground.

Authors Galbraith and Harrington already have tasted the fruits of success derived from cultivation of high ground in the Democratic Party. No one has told the story of that success more accurately than Arthur M. Schlesinger Jr. in his book "A Thousand Days" about the Kennedy Administration. Author Schlesinger writes (page 1010):

> It was not till toward the end of the [1950's] decade— and especially with the publication in 1958 of Galbraith's "The Affluent Society" and its chapter xxiii on "The New Position of Poverty"—that chronic poverty began to impinge on the national consciousness as a distinct issue. . . . Then in 1962, "The Other America," a brilliant and indignant book by Michael Harrington, translated the statistics [on poverty] into bitter human terms. If Galbraith brought poverty into the national consciousness, Harrington placed it on the national conscience.
>
> Kennedy read both Galbraith and Harrington; and I believe that "The Other America" helped to crystallize his determination in 1963 to accompany a tax cut by a poverty program. Galbraith's unremitting guerrilla warfare in support of the public sector certainly played its part too.

Since Galbraith still was "in the closet" during the Kennedy Administration, it is unlikely that President Kennedy was aware of Galbraith's real affiliation.

The goal of the 70's Left—says Michael Harrington—is "the free provision of the necessities of life to the people." Along with socialized medicine to be paid for by progressive income taxes, he calls for free housing, food and clothing. In their official printed call "Toward a Socialist Presence in America," the new Democratic Socialists declare that as a final goal "we posit a socialist world." How do they intend to achieve it?" "Tactically," they declare, "we move toward these goals by way of coalition politics. . . . In the Congressional elections of 1974 and the Presidential election of 1976, the serious choice between Left and Right will counterpose liberal Democrats to reactionary Republicans and the latter's Dixiecrat fifth column in the Democratic Party. In that conflict, we will side with the liberals against the conservatives—which is to say with the mass Left against the mass Right. . . . We act, then, as part of the Left wing of the Democratic Party in order to change the Party itself, to turn it into a new kind of mass political party in America. . . ."

The new Democratic Socialists announce, "We are trade unionists, students, intellectuals, black and white. Almost all of us are veterans of the movement to end the unconscionable American war in Vietnam and of the McGovern campaign of 1972."

In the 1972 McGovern campaign, radicals took effective control of the Democratic Party. The new Democratic Socialists intend to form a powerful caucus able to take control of the radicals and use the Democratic Party as an instrument for turning our country into a socialist state. "We are looking to the United States of the 1970's and beyond," says Michael Harrington.

"The new socialism," writes John Kenneth Galbraith, "allows of no acceptable alternatives; . . . The new socialism is not ideological; it is compelled by circumstances."

Both Communists and Democratic Socialists proclaim the inevitability of socialism due to circumstances. Neither Communists nor Democratic Socialists will tolerate the free market, the sole guarantor of individual freedom. What John Kenneth Galbraith and Michael Harrington are trying to do is to force every American to choose between Left and Right. In 1972, Americans—Republicans and Democrats—overwhelmingly rejected the Left. If they do not do so in 1974 and 1976, our country will begin its third century of existence under a Socialist President.

Appendix 15

August 26, 1970

Mr. Floyd Smith
International President
International Association of
Machinists & Aerospace Workers
AFL-CIO
1300 Connecticut Avenue, N.W.
Washington, D.C.

Dear Sir and Brother:

This letter is to make a personal appeal to you with regards to a very critical situation that has arisen in my campaign for re-election to the United States Senate.

I need not emphasize to you my voting record in the Senate in behalf of Labor, nor do I have to remind anyone of the consequences in the loss of another liberal Senator in this year's campaign.

The situation I mentioned above is one in which we have approrimately 8,000 Negro residents in Bernalillo County. The first problem, of course, is to get them all registered as we feel that this would be a solid block vote in my behalf. Voter registration in the State of New Mexico ends September 22. Unfortunately, we don't have, at this time, the cohesive Negro leadership necessary for a crisis registration drive.

Our next problem, of course, is in getting out the vote in these precincts for the reasons as stated. I am making a personal request that you allow and assign Grand Lodge Represtntative, Herbert Ward, to work in my campaign for as much time as you can possibly spare him. I am sure, of course, that his time is needed on other matters that directly affect your organization. I would appreciate your personal consideraion on granting this request, as I am sure Mr. Ward's assistance would add greatly to our carrying this block vote which is much needed in my campaign.

Thanking you for your consideration.

Fraternally yours,
/s/
JOSEPH M. MONTOYA
United States Senator

Appendix 16

Excerpts of a Brief Report Concerning Wyoming's Registration Drive with Particular Emphasis on the Role of the Computer

Rod Crowlie, Associate Staff Director, Senate Post Office and Civil Service Committee

The registration drive in Wyoming is concentrated on 111 key precincts where candidates like Senator McGee get most of their votes. The selection of those precincts is based primarily upon an analysis by Joe Moore of our staff of the voting returns since 1960.

The thrust of Moore's report is that Republican candidates in Wyoming in every Federal election secure roughly 65,000 votes. Thus, it is safe to assume that in 1970, Republican candidates will go into the election with 65,000 votes in hand. Obviously, Democratic candidates must garner something more than 65,000 votes if they are to win. *The disturbing fact in Wyoming elections since 1966 is that vote totals have dropped to below 130,000.*

Despite the fact that Wyoming is one of four states which has lost population since the 1960 Census, Moore's analysis shows that Democratic support still remains in the 111 precincts but there are a disturbing number who are not registered.

Since late spring of 1969, the AFL-CIO in Wyoming, some of Senator McGee's staff and other interested parties in Wyoming have been at work on the registration problem. Moore's report reinforced this concern. As a consequence, all parties have been at work developing an elaborate card file system as a location device for unregistered voters.

At this point, headquarters with telephones have been established in the 13 towns which encompass the 111 precincts. The card file system was made from 3 basic data sources—the city directory where available, the telephone book and voter registration lists. In all 111 precincts, the card file has been updated by at least two telephone call-throughs. We are now in the door-to-door verification phase.

COPE has played an unusual and almost immeasurable role in the success of the registration effort so far. Walter Markham, Don Ellinger, and Bill Holayter have been helpful beyond compare, particularly in the computer phase of the operation. Their advice and material aid kept the whole registration system from going under. It is at the computer and computer print-out level that the remainder of the report concerns itself.

Late in 1969, we had finished developing a master file in the 111 precincts. The problem of duplicating that master file then arose. COPE and the International Association of Machinists were able to offer their computer services. From our standpoint, we looked upon the computer primarily as a duplicating device.

The concept within which the registration and get-out-the-vote effort in Wyoming operates is as follows. Files are developed as a locating device for unregistered voters and as a record of who is at a particular address that is eligible and likely to vote. In view of this concept, the goal is to make the task of the precinct worker as simple and as explicit as possible. Thus, throughout the registration system is a built-in shrink factor.

For example, our file not only provides us with registration information on residents but allows us to set aside the verified unregistered Republicans so that the door-knocker has a much smaller and precise task in pursuing registration of the unregistered. No shotgun approach—all our shots are rifled in. The telephone operation is another case in point—every verification as to location of an unregistered voter by telephone is one less place the door-knocker has to go to in the verification process. (Of course, he will be at the door when the registration phase becomes operative.) This is to say nothing of the benefits of cross checking implicit in such an approach.

In view of the above operational concept, duplicate cards and lists become vital instruments to accomplish precise location with ease.

The IAM computer program and print-out format was both a blessing and a burden from our standpoint. On the one hand, it provided us with quick multiple copies of our master file. On the other hand, we were unable to include important data in the print-outs (i.e. long addresses such as trailer courts were not compatible with the computer's program) and we were forced to include data not particularly relevant to our operation (i.e. zip codes). Despite these difficulties, the contribution of COPE and the IAM in providing duplicate print-outs is magnitudinous. Because of this contribution, we are able to provide a set of street order cards for precinct (red borders), a set of alpha cards for headquarters personnel (green borders) and our master file as our security file.

Moreover, the provision for print-out lists has been of great value. Precinct workers have at their disposal a street order list which makes the operation at the door-knocking level a great deal more efficient and easier. The print-out list alphabetized within precinct willl be used by checkers at the polls in both the primary and general elections. The alpha list within county has been of great use to us since it enables us to determine almost at a glance where our duplications exist.

Another word about the lists. Because of programming problems, we were unable to secure a street order list with sufficient space between the names to make it easy for the door-knocker to add new information concerning an address (i.e. change of occupants, other family members who are eligible to vote, etc.). Here, too, there was information on the list that was not particularly relevant to our needs (i.e. zip codes, identification numbers, etc.).

When the print-outs first became available there was some discussion about the number of duplications that seemed present in the alpha list by county. Some felt that the duplications were going to run well over 20 percent—in short, that our master file had been badly in error. This has not been borne out by the telephone verification process. While our ball-park estimate about how many people were in the 111 precincts was around 65,000, the fact is that it is much closer to 80,000 and that the duplication we feared in our input has not been borne out.

The duplication error is not running at the 20 percent error level, but more at the 5 percent error level. Be that as it may, the point is that our original hypothesis that the mother load of Democratic support is in the 111 precincts now takes the shape of a bonanza . . . if we continue to exploit what is there.

There are some intangibles regarding the computer phase that bear mention. For one thing, there was some disagreement among the Wyoming leadership and within the McGee staff about viability of computers under any circumstances. That is to say, some were not all convinced that the computer was useful. This had some effect on the directness of our execution in utilizing computer services. I am happy to say that our experience has diminished that conflict to nearly zero.

This does not gainsay the fact that there are some problems about persuading volunteers about the efficacy of the print-out cards and lists. Like everything else, however, in the field or organization politics a great deal of teaching is a necessary ingredient. I am proud to say that people like Joe Moore, Dennis Guilford, and John Holaday have become remarkable teachers.

One further point needs to be made—that is—the weakest aspect of the computer operation is the problem of rapid update. We all recognize that the computer has other clients and is not there for our exclusive use. Therefore, the requirement for update in the various phases of our operation has been done by hand by volunteers at our various headquarters.

At the risk of repetition, I need to say once more how helpful COPE and the IAM have been in all this. Not only have they contributed hardware and print-outs but they have added a much more important ingredient—that is advice and counsel. We have all learned a great deal more about registration as well as the role of the computer. We are more convinced than ever that because of your role, Senator McGee's election in November is much closer to becoming fact.

Appendix 17

Excerpts of "The Computer's Role in Getting Out the Vote" *

The accurate, up-to-date "precinct walking list" has for years been the political Lost Dutchman gold mine, searched after by organizations engaged in the American electoral process. By use of a newly expanded, increasingly sophisticated computer program, tht AFL-CIO Committee on Political Education is attempting to break through the thickets barring the way to this long-sought goal.

The goal is a "walking list" of union members that can most effectively bring labor's political program directly to union members in their homes across the country and help dramatically to increase member participation in the democratic process. . . .

While the "walking lists" constitute the single most valuable potential computer output, its benefits and impact spread importantly into other facets of labor's political programs. The computer becomes, in effect, the ultimate mailing list, making possible fast, accurate mailings, as the need arises, to union members in almost any selected political subdivision in the nation. As well, it provides 3×5 index cards for precinct work.

And inside the computer is a two-way street, pouring traffic not only out of the computer to the state and local COPE groups, but routing new traffic, new data and new names into the main computer from those same state and local bodies. Continually the computer requires considerable specific information, and it will keep sending printouts back to the field until a satisfactory amount of information is returned.

The project, which involves the participation of 88 of the 116 international unions affiliated with the AFL-CIO, also requires constant updating for accuracy. In its formative stages, it has also required an education process for local COPE activists, union officials and volunteers on the use of the potential.

A major milestone was passed in January 1973 when the operation was moved into the AFL-CIO Data Processing Department for the first time. Previously, COPE had used the

*Rex Hardesty, *Federationist* (official AFL-CIO monthly publication), September 1973

computer facilities of tht Machinists and rented time on other computers in the Washington area.

At mid-summer 1973, the COPE project had about 8.9 million names committed to the computer memory bank, putting the program ahead of schedule on its goal of 10 million before the 1974 elections.

Periodic updatings and processing to compile more information—or more detailed information—are going on constantly.

It has taken almost eight years for the COPE computer program to develop to its present level and probably forever the "potential" of the program will lie just ahead of its reality. A few unions are forbidden by their constitution to provide their membership lists to the program—or at least the international union is forbidden to provide them. In many of these unions, locals are under no such restraint, so a list can be provided by the locals within a given state. Overall, it is turning out that about 80 percent of the union members' names can be compiled in a given state. . . .

Lists—or at least partial lists—have been compiled on about 34 states, mostly from among the heavily populated corridors of the northeast, the upper midwest and the west coast. That total is expected to reach 37 states by the end of 1973.

Eight years ago, the program was born from an experience in New Jersey in the 1964 elections—the election in which the most liberal of recent Congresses, the 89th, was elected along with Lyndon Johnson. As part of the labor effort in 1964, the response to an appeal to unions with sizable memberships in New Jersey produced a list of 400,000 names of union members.

After the election, that list, compiled and maintained totally by hand, was still around. In 1965, COPE spotted the potential of computerizing such lists and COPE Director Al Barkan launched the project on its first halting steps. As a pilot project for the future, work was begun on a similar list for Pennsylvania. As befits its status of a highly unionized state, Pennsylvania has remained a mainstay throughout the program.

For the 1966 elections, experimentation was extended to a few more states and by the time that election was over, the computers borrowed at the Machinists building had membership lists from at least parts of seven more states—Maryland, Virginia, Ohio, Colorado, California and Texas. Even then, Pennsylvania was carrying a sizable total of between 800,000 and 900,000 names. Work in Texas produced a list of 300,000, with a high degree of sophistication in how the Texas state federation broke down the list.

In April 1968, there were about 3.2 million names in the computer for use in labor's all-out campaign drive of that fall.

It was in the wake of the 1968 elections that COPE Director Barkan turned the data processing effort into a year-around project. An additional assistant director, John Perkins, came from the COPE field staff at that time, with the data processing project among his responsibilties. To coordinate distribution and fieldwork, Perkins has incorporated the computer project into an overall pre-election preparation known as the "critical path" method, designed to assist state AFL-CIOs and central bodies in planning, scheduling and controlling data processing activities.

"Critical path" isn't much different from the way a construction superintendent might organize work crews to make sure the forms are finished before the cement arrives, or the system an airline ground crew might employ to get the gasoline and meals aboard the right flights. This method is important to the data processing because it spells out deadlines well in advance and incorporates the concept of activities which are simultaneous but with separate deadlines.

The program has to be keyed from the start to the election laws and habits of a given state—the words county, ward and precinct aren't used everywhere and registration isn't required in small towns and rural areas of some states. The data processing also depends on who keeps the voter registration planning information—county, city or township; how that information is organized; what kind of access to it is allowed by law; and full details on the voter registration requirements. You can't build a big program for on-the-job worker registration, for instance, if the state allows registration only at the court house and forbids deputy registrars.

For example, when a computer file is "passed" to be printed out and sent to the field for the processing of political data, the cards are put in a sequential sort by county for areas with county government. But in New England and other parts of the country where the registration lists are kept by town, an assignment is made either by the name of the post office or the political subdivision and the sorting is done accordingly.

Consequently, a registration survey has to be conducted in the field to determine which sort is necessary for the computer to print out a format that can be easily processed against the local, county or city registration lists.

The combination of critical path and data processing has enabled COPE representatives in the field to determine the location of union members, the work loads that are involved in determining their registration status and costs in capturing telephone numbers and other critical political data. It provides those in charge with an overview, helping them allocate their resources for the maximum impact on election day.

Ironically, Perkins has found that the political workers who are the most accomplished in working with precinct lists are sometimes the most reluctant to utilize the computer's full potential on the next step. That's because they know how valuable the lists are and are reluctant to part with them for further revision.

That's why he urges the wider use of 3 × 5 cards. They can be bursted into sections, passed out to volunteers, marked on and generally folded, spindled or mutilated. A fresh supply, incorporating the new information marked on them, can be sent quickly—and often at far less cost than the new information can be manually updated in the field. But the naked feeling of being without the lists for even a limited amount of time is hard to overcome for some. . . .

Lists from the unions arrive at COPE in a wide variety of ways, from lists already committed to computer (magnetic) tape, to addressograph, scriptograph or other semi-automated lists which while containing most of the needed information, still have to go through the keypunch process before being committed to magnetic tape. And of course the same is true of typewritten lists.

Of the 88 unions which have members enrolled in the program, 61 of them provided membership lists from the union's international headquarters. . . .

Once the starting list has been received at the AFL-CIO in any form, it is keypunched to be added within the proper state and coded with an 18-character top line for future computer reference. . . .

Once the list is verified, the hard work begins. A printout is made, most likely on 3 × 5 cards, and is sent to the state AFL-CIO for the first compilation of "below-the-line," or political information. There's no substitute for the local voting list, a map, a phone book and precinct locator in compiling the next information; ward, precinct, party affiliation, registration status and phone number. If a voter is registered, a lot of that information comes quickly off election rolls in jurisdictions that make them public. But if all you have to go in is an address, identifying the unregistered by precinct requires a map and a lot of work. . . .

Once the political information is filled in as accurately as possible, the new information is re-coded to fit in with all other union members in the state. At this point, it is available for a printout in any form the state or local COPE may call for—mail labels, lists, 3 × 5 cards—and organized under vari-

381

ous identifying characteristics—by county, unregistered voters only, by union and so on.

At this state, the computer is also capable of giving COPE officials, locally or nationally, a quick overview. This can show the number of union members in each county in the state, the number unregistered or the ones on whom phone numbers are still not available. This keeps them ahead of their "critical paths" and provides a constant check on overall COPE activities. . . .

The potential of the program is considerable, but political observers know it's risky to start counting potential voters and predicting victory margins. When you look back at a close race, you can find the group that provided the margin almost anywhere you want—even attributing it to the left-handed Lithuanians, as election analyst Richard M. Scammon often says.

But since labor's strategy has always been the simplest of formulas—get workers registered and out to vote—the numbers game is a little more germane, if no more accurate, in predicting an outcome.

The examples are legion:

In two congressional districts of Connecticut, for example, COPE-endorsed candidates won one and lost one in 1972 by margins on which the unregistered union members could have had a distinctive impact. In the fifth district, the COPE-endorsed candidate lost narrowly in a district which has 29,364 union members on the data processing list. Of that total, only 18,828 were registered and 10,536 were not—almost twice the 5,436 margin by which the COPE candidate lost.

In Connecticut's third district, the COPE candidate won with 53.3 percent of the vote. That was a margin of 14,904 votes, but another 9,511 union members in the district were not registered. Had they been, and had they voted in the usual 7–3 range in favor of COPE-endorsed candidates, the 53.3 percent margin could have been much wider.

Similar examples abound, but of course the industrialized states—and working class districts—are the most important. With one-man, one-vote setting fairly tight population limits of 500,000 for a congressional district, the rule of thumb is that two-thirds of that population will be eligible to vote. That's an electorate of nearly 350,000 for any congressman, but only 164,000 turned out in 1972, for instance, when COPE-endorsed Rep. James O'Hara squeaked to re-election with 50.8 percent of the vote in his Michigan district, a margin of 2,684. One Massachusetts district was even closer, with the COPE-endorsed candidate winning by only 1,206 votes out of 234,300 cast. . . .

In sheer speed the computer is awesome. In sorting information, the computer can read 350,000 numbers per second off a disc. When information is going out, the computer performs equally prodigious feats: in one hour, it can turn out 30,000 of the 3 × 5 cards, 66,000 lines on a listing of 75,000 mail labels. A lot of volunteers have to do a lot of typing to match that.

What the computer means to improved political work is equally impressive:

• In the past, when a state COPE made endorsements for such races as state representative, it would have to combine several districts, perhaps all from one county, in the mailing to union members informing them of the endorsement. Or it would be necessary to send a cumbersome list covering endorsements in the whole state—in either case leaving the union member to dig out his own district. Now, by calling for a printout by ward or precinct, a very specialized mailing can be made on each district.

• In voter registration drives, the multiple available listings make it possible to reach some members at their home through street or telephone lists; others on the job by calling for a printout by union, then publicizing a date when deputy registrars will be at the plant—or some combination of both methods.

• In metropolitan areas where both the election board's registration lists and the telephone company's subscriber lists are available on magnetic tape, Perkins expects that within a few years, the AFL-CIO will be able to pass the COPE file of union members against those lists (in the same computer) and electronically capture the information on union members and their telephone numbers without a human hand being lifted. When COPE volunteers can throw away all the phone books, precinct locators and the like, the time and cost savings will be tremendous.

• On election day, it is possible for a precinct worker to draw up a list of the voters in triplicate, then tour the polling places periodically during the day. Union members who have already voted are scratched off, with the remaining names turned in to the COPE telephone bank for calls. The same can be done on the carbon copies later that day, so by dusk every union member in the precinct may have been reminded, or provided transportation to vote.

Appendix 18

UNITED STATES DISTRICT COURT
SOUTHERN DISTRICT OF CALIFORNIA

HOWARD ELLIS, et al.,
    Plaintiffs,
v.
BROTHERHOOD OF RAILWAY,
AIRLINE AND STEAMSHIP
CLERKS, et al,
    Defendants.
	Civil No. 73-113-N
	Consolidated with
	Civil No. 73-118-N
	
	INTERLOCUTORY
	SUMMARY
	JUDGMENT

ALLAN FAILS, et al.,
    Plaintiffs,

v.

BROTHERHOOD OF RAILWAY,
AIRLINE AND STEAMSHIP
CLERKS, et al,
    Defendants.

In accordance with the Findings of Fact and Conclusions of Law in this matter and with Rule 56(c) of the Federal Rules of Civil Procedure, and the Court having determined that there are no genuine issues of material fact as to the issue of liability alone,

IT IS HEREBY ORDERED, ADJUDGED AND DECREED as follows:

1. That an interlocutory summary judgment be entered for the plaintiffs and Fails class members (hereinafter collectively referred to as"plaintiffs") as to the issue of liability alone, the Court having found defendants to have breached their duty of fair representation as more fully set forth in the Findings of Fact and Conclusions of Law;

2. That summary judgment be denied as to each and every issue of damages, all such issues to be determined according to evidence to be presented at the trial phase of this litigation; and

3. That the pretrial conference for this litigation be held on May 3, 1976; all parties to conform to the dictates of Rule 9

of the Local Rules of Civil Procedure, Southern district of California.

SO ORDERED.

Dated: January 20, 1976.

/s/
LELAND C. NIELSEN,
United States District Judge

UNITED STATES DISTRICT COURT
SOUTHERN DISTRICT OF CALIFORNIA

HOWARD ELLIS, et al., Plaintiffs, v. BROTHERHOOD OF RAILWAY, AIRLINE AND STEAMSHIP CLERKS, et al, Defendants. ——— ALLAN FAILS, et al., Plaintiffs, v. BROTHERHOOD OF RAILWAY, AIRLINE AND STEAMSHIP CLERKS, et al, Defendants.	Civil No. 73-113-N Consolidated with Civil No. 73-118-N FINDINGS OF UNDISPUTED FACTS AND CONCLUSIONS OF LAW

This cause came on regularly for hearing and consideration before the Honorable Leland C. Nielsen on the motion of the plaintiffs, Howard Ellis, et al., Allan Fails, et al., individually and as class representatives, for summary judgment in the above entitled and consolidated cases, pursuant to Rule 56 of the Federal Rules of Civil Procedure. The Court, having considered said motion and the opposition of defendants thereto, and having examined and considered the entire record in the matter, including the pleadings, depositions, affidavits, and memoranda filed in support of and in opposition to the said motion, the Court now finds the facts and states the conclusions of law as follows:

FINDINGS of FACT

1. Plaintiffs at the commencement of these actions were citizens of the United States, residing in the State of California and employed by Western Airlines at various locations in the

State of California, including Los Angeles, San Francisco and San Diego.

2. Defendants Brotherhood of Railway, Airline and Steamship Clerks, Freight Handlers, Express and Station Employees and its subsidiary organizations, System Board of Adjustment No. 451, Skyliner Lodge Local 3001, Sky Harbor Lodge Local 3014, and Arrowliner Lodge Local 3049, are unincorporated associations and labor organizations whose purpose, in part, is the representation of employees for collective bargaining over wages, hours and working conditions within the meaning of Section Two of the Railway Labor Act. Defendant California State Legislative Committee of the Brotherhood of Railway, Airline and Steamship Clerks, Freight Handlers, Express and Station Employees is an unincorporated association, subsidiary to and affiliated with the Brotherhood of Railway, Airline and Steamship Clerks, Freight Handlers, Express and Station Employees, which has as its purpose, in part, the sponsorship of legislation in the State of California. Defendants are hereinafter collectively referred to as "BRAC."

3. Defendants Local Lodges 3001, 3014 and 3049 are subsidiary to Defendant System Board No. 451, which is in turn subsidiary to the Grand Lodge of the Brotherhood of Railway, Airline and Steamship Clerks.

4. Western Airlines is a corporation authorized to and doing business in the State of California, engaged in the transportation of passengers and freight in interstate commerce.

5. At all times material, Western Airlines has maintained a collective bargaining relationship with BRAC governing the terms and conditions of employment of plaintiffs and Fails class members and BRAC has been, and is, the exclusive bargaining agent for the craft or class of employees in which they are employed.

6. Under the terms of the collective bargaining agreement in effect between Western Airlines and BRAC, effective October 1, 1969, and the Letters of Agreement of October 27, 1966 and February 26, 1971, made a part of and incorporated into the collective bargaining agreement, each employee in a classification under the agreement was required to acquire and maintain membership in BRAC as a condition of employment after completion of the sixtieth day of employment, except that employees who were hired prior to October 27, 1966 and were not members as of that date were not required to acquire and maintain membership but only to tender to BRAC an agency fee equal to the initiation fee and monthly dues uniformly imposed on union members.

7. A communication issued by BRAC International President C. L. Dennis and published in the November, 1975

issue of the *Railway Clerk/interchange* construed the BRAC Constitution as not requiring any employee represented by BRAC to become a formal union member as a condition for retaining his job rights or for qualifying for other generally available union benefits.

8. Plaintiffs Fails, Frost, Johnson, Erkman, Taylor, Brown, Nelson, Damante, Ryan, Grote, Ballard, Young, Douglas, Emminger and Wisor, hereinafter collectively referred to as the "Fails plaintiffs," are or have been members of defendant BRAC, employed by Western Airlines. On March 23, 1973, the Fails plaintiffs filed Case No. 73-118-N, for themselves and as class representatives.

9. The Fails plaintiffs' motion for determination of class action determination of all issues was granted in orders entered by this Court dated September 14, 1973 and April 8, 1975. The class includes all BRAC members employed or formerly employed by Western Airlines who submitted written objections as stated in paragraph 13 of the Fails complaint. Subsequent references to the "Fails plaintiffs" include the class members.

10. Plaintiffs Ellis, Balian, Sauls, Dean, Payne, Fontaine, and Loudin, hereinafter collectively referred to as the "Ellis plaintiffs," are or have been employees of Western Airlines who have declined to become members of defendant BRAC, but who have been obligated, as a condition of their employment, to tender agency fees to defendant BRAC equivalent to the membership dues and fees paid by members of defendant BRAC. On March 20, 1973, the Ellis plaintiffs filed Case No. 73-113-N.

11. Subsequent references to "the plaintiffs" include the Ellis plaintiffs, the Fails plaintiffs, and the Fails class members.

12. Except for the class allegations in Case No. 73-118-N, the allegations of the two complaints are essentially the same. The plaintiffs alleged that defendant BRAC expended compulsory dues and fees exacted from plaintiffs, over their written objections, for political and various other non-collective bargaining purposes. Plaintiffs alleged that these expenditures over their objections deprived them of their rights under the Railway Labor Act and the First, Fifth and Ninth Amendments to the United States Constitution, and constituted a breach by defendant BRAC of its duty of fair representation owed to plaintiffs. Plaintiffs further alleged that defendant BRAC's existing three and one-third cents dues reduction procedure was unavailable to plaintiffs and further that the procedure was arbitrary and discriminatory because it did not correlate with defendants' political and ideological expendi-

tures. Plaintiffs sought declaratory and injunctive relief, money damages, attorneys' fees, and costs.

13. Plaintiffs and those class members falling within the territorial jurisdiction of the Defendant Local Lodges 3001, 3014 and 3049 pay dues and fees to the appropriate Local Lodge, to System Board No. 451, and to the Grand Lodge. Each Local Lodge remits 30 cents per person per month to the California State Legislative Committee. The remaining class members pay dues and fees to Local Lodges in their area, to System Board No. 451, and to the Grand Lodge. Thirty cents per month from their dues and fees is similarly sent to a State Legislative Committee.

14. Each plaintiff and class member has sent a written protest to BRAC, objecting to the contractual requirement compelling the payment of wages as union dues and fees. The language of each such protest is as follows:

As an employee of Western Airline, I feel that the Brotherhood of Railway, Airline and Steamship Clerks does not properly represent my interests and I protest the compulsory "agency fee" I must pay the Brotherhood of Railway, Airline and Steamship Clerks, in order to retain my job. In addition, I hereby protest the use of these fees for any purpose other than the cost of collective bargaining and specifically protest the support of Legislative goals, candidates for political office, political efforts of any kind or nature, ideological causes, and any other activity which is not a direct cost of collective bargaining on my behalf. I demand an accounting and refund from the Brotherhood of Railway, Airline and Steamship Clerks of all fees exacted from me by the so-called "agency fee."

15. Each such protest was sent by certified mail. In some instances, delivery was refused; in others, the letters were discarded; in still others, the letters were received but not opened. Defendants did not respond to any of these protest letters.

16. When the protest letters were sent by plaintiffs, the BRAC Constitution contained the following refund device:

Any member who does not desire to contribute to the Legislative Fund Account may have his dues reduced three and one-third (3⅓) cents per month, by notifying his Financial Secretary in writing and paying his dues direct to said Financial Secretary. Reduction in dues becomes effective with the month following the month in which the member notifies the Financial Secretary in writing and cannot be retroactive. The Financial Secretary will acknowledge receipt of notice.

17. None of the plaintiffs' dues were reduced or refunded in the amount set forth in the BRAC Constitution. Plaintiff Ellis specifically requested the 3⅓ cents per month reduction, but was told that non-members could not participate in the reduction scheme.

18. Approximately nine months after these suits were commenced, BRAC promulgated a Policy Statement (dated January 24, 1974) which established a procedure whereby objecting members and agency fee payers could secure a refund of that portion of their dues and fees which was expended upon "political purposes not germane to collective bargaining." Plaintiffs thereupon sought and obtained leave to amend their complaints.

19. The amendments allege that provisions of the Policy Statement are inconsistent with those of the BRAC Constitution, and that the Policy Statement is consequently invalid, as it was not adopted as a constitutional amendment. It is charged that the Policy Statement is part of a continuing bad faith effort by BRAC to deprive plaintiffs of constitutional and statutory rights. In addition to the relief requested in the complaints, plaintiffs pray:

(1) for an order determining that the adoption of the Policy Statement is void;
(2) for an order restraining defendants from subjecting persons represented by BRAC to the Policy Statement;
(3) for an order releasing objectors from any obligation to pay dues, fees, or assessments to defendants or any subordinate or affiliated organizations as a condition of employment;
(4) for damages, attorneys' fees, costs, and such other relief as the Court may deem proper.

20. Defendants raise the following affirmative defenses to the complaints, as amended:

(1) failure to state a claim upon which relief may be granted;
(2) failure to exhaust internal and administrative remedies;
(3) the bar of various statutes of limitations;
(4) preemption by the System Board of Adjustment, with regard to those claims arising out of the interpretation or application of the collective bargaining agreement.

21. Case No. 73-113-N and Case No. 73-118-N, pursuant

to the stipulation of the parties and the order of this court, have been consolidated for purposes of discovery and trial.

22. BRAC has engaged in the following activities since June 30, 1972:

(1) Recreational, social and entertainment expenses for activities not attended by management personnel of Western Airlines.

(2) Operation of a death benefit program.

(3) Organizing and recruiting new members for BRAC among Western Airlines bargaining unit employees.

(4) Organizing and recruiting new members for BRAC, and/or seeking collective bargaining authority or recognition for:

   (a) employees not employed by Western Airlines;

   (b) employees not employed in the air transportation industry;

   (c) employees not employed in other transportation industries.

(5) Publications in which substantial coverage is devoted to general news, recreational and social activities, political and legislative matters, and cartoons.

(6) Contributions to charities and individuals.

(7) Programs to provide insurance, and medical and legal services to the BRAC membership or portions thereof, other than such programs secured for its salaried officers and employees.

(8) Conducting and attending conventions of BRAC.

(9) Conducting and attending conventions of other organizations and/or labor unions.

(10) Defense or prosecution of litigation not having as its subject matter the negotiation or administration of collective bargaining agreements or settlement or adjustment of grievances or disputes of employees represented by BRAC.

(11) Support for or opposition to proposed, pending, or existing legislative measures.

(12) Support for or opposition to proposed, pending, or existing governmental executive orders, policies, or decisions.

23. Funds for the activities listed in paragraph 23 are derived in part from the dues and fees plaintiffs are compelled to pay BRAC.

24. A portion of plaintiffs' payments to the Grand Lodge are placed in general fund accounts. The defendants have been affiliated with various non-BRAC organizations at times material hereto, and have contributed amounts from general

funds to said organizations. Included among those organizations are:

the AFL-CIO, the Canadian Labour Congress, the Congress of Railway Unions, the Council of AFL-CIO Unions for Professional Employees, the Union Label and Service Trade Department of the AFL-CIO, and Canadian Railway Office of Arbitration, the Canadian Railway Labour Association, the Cooperating Railway Labor Organizations, the Canadian Non-Operating Railway Unions, and the San Diego-Imperial Counties Labor Council.

The foregoing non-BRAC organizations engage in fraternal, social, and political activities; and they espouse positions on economic and ideological issues, through publications and other means.

25. The Railway Clerks Political League (RCPL) is an unincorporated association affiliated with BRAC. Its officers are all BRAC officers, and its activities are conducted by officers and employees of BRAC, whose compensation is paid entirely by BRAC. Office space, computer services, and other operating supplies and facilities are provided by BRAC at no charge. The funds for such undertakings are derived from the BRAC General Fund, into which a portion of plaintiffs' dues and fees is commingled.

26. The RCPL supports or opposes political candidates, causes and legislation.

27. Funds for the RCPL are solicited by paid officers and employees of the Grand Lodge of BRAC and its subordinate and and affiliated organizations, including the remaining defendants. These fund-raising activities include publications in the BRAC magazine, *Railway Clerk/interchange,* and personal appeals at System Board and local lodge meetings. The direct and indirect costs of such fund-raising activities are paid by BRAC from general funds, and RCPL makes no reimbursement therefor.

28. Some amounts collected for RCPL are transmitted through the General Fund accounts of the Defendant Local Lodges, System Board #451, and Grand Lodge. RCPL funds have been utilized for the payment of employee salaries and other BRAC Grand Lodge operating expenses since prior to January 1, 1972.

29. BRAC has incurred costs for political activities from its General Fund for at least five to ten years.

CONCLUSIONS OF LAW

1. This Court has jurisdiction over the parties hereto, and over the subject matter hereof, under 28 U.S.C.§ 1337.

2. Fails et al. v. BRAC, Case No 73-118-N, is properly brought as a class action.

3. BRAC owes each plaintiff the fiduciary duty of fair representation.

4. Section 2, Eleventh of the Railway Labor Act, 45 U.S.C. § 152 *et seq.*, as construed by the United States Supreme Court in *International Association of Machinists* v. *Street*, 367 U.S. 740, 81 S.Ct. 1784 (1961), is intended to force all employees covered by the Act to share the costs of negotiating and administering collective agreements, and the costs of the adjustment and settlement of disputes.

5. The Railway Labor Act prohibits the use of fees and dues for non-collective bargaining purposes and activities, over protest from a represented employee.

6. Those activities listed in Paragraph 22 of the Findings of Fact are non-collective bargaining activities as that term is defined in *Street, supra*.

7. BRAC's use of dues and fees of protesting employees for non-collective bargaining activities and purposes constitutes a breach of the fiduciary duty of fair representation BRAC owes to each plaintiff.

8. BRAC has further breached its duty of fair representation to plaintiffs by the following:

(1) refusing delivery of some of plaintiffs' protest letters, discarding some letters, and ignoring the balance of such letters;

(2) failing to make dues reduction of 3⅓ cents per month to Fails plaintiffs and class members, as provided in the BRAC Constitution;

(3) excluding agency payers such as plaintiff Ellis from eligibility for the 3⅓ cents dues reduction because of their non-membership.

(4) maintaining provisions in its constitutions (1967 and 1971) which were not good faith efforts to comply with its lawful obligations.

Dated: January 20, 1976.

/s/
LELAND C. NIELSEN,
United States District Judge

Author's Acknowledgements and Notes

In 1973 the Center for the Public Interest of the Robert M. Schuchman Memorial Foundation, Inc., offered me a grant to conduct research into campaign financing. Specifically, I was to trace union political spending and activity (a previously neglected area of research) to wherever they might lead—and I found they ultimately led to both the Republican Party and the Democratic Party, although 90 percent goes to the latter. I welcomed this opportunity to take leave from my private law practice to undertake the Center's nonpartisan public interest research project because I felt the saga being told by Watergate of corporate campaign contributions, while deplorable and true, was too one-sided and that an equally interesting and revealing story could be told of union political spending.

I am indebted to the Schuchman Foundation for making it possible for me to undertake the research project, especially to Daniel Joy and Robert Feinberg, whose encouragement and advice were invaluable. Three other persons to whom I am extremely grateful are Washington attorneys John L. Kilcullen and Raymond La Jeunesse, and the latter's former paralegal assistant, Ms. Jade West.

This book is concerned with the general subjects of union political spending and activities as related to campaign financing reform. It is not concerned with any specific legal case or litigation or with any specific bill before Congress. While the basic research material was drawn from a wide variety of sources, some of the information comes from legal papers, correspondence, documents and depositions in the case of *George L. Seay, et al. v. Grand Lodge International Association of Machinists and Aerospace Workers, et al.*, 360, F. Supp. 123 (CD Calif. Dec. 19, 1973) filed in the United States District Court for the Central Division of California. The case was dismissed on December 19, 1973 by U.S. District Judge Harry Pregerson. While the case was before him, Judge Pregerson twice denied motions which would have placed the case's documents under a protective seal, the net effect ultimately being that all of these are now in the public record.

The book also draws upon a thoroughly documented affidavit filed by Professor Sylvester Petro of Wake Forest School of Law in his capacity as an expert witness in the case of *Gerald M. Marker, et al. v. John B. Connally, et al*, 337 F Supp 1301 (D.D.C. 1972).

The author of this research project does not comment on the issues raised by or on the outcome of either the *Seay* or *Marker* case, and has scrupulously taken care to cite only material or information disclosed in either case which is a matter of public record and available for public inspection in the cases' files located in the offices of the clerks of the district courts in Los Angeles and Washington, D.C., respectively.

CHAPTER 1

COPE: The Nation's Most Powerful Political Machine

1. Stipulation signed by J. Albert Woll of Woll and Mayer, Washington, D.C., and by Thomas E. Harris, Associate General Counsel, AFL-CIO (*Seay* exhibit 3889).
2. Quoted from the Petro affidavit, which cited the *National Journal,* December 12, 1970, p. 1965.
3. *Washington Daily News,* April 29, 1971.
4. Proceedings of the Tenth Consitutional Convention, AFL-CIO, October 18, 1973, p. 28.
5. Quoted from the Petro affidavit, which cited Barkan, "Political Activities of Labor," 1 *Issues in Industrial Society* 23, (N. Y. State School of Industrial Relations at Cornell, 1969), hereinafter referred to as "Barkan."
6. Quoted from the Petro affidavit, which cited *National Journal,* December 12, 1970, p. 1966.
7. Quoted from the Petro affidavit, which cited the *Washington Post,* August 31, 1970.
8. Quoted from the Petro affidavit, which cited the *National Journal,* August 12, 1970.
9. Memorandum of February 26, 1970, to Eugene Glover from Don Ellinger (*Seay* exhibit 1131).
10. *Report of the AFL-CIO Executive Council to the Eleventh Constitutional Convention,* October 1975.
11. *Seay* exhibit 370.
12. Quoted from the Petro affidavit, which cited the *Philadelphia Evening Bulletin,* November 8, 1967.
13. Ibid.
14. Quoted from the Petro affidavit, which cited "Barkan."
15. Ibid.
16. Ibid.
17. Ibid.
18. *Seay* exhibit 344.
19. Quoted from the Petro affidavit, which cited "Barkan."
20. Ibid.
21. Stipulation signed by J. Albert Woll and Thomas E. Harris (*Seay* exhibit 3889).
22. Letter of September 23, 1968 (*Seay* exhibit 348).
23. Quoted from the Petro affidavit.

24. Ibid.
25. Syndicated column of June 10, 1969.
26. Letter of May 7, 1969, to Don Ellinger, Director, Machinists Non-Partisan League (*Seay* exhibit 576).
27. *Seay* exhibit 1085.
28. Memorandum of June 15, 1970, to President Meany from Al Barkan (*Seay* exhibit 1084).
29. Ibid.
30. Letter of May 15, 1970 (*Seay* exhibit 904).
31. *Seay* exhibit 905.
32. Quoted in *Human Events*, November 28, 1970.
33. Quoted from the Petro affidavit, which cited the *New York Times*, September 22, 1971, p. 47.
34. Memorandum of September 3, 1969 (*Seay* exhibit 518).
35. Letter of August 18, 1970, to Don Ellinger, Director, MNPL (*Seay* exhibit 926).
36. Quoted in Haynes Johnson and Nick Kotz, *The Unions* (New York: Pocket Books, 1972), pp. 75-76.
37. Letter of November 17, 1970, to Don Ellinger, Director, MNPL (*Seay* exhibit 1174).
38. *Seay* exhibit 1173.
39. Memorandum of August 9, 1971, to the MNPL Executive Committee from Don Ellinger (*Seay* exhibit 1266).
40. Memorandum of December 1, 1971, to Al Barkan from MNPL Director Don Ellinger (*Seay* exhibit 1900).
41. *Seay* exhibit 1884.
42. Letter of December 3, 1971 (*Seay* exhibit 1883).
43. Letter of December 13, 1971, from William Holayter, Assistant Director, MNPL (*Seay* exhibit 1906).
44. Letter of July 25, 1972, from Claude Ramsey (*Seay* exhibit 2468).
45. *Chicago Daily News*, July 11, 1972.
46. *Washington Post*, July 12, 1972.
47. *National Observer*, May 5, 1973.
48. *Fresno* (Calif.) *Bee*, November 2, 1972.
49. *San Francisco Examiner*, September 21, 1972.
50. Ibid.
51. Memo from COPE, November 13, 1972.
52. *U.S. News & World Report*, November 27, 1972.
53. *Washington Post*, October 30, 1972.
54. *Boston Globe*, February 22, 1973
55. *Human Events*, November 28, 1972.
56. Common Cause News Release, November 30, 1972.
57. *National Journal*, July 22, 1972.
58. UAW Administrative Letter No. 3.

CHAPTER 2

The AFL-CIO Today

1. *Report of the AFL-CIO Executive Council to the Tenth Convention,* pp. 64-67.
2. Interview in the *National Observer,* May 5, 1973.
3. "Meany Lauds Union's Political Organization," *Boston Globe,* February 22, 1973.
4. "A New Face on Organizing," *Business Week,* August 25, 1973.
5. *Report of the Appeals Committee to the Tenth Convention,* p. 2.
6 Ibid., p. 9.
7. Ibid., p. 37.
8 "The Union Lobbying Machine," *Nation's Business,* May 1969, p. 69.
9. Ibid.
10. *Report of the AFL-CIO Executive Council to the Tenth Convention,* pp. 370-380.
11. Haynes Johnson and Nick Kotz, *The Unions* (New York: Pocket Books, 1972),. p. 54. I highly recommend this book for additional reading. The book is adapted from a series of articles that orginally appeared in the *Washington Post.*
12. Ibid., p. 69.
13. Jerry Wurf, "Labor's Battle with Itself," *Washington Post,* October 14, 1973.
14. Ibid.

CHAPTER 3

Labor and the Democratic Party

1. *Newsweek,* November 22, 1971.
2. *New York Times,* November 13, 1972.
3. *Detroit Free Press,* April 15, 1971.
4. *Seay* exhibit 515.
5. *Seay* exhibit 516.
6. *Seay* exhibit 517.
7. *Seay* exhibit 571.
8. *Seay* exhibit 572.
9. Letter of March 14, 1969, to Don Ellinger, Director, MNPL (*Seay* exhibit 570).
10. *Seay* exhibit 573.
11. *Seay* exhibit 604.
12. Letter of December 12, 1969, to Don Ellinger, Director, MNPL (*Seay* exhibit 548).

13. Letter of July 16, 1970, to business representative Philip Zannella, District Lodge 54 in Ohio, from Don Ellinger (*Seay* exhibit 917).
14. *Seay* exhibit 2415.
15. Memorandum of February 23, 1972, from William J. Holayter, Director, MNPL, to Francis Meagher, Vice President, IAM *Seay* exhibit 2275).
16. *Seay* exhibit 1875.
17. "Watergate Has Undone the Republicans, Right?" by Harry McPherson, *New York Times Magazine,* September 9, 1973.
18. Interview in the *New York Times,* November 14, 1972.
19. *U.S. News & World Report,* September 10, 1973.
20. *New York Times,* October 22, 1973.
21. *Washington Star,* July 21, 1973.
22. *New York Daily News,* August 12, 1973.
23. *Washington Star-News,* August 13, 1973.
24. Column of December 11, 1972.
25. *Washington Post,* August 2, 1973.
26. *Seay* exhibit 1175.
27. *Seay* exhibit 1280.
28. *New York* magazine, December 17, 1973.
29. *U.S.A* (530 East 72 Street, New York, NY. 10021), October 1973.

CHAPTER 4

How the IAM and MNPL Are Organized

1. Sworn deposition in *Seay* of Floyd E. Smith, June 9, 1971, p. 12.
2. Letter of October 14, 1971, to All Stewards in Local Lodge 56 (*Seay* exhibit 1367).
3. Letter of March 20, 1972, to All Local Lodges in the U.S. from MNPL Co-Chairmen Floyd Smith, Eugene Glover, and Charles West (*Seay* exhibit 2323).
4. *Machinist,* February 12, 1971.
5. Sworn deposition in *Seay* of William Holayter, February 11, 1972, p. 16.
6. Ibid.
7. Letter of April 4, 1968, to Postmaster, District of Columbia, (*Seay* exhibit 341).
8. Letter of April 30, 1968, to Postmaster, Washington, D.C. (*Seay* exhibit 340).
9. Memorandum of February 29, 1972, to Chief Accountant Parker O. Jones from General Secretary-Treasurer Eugene Glover (*Seay* exhibit 1597).

10. Memorandum of February 4, 1972, to MNPL Co-Chairmen Smith, Glover, and West (*Seay* exhibit 1876).

11. Memorandum of October 24, 1967, to International President P. L. Siemiller (*Seay* exhibit 424).

12. Letter of April 12, 1972, from IAM General Counsel Plato Papps to Comptroller General of the U.S. Elmer Staats (*Seay* exhibit 2574).

13. Affidavit of December 15, 1964, of International President A.J. Hayes (*Seay* exhibit 1432).

14. Memorandum of June 3, 1971, to the MNPL National Planning Committee Members and State Council of Machinists Officers (*Seay* exhibit 1576).

15. Brochure titled "MNPL, the Union's Other Arm" (*Seay* exhibit 17).

16. Sworn deposition of Floyd E. Smith, June 9, 1971, pp. 34-39.

17. Letters of February 23, 1972, (*Seay* exhibits 1594, 1595, 1596).

18. Letter of November 2, 1967, from GVP Gilbert Brunner to Business Representative William Nellis of District Lodge 91 in Connecticut (*Seay* exhibit 631).

19. Letter of October 23, 1969, from GVP L. Ross Mathews to District 58 Business Representative Justin J. Donohue in New York (*Seay* exhibit 608).

20. *Seay* exhibit 1514.

21. *Seay* exhibit 1511.

22. *Seay* exhibit 1508.

23. Memorandum of February 27, 1970, to All Full Time IAM Staff Members (*Seay* exhibit 58).

24. Letter of June 18, 1970, from GVP Robert Simpson to All Grand Lodge and Special Representatives, et al. (*Seay* exhibit 1546).

25. Letter of May 30, 1972, to Secretary-Treasurer Thomas Elliott of Local Lodge 1903 in California (*Seay* exhibit 2416).

26. Letter of July 16, 1971, from F. B. Wisner, Jr. of Local Lodge 100 in Montana (*Seay* exhibit 1219).

27. Letter of September 5, 1968, to General Chairman M. E. Melvin of District Lodge 19 in California (*Seay* exhibit 118).

28. Letter of February 17, 1972, from Illinois MNPL Chairman Kenneth Holland to MNPL Secretary-Treasurer Howard Dow (*Seay* exhibit 2311).

29. Letter of May 29, 1968, to Business Representative John Heidenreich of District 10 in Wisconsin (*Seay* exhibit 326).

30. Memorandum of March 21, 1968 (*Seay* exhibit 394).
31. Letter of March 20, 1968 (*Seay* exhibit 231).
32. Memorandum of December 9, 1968, from MNPL Co-Chairmen Siemiller, DeMore, and Mathews to All Local and District Lodges in the U. S. (*Seay* exhibit 1498).
33. Memorandum of April 18, 1968, to International President Siemiller (*Seay* exhibit 1002).
34. Letter of August 1, 1969, to Texas AFL-CIO Secretary R. Evans (*Seay* exhibit 996).
35. Letter of November 3, 1970, from GLR Philip Van Gelder and Business Representative Patrick O'Brien of District Lodge 12 in Maryland (*Seay* exhibit 844).
36. Memorandum of April 22, 1970, to All IAM Staff Members (*Seay* exhibit 1554).
37. Letter of July 28, 1970, (*Seay* exhibit 1542).
38. Letter of February 24, 1971, to All Business Representatives and Organizers in the Northeastern States Territory (*Seay* exhibit 1584).
39. Letter of February 5, 1969, to General Business Representatives DeWayne Williams in California (*Seay* exhibit 670).

CHAPTER 5

The MNPL Executive Committee and the National Planning Committee in Action

1. *Seay* exhibit 10.
2. Schedule of MNPL Educational Fund expenditures (*Seay* exhibits 3918, 3920).
3. MNPL Constitution, Article VII (*Seay* exhibit 2).
4. Letter of October 29, 1971, to Steve Bancroft, Institute of Labor and Industrial Relations, University of Illinois (*Seay* exhibit 1356).
5. Sworn deposition of Floyd E. Smith, June 9, 1971, p. 17.
6. Letter of October 1, 1969, from MNPL Co-Chairmen Smith, Glover, and West to GVP Fred Purcell (*Seay* exhibit 1142).
7. Memorandum of November 26, 1969, to Liaison GLRs (*Seay* exhibit 1138).
8. Letter of November 15, 1969, addressed "Dear Sir and Brother" (*Seay* exhibit 1140).
9. Letter of December 11, 1967 (*Seay* exhibit 407).
10. Letter of December 11, 1967 (*Seay* exhibit 408).
11. Sworn deposition of W. Don Ellinger, February 10, 1972, p. 13.
12. *Seay* exhibit 1920.

13. "The 1969 National Planning Committee" (*Seay* exhibit 1143).
14. *Machinist,* February 18, 1971.

CHAPTER 6

Assignment of the Union's Staff to Political Activity

1. The MNPL National Planning Committee 1968 Reports, p. 10 (*Seay* exhibit 8).
2. Ibid.
3. Memorandum of January 18, 1971, to Dean Ruth (*Seay* exhibit 1257).
4. Sworn deposition in *Seay* of Smith, p. 82.
5. Letter of April 17, 1972, to All Local Lodges, Ladies Auxiliaries, and District Lodges of the International Association of Machinists and Aerospace Workers in the State of Georgia, from T. S. Walters, Jr., Secretary-Treasurer, Georgia State Council of Machinists and Aerospace Workers (*Seay* exhibit 2360).
6. Sworn deposition of William Holayter, February 11, 1972, p. 55.
7. *Seay* exhibit 262.
8. *Seay* exhibit 252.
9. Official minutes of the October 10-13, 1968, meeting of the California Conference of Machinists (*Seay* exhibit 78)
10. Official minutes of the July 17, 1968, meeting of the California Conference of Machinists (*Seay* exhibit 83).
11. Official Minutes of January 14-17, 1971, meeting of California Conference of Machinists (*Seay* exhibit 92).
12. Ibid.
13. Official Minutes of the August 22, 1964, meeting of the Executive Board of the California State MNPLO (*Seay* exhibit 87).
14. Official minutes of the May 1, 1971, meeting of the Executive Board of the California State MNPL (*Seay* exhibit 90).
15. Official minutes of the October 10, 1964, meeting of the Executive Board of the California State MNPL (*Seay* exhibit 86).
16. *Seay* exhibit 80.
17. Separate letters of June 20, 1966, to GVPs White, West, Glover, Brunner, and Smith from P. L. Siemiller (*Seay* exhibits 1488-1492).
18. Memorandum of November 3, 1966, to P. L. Siemiller (*Seay* exhibit 427).
19. *Seay* exhibit 428.

20. Letter of February 20, 1968 (*Seay* exhibit 2168).
21. Letter of February 29, 1968 (*Seay* exhibit 2164).
22. Letter of June 24, 1968 (*Seay* exhibit 189).
23. Letter of October 13, 1968 (*Seay* exhibit 187).
24. Letter of October 9, 1968 (*Seay* exhibit 109)
25. Letter of November 11, 1968 (*Seay* exhibit 99).
26. Letter of August 19, 1968, to Don Ellinger (*Seay* exhibit 160).
27. Letter of September 9, 1968, to Ed Whalen, President, Oregon AFL-CIO (*Seay* exhibit 268).
28. Letter of November 13, 1968 (*Seay* exhibit 1501).
29. Letter of February 5, 1968, to Charles A. Jimenez, District Assistant to Congressman Thomas Foley (*Seay* exhibit 312).
30. Letter of October 24, 1969 (*Seay* exhibit 659)
31. Letter of May 26, 1969 (*Seay* exhibit 527)
32. Letter of November 7, 1969, from John Giacone Executive Vice President Wisconsin State AFL-CIO (*Seay* exhibit 607) .
33. Letter of November 3, 1969, to General Chairman Robert A. Lucas of District Lodge 100 (*Seay* exhibit 566)
34 Memorandum of September 22, 1969 (*Seay* exhibit 615).
35. Ibid.
36. Memorandum of October 6, 1969 (*Seay* exhibit 652).
37. Memorandum of December 23, 1969 (*Seay* exhibit 1569).
38. Letter of May 20, 1970 (*Seay* exhibit 799).
39. Letter of April 21, 1970 (*Seay* exhibit 800).
40. Letter of July 23, 1970 (*Seay* exhibit 913).
41. Letter of October 23, 1970 (*Seay* exhibit 891).
42. Letter of May 22, 1970 (*Seay* exhibit 1008).
43. Letter of June 9, 1970 (*Seay* exhibit 1007).
44. Letter of October 6, 1970 (*Seay* exhibit 779).
45. Letter of August 26, 1970 (*Seay* exhibit 933).
46. Memorandum of September 16, 1970 (*Seay* exhibit 1121).
47. Letter of June 16, 1970 (*Seay* exhibit 1112).
48. Letter of January 14, 1970 (*Seay* exhibit 1115).
49. *Seay* exhibit 963.
50. Letter of April 23, 1970 from Tommy Powell, President, Memphis AFL-CIO Labor Council (*Seay* exhibit 957).
51. Letter of August 21, 1970 (*Seay* exhibit 953).
52. Letter of May 19, 1970 (*Seay* exhibit 1550).
53. Letter of May 28, 1970 (*Seay* exhibit 820).
54. Letter of April 6, 1970 (*Seay* exhibit 824).
55. Letter of August 22, 1970 (*Seay* exhibit 1109).
56. Letter of August 27, 1970, to Joseph Rourke, Assistant Director, COPE (*Seay* exhibit 1110).
57. Updated letter (*Seay* exhibit 1170).

58. Letter of September 21, 1970, to Don Ellinger (*Seay* exhibit 832).
59. Letter of November 5, 1970 (*Seay* exhibit 845).
60. *Seay* exhibit 1077.
61. Memorandum of November 22, 1971 (*Seay* exhibit 1242).
62. Memorandum of December 27, 1971 (*Seay* exhibit 2203).
63. *Seay* exhibit 2204.
64. Letter of January 24, 1972 (*Seay* exhibit 2230).
65. Letter of May 5, 1972 (*Seay* exhibit 2388).
66. Letter of May 8, 1972, from Louis A. Romano, President, Connecticut State Council of Machinists (*Seay* exhibit 2406).
67. Letter of June 6, 1972 (*Seay* exhibit 2431).
68. Letter of June 20, 1972 (*Seay* exhibit 2430).
69. Letter of September 22, 1972 (*Seay* exhibit 2481).
70. Memorandum of September 25, 1972 (*Seay* exhibit 2482).
71. *Seay* exhibit 3947.
72. Ibid.

CHAPTER 7

Voter-Registration and Get-Out-the-Vote Campaigns

1. Sworn deposition of Don Ellinger, January 10, 1971, p. 20.
2. Telegram of October 29, 1968 to International President P. L. Siemiller from E. T. Kehrer, State Co-ordinator, Labor Committee for Humphrey-Muskie (*Seay* exhibit 166).
3. Letter of October 29, 1968, from Don Ellinger to GLR William Clitheroe in East Point, Georgia (*Seay* exhibit 165).
4. Letter of October 9, 1968, from Don Ellinger to GLR William Clitheroe (*Seay* exhibit 167).
5. Letter of August 14, 1968 (*Seay* exhibit 1509).
6. Letter of September 18, 1968, to Don Ellinger (*Seay* exhibit 114).
7. Memorandum of July 1, 1968 (*Seay* exhibit 391).
8. Memorandum of January 8, 1969 (*Seay* exhibit 1102).
9. Letter of May 23, 1969, to John Holaday, Executive Secretary, Wyoming State AFL-CIO from GLR Allin Walker (*Seay* exhibit 592).
10. Valentine, Sherman and Associates' Proposal of September 1969 to Minnesota DFL Party (*Seay* exhibit 883).
11. Ibid.
12. Letter of January 2, 1970 (*Seay* exhibit 880).
13. Letter of December 5, 1969 (*Seay* exhibit 598).

14. Letter of January 16, 1971, to Walter Burke, Secretary-Treasurer, United Steelworkers of America (*Seay* exhibit 877).
15. Memorandum of January 28, 1970, to Walter Burke, Steelworkers Political Action Committee; Al Barkan, Director, COPE; Members of the Steelworkers Political Action Committee (*Seay* exhibit 1167).
16. Letter of September 4, 1970, to GLR Al in Walker from John D. Holaday, Executive Secretary, Wyoming State AFL-CIO (*Seay* exhibit 761).
17. Letter of May 13, 1970 (*Seay* exhibit 1048).
18. Letter of August 20. 1970 (*Seay* exhibit 849).
19. Letter of September 1, 1970, from Don Ellinger (*Seay* exhibit 848).
20. Letter of August 19, 1970 to Don Ellinger from Herbert L. Ely, State Chairman, Democratic Party of Arizona (*Seay* exhibit 709).
21. Letter of August 27, 1970, to Herbert L. Ely (*Seay* exhibit 708).
22. Memorandum of May 16, 1972, to Fred Purcell (*Seay* exhibit 2398).
23. Letter of September 2, 1970, to Bernard Rapoport, President, American Income Life Insurance Company (*Seay* exhibit 816).
24. Letter of May 11, 1972, addressed to "Dear Brothers and "Sisters" (*Seay* exhibit 2400).
25. Letter of February 8, 1972 (*Seay* exhibit 2262).
26. Letter of October 26, 1972, from William Hill, President, Virginia State Machinists Council (*Seay* exhibit 2552).
27. Letter of November 1, 1972, to William Hill, President, Virginia State Machinists Council, from MNPL Vice Chairman George Kourpias (*Seay* exhibit 2551).
28. Memorandum of March 12, 1968, to Don E linger from Plato E. Papps, General Counsel (*Seay* exhibit 1524).

CHAPTER 8

IAM-MNPL's Cooperation with Political Groups, Liberal Candidates, and the Democratic Party

1. Memorandum of April 4, 1968, to IAM Executive Council, National Planning Committee, and Grand Lodge Representatives assigned to the Action Program (*Seay* exhibit 410).
2. Letter of June 11, 1968, to President John Schmitt of the Wisconsin State AFL-CIO (*Seay* exhibit 324).

3. Letter of June 13, 1968, to COPE Area Director Richard Fallow in Illinois (*Seay* exhibit 183).
4. Memorandum of January 12, 1970 (*Seay* exhibit 64).
5. Letter of January 13, 1970, (*Seay* exhibit 1133).
6. Letter of January 13, 1970 (*Seay* exhibit 1117).
7. Letter of January 17, 1970 (*Seay* exhibit 801).
8. Letter of September 18, 1968, to President Charles E. Edwards of the California Conference of Machinists (*Seay* exhibit 113).
9. *Missile-Aire* of October 15, 1968, published by District Lodge 1578 (*Seay* exhibit 1722).
10. Memorandum of October 2, 1968, from GLR W. G. Flinn (*Seay* exhibit 387).
11. Letter of October 22, 1968 (*Seay* exhibit 281).
12. Letter of December 17, 1968, to Don Ellinger (*Seay* exhibit 379).
13. Letter of October 25, 1968, from Recording Secretary Roland Lambert (*Seay* exhibit 294).
14. Telegram of November 1, 1968 (*Seay* exhibit 3681).
15. Memorandum of July 19, 1968 (*Seay* exhibit 266).
16. Letter of July 23, 1968 (*Seay* exhibit 337).
17. Letter of March 16, 1968 (*Seay* exhibit 439).
18. Letter of December 22, 1967, to IAM Business Representative Lloyd A. Wright from J. R. Bardsley (*Seay* exhibit 277).
19. *Seay* exhibit 279.
20. Letter of March 25, 1969, from Robert J. Keefe, Administrative Assistant to Senator Birch Bayh (*Seay* exhibit 491).
21. Letter of March 28, 1969, to Citizens for Bayh, Washington, D.C. (*Seay* exhibit 490).
22. Letter of February 26, 1969, to Virginia Machinists Council President Robert Spillane and Secretary-Treasurer W. E. Hicks (*Seay* exhibit 580).
23. Letter of March 27, 1969 (*Seay* exhibit 671).
24. Letter of April 28, 1969 (*Seay* exhibit 672).
25. Memorandum of July 8, 1969 (*Seay* exhibit 682).
26. *Seay* exhibit 685.
27. Letter of July 7, 1969 (*Seay* exhibit 810).
28. Memorandum of November 10, 1969 (*Seay* exhibit 1570).
29. Letter of September 2, 1970, from Business Representative Robert J. McFadden (*Seay* exhibit 725).
30. Memorandum of February 14, 1972, to IAM General Counsel Plato Papps from William Holayter (*Seay* exhibit 2257).
31. Letter of January 16, 1970 (*Seay* exhibit 752).

32. Letter of July 27, 1970, from E. J. Todhunter to Don Ellinger (*Seay* exhibit 736).
33. Letter of March 31, 1970 (*Seay* exhibit 1560).
34. Letter of April 7, 1970, from Business Representative Herbert A. Cooksey (*Seay* exhibit 748).
35. *Seay* exhibit 744.
36. Letter of June 10, 1970, to Congressman Richard Hanna from Don Ellinger (*Seay* exhibit 743).
37. Letter of November 30, 1970, to Don Ellinger (*Seay* exhibit 712).
38. Letter of July 20, 1970, to GLR Harold Shean from Secretary-Treasurer Elmo Hays of District Lodge 720 (*Seay* exhibit 729).
39. Letter of August 6, 1970, to Elmo Hays (*Seay* exhibit 728).
40. *Seay* exhibit 1587.
41. Letter of April 20, 1970 (*Seay* exhibit 946).
42. Letter of April 12, 1971, to Matthew E. Welsh, Volunteers for Hartke (*Seay* exhibit 1195).
43. Letter of January 20, 1971, to Don Ellinger (*Seay* exhibit 1196).
44. Letter of March 30, 1971, to Recording Secretary L. E. Walters, Local Lodge 694 in South Carolina (*Seay* exhibit 1231).
45. Letter of July 8, 1971, to Secretary-Treasurer E. T. Kirkland of South Carolina Labor Council (*Seay* exhibit 1230).
46. Memorandum of August 25, 1971, to MNPL Executive Committee from William Holayter (*Seay* exhibit 1343).
47. Letter of February 25, 1971, from MNPL files (no signature) to GVP Robert Simpson (*Seay* exhibit 1255).
48. Letter of December 22, 1971 (*Seay* exhibit 1909).
49. Memorandum of June 23, 1971 (*Seay* exhibit 1269).
50. *Seay* exhibit 1268.
51. Letter of October 15, 1971 (*Seay* exhibit 1366).
52. Letter of December 20, 1971 (*Seay* exhibit 2200).
53. Undated letter from MNPL files (no signature) on letterhead of Democratic National Committee (*Seay* exhibit 1300).
54. Undated letter from Robert B. Ryan of Local Lodge 1111 (*Seay* exhibit 1179).
55. *Seay* exhibit 2513.
56. *Seay* exhibit 2512.
57. Letter of January 19, 1972, to Joseph Dolan of Englewood, Colo. (*Seay* exhibit 1918).
58. Letter of February 9, 1972, to Business Representative John Roe(*Seay* exhibit 1924).

59. Memorandum of February 17, 1972 (*Seay* exhibit 2267).
60. Letter of February 18, 1972 (*Seay* exhibit 2268).
61. Letter of March 23, 1972 (*Seay* exhibit 2333).
62. Memorandum of April 5, 1972 (*Seay* exhibit 2345).
63. Letter of May 10, (*Seay* exhibit 2403).
64. Memorandum of meeting of May 15, 1972 (*Seay* exhibit 2436).
65. Letter of June 12, 1972, from Jack Sweeney, Staff Assistant, Harold Miller for Congress Committee (*Seay* exhibit 2435).
66. Letter of June 16, 1972, to MNPL from Charle O. Porter (*Seay* exhibit 2452).
67. Letter of July 20, 1972, from Secretary-Treasurer Marvin Kelso of Oregon MNPL (*Seay* exhibit 2451).
68. Letter of August 11, 1973 (*Seay* exhibit 2471).
69. Letter of October 18, 1972, to Secretary-Treasurer Joan Ranger of the Washington State Machinists Council (*Seay* exhibit 2529).
70. Letter of July 20, 1972 (*Seay* exhibit 2440).
71. Letter of September 27, 1972 (*Seay* exhibit 2490).
72. *Seay* exhibit 2492.

CHAPTER 9

Correcting an Imbalance in Our Political System

1. *Washington Post*, December 2, 1973.
2. Column of October 8, 1973.

Major Name Index

NOTE: This index does not contain the names of public officials, union leaders and others who are mentioned in the 18 appendices in the book. Since the index covers only the main body of the book, the reader is encouraged to consult the individual appendices where relevant.

What Really Causes Strikes Against Government?

The union bosses want us to believe that it is the lack of public sector collective bargaining.

All the logical evidence points to the conclusion that, rather than the solution, compulsory public sector collective bargaining is the cause of strikes.

What do you think?

For more information, send this coupon to Americans Against Union Control of Government to get your free copy of "Questions and Answers about Compulsory Public Sector Collective Bargaining."

Americans Against Union Control of Government is a division of the Public Service Research Council.

A Free Book with every four books you order!

A Free Book

with every four books you order!

of California. Covers his views on almost every national issue. "Reading these letters restored my faith."—*James Cagney*. **$1.25**

9. THE HUNDRED MILLION DOLLAR PAYOFF: HOW BIG LABOR BUYS ITS DEMOCRATS, Douglas Caddy. This classic available for the first time in paperback! (June). **$2.95**

10. THE LIBERTARIAN CHALLENGE: A NEW DAWN FOR AMERICA, Roger MacBride. The Libertarian Party presidential candidate calls for a return to first principles. (June). **$ .95**

11. THE MUNICIPAL DOOMSDAY MACHINE, Ralph de Toledano. "Forced unionization of public employees threatens American democracy. Toledano's book is must reading" —*Ronald Reagan*. **$1.95**

12. REFLECTIONS ON ECONOMIC ADVISING, Paul W. McCracken. The former Chairman of the President's Council of Economic Advisers shows how our economy is managed. **$ .95** (Pamphlet.)

13. THE POLITICIZATION OF ECONOMIC DECISIONS, Alan Walters, introduction by Harry Johnson. The economies of the West are being ruined by the substitution of politics for economics; the author shows how, and why. **$ .95** (Pamphlet.)

Green Hill Publishers, Inc.
Box 738
Ottawa, Illinois 61350

Please send me postpaid the following books:

(Circle numbers)   **1 2 3 4 5 6 7 8 9 10 11 12 13**

I understand that if I order four books, I get No.____FREE.

I enclose $_____*

_____

_____

_____Zip code_____

*Illinois residents please add 5% sales tax.

NOTE: Free book offer applies only when all books are shipped together. If not-yet-published books are ordered, entire order will be held until all books are available.

"The National Right to Work Committee . . . correctly interpreted the situs bill as a further intrusion into the individual liberties of American workers . . . led the fight (against it) . . . and deserves considerable credit," Sen. Paul Fannin, R-Ariz., after President Gerald Ford's veto of legislation to legalize coercive picketing at construction sites, January 1976.

"Outstanding service to the Nation and to the cause of personal freedom," Rep. David Henderson, D-N.C., in June, 1970, after the National Right to Work Committee led a successful grassroots campaign which resulted in a strong Right to Work provision being included in the postal reorganization act.

"The successful defense of 14(b) proved that, provided the leadership, millions of Americans . . . will take the time to stand up for freedom," nationally syndicated columnist James J. Kilpatrick, May 1966, following the year-long fight to preserve the Taft-Hartley labor act provision which authorizes state Right to Work Laws.

With nearly a million active supporters, the National Right to Work Committee is one of the largest public interest lobbies in the United States. For more than 20 years the Committee has provided vital leadership in the fight to protect working people against compulsory unionism. While the Committee supports the right of every citizen to voluntarily join a union, it also believes no one should be forced to do so in order to get or keep a job.

National Right to Work Committee
8316 Arlington Boulevard Dept. 100
Fairfax, Virginia 22038

I agree that union membership should be voluntary, not compulsory. Please send me additional information on how I can help.

Name_____

Address_____

City_____State_____Zip_____

Organized labor can be exposed by

THE HUNDRED MILLION DOLLAR PAYOFF

Organized labor is going all out this year to elect the most radical Congress ever. But a powerful weapon is available to expose the union bosses and their candidates—The Hundred Million Dollar Payoff by Douglas Caddy.

This book is the most devastating expose ever written of how the union bosses have bought and now rule a majority of both Houses of Congress. It shows how tens of millions of dollars in union dues are used to elect ultra-liberal and radical Congressmen.

The union bosses can be stopped and their candidates defeated if enough voters are alerted. Play a vital role: in the 1976 elections. Place your order today and lay plans now for the distribution of this important book.

QUANTITY PRICES

1-9 copies	$2.95 each	100-499 copies	$1.50 each
10-49 copies	$2.25 each	500-999 copies	$1.25 each
50-99 copies	$1.75 each	1000 copies and over	$1.00 each